BOYHOOD'S END

WILLIAM S.E. COLEMAN
LINDA ROBBINS COLEMAN

BOYHOOD'S END

MEMORIES AND A MEMOIR

Coleman Creative Services

ISBN 979-8-9885470-0-6 (Paperback Edition)
    979-8-9885470-1-3 (Hardcover Edition)

Library of Congress Control Number: 2023912247

Boyhood's End is a work of nonfiction. Names and identifying details of certain individuals mentioned in this book have been changed to protect their privacy.

Book Editing and Design by Linda Robbins Coleman
Cover design by Linda Robbins Coleman and William S.E. Coleman
    "Fallen Comrade" by William S.E. Coleman
Cartoons, illustrations, and photographs by
    William S.E. Coleman and Linda Robbins Coleman

Printed in the United States of America.
First printing 2023

Published by Coleman Creative Services
Des Moines, Iowa 50311
lindarobbinscoleman.com

Publisher's Cataloging-in-Publication data

   Names: Coleman, William S. E., author. | Coleman, Linda Robbins, author.
   Title: Boyhood's end : memories and a memoir /
      by William S.E. Coleman and Linda Robbins Coleman.
   Description: Includes bibliographical references. | Des Moines, Iowa:
      Coleman Creative Services, 2023.
   Identifiers: LCCN: 2023912247 | ISBN: 979-8-9885470-1-3 (hardcover) |
      979-8-9885470-0-6 (paperback)
   Subjects: LCSH Coleman, William S. E. | World War, 1939-1945--Personal narratives,
   American. | Soldiers--United States--Biography. | United States. Army. Infantry
   Regiment, 417th. | United States. Army. Army, 3rd--History. | World War, 1939-1945--
   Campaigns--Germany. | BISAC BIOGRAPHY & AUTOBIOGRAPHY / Military
   Classification: LCC D769.26 .C65 2023 | DDC 940.54/4973/092--dc23

Also by
WILLIAM S.E. COLEMAN AND LINDA ROBBINS COLEMAN

VOICES OF WOUNDED KNEE
WILLIAM S.E. COLEMAN, LINDA ROBBINS COLEMAN
COPYRIGHT © 2000
UNIVERSITY OF NEBRASKA PRESS ISBN 978-0-8032-1506-1 (HARDCOVER)
UNIVERSITY OF NEBRASKA PRESS/BISON BOOKS ISBN 978-0-8032-6422-9 (PAPER)

CONTENTS

PREFACE

Those who are looking to read a book that easily fits into the World War II genre will be disappointed. It isn't, nor was it ever intended to be, a book that only focuses on the war and its battles. It is not a scholarly tome, nor is it a comprehensive history of the era. Instead, this is a book about a time, and a young boy who grew up in that time. It is truly, as the subtitle describes, "memories and a memoir."

It was Bill's wish that his story provides a better understanding of how events and attitudes shaped the times and the culture he lived in, and how that impacted his life and the lives of his generation. It also details when and how this boy entered manhood, and how that determined the rest of his life and the choices he made.

His story is history.

INTRODUCTION

WILLIAM S.E. COLEMAN loved telling stories. It would be no surprise to anyone who knew Bill that he came from a family of storytellers, talkers, and teachers. As a young bride, new to the family, I was amazed at the amount of multi-generational reminiscing at his family gatherings. Although members of my own family were also talkers and teachers, events from our past were rarely shared with others. In fact, reminiscing about our family was almost unheard of, even within the family. In this way, Bill's family was almost the opposite of mine.

Over the years, I came to know Bill's history and stories better than my own. That was fine since it brought me closer to his family. I loved listening to his mother talk about Bill's youth and how, being an only child, he always had his nose in a book, listened to music, and seemed to be much older than his years. While Bill often felt that his Mom and Pop didn't understand him, he knew that they adored him. He was their "miracle baby." He was their legacy. He would keep the Coleman name alive into the next generation and beyond. This was vitally important to people of that era, and especially to his family.

From our beginning, I knew that my husband lived during a unique and powerful time in world history. Early on, he told me that he was a combat infantryman during World War II. Since he had dropped out of high school and enlisted in 1944 at the age of 17, he was one of the last age groups to see front line combat in that war. To try and appear younger later on in his life would have meant concealing those life-changing events that had such a profound impact on him. While I've heard about many WWII veterans who never discussed the war or their combat experiences, my husband spoke and wrote about it throughout his life.

When Bill and I met at a party in 1975, he was a tenured theatre professor, director, and playwright who was internationally known and admired for his many accomplishments. He also had just returned from a year-long sabbatical leave in London. Prior to that, I knew who he was and had attended some of his theatre productions. In 1973 I had even played piano in the pit orchestra for his production of *Gypsy*. But I couldn't really say that I *knew* him. To me, he was just a figure I occasionally passed in the hallways at the university, and a rather gregarious and intimidating figure at that.

That all changed in a hurry. I quickly learned that he was the father of two grown children and had been divorced for about a year. I was single, in the process of completing my undergraduate degree, and at the beginning of my professional life. Thankfully, his age didn't matter to me. I had always been attracted to older men, plus my father was considerably older than my mother so it didn't seem that unusual to me. By the end of that party, what I did know was that he was one of the most fascinating, interesting, attractive, and intelligent people I'd ever met. Much to my amazement, the attraction appeared to be mutual. We had one date, and it lasted more than forty years.

I was a post-war baby, so I had no memory of the Great Depression, the attack on Pearl Harbor, or World War II. But my parents did, and those events defined and shaped their lives, actions, and attitudes that they, in turn, passed on to me. It was no wonder that these events had the same effect – or greater – on young Bill. My father had been born the same year as Bill's mother, so many of our cultural references and attitudes were similar.

In 2002, after a long and illustrious career as Professor of Theatre Arts at Drake University, Bill retired in order to focus his creative talents and energies on writing (and going to baseball games). Although by now he was older than the normal retirement age, he was very young for his years and amazingly active. During his tenure at Drake – first as chair of the department for eight years having been hired to build the modern (post WWII) theatre department, and then as senior professor of theatre carrying an insanely full teaching and directing load – he hadn't always found the time to write much beyond scholarly articles, lectures and presentations, class textbooks, and, eventually, our non-fiction book *Voices of Wounded Knee*. The "publish or perish" onus was ubiquitous in the meritocracy of academe. Yes, he did write wonderful plays during those years, but they were not considered equivalent in value to scholarly research by the administration, and it was always a struggle to find the time and get into the creative flow while juggling his other duties and obligations.

In "retirement," he could finally and fully explore his passion to create new plays and screenplays. If I may interrupt to brag on him, Bill had more than a hundred productions of his plays throughout North America and abroad, and even as far away as Australia (at least three different productions in various cities). Many of his plays and screenplays received national and international awards, and a few of his screenplays were optioned. In 2013, at the age of 87, he became the oldest living playwright to receive an Off-Broadway debut with his plays. And this was only three years after a full Equity production of one of his comedies at the Mountain Playhouse in Pennsylvania! Just one week before his death, another one of his plays won an international competition, – complete with a cash award and a full production – in Toronto, Canada. Even posthumously, his plays continue to be read and produced.

During those wonderful years of amazing creative activity, I encouraged him to set aside some time to write down his family stories and history so that future generations could enjoy them long after we were dead and gone. I knew that legacy was important to Bill. Much to my delight, he heeded my request.

Bill's memoir wasn't an organized effort, nor was it a concentrated one. When he had a few minutes between projects, he'd write down some thoughts. Over the next few years, the file on his computer grew until it was about 900 pages long, and he hadn't even progressed past the point of his first marriage! When I expressed surprise at the length – it was long, even for him – he told me that he was writing more than just events, he was also writing about the times he lived in, the culture that he grew up in, and what it was like to be a young man at that point in history. I found that intriguing. He wanted his grandchildren to get a sense of the era, and to learn more about their own family and how it was affected by the culture, events, and societal views.

As time went along, I asked Bill if I could read some of his memoir. He was pleased at my interest and printed out the first half. As I browsed through the pages, I arrived at his memories of the attack on Pearl Harbor and his experiences in the army. Given that this was about the time of renewed interest in World War II and members of the Greatest Generation, I told him that this section might make a good standalone book, and one that would be of interest to more people than just his immediate family. Now it was his turn to be intrigued. I volunteered to help organize and edit it for him, knowing that this was one of his least favorite writing tasks.

At first, it was just something to do in his spare time. Slowly, the years began to catch up with him. In 2009 he was diagnosed with cancer along with other health issues. Even though the treatments seemed to bring the cancer under control, time became more urgent. By late 2012 he began to realize that he had better get serious about his memoir if he wanted to see it through. He began to shape the WWII section into a rough draft for a book. He printed it out and gave it to me.

Then, on June 26, 2014, our world came crashing down when he suffered a major heart attack and required open-heart surgeries. He almost died more than a dozen times. Later, when I drove him to medical appointments or physical therapy sessions, I carried along the manuscript (and my red ink pen) and worked on it while he worked on his recovery.

Editing the rough draft was a daunting challenge. Even though Bill was a superb writer, non-fiction was not his favorite genre. He much preferred writing plays and screenplays. Over the years I had learned that if he didn't like something, he often got sloppy with the details. He also hadn't written his memories in a systematic or chronological way. Most of the time he'd be working at his computer, something would jog his memory and he would jot down his thoughts in the "memoir" file, and then he'd close it and return to whatever script he was working on until the next memory churned to the surface.

As I worked on the manuscript, I quickly discovered that my biggest challenges would include organization, repetitions, and fact-checking. I also knew that a majority of people alive today don't have a personal recollection of the WWII era, so I had to be attentive to the history and culture of that time. If Bill glossed over something that might confuse younger readers, I would need to define and clarify that as well as introduce or describe many of the important figures who shaped those times.

In February 2015, Bill's cancer returned with a vengeance. The following month we celebrated our wedding anniversary. We tried to put on a brave face – "Let's go for 50 years!" – but deep down we knew better. By now we were hoping for months, not years. We received his terminal diagnosis later that spring, so we knew that our time together was both precious and fleeting. In early June we celebrated his 89th birthday, knowing it would be his last even though we desperately hoped for more.

By the middle of June, things began to cascade downhill. Bill gave me his blessing to complete *Boyhood's End*. He said that I had "captured his voice and style," and he knew the book was in good hands. I told him that since he had taught me most of what I knew, it made sense that I would complete the book and see it through publication. I promised to do my best and to make him proud.

On the days when he felt strong enough to sit at the computer, I would pull up a chair next to him and we would discuss and enter my edits and changes. Our goal was to have a rough draft of the first 100 pages to show his eldest son when he arrived for a visit. Wim is a brilliant writer, playwright, poet, and publisher. We were relieved that he liked what he read. Unfortunately, Wim also arrived just in time to see his father's health begin its final downward spiral.

When Wim returned to his home and Hospice entered our lives, it was obvious that the end was drawing near. I knew that I had to quickly read the remainder of Bill's draft so that I could ask questions and clarify his thoughts and wishes. After days filled with caregiving and tending to his medical needs, I stayed up most of the night for quite a few nights reading and making notes. I was running out of time.

I was so thankful that I got to the last page before Bill's pain required morphine and his body began to shut down. Knowing how much I believed in the book, how much I loved him, and that I would share his story with the world gave him a sense of peace as he began his journey to the Undiscovered Country. It also allowed him the release he needed to relax and gently let go of his cancer-riddled, worn-out body. It was the lasting – and last – gift I could give him. He might be gone, but his story would live on.

Bill died in my arms on July 8, 2015. I was absolutely devastated. Our love story had been unfolding for forty years. It continues to this day. We worked together, played together, loved together, and lived together. He was my life, my love, my heart, my partner, my best friend, and most of my reason for living. When he died, most of me died with him. I only stayed alive in order to keep the promises I made to him.

For more than a year I couldn't bear to even look at the manuscript. It was just too devastating. I would pick it up, sob, and set it down. Instead, I channeled my grief towards establishing a memorial in his name at the university. The William S.E. Coleman Memorial Fund became an all-consuming project that involved coordinating with the university and hundreds of theatre alumni, planning and hosting an all-theatre affinity reunion, re-naming a theatre, and establishing a guest artist series in his name.

By December 2016, those projects were beginning to slow down, and I was able to recover a bit and catch my breath. Once again, I picked up the book. I sobbed, but I did not put it down. I forced myself to try and work on it. Bit by bit, I began to make progress. Some days I could only work on a page or two before the tears blurred my vision and made reading impossible. As time went on, I could complete a section in a session.

By April 2017, it began to get easier. I soon discovered that spending time on the book was like spending an afternoon with Bill. As I sat at his desk, I could hear his voice in my ear and feel his laugh in my heart. I also loved doing the research to strengthen the book. I learned so much about Bill and his times. The process became a source of great comfort for me.

From there it took me more than a year to, as we say in the music business, "hit the double bar." Reading, researching, studying, organizing, editing, and writing became the focus of my life. During this time I was also attempting to restart my music business and resume my professional life. For almost twenty years I had put my own career on hold, first to care for my ailing mother and then to care for Bill. During my caregiving years I had put my personal life on hold as well. So much had changed in the world, and my learning curve was very steep. The world seemed very unreal to me. It still does.

Once I finished the manuscript, I immediately went back to the beginning and started over so that I could tighten it and pick up mistakes and repetitions that I had missed the first time through. This process was repeated at least five more times. In the autumn of 2018, I began finding, choosing, and inserting the graphics and photographs. By Christmas, I was ready to show the manuscript to my first readers.

The result of this whole experience is that now I feel even closer to My Sweet Bucarooo Billseye! I fell in love with him all over again. Working on this book did not reveal any great surprises for me since I'd already heard most of his stories, but seeing it all laid out in this way has provided me with a deeper understanding of who he was, why he was the way he was, and what motivated him. Knowing that he wrote this during a period of reflection when he knew he was living the final chapters of his life touched my heart. It also seemed to make him more willing to freely express himself, and to share his vulnerabilities and emotions much more openly on paper than he was prone to do in conversations or at other times in his life. When Wim read those first hundred pages, he said that he saw an openness in his father that probably wouldn't have been possible much earlier in his life.

Following his death and during this process, I have sensed Bill's presence numerous times. There were even times that I felt him guiding me to a source that resulted in the discovery of some letters and other materials I thought were lost. Whether or not he really is here and able to communicate with me doesn't really matter. The idea that he is gives me comfort, so I choose to believe it. I have always said that where love remains, life remains. He remains well-loved.

In many ways, I will be sorry to see this project end. It will be like another death for me. But I'm stronger now, thanks, in part, to this book. Many years ago, my mother used to describe me preparing to leave for a trip by saying, "She wants to go, but she hates to leave." Even now, this is true. I'm ready to complete this massive undertaking so that I can carry on with the long list of other projects that await my energy and attention. But I hate to leave *Boyhood's End*. I will carry it in my heart forever, just as I will carry my beautiful and beloved Bill with me until we are together again.

While I would love to live forever in the past with him and would give ten years of my life to have one more day – or even just one more hour – with him, I remind myself that, on his deathbed, Bill made me promise to take good care of myself and live my life to the fullest. He lived his life that way, and felt it was the best way he could honor all those who lost their lives. Some people would call this survivor's guilt. Whatever the case, it is up to me to do the same.

Even though I hate living without Bill, I will keep my promise and make the best of my life in the time that remains. I can only hope that more adventures await us in another time and place –

We'll meet again
Don't know where
Don't know when
But I know we'll meet again some sunny day.[1]

Linda Robbins Coleman

---

1 "We'll Meet Again" is a British song, written in 1939, with music and lyrics by Ross Parker and Hughie Charles. It was one of the most famous songs from the World War II era, made popular by singer Vera Lynn.

Billy Coleman, Age 15.
School photo taken October 1, 1941

PART I

A DATE WHICH WILL LIVE IN INFAMY

The Japanese have attacked Pearl Harbor, Hawaii
by air, President Roosevelt has just announced.
The attack also was made on all naval and
military activities on the principal island, Oahu.[1]

---

1   From the original radio broadcast from the CBS Radio Network, announced
by John Charles Daly, on the 2:30 (EST) of CBS's news and public affairs program,
"The World Today."

1

"We Interrupt This Program To Bring You A Special News Bulletin…"

On Sunday afternoon, December 7, 1941, Knox McBride, Jack Lemmon, and I played back alley basketball in Parnassus, Pennsylvania. The three of us had chipped in and bought a hoop, which we nailed to a plywood backboard above the door of the Lemmon's garage. Our court was narrow and pocked with potholes. It had rained the night before, so many were filled with muddy water that splashed us as we dribbled. Our parents, knowing this, made sure we were out of our Sunday best and into play clothes after our early afternoon dinner.

Jack was a fourteen-year-old kid who lived across the alley from me. He was lean, tall for his age, and had swarthy Celtic good looks. When he wasn't playing, he lived in the world of his imagination, a world shaped by movies, pulp fiction, and comic books.

Thirteen-year-old Knox lived in a fine frame house that was next door to our apartment over a four-car garage. He was small for his age and had to struggle to keep up with Jack and me. His parents were well to do. Ours weren't. His father was an executive with a major steel company in Pittsburgh. He was a squat, dour man who came home and disappeared into his house until he left for another day's work on the early morning train. He reminded me of Jiggs in the *Maggie and Jiggs* comic strip.

Knox's mother was imperious and intimidating. She was very much the lady of the manor. Knox was one of this odd couple's two children. His older brother seemed to be a carefree young man about town. Once he gave me a wonderfully worn tweed sport coat that smelled of tobacco. I wore it for many years. Like all classic tweeds, it wore like iron and was virtually indestructible. No matter how many times it was dry-cleaned, the tobacco smell remained.

At fifteen-and-a-half, I was the oldest. While I loved the rough and tumble of alley basketball, I wasn't very athletic, and I played without my glasses. Of the three of us, I was the most bookish and introverted.

I caught the ball on rebound and drove in for a lay-up. The ball spun around the rim of the basket. I didn't know that as it did, the delicate balance of my life teetered on the fulcrum of that historic day. On one side was my boyhood. On the other was what was to come.

Finally, my shot dropped through the basket. Knox grabbed the ball as it bounced to the ground and dribbled back, perhaps to take a long shot. Jack and I pressed him, but Knox drove past us. As he started to go up for a lay-up, I grabbed his belt. His shot fell short of the rim. Knox turned to me and shouted, "That was a foul!"

I threw up my hands and replied, "Ask the referee."

Of course, there was no referee to make a call, and blatant fouls were part of the game.

Knox turned to Jack, "You saw that, didn't you?"

Jack, who caught the ball on its rebound, dribbled as he replied. "I didn't see a thing."

Knox complained, "You guys don't play fair."

Of course we didn't! Nobody played fair in alley basketball.

While Knox complained, Jack picked up the ball and dribbled past us and scored. As he did, Jock Lemmon, Jack's father, his ever-present pipe in hand, ambled through the gate to their yard and into the alley. He was a dour Scotsman who said little. When he did, he spoke with his homeland's burr. His face was grimmer than his usual glum look as he watched our argument. His silence slowly pulled our attention to him. He quietly said, "Jack, you and the boys better come in and listen to the radio."

A few minutes later we sat in front of the Lemmon's large radio console. The yellow eye of its tuning window stared at us as the CBS Radio announcer, John Daly, reported that the Imperial Japanese fleet had attacked Pearl Harbor without warning. Ships had been sunk, and there were American casualties. A quiet anger swept through the room. This was treachery. The Japanese preemptive first strike resembled Hitler's attacks on smaller countries in Europe.

As the news spread, similar reactions exploded through living rooms across America. Our entire nation was infuriated. This, to us, was a cowardly act. Americans would never do such a thing. If we were provoked, we declared war and then attacked. We did not sneak up on our enemy and stab him in the back. We did not make what would later be called a preemptive first strike. We had been taught in school that America only went to war when it was attacked. This was not entirely accurate, but it was what we believed.

When regular programming resumed, Knox, Jack, and I went back outside into the alley. We had no wish to continue our game. Moments later my dad, his face grim, walked outside and asked, "Did you hear the news?"

We nodded. There was nothing to say. Our country was at war.

Later that afternoon, the three of us quietly walked south along the railroad tracks that fronted our neighborhood. In retrospect, that shared silence was a marvelous conversation. We sensed each other's thoughts. Perhaps it was our first step toward the taciturn manhood that characterized male friendships of our time. I have found that this characteristic male trait has always puzzled women and always will. During my long life my best male friendships have had that capacity for silence, of sensing what is unsaid, of not having a need to say anything. It's a very good thing.

Finally, Jack could contain himself no longer. He picked up a stone, angrily threw it into the brush, and shouted, "Those dirty yellow bastards will pay for this!"

Knox threw another stone and ruefully said, "It'll be over before we're old enough to fight."

Jack said, "We'll whip those yellow bellies in no time."

As we walked on, we agreed that one American soldier was worth ten of the enemy in battle. We had been told that was the reason why World War I ended so quickly after the entry of American troops. Years later, I learned in college that what our high school history teachers hadn't taught us was that 1918 Europe was war-weary and eager to end the bloodiest war to that point in time. Our entry merely tipped a balance between two exhausted powers. We had not single-handedly won the war.

I also remembered how badly the war had gone in Europe since Hitler's panzer tanks swept into Poland and across Western Europe in 1939. The British had been driven into the sea at Dunkirk in 1940. Much of their equipment was left behind. Their country was defenseless. From September 1940 until May 1941, London was bombed nightly. In October 1941, the

Nazis drove toward Moscow, Russia. Now, December 7, 1941, we were attacked throughout the western Pacific and at Pearl Harbor, Hawaii.

While we doubted the war would last long enough for us to become soldiers, we talked of enlisting, of avenging this act of treachery. I don't know what Jack and Knox thought, but I wondered if I would be brave enough to endure combat if the war lasted until I was eighteen. I was not strong, and I certainly wasn't athletic. Little did I know that in three years I would be tested under fire again and again.

Dinner – or supper as we called it then – was subdued. Finally, my father broke the silence when he angrily declared that he wanted to join the Army. He had ROTC training in college and was commissioned a Second Lieutenant. His commission had long since expired. My mother quickly quashed that idea when she pointed out that, at forty-one, Dad was too old for active duty. When he insisted that he was fit and ready to serve, she added that he had family responsibilities. Dad returned to his smoldering silence. It always bothered him that he was too young to fight in World War I. I also think he thought it would be better for him to fight than me. I was the only male Coleman child. Having that name live on was very important to my father – and the entire Coleman family.

I'm sure that similar dinner conversations took place all across America. As a people, we believed in fair play and sportsmanship. After supper we went to church again. I don't remember anything about the service except that it was somber. My mind wandered as our minister rambled a hasty reaction to our being at war. The hour-long service seemed endless. Worse still, I was missing some of my favorite radio programs.

When we returned home, Mom served us dessert as we listened to the eleven o'clock news. It was mainly a rehash of what we had heard earlier in the day. The damage done to our fleet and air forces at Pearl Harbor had been bad, but we weren't told just how bad it was.

I had a hard time going to sleep. I wondered how long the war would last. Would we be bombed? Would we lose the war? Of course not. We had never lost a war.

My world had changed.

Our country's world had changed.

I finally drifted off into a restless sleep.

"A State of War Exists..."

Thousands upon thousands enlisted at recruiting offices on the morning of December 8. Most were there out of a sense of patriotism, but more than a few wanted to select a preferred branch of service. Some who were underweight ate several bananas before they reported for their physical, and others purged themselves with strong laxatives. Later on, a few found other ways to fail their physicals. Some of the Greatest Generation were less than great, but most wanted to serve their country.

The manpower needed to fight a worldwide war was enormous. In time it would top 16,000,000. Fortunately, a military draft, which began in September 1940, was poised to go full blast. Our heavy industry still staggered from the Great Depression, but it awakened after President Franklin Delano Roosevelt declared we were the "Arsenal of Democracy" late in 1940. Even so, we weren't prepared for a far-flung deployment of troops.

Our classes at school stopped at noon so we could listen to President Roosevelt's address to a joint session of Congress. We sat in rapt silence as the nationwide broadcast began at 12:30 pm. After FDR was introduced, he began to speak in a measured cadence: "Mr. Vice President, and Mr. Speaker, and Members of the Senate and House of Representatives: Yesterday, December 7, 1941 – a date which will live in infamy – the United States of America was suddenly and deliberately attacked by naval and air forces of the Empire of Japan."

He continued, "The United States was at peace with that nation and, at the solicitation of Japan, was still in conversation with its government and its Emperor looking toward the maintenance of peace in the Pacific. Indeed, one hour after Japanese air squadrons had commenced bombing in the American Island of Oahu, the Japanese Ambassador to the United States and his colleague delivered to our Secretary of State a formal reply to a recent American message. And while this reply stated that it seemed useless to continue the existing diplomatic negotiations, it contained no threat or hint of war or of armed attack."

He admitted, "The attack yesterday on the Hawaiian Islands has caused severe damage to American naval and military forces. I regret to tell you that very many American lives have been lost. In addition, American ships have been reported torpedoed on the high seas between San Francisco and Honolulu.

"Yesterday the Japanese Government also launched an attack against Malaya. Last night Japanese forces attacked Hong Kong. Last night Japanese forces attacked Guam. Last night Japanese forces attacked the Philippine Islands. Last night the Japanese attacked Wake Island. And this morning the Japanese attacked Midway Island."

Then FDR's voice rose like a clarion call, "No matter how long it may take us to overcome this premeditated invasion, the American people in their righteous might will win through to absolute victory. I believe that I interpret the will of the Congress and of the people when I assert that we will not only defend ourselves to the uttermost but will make it very certain that this form of treachery shall never again endanger us.

"Hostilities exist. There is no blinking at the fact that our people, our territory, and our interests are in grave danger."

His voice soared, "With confidence in our armed forces - with the unbounding determination of our people – we will gain the inevitable triumph – so help us God.

"I ask that the Congress declare that since the unprovoked and dastardly attack by Japan on Sunday, December 7, 1941, a state of war has existed between the United States and the Japanese Empire."

In less than five minutes FDR called an angry nation to action. We sat at our school desks in silence as the Joint Session of Congress applauded and cheered. Then we spontaneously joined them. I have never before or since seen a classroom break into spontaneous applause. Our nation was unified. It was resolved that the treacherous attack on Pearl Harbor would be avenged.

FDR's skills as an orator had inspired us as we fought to survive the Great Depression. Now he put them to use as the driving power of our war effort. No political leader in my lifetime has equaled his ability to rally our nation. We didn't know he was confined to a wheelchair and that when he walked it was with the aid of canes and heavy metal braces. We did know that he was an inspiring leader. I remember movie audiences applauding and cheering when he appeared on movie screens during newsreels.

In the days to come FDR's eloquent speeches matched those British Prime Minister Winston Churchill made during the Blitz and repeated land and naval defeats. These two remarkable men rallied our allied nations to rise from defeat and began the long journey to victory.

The Attacks Widen

As President Roosevelt spoke on December 8, the Japanese Imperial forces launched multiple attacks across the western Pacific Rim. Their air attacks began in the Philippines ten hours after the attack on Pearl Harbor. Inexplicably, General Douglas MacArthur, the commander of the United States Armed Forces in the Asia-Pacific region, left the bulk of his air force lined up with proper military precision on Clark and Iba fields long after he learned of our military disaster at Pearl Harbor. After two waves of bombing, our ground troops lost the air cover they needed as they opposed the Japanese invasion of Luzon on December 10. As we retreated, the Japanese moved perilously close to Manila in the Philippines.

On the morning of December 11, the German *chargé d'affaires* and the First Secretary of the German Embassy in Washington delivered to the State Department and Secretary of State Cordell Hull a copy of the Declaration of War. We reciprocated by declaring war on Germany, Italy, Bulgaria, Hungary, and Romania. Churchill had the ally he sought as Hitler's forces conquered mainland Europe. Now World War II circled the globe.

Simultaneously, the Japanese seized Guam and made their first landing attempt against our tiny garrison on Wake Island. Invasions of Burma, British Borneo and Hong Kong followed. MacArthur withdrew from Manila and declared it an open city. His troops retreated into the Bataan Peninsula. Our troops on Wake Island surrendered after a gallant fight that ended on December 23. Their defense of this small island was compared to the Battle of the Alamo. British Hong Kong fell on Christmas Day as the Japanese advanced on British Singapore. Pearl Harbor had been the first step in a Japanese master plan that was designed to give Japan control of the western Pacific and much of Asia.

The Japanese attack on the Bataan Peninsula intensified during the first weeks of the New Year. MacArthur moved his command post to heavily fortified Corregidor, an island located at the opening of Manila Bay. On March 11, under orders from President Roosevelt, MacArthur left Corregidor in a torpedo boat and then was flown to Australia. Once there he was appointed Supreme Commander of the Southwest Pacific Theatre.

American and Philippine troops on Bataan, now under the command of Major General Jonathan Wainwright, were forced to surrender unconditionally on April 9. The 76,000 prisoners of war endured a brutal sixty-mile Death March in blazing sun with no food or water. More than 10,000 died. Some were mercilessly executed when they dropped by the wayside. We did not know about these atrocities until later, but we knew we had lost the Philippines.

This stream of defeats led us to question our belief in our national invincibility. We were losing the war in the Pacific, and we had not begun to fight in Europe and North Africa. Morale had never been so low in our country as it was in early 1942.

Finally, our spirits were raised on April 18 when sixteen B-25s were launched from the aircraft carrier *Hornet* and bombed military targets in the Tokyo area. Lieutenant Colonel James "Jimmy" Doolittle, a famous pilot and aviation pioneer, planned the daring raid. Flying a medium sized, bomb-laden bomber off an aircraft carrier was risky business. Returning to land on one was impossible. Our planes were forced to fly into China and the Soviet Union. Many had to crash land, but most of our five-men crews survived.[1] The Japanese captured only eight crewmen. Three were executed.

When FDR was asked where the bombers' airbase was, he wryly said they had flown from Shangri-La, the mythical Himalayan utopia in James Hilton's bestselling novel *Lost Horizon*. While it would be months until Japan was bombed again, the Japanese population had been warned that they were not immune to air attacks.

The tide of the Pacific War began to turn with the Battle of the Coral Sea, which raged off New Guinea from May 4 to 8. For the first time planes from aircraft carriers fought at long distance. We tactically lost the battle, but the Japanese advance toward Australia was stopped. A month later at the Battle of Midway torpedo planes and dive-bombers from the *Enterprise*, the *Hornet*, and the *Yorktown* destroyed four Japanese carriers and a cruiser, and badly damaged another cruiser and two destroyers. We lost the *Yorktown*, but this key battle allowed us to invade Guadalcanal and begin taking back the islands we lost during the first six months of the war.

---

1 Richard Eugene Cole, the last surviving participant of the Doolittle Raid, died in San Antonio, Texas on April 9, 2019 at the age of 103. He was Jimmy Doolittle's co-pilot in the lead airplane. He was born on September 7, 1915 in Dayton, Ohio. His memorial service was held at Joint Base San Antonio on April 18, the 77th anniversary of the Doolittle Raid. He was buried with full military honors at Arlington National Cemetery.

The reality of the war became immediate when my older friends turned eighteen and were drafted. Casualty reports began to stream in. Here and there in New Kensington and other American cities Gold Star[2] banners of mourning were hung in front windows. There would be many more in the months ahead.

I turned sixteen on June 7, 1942. The widening war and our slow progress in the Pacific began to make my going to war a possibility. I did not begin to imagine that I would be in Infantry combat in Europe before it was over. While I followed the war closely, I took time to be a typical American teenager. In looking back, it was a glorious time even though my adolescence had its heartbreaks and frustrations. It was not easy growing up in a world where few of my friends shared my growing interest in literature, music, and the arts. I managed to be so immersed in my boyhood world that I often ignored that I had unusual tastes.

Being a Teenager in a World at War

Many years before World War II began, the satirist Ambrose Bierce observed, "War is God's way of teaching Americans geography." Indeed, our knowledge of world geography exploded during those dark days at the beginning of 1942. We were inundated with exotic names of distant places. Rabaul, the Gilbert Islands, the Solomon Islands, New Guinea, Borneo, Java, Luzon, Corregidor, the Coral Sea, Marshall Island, the Dutch East Indies, Marcus Island, Guadalcanal, Darwin, Port Moresby, the Bay of Bengal, Mandalay, and a flood of other names jumped off headlines and were heard during radio news broadcasts. While we and our British allies suffered defeat after defeat in early 1942, our newspapers printed

---

2 Homes across America displayed service flags in their windows during the WWII. The flag or banner was a white field with a red border, with a blue star for each member of the family serving in the Armed Forces of the United States. A gold star represented a family member that died during service. The service banner was designed and established in 1917, during the WWI, and was later expanded to include "any period of war or hostilities."

During the 2016 presidential campaign, the father of Humayun Kuhn, a Muslim-American US Army captain who was killed in the Iraq War in 2004, brought renewed attention to Gold Star families when he spoke at the Democratic National Convention, calling out Republican candidate Donald Trump for his attacks on American Muslims. Khizr Kahn said that Trump had "sacrificed nothing and no one" in the fight against terror.

detailed maps with their stories. We quickly learned the geography of the Pacific Ocean.

I followed the war in the periodicals of the day – Henry Luce's *Time* and his newly created *Life Magazine*, the established *Newsweek*, flamboyant Bernarr Macfadden's *Liberty Magazine*, and our local and Pittsburgh newspapers. My parents subscribed to all of them from time to time. When they didn't, I read them in the library or at a neighbor's home. I added to my knowledge of international affairs by listening to radio newscasts and watching the newsreels at the movie theatres.

Newspapers became a big part of my reading life when I became a newspaper carrier at the age of twelve. First, I assisted a friend in delivering the *Daily Dispatch*, the New Kensington paper. His route included more than 200 customers in lower Parnassus. When he moved away, I inherited his route, but it was cut back to 120 customers so that another boy could have a route. Almost every house on my route subscribed to at least one daily newspaper. Some subscribed to two or more.

The local *Daily Dispatch's* coverage of the war was rudimentary, but I swapped extra copies with boys delivering the evening Pittsburgh newspapers. At that time, Pittsburgh had two evening newspapers, the sensational Hearst *Sun-Telegraph* – we called it the "*Sun-Telly*" – and the more responsible *Press*. My dad always brought the morning *Post-Gazette* home after work. Needless to say, we were well informed. The Pittsburgh papers cost a nickel. Everyone listened to radio news. Our nation had never been better informed.

The *Dispatch* – or the "Daily Disgrace" as it was nicknamed – cost three cents. We got one cent for each paper we delivered. A handful of people delayed paying their weekly bills, but I doggedly knocked on their doors again and again until most of them paid up. When it all added up, I made about seven dollars a week for seven hours of work. Mr. Dallyson, a kindly older man who supervised us, required us to place some of our profits into a secure bank savings account. We received our savings when we quit delivering newspapers. One perquisite of being a newsboy was the tips we received at Christmas. Most of my more than 120 customers gave me at least fifty cents. Many were more generous. I usually banked a hundred dollars when the holiday season ended. This was equal to two weeks of wages for a factory worker.

When the war started, I put any extra money into Savings Bonds. These cost about $18.75 and matured after a decade at $25. One could also buy savings stamps for as little as ten cents. I pasted these in a booklet until I had enough to buy a bond. Buying bonds was considered an act of patriotism. They also paid better interest than bank savings accounts.

While the *Dispatch* carried some international news, it concentrated on local news, sports, and society activities. Even though New Kensington was a true melting pot, our local paper focused its coverage on the social activities of white Protestants. A present-day researcher might wonder if any Italians, Syrians, Polish, Russians, Chinese, Czechs, or African Americans had lived in New Kensington during the 1930s and 1940s.

All of the Pittsburgh newspapers were politically conservative. The *Sun-Telly* was furthest to the right. They were not alone in their political bias. Almost all of the newspapers in the country leaned to the right. After all, they had to accommodate their rich advertisers. Even as we descended into the depths of the Great Depression, they persisted in defending an uncontrolled stock market. They ignored that its excesses led to the 1929 crash.

2

The Pre-War Years (1929-1939)

Survival

As a child of the Great Depression, I saw my dad's career as an electrical engineer end when Alcoa[3] downsized its Pittsburgh office. He ended up working as a janitor at the New Kensington Alcoa plant in a matter of days. He struggled to pay our rent and put food on our table. One night when I was in first grade, I overheard Dad telling my mom, "I'm going to feed my family even if I have to get a gun and rob a store." As I trembled with fear under the covers, I quietly shed tears. I didn't want Daddy to go to jail. I felt his bitterness and humiliation even though I was a small boy. The hardship and uncertainty of that time shaped my politics in the years to come. It also shaped my ambitions. I wanted security.

We were able to exist because of Dad's backbreaking work at the plant and the food we drew from my grandparents Coleman and Phillips' hundred-acre farms in Appalachian Ohio. As subsistence farmers who lived off their land, they produced enough food to feed themselves and sell. Dad squeezed out enough money from his earnings to buy a tank of gas for the hundred-mile drive to their farms. Once there, he helped with the seasonal slaughter of pigs and cattle and other chores while Mom canned vegetables, fruit, and meat. I learned how to milk cows, and I helped my grandmothers churn butter.

---

3 Alcoa (the Aluminum Company of America) was founded in Pittsburgh, Pennsylvania in 1888 by Charles Martin Hall and soon rose to become one of the world's largest producers of aluminum.

Many others in our town did not have a similar resource. Shabbily clad men often came to our back door. They offered to do chores if we gave them food. Downtown there were long lines at soup kitchens. Dozens of destitute men lived in lean-tos in the swampy area south of town. When we drove through Pittsburgh on our way to Ohio, I saw men wrapped in newspapers sleeping under piers by the three rivers. I remember a riot at a grocery down our lane when irate customers threw stones at the store because its owner had taken legal recourse to collect bills that were long past due.

Dad and Mom's brave struggles kept us from being part of the "ill-housed, ill-clad, ill-nourished one third of a nation" that FDR spoke of in his 1937 Second Inaugural Address. We survived. I never went hungry, but I wonder if my parents did.

My emerging left-leaning views were fueled by FDR's eloquence. I was not alone in this. His popularity soared. He was elected to second, third, and fourth terms. Conservatives fought his new programs, but they offered no solutions other than the poor should get to work and improve their situation. There was one very big problem with this opinion – there were no jobs.

FDR stabilized a country that could have plunged us into a revolution. I'm convinced that without his leadership, we, like Germany and Italy, could have descended into fascism. Depression fears were fueled by the promises of populist Huey Long, Nazi sympathizers lurking in German-American Bunds, the Ku Klux Klan substituting racist rage for economic despair, and the radio addresses of the fiery right-wing Catholic priest, Father Charles Edward Coughlin.

A devout Catholic family that lived down the lane accepted as Church doctrine Coughlin's solutions to our national problems. The Bunds were too narrow in their German ethnic background to be a major influence. While the Klan existed throughout the nation, it remained a relatively small group of angry and confused white men. Coughlin and Long threatened to run against Roosevelt in 1936, but Long was assassinated in 1935. Coughlin fell into disrepute when his open anti-Semitism led him to sympathize with Hitler and Mussolini in the late 1930s. When the war began in 1941, his radio program was cancelled, and his national voice was silenced.

There was slow economic recovery amidst this political turmoil. The Works Progress Administration (WPA) and the Civilian Conservation

Corps (CCC) provided employment for many. As it progressed, our infrastructure gradually improved. Results of this hard work can still be seen. At the time, the right-wingers denounced these and other programs as socialistic. I even heard some say FDR was a communist. Some called him "Russky-velt;" others ignored his Dutch ancestry and said he was a Jew. The majority of our nation accepted his leadership. No President in my lifetime has been more popular. His confident voice and elegant style of speaking gave our country hope and a sense of forward movement during his fireside chats on the radio.

During the slow recovery from the Great Depression, Dad was promoted from sweeping floors and taking out trash to the job of a skilled machinist and welder. My parents were never poor again, but they were never truly affluent. Dad was insecure in his job. He feared another Depression. This colored his thinking and how he handled money for the rest of his life. He often denounced the stock market as another form of gambling and declared that it was rigged. When he was able to save again, he kept his money in savings accounts. My view of economics was affected, too. As I grew older, I avoided taking risks. I sought security rather than wealth.

The Phillips farm in Appalachian Ohio.

My parents sent me to my grandparents' farms for a month every summer before and during my teenage years. Once there, I helped with the chores and went with my grandfathers to their work in the fields. As evening approached, I went with my Aunt Agnes Coleman to bring the cows in for milking. When we got to their pasture, Rover, their collie dog, rounded up the small herd and drove it through the gate and down the lane leading back to the barn.

At the Phillips farm, I played with my Uncle Bob. He was a few years older than I and became a big brother during my visits. I loved to jump from a beam into the deep hay in the barn's loft. Sometimes Bob and I went swimming in a nearby creek.

As I look back, I realize that I experienced how it was to live in the nineteenth century. They had no electricity at first, and room fireplaces heated their homes. After the chores were done on cold winter nights, we sat in front of the living room fireplace. Our backs were cold, but our faces were warm from the blaze. On some nights we made popcorn in wire-metal mesh poppers.

Grandpa Phillips, a rough-hewn giant of a man, loved to tell tall tales. Sometimes he played his fiddle. He also played the jug, but that talent was reserved for when he played with others at square dances. He spread warmth and generosity everywhere he went. If someone came down the road past their farm, he invited them in for a meal.

Grandpa Coleman with his cows.

The Colemans were reserved and had little to say. Grandpa Coleman was quite protective of me. I was the only grandchild who carried the Coleman name. Grandpa Coleman only allowed me to watch him work in his fields. To him I was the future of his family name. However, Grandpa Phillips allowed me to plow a furrow on my own. I was too small to fully control the horse-drawn plow, but I completed one irregular and quite jagged row. He also allowed me to ride his massive plow horses bareback. I am sure there was some despair in both families when I didn't marry until I was twenty-seven. By then most single men were called confirmed bachelors, a polite way of saying they were gay.

THE GROWING RUMBLINGS OF WAR

Harvest time in Ohio

Prior to the Second World War, I became aware that an oncoming tidal wave of fascism was sweeping across Europe, Africa, and Asia. At first Benito Mussolini and Adolph Hitler came off as figures for ridicule. Mussolini looked like a posturing egotist as he addressed the masses from balconies, and Adolph Hitler's ranting came off as melodramatic hysteria in newsreels. That view changed as their power grew, and they began to attack and seize smaller countries. My friends and I watched their acts of aggression closely. We divided the world into good guys and bad guys. Great Britain, France, and China wore white hats. The Germans, Italians, and Japanese wore black ones.

Mussolini's desire to create a new Roman Empire led him to attack Abyssinia in 1935. At first, tribesmen armed with spears and little else drove back the heavily armed invaders. The Italian army became a subject of international ridicule. The humiliated Italian generals retaliated with chemical weapons. Emperor Haile Selassie, the Lion of Judea who claimed to be descended from King Solomon and the Queen of Sheba, went before the League of Nations and pled for support. I remember seeing excerpts from his eloquent speech in newsreels. His plea was ignored. In May 1936, after a brave resistance, Abyssinia (now known as Ethiopia) fell and became part of Italy's empire.

The Spanish Civil War broke out that July. It began when the democratically elected Republican forces replaced a conservative monarchy. They fought against fascist Nationalists led by Generalissimo Francisco Franco who headed a rebel alliance that included monarchists and conservative Catholics. The Republican (or Loyalist) forces included members of the political left, communists, socialists, anarchists, centrists, and liberals. The general public in the United States treated this war as if it was just another small European war. Little did we know that it was a dress rehearsal for World War II.

Nazi Germany and Fascist Italy supported Franco and the Nationalists with arms and military advisors. The Soviet Union retaliated by supporting the Republican forces. Spain quickly became a testing ground for weapons and tactics. Atrocities on both sides included assassinations and bombing of civilian populations. Perhaps the most famous bombing was on April 26, 1937 when Nazi Germany's Condor Legion of the *Luftwaffe* began an aerial attack on the Basque city of Guernica. The attack devastated the town and shocked the western world. A new dimension of war was unleashed. Air power had been quite limited during World War I. Now it came into its own. In the years to come it was used again and again. This ruthless carpet-bombing of civilians[4] is remembered in Pablo Picasso's powerful painting, *Guernica*.

A number of anti-Fascist American volunteers joined the Republican's International Brigade. A few of its veterans can be seen in interviews during *Reds*, Warren Beatty's 1981 epic historical film depicting the leftist movements of that time. In the early 1980s, a few veterans appeared at a convocation at Drake University. It was a remarkable evening I will never forget. These grizzled old men had fought in the first battles that led to the Second World War. They gave a reality to the news reports of the Spanish Civil War that I had read about in my boyhood.

By 1937, American novelist and short-story writer Ernest Hemingway was one of the correspondents covering the war. He arrived in Spain with Dutch filmmaker Joris Ivens who was filming *Spanish Earth*,[5] a powerful documentary film that supported the Republican cause. Hemingway was

---

4 In the 21st century our military leaders speak of "precision bombing." I don't believe it exists. A bomb released at 25,000 feet cannot distinguish between a civilian and a soldier.

5 Orson Welles narrated the film, and Marc Blitzstein and Virgil Thomson provided the music score. After the Second World War ended, many who worked on *Spanish Earth*

brought in to replace John Dos Passos as screenwriter. Later that year Hemingway would write his only play, *The Fifth Column*, in Madrid as the city was being bombarded.

The Spanish Civil War raged until Franco's stronger armed forces prevailed. Between July 17, 1936 and April 1, 1939 more than a million soldiers and civilians died. Franco established himself as the dictator of a repressive regime that stayed in power until his death in 1975. Now Spain is a democracy, and one of the most liberal countries in Europe.

The rising tide of war was awash in Asia. The Imperial Japanese Army invaded Mainland China in 1937. In December, Japanese troops rampaged in an orgy of looting, rape, and murder for six weeks in what was called the Rape of Nanking. As many as 300,000 were slaughtered. Most were civilians. While most Americans were shocked by the bloody actions of the Japanese, I remember some adults saying they were not upset because "those people over there don't value human life."

President and "Generalissimo" Chiang Kai-shek led the Republic of China's opposition to the Japanese invaders. His wife, Soong Mei-ling, traveled throughout the United States in an effort to rally American support against Japanese aggression. No crowd was too small for her. I remember her coming to our Methodist church in New Kensington and speaking for her country's cause at a Sunday evening service. She was a tiny, beautiful woman who wore a sleek Chinese dress. It was the first time I saw a slit skirt. I also remember shyly shaking her hand.

Soong Mei-ling spoke convincingly about how she and her husband were devout Christians who were fighting a heathen, immoral enemy. We didn't know that Chang Kai-shek was corrupt, but we did know he was inept in defending his vast country. While a majority of Americans sympathized with Chiang Kai-shek's regime, we offered China little help. Our forus was on staying out of the war.

Back in Europe, Hitler annexed Austria in March 1938. By now he had moved from being a ridiculously melodramatic orator to a serious threat to peace. The Austrians tamely accepted becoming part of Germany. Despite this territorial gain, Hitler threatened a larger European war. The leaders of Great Britain, France, Italy, and Germany met in Munich and agreed that Hitler could annex Czechoslovakia's Sudetenland in exchange for a pledge of peace. The trustful and, some would say, naive

---

were called before Congress to testify before the headline hunting House Un-American Activities Committee. They were attacked for opposing a vicious right wing dictator.

British Prime Minister Neville Chamberlain arrived by airplane back in England
on September 30, 1938, after signing the
Munich Agreement. I remember seeing
this tall, awkward man in a newsreel as
he waved what would prove to be a piece
of worthless paper and declared, "peace
for our time."[6]

Billy in 1938

Hitler's aggression didn't end with
the Sudetenland. On March 15, 1939,
he seized the Czech provinces of Bohe-
mia and Moravia. As he did, Hungary
annexed the rest of Czechoslovakia. German troops seized part of Lithuania eight
days later. Now Hitler and his allies controlled a large part of Eastern
Europe.

Again, Great Britain and France clung to their policy of appeasement.
By spring, Hitler demanded the annexation of the Polish city of Danzig.
Finally, Great Britain and France guaranteed that they would defend
any intrusion on Polish territory. Europe teetered on the brink of war
throughout the summer of 1939. Then, on September 1, Hitler invaded
Poland. Great Britain and France honored their promise to defend Poland
and declared war on Germany.

World War II had begun.

A WORLD AT WAR

I vividly remember that fateful day. I heard the news on our car radio as
we drove to visit my grandparents in Ohio. I was thirteen. My youthful
perception was that the villains in black hats had made a cowardly attack
against a smaller country. To me they were like the bullies who plagued

---

6   In a speech that was meant to echo Prime Minister Benjamin Disraeli's words
following the Anglo-German Declaration in 1878, "I have returned from Germany with
peace for our time," Chamberlain concluded his remarks outside 10 Downing Street by
saying, "My good friends, for the second time in our history, a British Prime Minister
has returned from Germany bringing peace with honor. I believe it is peace for our
time. We thank you from the bottom of our hearts. Go home and get a nice quiet sleep."

me on school playgrounds. Now we call what Germany did against Poland a preemptive strike. I remember my dad muttering, "Those people over there can keep their wars." He reflected our country's reluctance to join the fray. After all, Europe was three thousand miles away.

When Winston Churchill replaced Neville Chamberlain as Prime Minister on May 13, 1940, he told a fearful nation, "I have nothing to offer but blood, toil, tears, and sweat." This brutally honest speech was broadcast on American radio. It was the first time I heard Churchill speak. It would not be the last. His deliberate, deep-pitched manner of speaking became familiar to Americans in the coming years. He became a living symbol of British bulldog courage. In fact, he looked like an English bulldog to me.

In late May and early June, the land war in Europe turned sour. The Germans' blitzkrieg panzer attacks swept around old fortifications, and the British and French forces were driven back to the beach at Dunkirk, France. Between May 27 and June 4, 1940, a total of 338,226 soldiers were rescued by a hastily assembled flotilla of over 800 boats that included warships, fishing boats, and even recreational craft. A majority of the British army and some of the French escaped, but their heavy equipment had to be sabotaged. England was virtually defenseless.

On June 4, after the evacuation known as the "Miracle of Dunkirk" was complete, Churchill thundered his country's resolve to persevere against impossible odds to the Houses of Parliament,

> We shall go on to the end. We shall fight in France, we shall fight on the seas and oceans, we shall fight with growing confidence and growing strength in the air, we shall defend our island, whatever the cost may be. We shall fight on the beaches, we shall fight on the landing grounds, we shall fight in the fields and in the streets, we shall fight in the hills; we shall never surrender.

I listened to a relayed broadcast of this powerful speech with admiration. I also remember seeing newsreels of the evacuation. While most Americans favored the British, they were reluctant to join the war. Joseph P. Kennedy, our Ambassador to England and the patriarch of the Kennedy dynasty, shared this reluctance. Even before the war started, he thought fighting Hitler was a losing cause. Now that the British beaches were defenseless and the war in North Africa intensified after Field Marshal Erwin Rommel's Afrika Corps replaced the stalled Italians, Kennedy thought England was doomed to defeat. He did not count on the dogged courage of Lieutenant-General Bernard Montgomery's British Commonwealth forces in North Africa. They drew away German forces that would be involved in any attempt to invade England.

Joe Kennedy was not alone in his opinion. The America First Committee led a nationwide isolationist movement. Many prominent Americans supported it. The best-known member was Charles Lindbergh. "Lucky Lindy," as he was called, became an American hero after making the first solo flight across the Atlantic in 1927 in the monoplane, *Spirit of St. Louis*. After the kidnapping and murder of their infant son in 1932, he and his wife Anne Morrow Lindbergh took their family to Europe. While there, he visited Germany. Hermann Göring, the Commander of the German Air force (known as the *Luftwaffe*), allowed him to study and even fly some of the *Luftwaffe's* newest aircraft. Lindbergh was convinced that German air power outclassed that of the British and the French. On his return, he spoke at huge public gatherings and accused President Roosevelt and the Jews of plotting to force our entry into the war. His was the strongest voice against our intervention. After so many years of admiring this larger-than-life figure, Lindbergh's anti-Semitism was devastating to hear. My boyhood hero was tarnished.

"London is Burning"

The Battle of Britain, the first massive air battle in history, began during the summer of 1940. On June 18, just over a month after he became Prime Minister of the United Kingdom, Winston Churchill delivered a speech to the House of Commons of the Parliament. The speech lasted 36 minutes and addressed the noble causes Britain was fighting for including freedom, civilization, and the rights of small nations. In the peroration Churchill warned,

> What General Weygand has called the Battle of France is over… the Battle of Britain is about to begin. Upon this battle depends the survival of Christian civilization. Upon it depends our own British life, and the long continuity of our institutions and our Empire. The whole fury and might of the enemy must very soon be turned on us. Hitler knows that we will have to break us in this island or lose the war. If we can stand

up to him, all Europe may be freed, and the life of the world may move forward into broad, sunlit uplands.

But if we fail, then the whole world, including the United States, including all that we have known and cared for, will sink into the abyss of a new dark age made more sinister, and perhaps more protracted, by the lights of perverted science. Let us therefore brace ourselves to our duties, and so bear ourselves, that if the British Empire and its Commonwealth last for a thousand years, men will still say, "This was their finest hour."

Shortly after Churchill's defiant speech, Paris fell. France surrendered. England stood alone. With the exception of Sweden and Switzerland, mainland Europe was in the grip of Hitler, Mussolini, and Franco.

From July through October the *Luftwaffe* attacked British shipping convoys, ports, coastal cities, and fortifications.[7] The Royal Air Force (RAF) gallantly fought back. Hitler, thinking the intensive bombing would soften British resolve, ordered the preparation of *Seelöwe* (Operation Sea Lion), an amphibious and airborne invasion of England. By mid-August bombs were falling in suburban areas around London. The bombing intensified on September 7, 1940, when the Blitz on London began.

We listened nightly to the radio to hear Edward R. Morrow's first-hand accounts of the bombing of London. As we heard the sound of exploding bombs, we were told that civilians took refuge in deep Tube (subway) stations. Thousands of Londoners were killed, and hundreds of city blocks

---

7   The Royal Air Force Museum "Introduction to the Phases of the Battle – History of the Battle of Britain – Exhibitions & Displays – Research" *RAF Museum* states that five main phases can be identified:

26 June – 16 July: *Störangriffe* ("nuisance raids"), scattered small scale probing attacks both day and night, armed reconnaissance and mine-laying sorties. From 4 July, daylight *Kanalkampf* ("the Channel battles") against shipping.

17 July – 12 August: daylight *Kanalkampf* attacks on shipping intensify through this period, increased attacks on ports and coastal airfields, night raids on RAF and aircraft manufacturing.

13 August – 6 September: *Adlerangriff* ("Eagle Attack"), the main assault; attempt to destroy the RAF in southern England, including massive daylight attacks on RAF airfields, followed from 19 August by heavy night bombing of ports and industrial cities, including suburbs of London.

7 September – 2 October: the Blitz commences; main focus day and night attacks on London.

3 October – 31 October: large scale night bombing raids, mostly on London; daylight attacks now confined to small scale fighter-bomber *Störangriffe* raids luring RAF fighters into dogfights.

were leveled. Overhead, the outnumbered British fighter planes attacked the waves of bombers again and again.

The question everyone asked was, "When will Hitler invade England?" Fortunately, Operation Sea Lion was postponed and eventually cancelled since Germany wasn't able to gain air supremacy against the gallant RAF fighter pilots. The Battle of Britain was the first major defeat of Hitler's military forces. The key to victory was attributed to superior British air power. This victory was also significant in that it began to shift the American opinion about the war.

FDR, despite carping from Congressional Republicans, ignored Ambassador Kennedy and began to mobilize for war. In a speech on December 29, 1940, he proclaimed that the U.S. would become the "Arsenal of Democracy." He proposed selling military supplies to Britain and Canada as a way of providing aid without entering the war. Isolationist Republicans in Congress opposed this since they feared that it was pushing us towards involvement in what they considered a European conflict.

The bill passed. Not surprisingly, the vote in both houses fell largely along party lines. President Roosevelt signed the Lend-Lease Act into law on March 11, 1941. It permitted him to "sell, transfer title to, exchange, lease, lend, or otherwise dispose of, to any such government – whose defense the President deems vital to the defense of the United States – any defense article."

At this time, the Lend-Lease program was as far as most Americans wanted to go. One benefit of the mobilization was that, in building arms for England, we awakened our dormant industries. The program was extended to China in April, and to the Soviet Union in October.

As a fourteen-year old boy my sympathies were with the English; but, like most Americans, I had mixed feelings. I wanted to see the defeat of the forces of fascism, and I realized that the British could not do that alone. I also knew that if we entered the war, Americans would die, and some would be my older friends.

The horrors of war frightened me. I had seen movies about a world at war. While *The Fighting 69th* was filled with Hollywood heroics, it also showed the horrors of trench warfare. The movie version of Erich Remarque's great novel, *All Quiet on the Western Front,* was more powerful and realistic. I saw it in one of its many reruns. I immediately checked the book out of our public library. Its vivid characters, the brutality of trench warfare, and the close comradeship among ordinary soldiers as they struggled to survive overwhelmed me. Even though it was about German soldiers in World War I, the movie and the novel convinced me that I wanted no part of Infantry combat.

Veterans of our wars were all around me. My great-grandfather and six of his brothers fought in the Civil War on the Union side. Two didn't return. As a small boy, I remember seeing a handful of Civil War veterans marching in an Armistice Day parade. They were barely able to walk, but they refused to ride in cars. I remember tears welling in my eyes. These brave old men had fought to free the slaves and to preserve our Union. Veterans of the Spanish-American War marched behind them, followed by the many more survivors of World War I. My parents had friends who had fought in "the war to end all wars." One had been caught in a gas attack and had severe breathing problems. Another had a metal plate in his head.

One night at a Sunday revival meeting at our Methodist Church, a visiting stem-winding evangelist who had served in World War I gave a very graphic description of his battle experiences in the trenches and how it convinced him to come to Jesus. Even then, I found this absurd. I asked myself, why would you praise God for allowing you and your comrades to suffer so that you could find religion? That single sermon set me on a course that led to my questioning the validity of organized religion.

Even with all of the radio news reports, newsreels, newspapers, and magazines, the war in Europe remained an abstraction across a vast ocean to me. My interest in it ran about as deep as my interest in sporting events. The tragedy was that the team I rooted for was losing. I didn't imagine that in early 1945, I would cross the Atlantic as an Infantry replacement. While I was fascinated with what was happening in faraway countries, at that time I was even more interested in being a normal American teenager.

MUSIC, MUSIC, MUSIC!

Popular music was a big part of my teenage life before the war began. There was an avalanche of romantic songs and swing numbers during the late 1930s and early 1940s. They were recorded and played by the many big bands that toured nationally. We were partisans of our favorite bands and argued over their merits. Many specialized in danceable music set to a firm beat. Some of the best were Fred Waring and his Pennsylvanians,

Blue Barron, Glen Gray, Hal McIntyre, Horace Heidt and His Musical Knights, Jan Garber, Ray Noble, Guy Lombardo and his Royal Canadians, Shep Fields (and his Rippling Rhythm, including microphoned bubbling sounds blown with a straw into a fishbowl), Tommy Dorsey, Sammy Kaye, and especially the danceable Glenn Miller. I considered some of these "square," but I loved dancing to their music.

When I wasn't dancing, I preferred listening to the hard-driving swing bands. The best included Woody Herman, Ted Weems, Clyde McCoy, Stan Kenton, and two of my favorites then and now, Artie Shaw and Benny Goodman. Shaw added strings to some of his recordings to make them more romantic and suitable for dancing. Goodman supplied the best jitterbug[8] numbers of the time with "One O'clock Jump" and "Sing, Sing, Sing." All the bands of that time made artfully shot featurettes that were released as short subjects to accompany feature films. These were the "music videos" of their time.

Several Harlem and New Orleans bands had crossover hits. Edward Kennedy "Duke" Ellington wrote and performed many standards including "Mood Indigo," "Take the 'A' Train," and "Caravan." Other popular Black bands included the uninhibited Cab Callaway, Louis Jordan, "Count" Basie, Lionel Hampton, Louis Armstrong, and stride pianist Earl "Fatha" Hines.

Most of these big bands were made up of less than twenty musicians. Each had its own distinctive sound and style. All had one or more vocalists. I especially liked Buddy Clark's smooth style. The warm-voiced Ray Eberle, who launched his career with Glen Miller, and Dick Haynes had brief movie careers.

Bing Crosby, who had become the first multimedia star of the era in the 1930s, juggled recordings, radio broadcasts, and movie acting. His recording of Irving Berlin's "White Christmas," first introduced on a Christmas Day radio broadcast in 1941, remains the best-selling single of all time. His singing style influenced many of the male singers who followed him, and his popularity lasted for many decades. Frank Sinatra, who launched his career with Tommy Dorsey's band, became an enduring solo artist and an award-winning movie star.

---

8 The jitterbug is a kind of swing dance that gained popularity during the 1930s and is identified with World War II. Jazz artist Cab Calloway's 1934 recording of "Call of the Jitter Bug" popularized the use of the word. The style lasted until the early 1960s. The dance was characterized by its "extremely vigorous and athletic manner."

On the female side were Connie Boswell, Ethel Merman, Hildegard, Jane Froman, Martha Tilton, Helen Forrest, Bea Wain, Anita O'Day, Kay Starr, Margaret Whiting, Dinah Shore, Doris Day, and Rosemary Clooney. Ethel Merman had a dozen hit records, won four Tonys and a Drama Desk Award for her Broadway work, [9] and appeared or starred in dozens of movies, radio shows, and television shows. Doris Day's career as a singer, recording artist, radio and television star, and a major movie star spanned more than three decades.[10]

Most bands featured vocal groups, the most popular being the Modernaires and the Andrews Sisters. Each group had a unique sound. Some bands featured combos that were small bands within the band. The best were Benny Goodman's small groups, and Artie Shaw and the Gramercy Five. Shaw created a unique sound by using a harpsichord and an amplified guitar.

Lena Horne, Billie Holiday, and Pearl Bailey didn't tour with the white bands, but their recordings hit the charts again and again. As the war began, weekly Monday night broadcasts of the *Chamber Music Society of Lower Basin Street* showcased traditional Dixieland and Blues songs. This series made Dinah Shore a star. When she left to join Eddie Cantor's radio show, Lena Horne took her place.

The Basin Street show featured two resident bands. Trumpeter Henry Levine's Barefoot Dixieland Philharmonic was an octet that played old jazz standards such as the "St Louis Blues," "Basin Street Blues," "When My Sugar Walks Down the Street," and other jazz standards. Paul Laval[11] and his Woodwindy Ten alternated with Levine's combo. Levine featured jazz greats such as Bobby Hackett, Jelly Roll Morton, and Benny Carter. I was devoted to this weekly program. These programs whetted my lifelong enthusiasm for classic jazz. Their recordings still give me great pleasure.

My parents didn't own a record player, so I had to listen to my favorite pop songs by feeding nickels into jukeboxes at soda fountains, visiting

---

9   Ethel Merman (1908-1984) received Tony Awards for Best Performance by a Leading Actress in a Musical in 1951 for *Call Me Madam*; in 1957 for *Happy Hunting*; in 1960 for *Gypsy*; and a special Tony Award in 1972. Her Drama Desk Award was for Outstanding Actress in a Musical in 1970 for *Hello, Dolly!*

10   Doris Day, born in 1922, lived until May 2019.

11   Paul Laval (1908 -1997) used his birth name, Joseph Usifer, until sometime around 1938 then changed it to Paul Laval. Some suggest that he changed his name from Laval to Lavalle in 1943 so as not to be associated with French politician and war criminal, Pierre Laval, who was executed for treason in 1945.

friends who played records for me, "previewing" records in listening booths at Cooper's Music Store, and listening to the many remote broadcasts from ballrooms across the country on the radio. My favorite was the weekly *Your Hit Parade* sponsored by Lucky Strike cigarettes. It opened with the chatter of a tobacco auctioneer and began a countdown of ten current hits. There were one or two extras along the way. I eagerly waited to find out what was the most popular song in the nation. I bought the sheet music for my favorite songs with my earnings as a newsboy and played them on my violin.

As the war raged in Europe, we looked forward to the newest Hollywood musicals and wondered which new songs would make their way to the *Hit Parade*. I enjoyed 20th Century Fox's Technicolor *Down Argentine Way* and *Moon Over Miami*. Both starred Betty Grable, who was famed for her stunning figure and beautiful legs. She became the number-one "pin-up girl" to American soldiers during World War II.

My favorite musical was the black and white *Sun Valley Serenade*. It was released while the Battle of Britain was at its height and teemed with great music played by the Glenn Miller Orchestra. It featured Miller's signature song "Moonlight Serenade" and the swing classic "In the Mood." It introduced "At Last," one of the great romantic ballads of that time.[12] The movie's biggest hit was "Chattanooga Choo Choo," a great swing number designed for jitterbugging, performed in an extended musical sequence by the Miller orchestra, Tex Beneke, and the Modernaires. The production number continues towards its climax with the band accompanying singer Dorothy Dandridge and the acrobatic dancing of the Nicholas Brothers. Sadly, the number was designed so that the performances of the three African-Americans – Dandridge, and Fayard and Harold Nicholas – could be cut when the movie was shown in the South.

MGM's *The Wizard of Oz* was released on August 15, 1939, just two weeks before the war started in Europe. Judy Garland was a perfect Dorothy. The ensemble that supported her was perfectly cast. Ray Bolger's eccentric dancing as the Scarecrow, Jack Haley's rusty clanking as the Tin Man, and Bert Lahr's wide vibrato singing as the Cowardly Lion were comedy landmarks. This great film's vivid color and imaginative

---

12 On January 21, 2009, the timelessness of the classic song, "At Last," found a new audience when mega-star pop singer/entertainer Beyoncé (Beyoncé Giselle Knowles-Carter) performed her Grammy Award-winning cover for the first dance at the Inaugural Ball of President Barack Obama and First Lady Michelle Obama.

set designs have never been matched. Judy's popularity soared when she co-starred with Mickey Rooney in *Babes in Arms* and *Strike Up the Band*. I felt that Mickey was a bit of a show-off.

At the time, popular music allowed us to escape the worry of a world at war. Much of the music of my teenage years stands the test of time. I didn't realize the greatness of so many of the popular songs of my youth until I was much older. I often play their recordings now. They awaken old memories. They also remind me of how romantic we were back then.

GOTTA DANCE!

A teenager who didn't know the basic ballroom steps couldn't function socially in the 1940s. Some of my friends learned to dance by trial and error at sock hops; but when I turned fifteen, my parents enrolled me in Mrs. Leahy's weekly evening classes in ballroom dancing. They were held in the Mount Vernon Grade School gymnasium. There we learned a variety of steps that ranged from foxtrots to waltzes, and from rumbas to a discreet form of jitterbugging.

While the prim and proper Mrs. Leahy demanded that we dance at arm's length, we were still able to hold our partner's hand and place our other hand on her waist. Any touch of a female body sent a thrill through me. I fondly remember placing my right hand on soft, undulating hips during a rumba. Mrs. Leahy made sure we never danced with the same partner twice.

We put our new dance steps to use at after-school sock hops in the Parnassus Junior High School gymnasium. On Saturday nights we danced at the New Kensington YMCA. There was coed swimming in the Y's indoor pool before the dancing began. It was very popular with us boys since we could ogle the girls in their swimsuits. Now their swimwear would be considered discreet, but back then a tight one-piece suit was titillating.

We especially admired a curvaceous young woman of Polish descent named Teresa. My parents had cautioned me about the dangers of being attracted to "foreign girls" and told me not to dance with them. I suspect our Catholic counterparts received the same admonition. Teresa always wore a black, clinging one-piece suit that revealed all her considerable physical attributes. To use the male slang of that time, "You could see everything she's got."

Male humor then was more physical than it is now. Goosing other men was not unusual, especially when we knew the victim would have an uncontrollable reaction. Some men were extremely touchy and screamed and leapt in the air. They were frequently goosed, especially when we were in public crowds. During our horseplay one Saturday night, John, my closest friend, dove under water with the intent of goosing me. I saw him coming and paddled to one side. He came up under an unaware Teresa and grabbed her crotch. She rose out of the water screaming and pounding on the back of a sputtering and very sheepish John. I am sure he was the first of us to have the distinction of touching a young woman's crotch! They were strictly off limits in those days.

After an invigorating swim, we dried off, dressed in our Saturday best, and went upstairs to the ballroom where a glitter ball sent a silvery shimmer of light through the darkened room. We boys stood together on one side of the room, and the girls clustered together on the other. As a disk jockey cued a record, we walked to one of the girls and asked her to dance. Some refused the invitation. It was humiliating to be turned down after I had mustered the courage to ask an especially attractive girl to dance, but I still enjoyed a number of willing partners.

Each dance set contained three numbers. The first was slow, the second faster or very fast, and the last was slow. I wasn't very good at the acrobatic form of jitterbugging, but I developed a discreet style that got me through fast numbers. Nobody danced like the jitterbuggers in movies. I never saw a girl flip over her partner's back, or any boy do the splits.

Some girls allowed us to dance cheek-to-cheek during slow numbers. They were much sought-after dancing partners. Close dancing allowed me to explore the evolving female body. The varying resilience of their bodies initiated me into heterosexual yearnings. Years later when I heard Shakespeare refer to Cleopatra's "infinite variety" I knew what he meant. Some girls remained lean and hard as they matured. Others became pillow-like in their softness. We would not have described social dancing as erotic then, but it was.

Sometimes it was quite sexual. One pretty and shapely blonde, who will remain nameless, maneuvered her legs astride mine during slow, romantic ballads. That sort of proximity causes real problems when boys enter their teens. When I danced with her the first time, the closeness and heat of her body was exciting. I immediately had an unstoppable erection. It was all I could do to control myself! She didn't seem to mind what was happening to me. Instead, she clung closer to me. Her warm, lush body was softly against me, and her crotch rode sensuously on my leg. As we danced her breathing became ragged. Her open sensuality frightened me even though I did not fully understand what was happening to both of us. I suspect she didn't either. In looking back, I believe she didn't realize what effect she had on boys and, perhaps, on herself. I never had the nerve to ask her to a prom or out on a date. While she became a regular dance partner, I wasn't sure I could handle a full evening of dancing with her – or what might happen after I walked her back home.

The last set of dances ended with recordings of either Artie Shaw's version of Hoagy Carmichael's "Star Dust" or Ray Noble's hotel band playing "Good Night Sweetheart." After we entered the war, it was an emotionally powerful moment to those who were seventeen and eighteen. Some had received their draft notices. Others knew they soon would be called into the service. As they danced, they wondered how many more Saturday dances were left in their young lives. But to those of us who were in our mid-teens, it was just the end of the evening.

Being young and inexperienced, we were too shy to ask our last dancing partner if we could walk her home. Instead, the girls walked home together. We teenage boys traveled in small and rowdy packs. I never walked a girl home until late in my junior year. I was not alone in this. I waited until my senior year to walk hand-in-hand to a girl's porch. If we were lucky, there was a discreet goodnight kiss at the front door. If the weather was warm, we sat next to each other on a porch swing. It took a great amount of courage to venture putting my arm around her shoulders. On subsequent evenings, if we walked together again, we began the long, slow trek toward necking and an even a longer one to what was then called petting.

My older friends told me that a sure way to get a date to a formal was to join the DeMolay, a Masonic organization for young men. Their dances were the most prestigious teenage social events in the valley. My father, a Mason, was pleased when I decided to become a member of the DeMolay. He harbored the hope that I would become a Mason when I was older. I was alarmed when he signed up to be a "Dad" – an adult sponsor who attended all meetings and social events.

The "secret" initiation was a ritual filled with poetic language. It was climaxed by a one-act play that depicted the torture of Jacques de Molay by the Inquisition in 1307. Older members, dressed in period costumes, acted how he resisted revealing his organization's secrets. The performance was filled with luridly lit overwrought acting. The melodramatic play impressed me. It was quite different from the polite comedies that our school dramatic groups performed. Jacques' suffering was an early stepping-stone to my lifelong interest in theatre.

After we watched the play, we were sworn to keep the DeMolay rituals secret. These secrets, to me, were ridiculous pseudo-poetic gobbledygook. I imagined being tortured to the point where I gave away the DeMolay rituals and envisioned my tormentors saying, "We put him through all that pain just to get bad poetry?!?!"

Seasonal formals, sponsored by the public schools, were a social highlight. I had to muster up a lot of courage to ask a girl to be my partner for a full evening of dancing. Some of the girls I asked already had a date. Some politely turned me down, but I managed to get a date for every formal throughout junior and senior high school.

My first prom was one of my most memorable. In my ninth-grade class was a very pretty and shapely girl named Ellen. She had a mature hourglass figure and a degree of fame. She played piano interludes for our local radio station. She was very popular at sock hops and Saturday dances. We danced together now and then, but we barely spoke to each other at school. I was painfully shy so my conversation with girls was limited, and probably very boring.

My older friends, who admired Ellen's physical assets, encouraged me to ask her to the spring prom. It took a great deal of courage to ask her to be my date. Much to my surprise she accepted my invitation. I rented a tuxedo. I wanted to take her to the dance in a taxi, but my father insisted on driving us. We picked her up at her doorstep. I presented her with a corsage, and we got in the car. We rode in silence to the dance as my dad kept an eye on us in the rearview mirror. Of course, we sat discreetly apart going and returning. There was no handholding or goodnight kiss when I walked her to her front door.

In those days each prom had ten sets of three dances. Tradition dictated that you danced with your date on the first, middle, and last set. For the rest of the dances, we exchanged our partners with friends and their dates. Only those who were going steady danced more dances with their dates. Going steady back then didn't happen until one's senior year – if then.

That changed when we entered the war. Eighteen-year-olds were drafted, so couples rushed to become serious. Some married. Many of those who did soon became parents. The rationale was that when the young man was leaving to face unknown dangers, he often wanted to preserve something of himself in case he was killed. His bride often wanted something to remember of him if he did not return home. More than a few Hollywood movies romanticized this desire to leave an heir behind when young men went to war. That seemed cruel to me. Those who married in their late teens would leave behind young widows who would have to support a child.

As the war intensified there was sadness along with the joy of holding one's dance partner close.

3

BEING A TYPICAL AMERICAN BOY

M Y INTEREST IN the wars spreading throughout the world continued; but it was offset with the rich variety of boyhood activities. In addition to my growing interest in girls and dancing, I took
time to be a typical American boy. My friends and I spent a lot of
time walking and, as we called it, "shooting the shit." Sometimes we
walked along the railroad tracks that ran through town. Sometimes
we wandered into wooded areas and a swamp south of town.

I bought an old bicycle for ten dollars from the money I earned as a
newsboy. It was creaky and slow, but it served its purpose. Better than
that, it strengthened my legs even though they were well developed from
carrying a bag of newspapers on my route. That allowed me to bicycle
with friends to outdoor swimming pools near town or even down the
river to a luxurious pool in Oakmont, eight miles away.

Life by the Allegheny River gave me a sense of living in Mark Twain's
world. This wide, fast flowing river is a vital part of the arterial system
that holds our country together. It and the Monongahela River combine
at Pittsburgh's Golden Triangle to form the Ohio, which flows west and
joins the Mississippi. It seems appropriate that now I live between the
Mississippi and the Missouri.

My friends and I often walked along the riverbank. Its dark green
depths had a sense of mystery. By the time its waters reached New Kensington it was polluted, but a mile or so upstream the waters were safe
for swimming. We rarely did that, but during spring physical education
classes we often swam in a creek that flowed into the Allegheny. Its waters

were yellow from mine sulfur,[13] but our gym teacher assured us it was
safe to swim in.

New Kensington flood event. Note the house floating down the river.

Every spring brought at least one flood event. Dark, dirty brown and
turbulent waters rose and moved into lower Parnassus, flooding houses
close to the banks. Once a flood filled the basement of Parnassus Junior
High School and ruined the gym floor. We spent hours walking along
the river's edge watching debris float by. Once in a while we would see
an entire house head downstream. Another time the raging waters broke
into the Schenley Brewery upstream, and hundreds of whiskey barrels
floated by. Thirsty men tried to catch them in hope of getting a free drink.

One summer three of us secretly bought an old canoe. Each of us put
in five dollars. My share came from money I secretly withheld from my
earnings delivering newspapers. We didn't have lifejackets, but the canoe
had long flotation tanks along each side, so it was quite stable. One day
we rode the waves that fanned from a paddle-wheel steamboat. I loved
to watch these elegant tugs push barges by us. To me, they are one of the
most beautiful things our country created.

---

13 In Parnassus, New Kensington, and throughout Westmoreland Country in western
Pennsylvania, there were rich seams of bituminous coal. Coal mines were – and continue
to be – an important part of the economy, providing the largest source of domestically
produced energy in America. In the mining process, waste would drain into streams and
creeks, turning the waters orange or yellow. These were referred to as "sulfur creeks."
It usually meant that the stream was dead since the toxins would smother the flora and
poison aquatic life. In 1977 the Surface Mining Control and Reclamation Act (SMCRA)
was passed by Congress, requiring mine operators to take responsibility for their impact
on the environment, repair the damage the mining process caused, and restore the land.

On another summer day we ventured downstream to one of dams that held back the swift-running Allegheny. There we stopped before we were swept over the dam, paddled to shore, and watched a steamboat and its barges go through the lock. Usually, we just went out on the river and rowed upstream and down. I remember the summer of 1942 – the Canoe Summer – as a time of grand adventure, a time when I became part of the river. My parents never knew about the canoe.

I enjoyed playing sports in season. Each summer our church sponsored a softball team. We played a regular schedule with boys from other churches. Our coach was our Sunday school teacher, a gaunt man who knew little about teaching us how to play. We usually lost to stronger teams. One day I hit a triple during a winning game. I kept a newspaper clipping of the box score for many years. It was the first time my name appeared in a newspaper.

In addition to the church team, we also created our own leagues. No adults were involved. Little Leagues and American Legion Leagues didn't exist. We played pick-up tackle football (without pads), baseball, softball, and alley basketball. Each area in town had a team. If we wanted a game with another team, we challenged a rival at school. If we didn't have enough players to make up two teams for baseball and softball, we played rounders. After picking positions, we took the field. The first player batted. If he had a hit, we had one less player in the field while next player batted. Everyone moved up a position as the game progressed.

Since I wasn't allowed to wear my glasses while I played,[14] I wasn't very athletic, but I persisted. I remember having a feeling of rejection when sides were being selected for a pick-up game. I was always one of the last chosen. However, everyone played. When I went out for a pass, I hoped the ball would be thrown to me. It rarely was. In baseball and softball, I was relegated to right field. The ball was rarely hit there. In softball I was often the catcher since there was no stealing. Once in a while I was allowed to play second base; and just once, I pitched a few innings.

Most of us owned a glove, a ball, and a bat. I kept my well-oiled baseball glove for many years. The ball and bat were perishables. Usually the baseballs were ten-cent rockets we bought at a five and dime. They quickly became misshapen from being hit. We repaired them by wrapping them

---

14 This was a matter of practicality and financial consideration. Eyeglasses were expensive and involved a wait time of at least a week. There were no one-hour optical stores in those days, and lenses were made of glass.

in black electrical tape. Broken bats were cobbled together with finishing nails and were also wrapped with black electrical tape. Repaired bats sent shocking vibrations up your arms when you had a solid hit.

There were several small, open fields suited for softball, but finding a field large enough for baseball wasn't easy. The best was in Parnassus Junior High's football stadium. Our local semi-pro baseball team, the Corbins, played their summer season here. When the field was not in use, its gates were locked. When two pickup teams met, we scaled a high chain link fence and started our game. Our ground rules were simple. We played until a janitor caught us and ordered us to leave. When the janitor was off duty, the games went on for many innings. Sometimes the game lasted for just a few minutes. Then we scattered and sought out a smaller field nearby and resumed playing, this time with a softball.

During the early evening we attended the Corbins' games. A local grocery store owner sponsored them. The team was made up of mill workers who received a pittance per game. While most were men too old for the draft, they usually were quite good. Admission for boys was a quarter, but we were seated so we looked into the early evening sun.

Barnstorming teams occasionally played exhibition games with the Corbins. We were treated to the House of David, a group of college students who grew beards and pretended to be religious. The most bizarre team played on donkeys. When a player hit the ball, he jumped on a waiting donkey and tried to gallop to first base as another player pursued the ball while riding on a balking donkey. It wasn't baseball, but it was a great deal of fun.

One visiting team starred the one-armed outfielder, Pete Gray. As the war progressed, he played most of a season as an outfielder for the St. Louis Browns in the American League where he hit .218 in 77 games. His fielding average in center was a respectable .958. He had one day of glory when he had five hits against the Yankees in Yankee Stadium on May 19, 1945. He returned to the minor leagues after he was released at the end of the season.

Pete Gray couldn't muster the leverage to hit home runs, but at the minor league level he was a solid hitter and an expert bunter. I remember him daringly run out a triple. It was exciting to see him playing the outfield. When a fly ball came in his direction, he caught it one handed, tossed his glove in the air, and in one motion pegged the ball to the infield. He was quite accurate when it came to throwing out base runners. Years later, I asked Cleveland Indians Hall of Fame pitcher Bob Feller about him. Feller tersely replied, "He couldn't hit a change-up." Indeed, when Gray started to swing with one arm, he couldn't stop. I'm pleased to have a baseball he autographed. They are very rare.

The most exciting teams were from the Negro League. They barnstormed up and down the Allegheny when they weren't playing on their home field. Two of these teams, the Homestead Grays and the Pittsburgh Crawfords, were local. James "Cool Papa" Bell, Josh Gibson, Buck Leonard, and Satchel Paige were among the greats that played our Corbins. All ended up in the Hall of Fame. I vividly remember Josh Gibson – known as the "Black Babe Ruth" – smashing a towering and Homeric home run that sailed over our right field fence, beyond the adjacent railroad tracks, and over the river embankment until it splashed down in the Allegheny River. I also remember the gangly, loose-limbed Satchel Paige throwing unhittable heaters. He completely confused our local batters.

Paige was the only one of these remarkable players who made it to the major leagues, signing with the Cleveland Indians on July 7, 1948, which also happened to be his birthday. His $40,000 contract was for the three months remaining in the season. Two days later, at the age of 42 years and two days, he became the oldest man ever to debut in the major leagues. He was the first Negro pitcher in the American League and the seventh African American to join the big leagues.

All of these players were legendary figures. All should have had the opportunity to play major league baseball. Sadly, it wasn't until Jackie Robinson (who played briefly with the Kansas City Monarchs in 1945) broke the color barrier when he made his major league debut with the Brooklyn Dodgers at Ebbets Field on April 15, 1947.

Years later, I met a few of the Negro League players at our local Iowa Cubs Fanfest and collected their autographs. They included Ernest "Schoolboy" Johnson and William "Lefty" Bell, Jr. (also known as "Baby Bell"), who played for the Kansas City Monarchs, and Art "Superman" Pennington who played for the Chicago American Giants and the Pittsburgh Crawfords. The most colorful and charismatic of these was John Jordan "Buck" O'Neil. He played first base and managed the Monarchs. Later, in 1962, he became the first African American coach for Major League Baseball, signing with the Chicago Cubs. In 1990, O'Neil became the driving force to establish the Negro Leagues Baseball Museum in Kansas

Forbes Field

City and served as its honorary board chairman until his death in 2006 at the age of 94.

I saw the Pittsburgh Pirates play at old Forbes Field at least once a season. Once in a long time I went to a game with my father. While admission to a good seat was only a little more than a movie ticket, he was not inclined to spend money seeing a sporting event. Usually, I went with a friend's family or on a spring school outing. I do remember that Dad took me to one of the first night games. This was a real treat. A special train took us to the Shadyside Station. It was a long walk to old Forbes Field. Once there, I was thrilled to see agile shortstop "Arky" Vaughan skillfully turning double plays, and Paul and Lloyd Waner patrolling the deepest outfield in baseball. All three are in the Hall of Fame.

The Pirates infield coach was an old, bandy-legged, hawk-nosed man. Yes, it was Honus Wagner. I remember him hitting fungoes to infielders during warm-ups. I also remember visiting his sporting goods store in downtown Pittsburgh. While I looked at a display, a big hand grabbed my shoulder and an old voice said, "Hi, kid." The greatest shortstop who ever lived had touched me. I will always regret not asking him for his autograph!

I followed the Pirates on the radio. The voice of the Pirates was Albert Kennedy "Rosey" Roswell, who worked as the first full-time play-by-play announcer for the club from 1936 until his death in 1955. Roswell was also a folk poet and author whose work resembled that of Edgar Guest. Rosey covered the home games from a box in Pittsburgh, but he didn't travel with the team. Instead, he re-created away games by using the information that came over the wire via the very audible ticker tape machine. This information was usually an inning or two behind what was happening on the field. I am sure he embellished the terse descriptions he received.

Rosey had a unique broadcasting style. He always called the Pirates "Buccos." He would describe a double play as "put 'em on and take 'em off," and loaded bases as "They're F.O.B." (Full of Bucs). His most memorable descriptions involved calling out to an imaginary relative.

When a Pirate hit a home run, he shouted, "Raise the window, Aunt Minnie! Here it comes, right into your petunia patch!" This was followed by the sound effect of a big crash of broken glass. "That's too bad," he would then exclaim, "Aunt Minnie never made it in time." Rosey was a beloved figure. I remember him speaking at our church on a Sunday evening.

All these boyhood activities were interrupted by churchgoing at least three times a week. That began with an hour of Sunday school. Boys and girls were segregated. We were usually taught by an eager but badly informed adult. Then we went upstairs to the sanctuary for the main service. Our choir was excruciatingly bad, but I liked singing hymns. The sermons, while only half an hour long, seemed to go on endlessly. We were Methodists so there was little fire and brimstone. Sometimes, I sat with friends my age. We quietly passed hymnals back and forth as we imagined their song titles ending with "between the sheets." We had to repress our giggles.

Families sat in their usual pews. Sitting next us was an elderly and rather distinguished gentleman. I was usually quite flatulent after a big Sunday breakfast, so I became adept at releasing a quiet fart. After I let one slide, I stared accusingly at the distinguished old gentleman. He was oblivious to my stare, but he gained notoriety for his Sunday flatulence.

We usually went to a Sunday evening service and a Wednesday evening prayer meeting. This incessant churchgoing drove me towards my growing agnostic views. As I entered my teens, I began to see many of the miracles in the Bible as the equivalent of witchcraft.

Occasionally we drove down to Pittsburgh to attend an organ recital in Carnegie Music Hall on Sunday evening. Once a choir and small orchestra presented *The Seasons,* a thrilling oratorio by Franz Joseph Haydn. These first experiences with live music whetted my lifelong taste for classical music. Attached to the hall was a museum of natural history that included dinosaur skeletons. I was excited by these remnants of prehistoric monsters. There was also an art museum nearby. It had an exhibition of new American art every other year. I got to see the recently created works of Grant Wood, Stuart Davis, Thomas Hart Benton, Reginald Marsh, Ivan and Malvin Albright, Peter Hurd, Willem de Kooning, and many others. It was an exciting time in the art world.

Nearby Carnegie Tech had annual open houses. My parents dropped me off at an intimate proscenium theatre where theatre arts students presented truncated versions of the classics while Dad went on to technological displays. This was my first taste of quality live theatre. It seemed magical to me, a wonderland, a place that intrigued my young imagination. I had no idea that I would spend most of my adult life teaching, writing, and making theatre.

BEING BOOKISH

I read voluminously. While I was an active boy, I was also an only child. This meant that when I was home, I was alone. I spent a great deal of that time reading. We had few books of our own, but my parents still had their schoolbooks. Much of what I read was checked out of the school and town libraries. I had no guidance in selecting what I read. My choice of books was based on impulse. There was no structure to this aspect of my becoming an autodidact,[15] but somehow most of what I read shaped what I needed to know in my adult life. I remember a conversation I overheard between my parents with visiting friends. I remember one sentence, "He's older than his years."

Movies were my escape from reality, but books were my wonderland. They transported me into great adventures, trips to far away and imaginary places, our historical past, biographies of people more interesting than me, and scientific advances. I read the usual boys' books – Mark Twain's *Tom Sawyer* and *Huckleberry Finn*, Booth Tarkington's *Penrod* and *Penrod and Sam,* and Robert Louis Stevenson's *Treasure Island.* Tarkington's genteel comedy has become dated, but I read and reread the Twain and Stevenson masterpieces. Hollywood has never done Twain justice, but the 1934 adaptation of Stevenson's *Treasure Island* caught the spirit of the book.

I read as much of Rafael Sabatini as I could find. His lurid swashbucklers thrilled me. I didn't stop with *Captain Blood* and *The Sea Hawk.* I sought out more of his novels and stories at the library. All had cliff-hanging chapter endings that swept you through his books. I fondly remember the opening sentence of *Scaramouche* in which he described his hero: "He was born with a gift of laughter and a sense that the world was mad." That single sentence helped form my lifelong satirical sense. *The Sea Hawk* and

---

15   A self-taught person.

Captain Blood were made into fine swashbuckling films in the 1920s and 1930s. I have seen both of these films many times over the years.

I devoured the novels by Jules Verne. The most memorable were *Twenty Thousand Leagues Under the Sea, Journey to the Center of the Earth, Around the World in Eighty Days*, and *From the Earth to the Moon*. Verne introduced me to science fiction. His writing style was ornately Victorian, but he had a knack for telling a compelling story. I sought out other science fiction novels by other writers. The best were by H.G. Wells. The notoriety of Orson Welles' 1938 radio adaptation of The War of the Worlds started my journey through H.G. Wells' books. Three more of my favorites were *The Time Machine, The Invisible Man*, and *The Shape of Things to Come*. I saw the movie version of *Things to Come* when it was re-released just as the Second World War began in Europe.

Just before I entered my teens, I bought a complete collection of A. Conan Doyle's Sherlock Holmes novels and stories with my newsboy money. I read it from cover to cover. It remains in my personal library. Even now I return to favorite stories from time to time. Doyle's description of Holmes' self-education in the first novel, *A Study in Scarlet*, inspired me to become an autodidact. I didn't realize it at the time; but my education was on two tracks – one at school, and the other in my reading.

Thick historical novels were quite popular. Most became best sellers, so I had to sign up on a waiting list at the library. I read most of them, but I remember two vividly, Walter Edmund's very readable and exciting *Drums Along the Mohawk* and Kenneth Roberts' *Northwest Passage*. Of course, I read *Gone with the Wind* even though my parents worried that it was too daring for my young eyes. The movie version cost a dollar when it first came out early 1939. I remember my father grumping, "I'm not paying a dollar to go to a movie. We'll wait until it comes back." When it returned six months later, the admission was half a dollar. We went. I was caught up in its epic sweep. I'll never forget the lurid red lighting and soaring music when Scarlet O'Hara returned to Tara just before intermission. Now I find much of the film repugnantly racist. Few have noted the similarity of its plot to D. W. Griffith's *The Birth of a Nation*. I suspect I would feel the same about the book if I reread it.

These and other historical novels, my parents' old history textbooks, and my history classes sent me on a life course that led to my doctor-ate in theatre history, publishing numerous articles, giving convention papers, and creating with my wife Linda *Voices of Wounded Knee,*[16] our non-fiction book that dealt with the events that led to the 1890 Massacre at Wounded Knee, South Dakota.

Two adult novels that grabbed my attention from page one were Richard Llewellyn's *How Green Was My Valley* and Henry Bellamann's *King's Row.* The first vividly depicted a small boy and his relationship to his family of Welsh coal miners. It veered from warm-hearted comedy to tragedy. It seemed like life itself. The film version, released just before we entered the war, caught the essence of the novel. Walter Pidgeon became a father figure to me, and Maureen O'Hara became the essence of womanhood. Donald Crisp, the father of the family, was a wise grandfatherly figure. I've watched the film many times. It always moves me.

King's Row fascinated and puzzled me. It dealt with adult matters I didn't quite understand. While I realized that the key characters, including the hero, had illicit sex and there was incest between a doctor and his daughter, it was far from explicit. Sex in novels of that time was vague and hazy. Even so, it was sensual and gave a hint of what could happen when I became an adult. The 1942 movie version, starring Ann Sheridan, Robert Cummings, and Ronald Reagan, was even more vague in its treatment of sex.

Many of the novels by the great 19th century English writer Charles Dickens also dealt with boys growing up. I read and loved *David Copperfield, Oliver Twist,* and *Great Expectations. A Tale of Two Cities* was taught in my junior high school literature class. Every year from seventh grade onward we also read two plays by William Shakespeare. In addition to that we read short stories and poetry.

These books laid the foundation stone of my fascination for the *Bildungsroman,* books that deal with the rites of passage from boyhood to manhood. While their central figures experienced more vivid lives than I had at that time, they explained my growing pains to me. They led me to the realities of manhood.

I also enjoyed travel books that took me to exotic and sometimes dangerous places. Richard Halliburton, a daring world traveler, wrote some of my favorites. In spite of an early death at sea, he left a rich legacy of travel books. I remember checking *The Royal Road to Romance* and *The Glorious Adventure* out of the Parnassus Junior High School library.

---

16 University of Nebraska Press, 2000. It remains in print in quality paperback and is available through UNP or Amazon.

The first covered his visits to many countries from England to Japan; the latter traced the epic Mediterranean journey home by the Homeric hero, Ulysses. His well-written books made me long for world travel in faraway countries.

I Married Adventure, the 1940 autobiography by Osa Johnson, was a best-selling non-fiction book. She and her husband Martin were explorers and documentary filmmakers. Her book and their films took me to jungles in Africa and Borneo and the New Hebrides and Solomon Islands. I saw many of the films the Johnsons made.

I also enjoyed reading a variety of mysteries, thrillers, and stories of high adventure. They ranged from the Ellery Queen stories and novels to exotic Sax Rohmer Fu Manchu novels, and from Leslie Charteris' novels about Simon Templar's alter ego the Saint, to Edward Phillips Oppenheim's *The Great Impersonation.* Our library didn't carry the Tarzan books by Edgar Rice Burroughs since they were not considered literary, so I had to borrow copies from friends. Sometimes when my parents visited friends, I read one straight through as the adults chatted, sipped their coffee, and munched cookies and snacks.

Adventure became a reality when the world went to war. I began to learn about the realities of war from the non-fiction books that began to appear. William L. White's *They Were Expendable,* a national bestseller in late 1942, offers an account of the heroic actions of Motor Torpedo Boat Squadron Three during the fall of the Philippines. War correspondent Richard Tregaskis' *Guadalcanal Diary* was published shortly after that bloody campaign ended in January 1943. It recounts the author's time with the United States Marine Corps during the jungle battle that began in 1942, recording the heroism of the men who turned the tide of the land war in the Pacific. Before the year ended the book was turned into one of the better war movies of that time. I remember hoping that if I had to go into combat, it would not be in the Pacific. Most young American men felt the same.

Guadalcanal Diary was one of the first films to create the formula of a widely diverse group of characters of various ethnic and societal origins joined in a combat operation. The formula included a wise-cracking big city guy, a buffoonish character from New York (preferably from Brooklyn), a devout Catholic who is thinking of becoming a priest, a simple farm boy, and flamboyant or moody Italian (preferably first-generation American), a sensitive scholarly type, a husband who misses his wife, and a nice guy who was Jewish. I soon got to know that when one of these characters had a long speech about his longing for home, he was going to die in the next battle sequence. With few variations, that formula still exists.

My reading inspired me to take tentative steps toward becoming a writer. I still have a small ring-bound book of poetry I wrote before I entered my teens. Most were modeled after Robert Louis Stevenson's *A Child's Garden of Verses*. They're callow and clumsy, but they were heartfelt. I still write poetry from time to time, but it's for private expression rather than publication.

OTHER SOLITARY INTERESTS

When I was alone and not reading, I found many ways to entertain myself. I played with my Erector, chemistry, and microscope sets. While the Erector set had a booklet of models to build, I liked to enhance them or even construct my own machines. I had a motor to propel my constructions, but they had a limited range because the motor had to be plugged into a wall socket. My parents weren't amused when I appropriated an extension cord that was in more important use.

Another interest of mine was making model airplanes. I favored making the warplanes of the time. Cutting out the balsa wood parts, gluing them together, and covering them with tissue paper took a great deal of skill. We hadn't figured out we could get a high by sniffing the glue we used. When finished, they were light enough to fly if they were properly weighted. Some were gliders; others were propelled by rubber band motors. My pride and joy was a two-motored version of the British Blenheim bomber.

My fascination with the comic strips of the day led me to think about becoming a cartoonist. I admired the draftsmanship of Milton Caniff's *Terry and the Pirates*, Hal Foster's beautifully drawn *Prince Valiant*, Burne Hogarth's dynamic *Tarzan*, Zack Mosley's *Smilin' Jack*, William Ritt and Clarence Gray's *Brick Bradford*, and Alex Raymond's *Flash Gordon*. Raymond's drawing skill and storytelling exceeded that of *Buck Rogers*, a popular sci-fi strip set in the 25th century. I also liked to look at Raymond's scantily clad women. One sequence in *Brick Bradford* posited the idea that the atoms within us are solar systems within a tiny universe and we, in

turn, are part of a larger being. It was inferred that there was an endless
chain of ever-larger beings. I was fascinated by this idea – and still am.

In addition to these adventure strips, there were comic strips that were
really comic. I laughed out loud at Rudolph Dirks and Harold H. Knerr's
Katzenjammer Kids, E. C. Segar's *Popeye*, and Bill Holman's surreal
Smokey Stover. George McManus' *Bringing Up Father* featured Maggie
and Jiggs, a middle-aged *nouveau riche* couple. Jiggs penchant for partying
and staying out late and their bungled social aspirations were hilarious.
Walt Disney allowed some of his beloved characters to star in a *Mickey
Mouse* strip. All comic strips had their merits, but only Chic Young's

"SCOTTY DON'T THINK WASHINGTON COULD
THROW THE DOLLAR ALL THE WAY ACROSS THE
POTOMAC!"

Blondie has held up over the years.
It first appeared in 1930, but it still
delivers daily laughs in more than
2,000 newspapers in 47 countries
and 35 languages.[17] *Li'l Abner*, Al
Capp's satirical chronicle of Appalachia Dogpatch, first appeared in
1934 and quickly became the most
popular comic strip of that time. It
ran for 43 years.

All these artists inspired me to
try my hand at drawing my own
cartoons. I bought a book about
cartooning techniques, borrowed
my dad's old drawing board, bought
pencils and a variety of pens, a bottle of India ink, and some drawing
paper and began to draw. I started
by copying my favorite characters.
Then I tried my hand at one-panel

Early linoleum block cartoon.

gag cartoons. Eventually I worked on an adventure strip. Like my poetry,
they were youthful works that are best forgotten; but in them I began to
develop a drawing style that would serve me well during the post-war
Occupation in Germany.

---

17   After his death in 1973, *Blondie* passed to Chic's son Dean who continues to
write the strip. Over the years *Blondie* has been drawn by various artists including Jim
Raymond, Mike Gersher, Stan Drake, Denis Lebrun, and John Marshall.

Another influence was Cy Hungerford, the Pittsburgh *Post-Gazette's* editorial cartoonist. One evening he visited our church and gave an illustrated lecture on how he created daily cartoons that commented on current events. He gave me one of the hastily sketched drawings he made during his talk. You must be able to caricature public figures if you want to be a political cartoonist. I could not. I quickly abandoned that ambition. Sadly, many newspapers no longer have resident editorial cartoonists. A skillfully drawn and thought-out drawing often sums up a political issue better than an editorial can.

On occasion I published cartoons in the school paper. Since engraving a drawing was expensive, I had to arduously carve my drawing out on a linoleum block. The result was stiff and lacked character. I preferred showing my drawings to my friends.

All these cartooning influences collided in my youthful mind. Could I become a cartoonist when I entered the adult world? That ambition seemed impossible, but it was my first thinking about a future career. After seeing the Great Depression's impact on my parents, I knew that I wanted a secure way of making a living. At this point, my interest in history pointed me towards becoming a high school teacher.

A Theatre for the Ears

Radio was the basic home entertainment. Everyone owned a radio whether it was a cheaper table model or a console. We owned an Atwater Kent console. I still have it, and it still works. Families then spent time together listening. I was addicted to fifteen-minute radio serials after I came home from delivering the afternoon newspaper. I quickly jettisoned *Little Orphan Annie*. Her adventures were too tame. Instead, I listened to *Terry and the Pirates* and *Jack Armstrong, the All-American Boy*. They presented rousing, cliff-hanging adventure tales. All used sound and music to vividly create the listener's view of what was happening.

As a family, we listened to news programs over dinner. This was often a subject of contention. My mother wanted to talk about her day, but my father wanted to concentrate on the news. Sometimes quarrels broke out and the news was drowned out.

After dinner we listened to Lowell Thomas's live fifteen-minute news-cast.[18] He and his announcer, Jimmy Wallingford, often went on laughing jags over Thomas' frequent mispronunciations and accidental spooner-isms. One was particularly funny. Thomas accidentally called Sir Stafford Cripps Sir Stiffhard Craps. When he and Wallington broke up, they had a very difficult time continuing. When Thomas began to read the next news item, he broke out into a choked, high-pitched giggle that exploded into loud laughter by both men. The broadcast ended up in a chaos of false starts and laughter.

Following Lowell Thomas was the fifteen-minute comedy program *Amos 'n' Andy*. Now it is considered racist, and rightly so. Its characters were clichés acting out clichés associated with African Americans. It was immensely popular from 1928 to 1943 as a nightly radio serial, and then as a weekly situation comedy from 1943 to 1955 when it moved to television. I still have a well-worn toy car that was part of a running gag in the show. *Amos 'n' Andy* was not alone in its blatant racial stereotyping. Jack Benny had his Rochester,[19] a valet and chauffeur played by Eddie Anderson, and there was a popular weekly minstrel show.

After *Amos and Andy* finished, prime time broadcasting began. Each network had a mix of comedy and dramatic shows. *The Lux Radio Theatre* presented aural versions of popular movies and stage plays. Film director Cecil B. DeMille was its host. They often used the original stars. *Grand Central Station* presented new radio plays that ranged from romantic comedies to lightweight dramas.

---

18 Lowell Thomas (1892-1981) was a writer, broadcaster, traveler, and businessman who was inducted into the National Radio Hall of Fame in 1989. Thomas' big break came during World War I when he was a war correspondent covering the actions of British Army Captain T.E. Lawrence during the rebellion of the Palestinians against the Turks. Thomas' film, newsreels, and stories about the man who became known as "Lawrence of Arabia" captivated the world and made both men household names. Thomas went on to have a long, award-winning career in both radio and television, and authored more than 50 books.

19 The character of Rochester van Jones was performed by Edmund Lincoln "Eddie" Anderson (1905-1977), who became the first African American actor to have a regular role on a national radio program. When the show moved to television, Anderson con-tinued in the role until the show ended in 1965. Rochester's popularity nearly equaled that of Jack Benny. Although Rochester was treated as a functional equal in the Benny household, after the war Benny made special efforts to remove stereotypical references from the character.

The quality dramatic show was Orson Welles' short-lived *The Mercury Theatre on the Air*.[20] This weekly hour-long show presented classic literary works like *Adventures of Huckleberry Finn* and *A Tale of Two Cities* featuring some of the best radio actors, with music composed or arranged by Bernard Herrmann. Its fame rests on the notorious *The War of the Worlds* broadcast on Halloween in 1938. I remember coming home from church to learn on the late news that hundreds of people had fled Pittsburgh during the broadcast. I still wonder how we would have reacted if we had been at home listening.

Suspense and *Lights Out* were two other programs that specialized in horror and the supernatural, but I especially enjoyed the scary *Inner Sanctum*. It opened with a creaking door and ominous organ music. That was followed with a silken male voice: "Good evening, I'm Raymond, your host." Then after a spooky tale ended, Raymond returned to ghoulishly intone, "Pleasant dreams."

A *Sherlock Holmes* series that starred Basil Rathbone and Nigel Bruce was immensely popular. Jack, Knox, and I would meet at one of our houses, turn down the living room lights, and listen as we stared at the light of the tiny tuning dial. I remember listening to a brilliantly performed *The Hound of the Baskervilles*. I also remember shuddering as that demonic hound howled in the distance. No one ever admitted they were scared.

There were a rich variety of comedy shows. The nation stopped to listen to Jack Benny, Fibber Magee and Molly (Fibber's overflowing closet provided the ultimate sound gag weekly), Joe Penner (whose catchphrase "Yuk, yuk! Wanna buy a duck?" entered the language), the wryly satirical Fred Allen, and Bob Hope with his rapid-fire one-liners tinged with hints of the risqué.

Many programs had feuds with other programs. The funniest was Fred Allen's running feud with ventriloquist Edgar Bergan's dummy, Charley McCarthy. I am sure few felt that they could become major radio and movie stars, but the roué dummy and his human sidekick became both. Indeed, many of the characters in radio programs went on to star in movies. It's a pity that this Golden Age of Radio no longer exists. It's much more real than most television programs.

---

20 The series was short-lived, running only 22 episodes. The success of Welles' Mercury Theatre provided opportunities in Hollywood where he would go on to make *Citizen Kane* in 1941, considered by many to be the one of the greatest movies of all time.

Going to the Movies

While radio listening was free, going to the movies was an inexpensive form of entertainment. More than 50% of the nation went the movies every week during the late 1930s and early 1940s. I was among them. The New Kensington and Arnold areas had five movie theatres. Two showed first-run movies. The rest ran old releases. They often had double features. I liked the bargain of watching two movies for the price of one.

First-run film theatres charged fifty cents for evening admission. There were reduced prices before six in the evening, and there were even lower prices for children and teenagers. Second-run movie houses charged thirty-five cents after six. Before six they charged a quarter, or less. Since I was small for my age, I tried to arrive before six and get in for the special price for children under twelve. Once when I was fourteen, I asked for a child's ticket. The box office attendant studied me and asked me what year I was born. I was not prepared for this question. I walked away and did the addition, but I ended up paying the adult price at that theatre from then on.

Third-run houses charged fifteen cents or a dime, depending on the time of day. The cheapest was the Dattola Theatre. It ran a low budget western every Saturday afternoon. By low budget, I really mean *low* budget. I can't begin to count the number of chases I saw through the same rock formations outside of Hollywood and the badly choreographed fist fights in the same redressed saloon. It was accompanied by a chapter of a serial, a cartoon, a slapstick comedy, and previews. Candy cost a nickel, but there were cheaper penny bars too. It had no restrooms, so boys peed on the floor while sitting in their seats. The theatre reeked, especially on summer afternoons. Finally, it was torn down and replaced with a luxurious first-run theatre. The third-run practice continued in a decrepit old theatre across the street. Thankfully, it had restrooms.

Playing times weren't printed in newspapers. Sometimes they were posted on a small card in the box office window. If you walked in during a showing, an usher with a flashlight found you a seat. You stayed for the next showing and caught up with what you missed. If you really liked the movie you stayed to see it again. There were no breaks between films except with rare "road show" films such as *Gone with the Wind*. For them the audience arrived on time and was ushered out after the film ended.

I had many favorite stars, and I enjoyed a wide range of genres. Most of the movies I saw were bad, but many were great. The late 1930s and early 1940s were one of Hollywood's golden ages. My parents took me to movies they considered educational or serious when I was a boy. I saw biographical films such as *The Story of Louis Pasteur* and *The Life of Emile Zola* and literary films such as *David Copperfield* and *A Tale of Two Cities*. They even took me to spectacles like *San Francisco* and *The Rains Came*. They made sure that I saw all the Shirley Temple films and dragged me to see Jeanette MacDonald and Nelson Eddy musicals. I liked the music, but I hated the operetta plots.

When I was allowed to go to movies on my own, I managed to see reruns of movies I missed because of parental disapproval. I was permitted to use some of my profits from delivering newspapers in place of an allowance. On some Saturdays I sat through a day of movies before I ended up at the swim and dance at the YMCA.

I had little use for "B" and "C" Westerns, and I especially disliked singing cowboys. I preferred big Westerns such as *The Plainsman, Stagecoach, Dodge City, Jesse James, North West Mounted Police, The Westerner, They Died with Their Boots On, The Santa Fe Trail, Western Union,* and *Buffalo Bill.*

Buffalo Bill, a 1944 biographical Western starring Joel McCrea and Linda Darnell, was a highly fictionalized version of William F. Cody's life, but it seemed like the real thing to me. It whetted my interest in this mythic frontier figure who, quite remarkably, became the most popular showman of the late Nineteenth Century.

However, my deep interest in Buffalo Bill really began when my beloved great uncle, Garrett Haught, told me that while he was wildcatting for oil in Oklahoma, he met Buffalo Bill. I was no more than ten on that memorable winter night when I sat with that weathered old man in front of a blazing fireplace in Grandpa Phillips' farmhouse. I immediately sought out Cody's often-fictional autobiography and other books about him. My lifelong fascination with Cody's life and performance career was underway long before I realized where it would lead me.

Pop Music Joins the Fray

Tin Pan Alley contributed to our morale with stirring patriotic songs. Don Reid and bandleader Sammy Kaye wrote the first big hit, "Remember Pearl Harbor." Its catchy lyrics and stirring martial tune became a national battle cry. It immediately soared to number one on *Your Hit Parade.* As it did, we poured our nickels into jukeboxes at soda fountains to hear it again and again. Its sheet music was printed in the newspaper. I still have the copy I cut out.

Other inspirational songs followed. Frank Loesser wrote "Praise the Lord and Pass the Ammunition" after he read that a Navy chaplain joined a gun crew during an air attack on a battleship. Kay Kyser's *Kollege of Musical Knowledge* big band's recording was an enormous hit. Some said the event never happened. That didn't matter. We believed it had.

Songwriters Jimmy McHugh and Harold Adamson created a fictional act of heroism with their "Comin' In on a Wing and a Prayer."

The departure of young men to military service inspired a rich stream of romantic ballads. All were declarations of undying love and promises of fidelity. Some of the best were "Don't Get Around Much Anymore," "Every Time I Say Goodbye I Die a Little," "I'll Walk Alone," "I'll Be Seeing You," and "I Don't Want to Walk Without You." All became instant hits. "Don't Sit Under the Apple Tree (With Anybody Else But Me)," "Goodbye Mama (I'm Off to Yokohama)," and Johnny Mercer's "Ac-cent-tchu-ate the Positive" were more upbeat. The British singer, Vera Lynn, sang of a world's longing for peace in "When the Lights Go On Again All Over the World," "There'll Be Bluebirds Over the White Cliffs of Dover," "We'll Meet Again," "A Nightingale Sang in Berkeley Square," and "There'll Always Be an England."

Spike Jones and his City Slickers, a raucous novelty band that toured nationally as The Musical Depreciation Revue, contributed to our morale with the impudent *"Der Fuehrer's Face."* Walt Disney animated this jazzy satire and its raucous refrain, *"Heil,* (razzberry), *Heil* (razzberry), right in *Der Fuehrer's* face!" and released it as a short subject. I was fortunate to see the City Slickers play in Indianapolis after the war. Their rapid-fire rhythmic hiccups and belches were accompanied by the sneezing of Billy Gilbert. Gilbert, a favorite movie and radio comedian and character actor, toured with Jones. It was a hilarious show. I sat through the bad movie that accompanied it and saw it again.

Many of the romantic ballads had a deep emotional impact on couples who were about to be separated. These parting lovers had their own songs of love and goodbye. World War II gave birth to the concept of "our song," a lover's tradition popularized by "As Times Goes By" in the movie *Casablanca.*

Pop composers reached beyond the charts to write official and unofficial songs for the various Army, Navy, Coast Guard, and Marine units. The best of these was the Army Air Force's[21] "Off We Go into the Wild Blue Yonder."[22] Tin Pan Alley composers rushed to cash in on the war effort, but the Infantry was overlooked. It still doesn't have its own song. At concerts we are represented by the stirring melody of the "U.S. Field Artillery March," known as the "The Caisson Song," written in 1917 by John Philip Sousa, based on a 1908 work by Edmund L. Gruber. On Veterans Day 1956 the current version, with an updated title and new lyrics by Harold W. Arberg, was dedicated. "The Army Goes Rolling Along" is now the official song for the entire Army.

HOLLYWOOD GOES TO WAR

Joseph Goebbels, Hitler's Reich Minister of Propaganda, enjoyed Hollywood films and studied them. It was said that Hitler shared that admiration. American producers avoided offending the Nazis even after their menace to the world became apparent. Germany was a huge market for American films until the war started in September 1939. The first major pre-war Hollywood film to attack the Nazis was Warner Brothers *Confessions of a Nazi Spy,* released in May 1939. It was a big hit, but Charlie Chapin's 1940 satire *The Great Dictator* played to even bigger audiences.

---

21   When World War II began there were four branches of the United States armed forces: the Army, Navy, Coast Guard, and Marines. The Air Corps was established in 1907 as part of the Army. In June 1941 it was renamed the Army Air Force. The United States Air Force did not become an independent branch of the U.S. military until September 18, 1947 – two years after the end of the war – as part of the National Security Act of 1947.

22   Originally titled "The Army Air Corps," the song was written by Robert MacArthur Crawford in 1938. Crawford, a professional musician billed as "The Flying Baritone," wrote both the music and lyrics. The song was first heard on national radio in 1939 at the National Air Races with Crawford singing. During WWII the song was renamed "Army Air Force" to reflect the change in the service name. When the Air Force became an independent service in 1947 the song was once again renamed to its current title, "The U.S. Air Force Song."

It was a mix of slapstick, heavy-handed satire, and the usual Chaplin sentimentality. That didn't matter to us. I guffawed at its broad comedy and was moved by Chaplin's idealistic speech at the end. I sat through it twice.

Alfred Hitchcock's *Foreign Correspondent* was a more sophisticated reaction to the rising tide of Nazism. It opened on August 1940 in the United States. The film ended with Joel McCrea broadcasting during a night bombing of London. Hitchcock and his writers anticipated the Battle of Britain air attacks that began in October, long before the nightly bombings of London.

One of my favorites was Fritz Lang's *Manhunt*. It was based on *Rogue Male*, a fine novel written by Geoffrey Household. A British big game hunter played by Walter Pigeon stalks Hitler at Berchtesgaden for sport with no intention of assassinating him. He's caught, escapes, and becomes the subject of a massive manhunt led by a suave and villainous George Sanders. *Manhunt* was a fine suspense film that made us wish someone would kill Adolf Hitler.

Hollywood released a number of movies that glorified pre-war military life. Most were action films such as the *Submarine D-1* and *Dive Bomber*.[23] That was before Congress, anticipating an entry into the Second World War, initiated the draft in September 1940. Bud Abbott and Lou Costello, who performed rapid-fire and absurd word games on their radio shows, became instant movie stars with the January 31, 1941, release of *Buck Privates*, a broad comedy about life in the peacetime Army. In it, the popular "Boogie Woogie Bugle Boy," sung by the Andrews Sisters became a very big hit with jitterbuggers. We ignored the fact that it was a low budget quickie because it was very funny. I remember standing in a long line as we waited for the audience from an earlier showing to file out. The audience demand was so great that we were not allowed to stay and watch it a second time.

Hollywood took off its gloves and churned out dozens of action and espionage films once we were a nation at war. I saw most of them since they predominated the market. Besides, I was tired of escapism fluff. Many of the first war movies were low budget quickies such as *A Yank on the*

---

23 Although *Dive Bomber* – directed by Michael Curtiz and starring Errol Flynn and Fred MacMurray – wasn't produced until 1941, after the draft was established, it was Warner Bros. Pictures' tribute to the pre-Pearl Harbor U.S. Navy. It is considered to be a historical document both in its footage of U.S. warships and aircraft, and of the prewar U.S. in 1941.

Burma Road and *Corregidor*. Established movie series soon followed suit. A reluctant Tarzan joined in the war effort in *Tarzan Escapes* after Nazi paratroopers invade his escarpment. I've never quite figured out what the Nazis were doing deep in the African jungles. *Sherlock Holmes and the Voice of Terror* and *Sherlock Holmes and the Secret Weapon* transported the great sleuth and his sidekick into the 1940s. Basil Rathbone and Nigel Bruce had not aged a whit as they fought against sabotage in wartime England.

John Huston's *Across the Pacific* dealt with a fictional Japanese plot to attack the Panama Canal. *Flying Tigers* dealt with American mercenaries who fought for China before we entered the war. Its realistic air combat footage was a clever mix of model shots, close-ups, and cuts from actual newsreels. *A Yank in the RAF* dealt with American fighter pilots who fought in the Battle of Britain before we entered the war.

One of the best combat movies of the time was *Wake Island*. It was a highly fictionalized treatment of our troops' heroic stand on that small, isolated island. The Marine detachment was attacked on December 7 and held out until December 23. It showed our troops fighting to the death against Japanese invaders. Our men did fight bravely, but many surrendered and became prisoners of war. The movie overrode historical fact. Wake Island was seen as our Alamo.

There were a several films about the gallant defense of the Philippines. *So Proudly We Hail* and *Cry 'Havoc'* dealt with the heroism of Army nurses as our soldiers retreated back into the Bataan Peninsula. *Bataan* ended with Robert Taylor machine-gunning dozens of Japanese soldiers as he bravely fought to his death.

The war in North Africa received Hollywood's attention, too. In 1943 *Sahara* dealt with tank warfare in North Africa. It's very well done, but it looked like a paraphrase of John Ford's 1934 classic, *The Lost Patrol*. *The Immortal Sergeant* in the same year also dealt with desert warfare.

Guadalcanal Diary, loosely based on Richard Tregaskis' non-fiction bestseller, and *Gung Ho!* dealt with the beginnings of our island hopping. The epic *Air Force* remains one of my favorites then and now. The air battles are well done, especially the final one featuring an air view of the Battle of the Coral Sea. The film is filled with implausibilities, but it's a fine action film that's filled with well-drawn characters.

In 1941 the British movie, *Dangerous Moonlight* (also released as *Suicide Squadron* in the U.S.) starring Anton Walbrook and Sally Gray, treated the courage of Polish airmen who continued to fight after the fall of their country. It introduced the "Warsaw Concerto" by Richard Addinsell and began the vogue for mini concerti in movies, usually portrayed by troubled artist characters. The English also created a classic of air warfare in 1942 with *One of Our Aircraft Is Missing*.

A few wartime films were set in North America. The best of these were *Northern Pursuit*, *The 39th Parallel*, *The House on 92nd Street*, and *Saboteur*. The first two were realistic suspense thrillers set in Canada. They were not Hollywood products. The last two dealt with espionage and sabotage in the United States. *The House on 92nd Street* was a precursor of the realistic crime thrillers that emerged after the war. *Saboteur* was Hitchcock deftly using iconic American locales on a cross-country pursuit. I am still haunted by that last scene at the top of the Statue of Liberty. All are watchable and rewatchable.

Another sub-genre of war films was set at sea. Some of the best were Hitchcock's 1942 *Lifeboat*, John Ford's 1940 *The Long Voyage Home*, and Noel Coward's 1942 epic *In Which We Serve*. Others included the Merchant Marine delivering war weapons to Russia in *Action in the North Atlantic* and claustrophobic submarine films such as *Destination Tokyo* and *Crash Dive*. There were many more, but I vividly remember these.

In *Lifeboat*, Hitchcock's daring was at peak form, and he was abetted by a fine writer, John Steinbeck. He dares to set almost all his film in a lifeboat lost at sea after a ship has been sunk. Hitch raised eyebrows with the open-mouthed kiss between John Hodiak and Tallulah Bankhead. That was a shocking Hollywood first. Usually, kisses were angled so mouths were masked.

The Long Voyage Home blended four of Eugene O'Neill's *Sea Plays* into a continuous story about a group of merchant seamen. It was moody and beautifully shot and acted. John Ford and his screenwriter Dudley Nichols transposed O'Neill's early one-acts to the dangers that convoys faced as we shipped goods to Great Britain. It is one of the best of Ford's films. His maudlin sentiment and male braggadocio are muted. He allows his film to give a glimpse of a great American playwright's early work.

Coward's very British *In Which We Serve* is one of the best patriotic films of its time – or any time. It delivers its message of the bravery of a destroyer's captain and his crew without overt preaching. As can be expected, Coward's script is elegantly written. He directed the film, starred in it, and wrote its background music. It was unusually spectacular thanks to production assistance by the British Ministry of Information.

Action in the North Atlantic, starring Humphrey Bogart and Raymond Massey, extolled the men who shipped supplies to our Russian allies. During the Red Scare after the war some of those who were involved in the production were called before Congress and accused of being Communist sympathizers.

Destination Tokyo, starring Cary Grant and John Garfield, a 1943 tribute to our submariners, was a thrilling suspense film about at attempt to get inside the Tokyo harbor. Its underwater miniatures were extremely realistic.

To me, the best of the war films was the 1942 classic *Casablanca*, starring Humphrey Bogart, Ingrid Bergman, Claude Rains, and Paul Henreid, with a timeless music score by Max Steiner. It mixed a story of a lost love with an imminent takeover by the Nazis. Its release was timely. FDR, Winston Churchill, and Free French leaders Generals Charles de Gaulle and Henri Giraud met in Casablanca in January 1943. Once there, they determined the war could end only with the unconditional surrender of the Axis powers. That these four world leaders could meet there contradicted the threat of the menacing Nazis in the film. My wife and I see it annually. I am sure many others do the same.

Casablanca set off a flurry of films dealing with the German occupation of conquered countries. John Steinbeck again took time away from writing novels to author *The Moon Is Down*. Errol Flynn transferred his swashbuckling derring-do to occupied Norway in *The Edge of Darkness*. In *This Land Is Mine* Charles Laughton was brilliant as an introverted teacher who made a stand against the Nazis who occupied his homeland. Hollywood didn't neglect our Russian allies. *Days of Glory, North Star, Song of Russia,* and *Mission to Moscow* showed the Russian war effort in a favorable light. Even though Russia was a brave ally and suffered far greater casualties than we did, following the war the House Committee on Un-American Activities accused their filmmakers of spreading Communist propaganda. Some of the actors, directors, and writers of these – and other patriotic films – were blacklisted. I was blissfully unaware if I was being brainwashed. To me they were good movies about brave men and women fighting against great odds.

Many Hollywood comedies and musicals ignored the war, but George Stevens' *The More the Merrier* was a hilarious and sophisticated farce about the crowded housing situation in wartime Washington. Director-writer Preston Sturges created two comic wartime masterpieces in *The Miracle of Morgan Creek* and *Hail the Conquering Hero*. Both pushed the Production Code to its limits.

These comedies and others were welcome escapes from reading the casualty lists that appeared daily in our newspapers. Some of those listed were older friends. The war was going much too slowly. I worried that I would end up on one of those lists.

That shadow of fear hovered over all of us as we moved toward our eighteenth birthdays. I wondered how I would be tested in the violence that raged throughout the world. Would I meet that test? Would I be badly wounded or maimed? Would I die before I turned nineteen? I'm very sure that my parents were more fearful than I was. I was their only son. More than that, I was the future of the Coleman name. My dad was the only male in a family of five children.

Parnassus Junior High School

Schools of the 1940s were very different from our modern educational system. The junior high seventh and eighth grade curriculums were lumped together. There were the basic courses in English, history, general science, mathematics, physical education, health and hygiene, shop, and very few electives. I first learned about the dangers of venereal disease in Coach Al Dunn's hygiene class. He also dared to venture into sex education.

I became aware that some of my fellow students were not doing well. After eighth grade they ended up in another section. More than a few didn't return for ninth grade. Even more never moved on to high school. Junior high school was seen as a place to sift out those who had less aptitude in their studies. The term "social promotion" did not exist.

We had a choice of four curriculums when we entered ninth grade. The most prestigious was the rigorous academic course of study. It required at least two years of Latin, four years of English, four years of history and social studies, four years of mathematics and chemistry, and four years of physical education. There was room for electives such as art or music. Those who entered this program were intent on going to college.

Those who took the commercial curriculum aimed at white-collar office work. It offered practical courses in typing, bookkeeping, and other clerical skills. Another group transferred to the vocational school, a separate building some distance from Parnassus Junior High. There they acquired mechanical and technical skills that allowed them to become apprentices in a skilled trade or to work on the floor of one of the industrial plants in our valley. The general curriculum was lowest in esteem. Its enrollees had no desire to go beyond high school. Many wanted to drop out and go to work.

I chose the academic course of study. My father took pride that he was the first member of the Coleman family to go to college. Mom finished a year of Normal School and qualified to teach in a one-room school that included first through sixth graders. Teaching there was a real juggling act. My mother did that for two years before she got married. Neither of my grandfathers had gotten beyond the third grade, but they could read and write. Dad often said after he came home from hard manual labor, "No son of mine is going to work on a factory floor."

While Dad and Mom assumed that I would go to college, higher education existed in a rarefied intellectual atmosphere that seemed to be beyond my grasp. I had many reasons for my inferiority complex. While my grades were above average in all my classes, many of my classmates did much better than I. In English and history classes I did very well, but I struggled in mathematics and science. Later when I was in college, testing revealed that I had a high aptitude in mathematics; but I never did well. I had a serious problem. Math bored me. It seemed pointless to do problems that had been done by generations of high school students. My boredom intensified when I took geometry and solid geometry. I suspect some of that boredom arose out of the fact that I was revolting against my father's wishes. He wanted me to become an engineer. My ambitions were vague, but I didn't want to go in that direction. My interests were in English and American literature, history of any period, playing my violin, and my rudimentary attempts at cartooning. Theatre, which dominated most of my adult life, never entered my mind as a vocation. It seemed distant. It seemed like something someone else did. I was not active in school plays. The idea of acting terrified me.

4

A Seething Melting Pot

My clumsiness in my early teenage social life gave me an inferiority complex that was provoked by where I stood in New
Kensington's economic class system. No one put it into words, but it
existed. Perhaps it still does. The children of the well-to-do dressed
better than I, and they had an assured flair in their manners and
social interactions.

Actually, there were two tracks in our class system. The first dealt with
economic differences and where we lived in town. The Great Depression
had dealt a devastating blow to employment and economic opportunities for many years, and recovery was taking a long time. My father had
begun a slow climb up the economic ladder after we entered the war; but
that was blurred by the fact we lived across the tracks in an apartment
over a four-car garage. I wasn't at the bottom of the totem pole, but I was
uncomfortably near its base.

The second tier of class-consciousness was geared to religious, ethnic,
and racial differences. New Kensington was a model of the festering melting pots that spread through the three-river area. White Episcopalians
were at the top. Most were affluent, and many had lineages that reached
back to the founding of our country. They were the town's aristocrats. A
descending order followed. It began with Lutherans and was followed by
the Presbyterians, Methodists, and finally, the Baptists. No one spoke of
being atheist or agnostic. There also was a Black Baptist church. It was
considered quaint and harmless. Sometimes their choir came and sang
at our church on a Sunday evening.

The Protestant churches were followed in class by the Orthodox churches in town. They included small groups of Greeks, Lebanese, and Syrians. They were considered "different" because their services were conducted in different languages and many of their members were "foreigners," a word used to describe first and second generations of immigrant families.

Our small population of Jews was outside this ethnic hierarchy. Anti-Semitism was rampant, but many bigots had a grudging acceptance of our town's Jews since many were well educated and affluent. Money often overcame prejudices. Some Jews owned downtown stores. Others were skilled professionals. The father of one of my Jewish friends owned a shoe store; another was the son of a highly admired surgeon.

There was only one Chinese family in town. They owned and ran a laundry and dry cleaning service. This was essential to white-collar workers. The air pollution in our valley made it necessary for a daily change of shirts. Bob Yee was the best student in my class. He was fully accepted into our teenage society. I had only one Black friend, Doug Waters. He was handsome, amiable, and popular. He joined us at Saturday dances at the 'Y,' but few white girls dared to dance with him. To do so was frowned upon by many. Among those many were a few of Doug's closest chums. He and I exchanged junior pictures. I still have it in a family album. Few other Black students made it into high school. Those that did were never allowed to play on our athletic teams. A breakdown in that taboo came after the war and long before it did in professional sports.

There were a large number of Catholics in town. They, too, had a class system. It included, in descending order, families that had resided in America for generations. Many of these were Irish. They were followed by the Czechs (some of whom were Protestant), Poles and other Slavic groups, and finally the Italians. Even if an Italian family was well to do, they were at the bottom of the ladder. In some ways they were below the Blacks in New Kensington society.

One of the reasons for this was that New Kensington was a Mafia town. We were seated in alphabetical order in high school. The Italian boy in front of me was a chum of mine. His father had been killed in a gang war. I will not go into the gruesome details. He studied law and represented gang members when he became an adult. The Italian boy in back of me eventually went to prison for running a gambling den. It was rumored that the red-light district near the gates of the Alcoa plant were run by the Mafia. It was also believed that two rival families ran these and other illegal enterprises.

These minorities formed a huge part of the workforce at the large Alcoa plant that sprawled on the East bank of the Allegheny River. There was a mix of common labor jobs, skilled positions such as welding and machining, and foreman supervisors. That meant there was a rivalry for better paying jobs and positions of authority. Old "American" workers felt that they should have prime supervisory positions.

As I grew up amidst this web of ethnic, racial, and economic complexities, I began to question these hierarchies of discrimination. I had male friends in all of these groups even though our parents forbade dating their sisters. We enjoyed each other's company, and we rarely discussed religion. Perhaps the real melting pot began to function amidst these teenage interchanges. They were good guys who were the same as me. I saw no difference in them. I didn't understand the open prejudice and the name-calling that surrounded me as I grew up.

KEN HI

In the fall of 1941, I felt very adult as I walked a mile uptown with friends to begin classes at New Kensington High School or, as it was better known, Ken Hi. I had enjoyed my three years at Parnassus Junior High School; but now, at fifteen, I felt I was taking a big step toward growing up. What lay ahead seemed to be a great adventure, but I felt tremors of doubt. Would I be equal to the advanced courses I would be taking? I even asked myself if I would be able to graduate from high school. There was no social promotion back then. You had to meet a mark. If you didn't, your future life was limited. You only had one shot at tomorrow. I feared

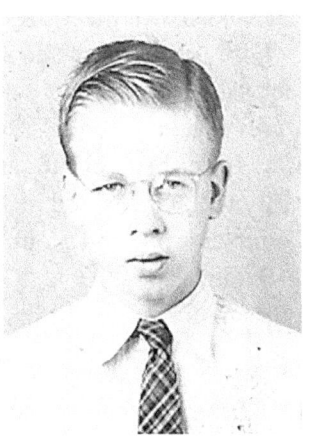

Bill in high school.

that I would reach a level where I could advance no further. Once there, I would have to settle for a lowly job that would possibly – just possibly – allow me to marry and raise a family. I had no idea of what I could attain in my adult years. I was unaware that my independent reading and other interests were preparing me to exceed my wildest dreams.

I remember little about my sophomore year in high school. One of the reasons for this was that I was in the traditional adolescent fog. The other was that I encountered no teachers who picked me out of the crowd around me. I do remember one event very vividly. A quiet Italian boy left a loud fart in our English class. It seemed to go on forever. The boy dropped his head on his desk and covered his face in embarrassment. The fart continued. It never seemed to end. Our teacher, a kindly but stern middle-aged woman, turned to the blackboard and began to write an assignment on it. As she did, her shoulders shook with repressed laughter. A few boys guffawed, but most of the girls sat with shocked looks on their face. Finally, our class resumed. The humiliated boy transferred to trade school the next day.

After he graduated and served in the Armed Forces, he ran his own beer garden. It was a quiet, well-run place that was frequented by workingmen and women who needed fortification before they went home. I stopped there many times in later years when I came home to visit my parents. He and I chatted about football and basketball games during our high school years, but I never mentioned what had happened in sophomore English class. Some things are better forgotten.

Girls, of course, acted as though they never farted; but we suspected they did so silently. There are some things in life that you can't avoid. Boys, however, rejoiced in releasing noxious gas when they were together and away from the opposite sex and their elders. We delighted in offending each other. One would lift a leg, leave one, and say, "Freedom!" Another would leave one and shout, "Fire one!" When they did, we ran away in all directions as we shouted, "Gas attack!" Others would surreptitiously release a lip fart in a crowded hallway at school and point at an unsuspecting friend. A few dared to release a back-row raspberry in class.

Some of my friends had a farting contest as we walked to school. One disqualified himself and had to go home and change his pants. Mastering the art of releasing voluntary farts was a goal for some – but not me! Another aspect of our boyish high spirits was impromptu wrestling matches – "rassling" or "horsing around," as we called it. If the winner could, he'd fart in the face of his subdued opponent. This ape-like victory signal was a primal expression of male dominance.

A public utility that served Western Pennsylvania bore the name People's Natural Gas. Young and old greeted that name with merriment. I recently noticed the company still bears that unfortunate name. With that I will end my boyhood fart stories. I think I have exhausted the subject.

There were the usual adolescent crudities as we went from class to class. Some of the bolder boys asked a well-built girl, "If I told you that you have a great figure, would you hold it against me?" This did not endear the boy to the girl. I doubt that she ever danced with him again. Most of us knew better. As for me, I was shy and tongue-tied when I was around girls my age.

We delighted in exchanging the dirty jokes older boys told us. New ones appeared almost daily. I theorized that somewhere in our land a wizened and very dirty old man thought them up and told them to a friend. A chain reaction began, and the new jokes spread like wildfire. The jokes ranged from adolescent to very adult and disgusting. Telling dirty jokes was a male pastime then. I first heard dirty jokes being told in mixed company when I was in my late twenties. I remember one adolescent joke that reflected our attitude toward Hitler.

"Why does Hitler wear long underwear?"
Answer: "To keep his Nutsys warm."

The most popular dirty jokes were about traveling salesmen stopping for the night at a remote farmhouse. There were infinite variations on this theme. Most jokes dealt with a lusty farm girl. One of the most hilarious dealt with two traveling salesmen, a traveling lady salesperson, and a pet polar bear. Other jokes dealt with innocent young men trying to buy condoms at drugstores or making a first visit to a house of prostitution. If you want to read some of the best jokes of that time, I refer you to G. Legman's two-volume *Rationale of the Dirty Joke*. In it he tells a classic joke and analyzes its social impact. Mr. Legman also published a collection of ribald limericks. Yes, that's his real name. As for me, I've kept a file of the punchlines for many of the dirty jokes I heard over the years. Two of my favorites were, "Run like hell! We're in the wrong room!" and "All is forgiven, just tell us where it is."

We were introduced to the highly popular "pin-up girls" in the stylized paintings of Alberto Vargas and George Petty. Both published their work in *Esquire*, the first quality men's magazine. Their women were scantily, but strategically, clad. Their slick paintings exceeded the reality of even the best female body. Their works were prototypes of the pin-up photographs popular with the Armed Forces. They were partly responsible for creating an impossible standard for female beauty. Airbrush techniques were used in photographs even then, although today's digital technology and computer apps achieve the same result. On the male side, what was handsome was determined by the movie stars of the time. That standard added to my inferiority complex. I looked young for my age, and I did not have classic good looks. Worse than that, I wore glasses.

Our pornography was limited to tattered *Tijuana Bibles* in which popular comic strip characters such as Maggie and Jiggs, Barney Google, Popeye and Olive Oyl, and Blondie and Dagwood were shown in explicit and outrageous sexual situations. Their eight pages were printed on cheap newsprint. Their origin was unknown, but it was rumored they were printed in Mexico and smuggled into the United States. They were furtively passed from hand to hand. They were quite disgusting.

A more innocuous source of titillation was *Sunshine and Health*, a nudist magazine we furtively scanned in the back aisle of a magazine store. It was filled with nude pictures of men and women. The genital areas of both sexes were airbrushed. Usually, these enthusiasts of nudity were shown as they enjoyed outdoor activities such as volleyball and table tennis. They were very ordinary people who were a far cry from Vargas and Petty's idealizations of the female figure.

In spite of my hazy remembrance of most of my sophomore year, a few things stand out. I remember that I enjoyed my history and English classes, and that second year Latin was the bane of my high school life. Even though four years of it was recommended for those who wanted to enter a better college or university, I stopped after two. Later in life I realized that those two years of Latin enhanced my vocabulary and allowed me to do well on standardized tests. I didn't dare suggest that I wanted to drop out of the academic math cycle after I completed sophomore trigonometry. I knew that request would have been vetoed. I reluctantly moved on to geometry in my junior year.

Japan's sneak attack on Pearl Harbor and our initial defeats in the Pacific stand in bold relief amidst my sophomore year memories. By now the older boys who supplied us with dirty jokes and pornography were being drafted. Some enlisted. It was sensible to enlist since one could choose his branch of the service. The Navy was preferred over the Army, but a few of the macho types joined the Marines.

Our local draft board was controversial. Some exemptions were questioned. It was rumored that some well-to-do fathers had gotten on the board in order to exempt their sons. Now we have no draft. This means that the poor are fighting our wars. While drafts are never popular, they are egalitarian in selecting those who will serve. While we have been labeled as the "Greatest Generation," we were flawed, but I like to believe that the majority of us wanted to serve our country in the war against the Fascist forces that were threatening the world.

My eighteenth birthday seemed far away, but I often wondered what it would be like to be in combat. I felt that combat was limited to the athletic and the especially brave. What little I saw of the realities of warfare in war movies convinced me that I would not be an ideal soldier.

I put those thoughts aside, enjoyed my summer vacation, and looked forward to my junior year.

The Summer of '42

As I turned sixteen my adolescent fog began to lift. I became more assured in my social life and my studies. A few of my friends began to date. I had a handful of pals, but I remained a loner. I still read on my own, and I went to the movies alone or with my male friends. I enjoyed dancing with a variety of girls on Saturday nights at the 'Y' and had attractive dates to DeMolay formals, but I had no longstanding girlfriend. Going steady with one never entered my mind.

Everyone I knew had a part-time job. My best friend, John, worked at the Keystone Dairy Ice Cream Parlor. His right forearm bulged with muscles from dipping cones. Others worked part-time as stock boys in stores. A select few worked as ushers in our movie theatres. As for me, I still carried the afternoon papers. That strengthened my legs, but it also made me a slow runner.

My junior year began well. I now had a circle of close friends. We played at seasonal sports and went to all the school football and basketball games. School spirit was rampant. We danced whenever we had the opportunity. I even began to strike up conversations with girls as we moved from class to class. I was on my way to becoming a "typical" teenager. It was a time of transition. Little did I know there was a wrenching and drastic transition waiting for me at the end of my first semester.

The tide of the war began to shift in North Africa and the Pacific, but our progress seemed glacial. Waging a world war was a titanic effort for a country that had just emerged from the Great Depression. Between 1941 and 1945 one eighth of our population, 16,000,000 men and women, joined our Armed Forces. They had to be equipped, clothed, and fed while they trained for combat. Then they had to be transported to far-flung battlefields. The workforce on the home front was depleted. Women rushed to gain new skills before they went to work in factories. New weapons had to be designed before they were manufactured. Hundreds of ships were needed to carry them overseas. Sunken battleships, cruisers, destroyers, submarines, and aircraft carriers had to be replaced. Shipyards hummed with activity. We had to create a vast aircraft industry since thousands of airplanes were needed, some for air support, and some for bombing the enemy. Our country rose to the challenge, and it did so with amazing rapidity.

Standing proud amidst all this activity was "Rosie the Riveter." In 1942 Tin Pan Alley immortalized women's war efforts, and the hit song's catchy lyrics and upbeat tune by Redd Evans and John Jacob Loeb became an instant hit. An idealized and defiant Rosie even appeared on the cover of the *Saturday Evening Post.*

My high school life continued. Our day began when we milled around in the morning outside Ken Hi until the doors were open. Our principal, the forbidding and dour H. B. Weaver, sat at a window in one of the two round towers flanking the entrance doors and balefully looked down on us. If he spotted an impropriety, he invited the culprit to his office. The usual penalty for misbehavior was time in a detention hall after school.

There was no cafeteria at Ken Hi, so I had to carry a lunch Mom packed for me in a colorful lunchbox that I felt was below my junior status. I joined my friends at a nearby drugstore during the lunch hour. The owner tolerated our eating our own lunches because we bought Cokes, root beer floats, and sundaes. I remember those lunch hours fondly. They were raucous escapes from our morning classes and gave us energy to face the afternoon.

When school let out, I dashed to the *Daily Dispatch* downtown office and picked up my newspapers. I delivered them quickly, so I had time to join my friends for play or to walk around "shooting the shit." While I never rode my bicycle to school, I often picked it up at home and rode it as I delivered my newspapers. I became quite adept at hurling folded newspapers with one hand onto porches as I sped along. We were forbidden to do this, but I did it anyway. It cut my delivery time in half.

There was an age-old custom then that we got a day off school when we defeated a major football rival. Arnold High was much smaller than Ken Hi and less of a football power. One chilly autumn night we soundly beat them. As we walked home together after the game, everyone agreed we deserved a day off. The next day we all stood outside chanting for an off day. H. B. came out and proclaimed that the custom only applied to major rivals. He reminded us that Arnold was a small town and that we usually beat their team. Nevertheless, we persisted. An ultimatum followed – come in to school or suffer a week in Detention Hall after school. A few went in, but most of us stayed out. It was the only time I played hooky.

Several of us walked out to a barn on Seventh Street Road and rented a basketball court that its owner built when he gave up farming. After picking sides, we decided to play until one team scored a hundred points. It was a long day since none of us was very good at basketball. When we returned to school the next morning, we were sentenced to seven hours of Detention Hall. I didn't mind. While it made me an hour late delivering papers, it gave me a chance to read, write, and draw.

My best friend John also played hooky and got detention. His angry father visited my dad and asked him how he was going to punish me for my part in the strike. Dad, who was quietly amused for my part in the event, said he planned to do nothing since I was receiving my punishment in Detention Hall. John's dad was not as forgiving. John was grounded for a very long time. Little did I know that I would soon owe Ken Hi three mornings of detention in perpetuity.

A Tearing up of Roots

One day near the end of the first semester of my junior year my father came home from work quite excited. Alcoa was building a new aluminum plant near Cressona, a small town in Schuylkill County in Eastern Pennsylvania. Dad was thrilled. His skills as an electrical engineer were needed. His years as a machinist and welder were over. His salary was greatly improved, but it wasn't enough to allow Mom to stay with me in New Kensington while I finished high school. I hid my feelings, but I was deeply upset. It was a great move for Dad, but I feared what this abrupt change in my life would bring. I was leaving my friends and the social structure I had grown into. It had its limitations and frustrations, but it was a reality I knew.

Dad went ahead of us to begin his work designing the electrical systems for the huge new plant. Since he wanted me to go to a large high school, he rented a spacious duplex house in a pleasant middle-class area on a hill above the downtown Pottsville business area. It was a short walk to Pottsville High School. It was a four-mile drive for Dad. Gasoline was strictly rationed, but since Dad was involved in the war effort, he would receive additional gas stamps.

Duplex in Pottsville

As my first semester ended, he drove back to New Kensington to pick up Mom and me – and our bulldog Peggy – arriving just as a huge moving van pulled up in back of our apartment in Parnassus. The drive to Pottsville was almost 250 miles. We took the newly built toll road, the Pennsylvania Turnpike, for most of the trip. By now we owned a 1936 four-door Chrysler. It was a great improvement over the wheezing 1928 Pontiac Dad kept working during the Depression. It was a pleasant ride. There were stops to eat at the Howard Johnson restaurants that had been licensed to operate on the Turnpike. We stayed in a hotel after our journey until movers arrived with our furniture. Dad could afford to be generous with our food and lodging since Alcoa paid for our moving expenses. I had rarely eaten in restaurants, and I had never stayed in a hotel before our move East.

We shared the duplex with the Choman family. They were second-generation Czechs. While the spelling was different their family name was pronounced just like ours. The father taught handwriting and was an expert calligrapher. It is a pity that this fine art has all but disappeared. They were a tight-knit family. My parents were apprehensive about living next door to "foreigners," but they soon found that the Chomans were good neighbors and not at all different from us.

I enrolled in the second semester of my junior year with some apprehension. I felt incredibly alone. I knew no one, and I was entering an unfamiliar school and facing new teachers. Even so, I sensed friendliness at Pottsville High. I quickly began to make friends. I enjoyed more social prestige than I had in New Kensington because I was the son of an Alcoa electrical engineer who was creating the electrical systems of a new plant that would supply many new jobs.

Pottsville, a town of less than 15,000, is nestled amidst the hills in Schuylkill County. Ninety-seven miles northwest of Philadelphia, it is surrounded by smaller Pennsylvania Dutch communities and is close to Fort Indiantown Gap, an Army induction center. The town centers on a sloping Main Street. Along it were stores, restaurants, two movie theatres, bars, and pool halls. Another movie theatre on a side street had weekly vaudeville acts. There I saw some of the classic acts in this last existing performance wheel. While I enjoyed seeing live acts, I had to endure the bad "B" movie that accompanied them. That didn't matter. I could see first run movies at the theatres on Main Street. I was witnessing the end of an era. In a few years, some of the acts I saw would appear in USO shows when I was in the Army. Later on, weekly television shows like the *Ed Sullivan Show* would give some acts a much wider audience, while other performers would disappear into the mists of time.

There were five vaudeville acts every week. One of the performers served as an emcee. There was a small pit orchestra made up of local musicians. Admission was the same as at the first-run theatres. The performers must have been paid a pittance. They cheated a little bit on that billing. A solo act would join another to form a third act. Then a duo act would combine with one of the solo acts to make it five. The acts were a mix of dancing, juggling, magicians, contortionists, acrobats, comics, and singing. The best was a group of beautifully trained dogs who built a small town on stage with minimum cueing. Most of my friends considered vaudeville old and "square," but I loved the acts I saw even when they weren't very good.

I soon learned that Pottsville had a dark history. Some of it was suppressed because it was scandalous and violent. Pottsville gained considerable fame when one of its sons, the novelist John O'Hara, wrote

Appointment in Samarra, a 1934 *roman à clef.* In it he vividly described the sharp business practices, corrupt local politics, and a variety of extra-marital affairs conducted by recognizable Pottsville citizens. Mr. O'Hara was hailed as an important American writer, but he was no longer welcome in Pottsville.

While the novel is largely forgotten, it deserves to be read. It, like Sinclair Lewis' *Babbitt,* is a vivid study of life in a small American town early in the 20th century. O'Hara's lean, laconic writing style is worth studying. This is especially true of his dialog. No other writer of that time managed to catch the conversations of men and women in the act of making love so well. Some critics hailed him as America's best short story writer. I soon learned that you did not mention his name in Pottsville.

A much older scandal lurked in Pottsville's past. It was the home of the late 19th century Molly Maguires, a secret society of Irish-Catholic miners who rebelled against child labor and the low wages paid by the Protestant owners of the anthracite coal mines in the area. The situation turned violent and the Pinkertons[24] were brought in. I soon found that no one mentioned this uprising socially. The revolt was never mentioned in our high school American history classes.

There was a book about the Molly Maguires in the town library, but it was not shelved. You had to ask for it over the frowning look of a librarian. It named names, and the names included many prominent families still in town. It's worth noting the Molly Maguires were fictionalized in A. Conan Doyle's early Sherlock Holmes novel, *The Valley of Fear.* A novel written in 1964 by Arthur H. Lewis, *Lament for the Molly Maguires,* was made into a movie starring Sean Connery and Richard Harris in 1970 and directed by Martin Ritt.

---

24 Allan Pinkerton founded the Pinkerton National Detective Agency in 1850. It functioned as a private security guard and detective agency for hire, and for a time was the largest private law enforcement organization in the world. It was used by the Department of Justice from 1871 until 1893, when the Anti-Pinkerton Act was enacted. Throughout its history it has been employed by railroads, mining and steel companies, and various other businesses and entities to exert greater control over their employees, protect strikebreakers, transport money, track down outlaws, bring criminals to justice, investigate possible criminal activity, and provide protection services. In the 1870s the agency was hired to infiltrate the Molly Maguires and bring down the labor organization. In 2003 Pinkerton's, along with the William J. Burns Detective Agency, was acquired by Securitas AB and became Securitas Security Services USA, Inc., one of the largest security companies in the world.

There were few minority groups in Pottsville. The town was almost equally divided between Irish Catholics and German and English-descended Protestants. The most affluent were the Protestants who owned most of the stores and businesses. The only exception was a small restaurant run by a Greek family. Their son, Gus Pallas, was one of my best friends. The Irish Catholics tended to work at low paying jobs, and the self-created aristocracy of Pottsville looked down on them. The American tendency to create class systems was inescapable. As for us, my dad was well paid for the first time in his life, but economically we were in the middle.

We immediately joined the Methodist Church. Of course, I had to go to Sunday School, the Sunday morning and evening services, and too many Wednesday prayer meetings. They struck me as a waste of my time, time that I would have used to go to a movie or to stay at home listening to radio programs.

Our minister, Reverend Cox, was an older man. His portly build and large mane of hair made him look like a Nineteenth Century tragic actor. His sermons were highly dramatic and emotional. He brought his parishioners to tears on many Sunday mornings with his stentorian voice as he orated and even acted out tales of woe and redemption. Of course, there was a climax, a rising peroration, where the suffering came to Christ. Churchgoers grew tired of these emotional onslaughts. They wanted a younger minister who would uplift their spirits. Reverend Cox was sent into retirement.

I joined the Epworth League at the church. High school students of both sexes attended it. The segregation of Sunday School was in the past. This allowed me to put one foot inside the high school social life because boys and girls whom I met in my classes attended these Sunday evening meetings. We rarely had an older advisor, so we were usually on our own. One evening, shortly after I arrived in town, we played "Post Office." I'd heard of this game, but I hadn't played it. Lots were drawn; and when you drew your turn, you went into another room. There a girl waited. You discretely – and sometimes not so discretely – kissed and returned to the main room. That game was a milestone for me. That evening, at sixteen, I kissed a girl for the first time. As I did, my right knee began to jerk and quiver involuntarily. It was a memorable moment. Unfortunately, word got out about our group's impromptu activity. From then on, we had an adult at our meetings. We had to find ways to kiss girls on our own.

As he resumed his long dormant career, Dad seemed happier than he had been in years. He was doing what he had set out to do when he left small-farm life and entered the electrical engineering program at the University of Pittsburgh. The new Alcoa plant was being built from the ground up, and Dad was deeply involved in the complexities of its wiring and lighting. While he never mentioned how much money he made, we lived better in Pottsville. The economic pressures of making ends meet were lifted. Dad was relaxed and genial, and his temper was not as quick to flare. He truly became a dad.

Pottsville High School was in a newer building that sat on a bluff overlooking the town. In many ways, it was a more pleasant place than Ken Hi was. Our principal, Mr. D.H.H. Lengel, was popular and genial. He ran the school smoothly. It was a happy place. The relaxed tone he gave to the school allowed us to open up our minds. He was certainly the best school administrator I've ever encountered.

Every morning we had all-school assembly. Sometimes we sang songs; sometimes there were skits and pep rallies, or a scene from a class play. Sometimes assemblies included surprise events. We never knew what to expect. On rare occasions classes were shortened so we could watch a feature film. I remember seeing the 1936 *Lives of a Bengal Lancer* there for the first time. It was exciting, but it had dubious educational value. I recently saw it again. Even though it's an exciting action adventure, it has a vicious racist tone that glorified British Colonialism in Northern India. This was the same colonialism that inspired the Japanese to try to conquer Asia and establish their own colonialism. I didn't understand the duality of wars then. It was much later, when I was in college and took a course in geopolitics, that I began to understand that all wars, even those that claim to be religious, are motivated by national needs for land and natural resources.

TURNING POINTS

The war reached a turning point for the Allies during the winter of 1942 and 1943. Our Air Force and the British RAF began nightly bombings of Germany. One of the prime targets was Berlin, but many other German cities suffered intense bombing. Thousand-plane air raids became the norm.

In Russia, after five months, one week, and three days, the Battle of Stalingrad ended on February 2, 1943. It was one of the largest and bloodiest battles in the history of warfare with nearly 2 million killed, wounded, or captured. More than 100,000 German troops surrendered. Only about 5,000 made it home. The defeat infuriated Hitler. His Russian adventure had ground to a bloody, humiliating halt. The Red Army immediately went on the attack. Stalin began to clamor for a British and American cross-Channel invasion.

A week after the defeat at Stalingrad dealt Germany a devastating blow in Russia, the first victory in the Pacific theatre came when Allied forces defeated Japan in the Solomon Islands. The Battle of Guadalcanal had raged from August 7, 1942, until February 9, 1943, for a total of six months and two days. Both of these battles were considered turning points in World War II. A few weeks later, in an air attack that lasted from March 2 through the 4th, our Navy destroyed a Japanese convoy of troops bound for New Guinea in the Battle of the Bismarck Sea. The fight for New Guinea was underway. After a year of defeats our morale was boosted.

Perhaps the war would end sooner than we thought it would. My concerns about military service faded into insignificance as I entered my new world. Shortly after we arrived in Pottsville, and just as I began enjoying my classes and making new friends, the unexpected happened. My new life was brought to an abrupt halt.

Mumps!

I caught the mumps. This could not have come at a worse time. I had suffered through measles, chickenpox, and other contagious diseases before I reached my teens. This was in the pre-vaccine[25] era, so all involved

---

25 The first mumps vaccine was licensed in 1948, but its effectiveness was very short term. An improved mumps vaccine was developed and licensed by vaccine researcher Maurice Hilleman in 1967. He used the mumps virus he isolated from his daughter Jeryl Lynn when she was ill with the mumps at the age of 5. This strain is referred to as the "Jeryl Lynn strain." Mumps vaccination is combined with measles, rubella, and varicella vaccines (MMRV) and is given in two doses, the first at 12-15 months of age and the second between 4-6 years of age.

In recent years, a controversial 1998 study asserted that vaccines were harmful and caused, among other things, autism. Even though the article was proved false many times over, the doctor who wrote it lost his medical license, and the medical journal that

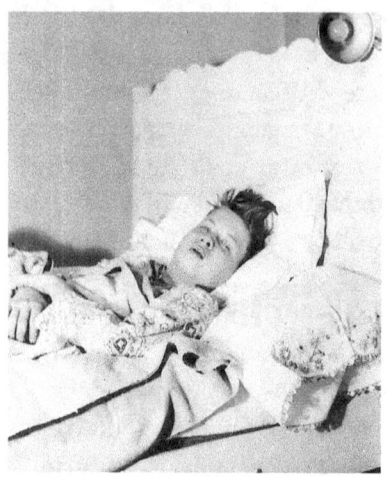

Bill with the mumps!

quarantines. Parents treated these diseases as something to get out of the way. That is, unless it killed you. Once you had one of these diseases, you were immune to it. More serious diseases such as smallpox and polio were feared. There was no cure for either, but polio was more fearsome. It was crippling or fatal. Many of those who survived its attack had to spend the rest of their lives in iron lungs.

Mumps meant a time of complete inactivity. It hit me very hard, and I was restricted to my bed for most of a month. My parents feared I would become sterile if my fever got too high. I was dreadfully alone and bored. To make matters even worse, I wasn't allowed to read. People feared that with the high fever that accompanied the mumps too much light would damage eyesight.

My room was darkened during my quarantine. Since I was confined to my bed, I could not go downstairs to listen to our Atwater Kent console radio. One thing saved me. My parents bought me a small table radio. During my quarantine – and after – I pursued my emerging interest in classical music. I listened to the several symphony broadcasts of the time. On Sunday evening the CBS Symphony – yes, radio networks had their own symphony orchestras – presented full concerts. The most famous radio orchestra was the NBC Symphony, which was led by the fiery Italian-born conductor, Arturo Toscanini. I soon got used to listening to long and complex musical works. I continued my interest in jazz by

---

published the article retracted the article, an anti-vaccine movement began to rise among certain groups of people. Sadly, because of this ongoing erroneous and dangerous assertion even with overwhelming evidence that vaccines are safe, some parents have chosen not to have their children vaccinated. As a result, diseases such as measles have seen a troubling and harmful resurgence. During the COVID-19 pandemic of 2020-2021, vaccines again dominated the news.

It is interesting to note that in 2018 a medical study has drawn the first direct link between the banned pesticide DDT and autism. This refutes the assertion of those who oppose vaccinations, claiming that it causes autism. Even though DDT has been banned from agricultural use since 1972, it remains in the environment.

listening to the weekly *Chamber Music Society of Basin Street*. At night I furtively listened to remote broadcasts by famous big bands from ballrooms around the country.

I listened to daytime soap operas such as the rambling *Vic and Sade*, the wonderfully Jewish *The Goldbergs*, and the melodramatic *Backstage Wife*. The latter opened with the announcer grandly intoning, "Now, we present once again, *Backstage Wife*, the story of Mary Noble, a little Iowa girl who married one of America's most handsome actors, Larry Noble, matinée idol of a million other women – the story of what it means to be the wife of a famous star."

I couldn't have cared less about Mary Noble's troubles, but the program was something to listen to every afternoon and listen I did. I was relieved when the evening prime time programs came on. I could spend my evening hours with old friends I had listened to since I was a young boy.

CBS condensed great novels for broadcast. One of my favorites was an adaptation of James Joyce's *Portrait of the Artist as a Young Man*. After my illness ended, I rushed to the library and devoured the book. Joyce's stream-of-conscious technique thrilled me. Reading that book was one of the formative experiences in my young life. I found that a young Catholic man could be just as disenchanted with his church as I was with my own.

Thanks to my illness I discovered one daytime radio delight, Don McNeill's Chicago based *Breakfast Club*. It was a variety show punctuated by the "Call to Breakfast" every quarter hour, when McNeill would instruct listeners to stand up and march to music around their breakfast tables. Its house band featured the great jazz violinist, Joe Venuti. I learned that a violin was a viable jazz instrument. I attempted some bluesy licks on my violin when I edged into my recovery. Venuti lived well into the long-playing stereo record era. I purchased many of his albums. His tasteful, swinging jazz improvisations remain listening delights that I regularly enjoy. They are kingpins in our extensive jazz collection.

Popular music continued to play a huge part in my social life. I listened to live broadcasts of my favorite bands during my recovery. The young women of the time were enthused about Frank Sinatra. He established his popularity with the Tommy Dorsey Orchestra. Dorsey and his brother, Jimmy, another bandleader, grew up in nearby Orwigsburg. All the boys, including me, thought Sinatra was a sissy. After all, he was only twenty-eight; and he hadn't joined the Army.

Young women adored Sinatra's boyish look and manner. Many swooned when he sang torch songs. Older singers like Russ Colombo and Rudy Vallée, the "Vagabond Lover," had enjoyed this same type of fame a few years earlier; but no other singer of Sinatra's time got that sort of reaction. Boys of my age resented Sinatra's sex appeal. I never heard such screaming and squealing again until years later, first with the young Elvis Presley and then with the Beatles. I suspect that some of that fainting was done to gain the attention of the singer on stage.

Some of my classmates made the hundred-mile train trip to Philadelphia to hear Sinatra perform with the Dorsey Band. The boys in the audience threw pennies on stage during Sinatra's first song. He stepped to the edge of the stage and said, "If you guys want trouble, come backstage. I got some big guys to take care of you." The boys hooted even louder and threw more pennies.

After my mumps quarantine ended, I eased back into school life. I lost some academic ground during my absence, but I caught up and finished my junior year with above-average grades. Again, I excelled in English and history. Again, I struggled in math and science, but I survived. I was happier than I had been in New Kensington. I liked the sense of spirit at Pottsville High. While I missed my old friends, I enjoyed a wider social acceptance now.

I quickly gained a new circle of male friends. They included Harry Roadarmel, Jack Malson, Bob Hildebrandt, Dick Fetterman, Bim Meyer, and John Gibson. Harry was strikingly handsome. His parents were Mom and Dad's closest friends, and we went to the same church. Jack had dark Celtic good looks. He was in superb physical condition from his gymnastic training. He became the state rope climbing champion in his junior year. Bob was blonde and had an incredibly cheerful smile. Dick was a joker who had a cheerful disposition and kept us laughing. Good humored and witty Bim Meyer was Pennsylvania Dutch and had a slight accent. He was an avid fan of the daily comics. His parents had gotten his name from the father in *The Gumps*, a popular one-panel comic of the time. Years later, his nickname inspired me to call my eldest son Wim.

John Gibson was the most bookish of our gang. He was deeply into baseball statistics and never played games with us. He and his brothers were honor students. The rest of us weren't. My closest friends were Harry and Jack. I happily adjusted into my new life as my junior year ended.

For the moment the war seemed far away. This was the happiest time of my young life.

One Last Summer on the Home Front

Allied victories began to mount as the summer of 1943 began. The British, bolstered by American troops, drove Rommel's German Afrika Korps and surviving units of the Italian First Army troops into Tunisia. More than 250,000 Axis forces surrendered on May 13. The war in Africa ended with an Allied victory. Rommel's reputation as a strategic genius was tarnished. He escaped to France. Once there he began to plan a defense against an anticipated invasion from England.

We followed up this great Allied victory in Africa by bombing major cities in Sicily and Sardinia, two possible stepping-stones to an invasion of Mainland Italy. As summer began the Russians were driving the German troops west. The loss of so many troops in Russia and North Africa weakened Germany's ability to launch attacks against our Allied forces on any front. After so many years as the offensive power, Germany was now in a defensive position.

British and American bombers attacked German cities. The bulk of their bombing runs concentrated on armament works, steelworks, coke plants, ten synthetic oil plants, and the Ruhr dams that supplied electricity for the German war industry. At sea, the Allied defense against U-boat attacks was so successful that German Admiral Karl Dönitz withdrew his submarines from the Atlantic. Now it was possible to cross the ocean with less fear of an enemy attack on the high seas. Plans for a Second Front in France could begin. We all asked when would that be?

*   *   *

Now that we had finished our junior year, we became concerned about the draft. Some of my friends were close to turning eighteen. There were no deferments to finish high school. When you reached draft age, you were inducted. Casualties were mounting, and more young bodies were needed to replace the fallen. I was safe. I didn't turn eighteen until June 1944, immediately after my high school graduation, but I sensed that if the war continued, this was going to be my last summer of freedom.

Since most of my friends had part-time jobs, I decided to join the workforce. I applied for work at a nearby Acme Grocery store and was hired as a stock boy. It was a pleasant job, but it paid a mere 35½ cents an hour. That was far less than I was paid for the hour I spent delivering newspapers, but I worked at least twenty hours a week once school was out.

I would have been happier seeing free movies if I worked as an usher at a movie theatre but working in a grocery store wasn't demanding. We stocked shelves, replaced produce, and helped customers. More often than not, we had little to do. We ate more than our share of grapes, fruits, cheeses, and cold cuts as we worked. The manager never chided us for this. I suspect he would have if he had come out of his office to see what we were doing. Fortunately, he wasn't a hands-on manager.

The Acme Grocery chain was notoriously cheap. Nothing went to waste. Some of it should have. One of our most revolting tasks was to sort out rotten potatoes from those that could still be sold. Rotting potatoes smell terrible. One of the guys I worked with resented this. When the manager stepped out, he heaved some of the most rotted potatoes into a ventilating fan. A wretched odor spread throughout the store. Customers arrived and left quickly. When the manager returned, he was puzzled by the smell. His only reaction was to retreat to his tiny office. He quickly exited. The smell had permeated his small space since it was linked to the ventilation system. He blamed the rotting potatoes in the back room for the wretched smell that permeated the store and ordered us to throw them in the garbage. He never found out what my colleague had done. Our nauseating days of sorting potatoes ended.

Our produce sales were lagging behind those of other stores in the Acme chain. Our manager, again keeping an eye on the bottom line, let the bins empty until he ordered again. Sometimes he kept the produce too long. By the end of the week too much was wilted and rotting. The district manager sent a man named Dave, a produce specialist, to increase sales. Dave was a jaunty, stocky man who was brimming with self-confidence. His first act was to order more produce and fill the display bins to the brim. The banks of multi-colored fresh produce were stunning. Sales soared. Our indolent manager was fired, and Dave became our manager. We liked him, and we worked harder for him than we had for his predecessor.

I learned a valuable lesson from Dave. To make money, you have to spend money. This is a lesson many of today's bean counters haven't learned or choose to ignore. If you give people value for their money, they will come back again and again. Dave quickly made us one of the most profitable Acme stores in the East. Many years later we learned that the economic theories of John Maynard Keynes were right. Austerity only causes more poverty.

After a few weeks on the job, my pay was raised to 37 cents an hour. I hardly noticed it when I received my weekly paycheck. I invested some of my modest earnings in war bonds, but I held back some for my entertainment and socialization. By now, my parents had a firm financial footing. By working, I cost them very little.

There were shortages of various kinds of food and staples at the Acme store. One week we would have toilet paper. The next week we wouldn't have enough. Another week we would be short of laundry detergent. The shortages varied from week to week. Hoarding was not unusual. Shopping housewives sidled up to us as we stocked shelves and quietly asked what the current shortage was and if we knew of any impending shortages. We grew to despise them.

When our biweekly delivery trucks arrived, dozens of wives filled the aisles as they waited for us to open boxes and begin to stock the shelves. Sometimes they rushed through the store opening boxes and filling their carts before we could. Sometimes they grabbed items from our hands before we could put them on a shelf. Their panic disgusted us. Worse still, they bought up more than they could ever use in the week ahead. It was unfair to customers who came to the store later.

We began to amuse ourselves with making up shortages that did not exist. Our questionable contribution to the war effort was to tell the hoarders that we were going to have a short supply of items that were in generous supply. They frantically cleaned off the shelves and bought items that were in abundance. More often than not, they bought groceries they didn't need.

For a while Dave was puzzled by these weird increases in sales. Then he discovered what we had been doing. He quietly urged us to continue our false reports. After all, increased sales of anything enhanced the regional office's opinion of Dave's management abilities. As for me, I wondered how long it would take a family to use up dozens of jars of pickles, large bottles of vinegar, and other staples. I remember us chuckling as one woman filled her cart to beyond the brim with toilet paper when we knew that a shipment of it was pulling up in a truck back of the store. I must admit I let my Mom know about real shortages. I told her not to tell her friends. One, in particular, was an avid hoarder.

Rationing was a part of life on the home front. Natural rubber tires were scarce since we no longer had access to the Pacific rubber plantations. Worn tires were retreaded or replaced with the newly developed synthetic rubber tires made of a copolymer of butadiene and styrene. Supplies of gasoline were scarce. My father received extra gasoline stamps so that he could drive to his work outside of town. However, because he had to nurse his use of gasoline, I wasn't able to learn to drive until after I got out of the Army. Not having a driver's license contributed to my ending up in the Infantry. I was not alone in this. Few eighteen-year-old soldiers had driver's licenses, so older draftees got to drive jeeps, trucks, and tanks. Another skill I failed to acquire in school was typing. That barred me from working as a desk clerk in the Army.

*   *   *

Our gang played the usual seasonal pickup games. There were no informal leagues in Pottsville, and our church didn't sponsor any sports. We just got some guys together and played. It was rough and tumble. I remember playing tackle football without pads in a vacant lot. One of the end zones was a cinder path. Scoring a touchdown meant cinder abrasions. I came home with more than a few. Gymnast Jack Malson was more muscular than the rest of us. We soon learned to tackle him with a knuckle driven into his thigh. This gave him an instant agonizing charley horse that removed him from the game. Fortunately, Jack was amiable about our dirty play.

I had my first semblance of a romance during the summer of 1943. A pretty girl my age came to stay with friends of our family. Their son was one of my best friends and introduced us. She had a pert figure and a lively manner. This charming summer visitor enchanted me. I was amazed when I got up the nerve to ask her out on a movie date. I was even more amazed when she accepted. It was a pleasant evening. She was well read, so we had something to talk about other than the movie we saw. I was rewarded with a lingering kiss as we stood at the front door. We agreed to another movie date.

Shortly after our second date, my parents sat me down and told me I was not to date her again. I was puzzled. She fit all their requirements.

She went to our church with the family she was visiting, and she was quite Anglo-Saxon. I resisted. They insisted. They gave no reason, but I suspect she may have been pregnant or had acquired a bad reputation and was sent away from home. She left later in the summer to points unknown. Nothing was said, and there were no rumors. What had she done? What kind of life did she lead after that summer? She is one of the many unfinished stories in my life.

I turned my eyes to other girls as I settled into my last summer of being just a boy. Teenage boys can be very disgusting. When a blossoming young woman was out of earshot, some described her as being "stacked." A cruder term was, "She's built like a brick outhouse." Sometimes this small building had a more excretory name. A low whistle of appreciation for a passing pretty girl was not considered out of line in those days. Young women considered it a form of flattery. Another phrase of admiration was, "Hubba-hubba!" A boy who relentlessly pursued girls was called a wolf. A wolf howl was considered less than cool, but some boys ventured one after a girl had passed by. I was too shy and proper to use any of these expressions of male approval.

MEANWHILE, BACK AT THE FRONT

British and American forces led by Field Marshal Bernard Montgomery and General George S. Patton invaded Sicily on July 10, 1943. It was a quick victory. Further north on the mainland of Italy on July 24, 1943, the Prime Minister was deposed by King Emmanuel III when the Fascist Grand Council voted no confidence in Mussolini. The next day *Il Duce* was removed from government, arrested, and spirited north to a mountaintop prison.

The island of Sicily was secured on August 17. Now we had a base for an invasion of Italy. The channel to the toe of Italy's boot was so narrow that landing craft could cross it on their own. It seemed like an easy jump to the mainland of Europe.

A serious complication emerged. While visiting a field hospital on August 3 and 10, General Patton slapped and berated two soldiers who suffered from what was then called battle fatigue. The news of these temper fits spread to Patton's superiors and were eventually reported by journalists in the United States. Army Chief of Staff George Marshall and

Supreme Commander Dwight D. Eisenhower ordered Patton to apologize to the men, his Seventh Army was disbanded, and he was not allowed to return to a combat command for almost a year.

The country was deeply divided. Many thought the soldiers were cowards who got what they deserved. Others disagreed and despised Patton for his actions. Post-traumatic stress disorder (PTSD) was not defined until long after World War II.[26] In fact, it did not enter the general public's consciousness until the 21st century. In the First World War it was called "shell shock." It was assumed that the explosion of a nearby shell injured the brain. The definition was expanded to include battle fatigue in World War II, but too many considered mental collapse during combat was due only to cowardliness.

The Germans could not believe that the brilliant Patton wouldn't be used in the invasion of Italy. Even though he was in the doghouse, our High Command used Patton as a decoy as they planned the Normandy invasion. Eventually he was given the Third Army in January 1944, but he was not allowed to be part of the Normandy landing. Once he returned to command, his army moved faster and farther than any other.

---

26 During WWII various terms were used including "battle fatigue," "shell shock," "battle stress," and "combat neurosis." In the 1950s it became known as "gross stress reaction" in the DSM-1 (Diagnostic and Statistical Manual of Mental Disorders). That diagnosis had similarities to our modern understanding and definitions of PTSD and contains language including "civilian catastrophe." The actual term "post-traumatic stress" was not adopted by DSM-III until the 1980s. Greater understanding of this condition came about during and after the Vietnam War as the experiences and conditions of the U.S. military veterans were recognized and acknowledged. The term post-traumatic (with a hyphen) stress disorder became more common when the International Statistical Classification of Diseases and Related Health Problems (ICD-10) was completed in 1992. The results of Post-Traumatic Stress Disorder (PTSD) on individuals did not become part of the general public perception until the end of the 20th and the beginning of the 21st centuries, and especially so as a result of the Persian Gulf wars in Afghanistan and Iraq. More recent public awareness of "Trauma and Stressor-related disorders" has expanded to include trauma, anxiety, and stress resulting from events on civilian populations such as the Oklahoma City bombing in 1995; the September 11, 2001, attacks; and Hurricane Katrina in 2005; as well as individual traumatic events such as rape, sexual molestation, physical attack, being threatened with a weapon, and abuse.

It must be noted that there is a difference between post-traumatic stress, and post-traumatic stress disorder, even though there is considerable overlap in symptoms between the two conditions. To learn more about the differences, and the treatments for each, please visit the link: https://www.brainline.org/article/what-are-differences-between-pts-and-ptsd. This *BrainLine* website for information about traumatic brain injuries is sponsored by the Bob Woodruff Foundation, with the stated purpose of "investing in the Next Chapter for Our Veterans."

Little did I know in that summer of 1943 that I would join the Third Army as a rifleman and become part of its daring advances in the last months of the war. I never saw Patton in person, but he had a great impact on my young life. In fact, I believe I am alive because of his tactics. I will speak more of that later.

The Allied Invasion of Italy began on September 3, 1943. Italy secretly began negotiating a surrender on the same day. British General Harold Alexander's 15th Army group, comprising Lieutenant General Mark Clark's U.S. Fifth Army and General Bernard Montgomery's British Eighth Army, were assigned the task of invading Italy. Montgomery led his forces north from the toe of the boot while the bulk of the British and American troops landed on beaches near Salerno. Clark's caution once his troops landed gave the Germans time to counterattack. He was not helped by Montgomery's slow advance from the boot even though he met little resistance.

Our invasion of Italy was bogged down. I believe that if Patton hadn't slapped those two soldiers, the beginning of the Italian campaign would have been much different. If he had landed at Salerno, he would have gotten off the beaches quickly. The Nazis wouldn't have been able to build up their forces and contain the beachhead for almost two weeks. If Patton had landed at any point on the foot of the boot, his Seventh would have sped north and cut off the German forces rushing to stop the Salerno invasion. However, the High Command's choice of discipline also punished the gallant soldiers who were forced to fight under the cautious generals, Mark Clark and Bernard Montgomery.

The Italians surrendered on September 3, and Marshall Pietro Badoglio was named Prime Minister of Italy. The surrender was not formally announced until September 8 over fears of the German response to the Armistice. The next day, following hostile German actions, King Victor Emmanuel, Prime Minister Badoglio, and some military ministers and staff members escaped to Brindisi and Pescara seeking Allied protection.

The Salerno beachhead was still contained when Winston Churchill spoke to the British Parliament on September 12. His observation was almost surreal: "This is not the end. It is not even the beginning of the end. But it is, perhaps, the end of the beginning."

On the same day, German SS troops led by Otto Skorzeny rescued Mussolini from his mountaintop prison. Hitler declared his old ally head of the puppet Italian Social Republic. A few Italians remained loyal to him, but most accepted their nation's surrender to the Allies. Clark's forces finally broke out of the Salerno beachhead on September 19 and began a slow advance on Naples against heavy Nazi resistance. The long and bloody slog up the boot began. On September 23 a longer version of the Armistice was signed in Malta. Finally, on October 13, Badoglio and the Kingdom of Italy, rather belatedly, officially declared war on Nazi Germany.

To most Americans the war in Italy was a sideshow. Everyone wondered when we would cross the English Channel and invade France. As I entered my senior year in the fall of 1943, I wondered how long the war would last. I was not deeply concerned since I would not turn eighteen until June 1944.

5

An Interrupted Senior Year

MY SENIOR YEAR began well. I enjoyed my classes in English and Problems of Democracy. Chemistry was bearable, but geometry was a struggle, even from the beginning. Physical education was mandatory. It was lazily taught by a coach who preferred spending time in his office while we exercised on our own. I got out my violin and joined the orchestra. I was not first chair material, but I liked being part of an ensemble.

Our conductor was Mr. Minnichbach, an older man inclined to schmaltzy interpretations. I remember that he prepared us to play the Strauss waltz, "Roses from the South," with a prominent guest conductor, Dr. Peter Buys. There was a passage he took very slowly. He made it wail with an anguish worthy of Tchaikovsky. When the guest conductor took over, we wailed out the section. He stopped in dismay and insisted that we play it brightly. It sounded much better. Poor Mr. Minnichbach stood to one side quite crestfallen.

Art was my favorite elective. The teacher was Isabelle Zerbe,[27] a willowy beautiful woman who was in her early thirties. She was an excellent teacher who quietly motivated you to strive to be better. At first, we sketched from still life and plastic models that were artfully arranged on

---

27 Isabelle Zerbe was born May 24, 1906. A coal miner's daughter, she grew up in Newtown and rode a stagecoach to classes at Pottsville High School where she graduated in 1923. She received her bachelor's degree from Edinboro State University and then went to George Peabody Art School (now part of Vanderbilt University) in Nashville, Tennessee for her master's. She taught at Pottsville High School from 1929 until 1950. She taught for another 20 years at Council Rock High School in Bucks County. She was considered a good artist and one of Schuylkill County's greatest art teachers. Isabelle Zerbe Westberg died on September 23, 2003.

a table. We progressed to a male model wearing bathing trunks. I was frustrated. My drawings of the human figure were stiff.

One day Miss Zerbe noticed that I was entertaining my classmates with cartoons I drew. Some satirized high school life and my friends. Some made fun of my teachers. Fortunately, Miss Zerbe was amused. She wisely told me to stop struggling with reality and concentrate on my cartooning. Until now, I had never had a teacher who took such a bold step to allow me to realize my talents. I became very productive. Once I had a body of work, I was given my own bulletin board in the upper hallway. I drew several cartoons each week and posted them. I was gratified to see

Pottsville High School cartoon,
November 22, 1943.
Note the name of Miss (Florence) Short
in the upper right-hand area.

the hallway jammed with students and faculty members looking at my newest work. This was my first moment of fame.

Some of my cartoons lampooned controversial moments of the week. It is to Miss Zerbe's – and the administration's – credit that I was never censored. My friends contributed ideas. Even the teachers became involved. When I drew a cartoon lampooning one teacher's foibles, he or she would ask me to draw one about one a colleague. I complied. The academic teachers seemed to enjoy my work. The jocks were less amused.

My most famous cartoon was drawn in the winter of 1944. One day the lazy coach/gym teacher I mentioned earlier made us exercise outside in gym shorts during a freezing day while he wore an overcoat and earmuffs. I recorded this moment and posted it. The coach was infuriated, even though all I had done was record an actual event.

At the end of each week, I took down the cartoons that hadn't been stolen and put them away. Many survive. Some portray long ago events. Some still retain their humor. I think they give a sense of a different high school era. While they were drawn

Obstacle Course

Rough draft sketch for USO Mural.

in time of war, a time when many of my friends turned eighteen and were drafted, they are devoid of any reference to the fears we all shared. Somehow, we managed to preserve our innocence.

My fame as a cartoonist spread into town. I was asked to draw a mural on a large wall at the downtown USO, a recreational facility set up for visiting servicemen and women. It was a big project, but I enjoyed it. First, I drew a panoramic cartoon on two standard sheets of paper. Then I sketched this out on the wall with charcoals. When I felt it was ready, I filled my work in with paint. My mural was filled with lecherous soldiers pursuing townswomen. No one seemed to object to its ribald content, probably because it was true!

My favorite English teacher at Pottsville High School was Florence Short (b. 4/19/1889-d. 9/1/1963), a formidable single woman then in her middle years. While stern, she was a fine teacher. She noticed my writing ability and encouraged it. It is amazing how just a little encouragement will set one on a path that could be realized many years later. I owe a lot to her. She encouraged my writing and expanded my reading interests.

I did receive one reprimand from her regarding my reading outside of class. Drugstores had lending libraries specializing in recent best sellers. I checked out Stuart Cloete's *Congo Song*. It dealt with a dissatisfied young wife who lived with her indifferent husband in an African jungle village. It was implied she had an affair with a gorilla. It was so vaguely written that I was unsure of what really happened between her and the gorilla. I brought the book to school, so that I could have something to read in study hall. Miss Short noticed what I was reading and reprimanded me. It, I found, was considered a "dirty book." Now it would be considered quite tame.

I haunted the school and town libraries. Somehow, I began reading stage plays. At first, I read the *Best Plays Theatre Yearbook* series by Burns Mantle. These were annual collections of the ten best Broadway plays and a record of the entire season. Instead of printing the entire play, Mr. Mantle, a noted critic, condensed them by mixing some dialog with narration. They were quick and easy reads. I was surprised to learn that some stage plays treated certain subject matter in more adult ways than movies did. Broadway had no Hays Office or a Motion Picture Production Code.[28] This freedom intrigued me. After reading through several

---

28   From 1930 to 1968 a set of moral guidelines, known as the Motion Picture Production Code, was applied to movies in the United States. This was also known as the Hays Code, named after Will H. Hays, the President of the Motion Picture Producers and Distributors of America (MPPDA) from 1922 to 1945. The MPPDA later became known as Motion Picture Association of America (MPAA). The Production Code was adopted in 1930 and began to be strictly enforced in Hollywood under the administration of

seasons of condensed plays, I was inspired to read entire plays. These were in short supply, but I read every one I could find. While I was not involved in high school dramatics, I had an interest in theatre that was almost instinctive. I owe an immense debt to Burns Mantle. He set me on a course that eventually led me to a long life in theatre teaching and production, theatre history, and playwriting.

The elderly, or so he seemed to us, "Pop" Gaskins taught algebra and geometry. He was a grumpy old guy with a quick temper. Some of the boys openly teased him. He was quite indignant when we did not do our assignments well. He had good reason to lose his temper with me. I was not very good at math, and I was even worse in geometry. I was headed toward failing his course in solid geometry as I began the second semester of my senior year. The only thing that saved me was that I enlisted in the Army in February and never finished the course.

The most popular teacher at Pottsville High was Pete (as we called him privately) Sterner. His Problems of Democracy class was equally popular. He required us to subscribe to *The New York Sunday Times*. By doing that, he established a lifetime habit that I still enjoy. P.O.D., as

---

Joseph Breen in 1934. It spelled out what was and was not acceptable content for motion pictures produced for the public in the U.S. Profanity, suggestive nudity, sex hygiene and venereal diseases, ridicule of the clergy, drug trafficking, miscegenation, White slavery, perversion, childbirth, and children's sex organs were among the things strictly forbidden. Other depictions like sedition, sympathy for criminals, arson, cruelty to children and animals, rape, a man and women in bed together, etc., had to be presented with special care "to the end that vulgarity and suggestiveness may be eliminated, and that good taste may be emphasized." Over the years many directors and screenwriters attempted to get around the Code using various tricks and techniques, such as Alfred Hitchcock's 1946 film *Notorious* where the screen kiss between Cary Grant and Ingrid Bergman extended far beyond the three-second limit through skillful acting and clever editing. More often than not, however, filmmakers were at the mercy of the Hays Office rulings on content, and many had to reshoot or cut scenes in their movies before they could be distributed, since all films needed the seal of approval to be released. The Code began to weaken in the late 1950s and was abandoned by the late 1960s. The Hays Office closed in 1966. In 1968 it was replaced by the MPAA with the rating system that included *G* for general audiences, *M* for mature content, *R* for restricted (under 17 not admitted without an adult), and *X* for sexually explicit content. In 1970 the *M* rating was changed to *GP* and then in 1972 altered to the current *PG* – parental guidance suggested – and in 1984 the middle tier *PG-13* rating was created in response to extreme violence and horror elements in some films. In 1990 the *X* rating was replaced by *NC-17* (under 17 not admitted), which became a rating that was often the "kiss of death" at the box office due to social stigma. The *X*, *XX*, and *XXX* symbols are not part of the MPAA film ratings and are normally used by pornographic bookstores and theatres.

students affectionately called the course, moved beyond history to politics. It raised my political awareness and related it to my interest in history. It capped twelve years of social studies and history courses. Mr. Sterner allowed free rein to class discussions, but he withheld his own opinions. The freedom to express my leftist views in class allowed me to formulate my political attitudes in the years to come.

Mr. Sterner liked my cartoons. His best encouragement to me was when he said I had a "fine sense of the ridiculous." This satirical sense has been with me as long as I can remember. It reaches back to when I was a small boy who found amusement in adult pretensions and mannerisms. This sense of the ridiculous has served me well, first as a cartoonist, then as a writer and stage director. It also got me into trouble more than once.

After I enlisted and before I left for Army duty, Mr. Sterner told me he was a friend and classmate of Russ Westover, the creator the then-popular comic strip *Tillie the Toiler*. He told me that when I returned home after the war, he would put me in contact with Westover. There might be the possibility that he needed an assistant. Cartoonists then and now have at least one assistant. They are usually relegated to lettering and doing repetitive detail work. These assistants inherited the script when the cartoonist retired. This possible opportunity never worked out, but that was my fault. By the time I got out of the Army I was intent on going to college and becoming a teacher. My dreams of becoming a cartoonist seemed remote and impractical. However, my experience as a cartoonist served me well while I was on occupation duty in Germany after the war in Europe ended.

While the shadow of a raging war that was going much too slowly hovered over us, we concentrated – perhaps too much – on being teenagers. My friends and I traveled together as a pack until we broke off into dating. We went to movies together. The main movie theatre confined teenagers to the balcony. There was a good reason. Boys can be rowdy. Too often there was a running commentary on a movie. I remember one Pennsylvania Dutch boy who went with us, chiming in with his guttural voice and quaint accent at moments on the screen. His comments often sent the balcony into gales of laughter. The movie was *I Wanted Wings*. It was a wartime tribute to the Air Corps that was also an action movie. It was Veronica Lake's first starring role. In one scene she wore a dress that was deeply cut almost to the navel. When she moved, we got tantalizing but brief glimpses of the swell of her breasts. Her exposure was a little

more than the Hays Office usually allowed, but some production standards were lowered after the war began. Amidst hooting and whistles,
our friend shouted, "Did you know she has TB?" Silence. Then he added,
"Two beauts."

The theatre exploded into laughter. That included the downstairs adults.
Our ribald friend turned eighteen just as he was about to begin his senior
year. He died in combat on a little-known Pacific Island less than half a
year later. I will always remember that odd voice. I will always remember
his wide smile. I will always remember his quaint Pennsylvania Dutch
accent. I wish I could remember his name.

Our gang always went to Saturday night dances together. They were
held in the high school gym, but we had a glitter ball that was hung just
for our dances. A disk jockey usually spun records, but sometimes we
had a live combo. They cost an extra fifty cents. Once we were favored
with a combo led by Chick Webb, the composer of "The Dipsy Doodle,"
a jump standard popular with jitterbuggers.

Our Saturday dances were much like the ones I enjoyed in New Kensington. The gym was darkened, and the glitter ball sent shimmers of
light through the cavernous space. At first, the girls stood on one side,
the boys on the other. The boys walked across the floor when the first
number began to play. If another boy took the girl of his choice, he veered
toward his second choice, or even his third. We tried to walk so the girls
couldn't see our aim. No girl wanted to play second fiddle. The segregation broke down by the third or fourth number. Couples began to form.
Others, like me, were stags that changed partners from dance to dance.
It was considered a subtle commitment if you asked a girl to dance more
than twice. I didn't. Instead, I enjoyed a delightful smorgasbord of young
women. As my senior year began, the draft drew close. I wasn't interested
in rushing into marriage. My practical streak told me that I was unable
to support a family.

I quickly discovered that the girls in Pottsville danced even closer than
their counterparts in New Kensington. The pneumatic girls were the most
popular dance partners. One of the most popular was Gloria Mosolino.
She was two years younger than me. Generally, we stuck to dancing with
girls from our class. Once in a while we deigned to dance with a junior. It
took a bit of courage to ask a mere sophomore to dance, but Gloria acted
older than her age. She was a striking blonde with a Madonna-like face.
Her large eyes were warm and inviting. She had a slightly ribald sense of

humor. She liked to dance close. I fondly remember those breasts cushioned against my chest as our bodies moved intuitively about the dance floor.

There were few Italians in Pottsville. They seemed exotic to me. My friendship with Gloria was furtive. My parents would have been greatly upset if they knew that I was dating an Italian girl. She was more worldly than I was, more forward. We never spoke of religion, but I suspect that she was breaking away from her Catholic upbringing. We never got serious. I lost contact with her once I was in the Army.

After high school graduation, Gloria went to college and lived in Greenwich Village. During the early days of television, she was the aged Arthur Murray's dance partner on the popular *The Arthur Murray Party* dance show. Her appearances on television led to her working as Marilyn Monroe's stand-in during the making of *The Seven Year Itch* and for Eva Marie Saint during the shooting of *On the Waterfront*. In 1957 she married James Jones, the noted author of *From Here to Eternity*. Their marriage lasted until his death in 1977. She died in 2006 at the age of 78. I remember seeing her in a television interview many years later. Her exotic beauty had weathered the years.

None of us had access to a car. Gas rationing tightened and prevented any nonessential use of automobiles. That mobile alternative to the boudoir, the back seat of a car – if you could maneuver your date there – was not available until the 1950s. Dating was a slow, almost formalized ritual. It began with walking a girl home after a Saturday dance. If a girl seemed congenial, I blurted out a request for a weekday movie date. Some said they had one. That was probably a polite way of rejection. Some agreed. That was a big first step. It could lead to nothing or proceed on to courtship and marriage. As for me, I never had a chance to pursue one girl long enough to move through the next steps in courtship.

There was little else to do in Pottsville, so most dates started with a movie. It was expected that it would be a first-run movie. For some reason it was bad form to take a date to the vaudeville house even though the routines were squeaky clean. There were two first-run houses to choose from. You didn't take a date to a second-run movie house or a double feature. It couldn't be an action or horror movie. Romantic comedies and glitzy musicals were preferred. The choice of movie was agreed upon beforehand.

"YOU MUST REMEMBER THIS..."

There is one movie date I remember vividly. I was attracted to a pretty honey blonde who had strong, Germanic good looks. Her name was Ruth. We belonged to Epworth League and shared a number of classes. She was intelligent and had a quick wit. Better still, she was an excellent dancer who seemed to like to dance with me. One evening, while I walked her home from a Saturday dance, I asked her out on a midweek movie date. She agreed. I was pleased and a bit surprised.

The standard attire for a movie date was a sports jacket, shirt, and matching slacks. A tie was mandatory. My parents teased me as I dressed. I hated that, but it was part of their country humor. Fortunately, they approved my dating her. Her family went to our church, and she came from solid Pennsylvania Dutch stock. What bothered me most was that my parents treated a first date as a prelude to marriage. As for me, I felt I would be lucky if there was a second date. Two previous dates with other girls had not gone well. I enjoyed one, but I hesitated too long to ask for a second date. Another guy moved in, asked her out, and ended up going steady with her. The other date bored me. We had nothing in common except that we attended the same high school.

I had to time my arrival at Ruth's doorstep close to the arranged time. If I was too early, it signaled I was too eager. Being late meant I was careless or only mildly interested. Five minutes late seemed casually correct. It was a short walk to her home, and a little longer one to the downtown movie theatre. That made timing complicated.

It was a pleasant twilight evening in late October. The trees had changed to a riot of colors. Many leaves had fallen, so my feet swept through their crispness as I walked. I checked my watch when I came to her block. I was five minutes early. That would never do. I turned and walked a block back. That took five minutes. Five minutes back, and I would be fashionably late.

I walked up on Ruth's front porch with an intense feeling of awkwardness and rang the bell. I waited patiently. No response. I rang it again. That was enough. Finally, her father answered the door. He was a large, imposing man; but he greeted me cordially and asked me to step in.

"Ruth's running a little late," he said.

I had no answer to that. Awkward silence.

I wondered, is she being a "little late" a tactic? A way of putting me at a disadvantage? The thought went away quickly. Girls took longer to dress than men.

He added, "It takes a while for a girl to put on her face."

No answer for that either.

"Nice evening," he said after another awkward pause.

Finally, I had something to say. "It's really warm for late October. I almost didn't need a jacket."

"Indian Summer. One of the most beautiful times of the year. Leaves changing."

"All those colors," I added.

"It's a shame we have gas rationing," he said. It'd be a good time to take a drive in the country. Used to do it all the time. The hills around here. All those colors. And you wish you had a color camera. One of these days we will.

"I'll have to get out the rake Saturday. Can't let them get ahead of you. You never know when the first snow will come."

"I kind of like raking leaves," I replied.

After he smiled in approval, he said, "That's what sons are for. Wish I had one." Then he asked, "What are you going to see?"

I replied, "*Coney Island.*"

Ruth and I had previously discussed our limited movie options. One was *The Ox-Bow Incident*, a grim tale about a frontier lynching of suspected cattle rustlers. I didn't mention it, partly because I had just seen it, and partly because it was eons away from being a first date movie. I had read the novel before I saw the film. Both were relentlessly powerful, fine statements against lynching. There was no way I would take Ruth to see it. We were left with one choice, the newest Betty Grable musical, *Coney Island*. I liked the blue and pink hues of 20th Century Fox's Technicolor musicals, and I liked Betty Grable's legs even more. It was set in the Gay Nineties and contained old and new songs, two of which had made the *Hit Parade* radio show. George Montgomery for her, Grable for me, lots of music and dancing, comedy by Phil Silvers, clichéd romance, and vivid color – *Coney Island* was an unbeatable choice for a first movie date.

"Good choice," her father observed before he added, "I've been thinking about taking the old lady out to see that. When does it end?"

"Tonight."

"Guess we'll have to wait until it comes out in a rerun. Hey, maybe we can catch the second show together. It'll take a while for the missus to get all gussied up."

It was then that Ruth made her grand entrance down the stairs. It was just in the nick of time. The last thing I wanted was a double date with Ruth's parents on our first date.

I stood awkwardly in the foyer of the living room. I tried to think of something appropriate to say. Usually, I blurted out a banality. This time I kept quiet.

She wore a dress that was slightly better than the ones she wore to school. Under it she wore the requisite chastity protection, a girdle. An uplift bra, of course, was a prerequisite then, even when girls didn't need one. They were part of her armor against unwelcome – or even welcome – advances. She looked much different than she did at school since she wore pancake makeup, artfully placed rouge on her cheeks, and a livid red lipstick. The lovely face that had been part of her attraction was still there, but it was smoother and quite different. It, too, served as a preventative measure. Girls didn't remove their lipstick until at least the third date.

As for me, I didn't want to go home with the remnants of lipstick or makeup on my collar. My parents would never let me hear the last of it if I did. My parents began teasing me when I announced I had a date. It didn't stop there. If I called to ask a girl for a date or to a dance, they were nearby listening. This inhibited me so much that I often messed up the call. If I was turned down, the teasing intensified. My parents were not alone in this damaging behavior. Elders of the generation before me had no concept of interpersonal psychology. Their teasing did great damage to my security in the mating game even after I left home and was on my own.

Ruth's father took a light fall coat out of the closet and handed it to me. It was another awkward moment. I had to be careful not to muss her carefully coiffed hair. Finally, we were ready to leave. As we started to walk out the door, he said, "Mind you, Ruth needs to be home by ten. No later. Okay?"

Ruth and I looked at each other with a teenage roll of our eyes. Then we nodded gravely in agreement and exited.

Once we were out of her house and away from parental eyes, we could talk freely. That presented another problem. What do you talk about with someone you barely know? Her high heels clicked on the sidewalk as we sparred at making small talk. Talking about our classes in school was boring. Gossip about our classmates was a safe topic of conversation. Who was dating who? Who had just decided to go steady? What about that teacher who had a drinking problem? Current movies, too, were conversation fodder. I soon learned to tiptoe through talking about current best sellers. My taste for classical music was off the boards. My interest in that topic made me a bit of a freak. Fortunately, Pottsville was a small town, so the walk to a movie theatre wasn't too long.

Once there, Ruth stood to one side as I bought our tickets. Nothing was Dutch[29] in those days. The male paid. Once inside, an usher, using a flashlight, directed us to our seats. Since we were a couple, we were allowed to sit on the ground floor. More quandaries arose once we were seated. Should I hold her hand? Did I dare to put my arm around her shoulders? No, this was a first date. I had to wait for cues from her. I made sure that she possessed the seat arm between us. If she didn't lean toward me, I would watch the movie and contain myself to my own seat area. Later in the movie, I slowly let my hand wander, so that it was placed over her hand. There was no rebuff. I was holding her hand! An important first step had been taken. I decided that was as far as I was going to venture. I resolved to ask her out on another date. Being allowed to take her hand assured me that she liked my company.

After the movie we went to one of the two ice cream parlors on Main Street. Once we were seated across from each other, we finally had something to talk about. The movie. Fortunately, we both liked it. There were no waiters, so I had to go to the counter and place our order. Once again, I paid. Our conversation resumed once I returned to the table with our treats.

As we came out of the ice cream parlor, we saw her parents buying tickets for the second showing of *Coney Island*. Her Mother waved to us. Her dad looked at us and tapped his wristwatch as a reminder of Ruth's curfew. Seeing them going to the movie added a new complication. I was walking Ruth home to an empty house. Would she ask me in? Even so,

---

29 "Going Dutch" was a term that meant each person participating in a group activity would pay for their own expenses rather than have one person pay all the costs. There were other variations of this idea, including "Dutch treat," "Go Dutch," "Dutch courage," and "Dutch date." Some think that the idea originated from the concept of a Dutch door, where the upper and lower halves can be opened independently. The *Oxford-English Dictionary* connects the term to the 17th century, during the period of the Anglo-Dutch Wars.

walking her home was easier. A little bit of the ice had been broken, but it was surrounded by a skating rink of ambiguity. She took my arm as we walked and talked. The next moment of uncertainty came when we walked up to her front door. The porch light was on, but there was only one light inside, a living room lamp. When you're with an attractive young girl, an empty house was both forbidding and enticing.

She politely told me she had enjoyed the evening as we stood at the door. I agreed. Should I lean toward her as a first step toward a goodnight kiss? No, I kept a discreet distance. Then she leaned to me and chastely kissed me on the cheek.

"Thank you for the lovely movie, the sundae and coke."

There was an awkward pause. Gulp! Should I ask her for another date now? Or should I wait until later? I took the plunge.

"There's a Monte Wooley comedy coming next week."

"I liked him so much in *The Man Who Came to Dinner*."

"Me, too."

Another awkward pause while I gathered my courage.

"Would you like to go?"

"I think I'd like that very much," she said with a warm smile.

Then she turned, opened the unlocked door, and entered. Once she was inside, she turned back and blew me a kiss. Then she closed the door. I stood alone on the porch for a moment. I had a second date. And she had kissed me on the cheek. Best of all, my first date with Ruth hadn't been a clumsy disaster. It was a happy walk back home, but I dreaded the teasing and cross-examination from my parents that was sure to follow.

Dating protocol in the 1940s followed a strict sequence. A second date often ended with a polite kiss on the lips. On the third it was a lingering kiss. If the parents were out after the fourth date you might be asked inside, but if it was a warm night, you sat on the porch swing. Petting was underway by the fifth if mutual interest continued. It was then that some girls unfastened their bra. Most continued to wear their blouse or dress. Petting then grew more intense.

Usually, the couple was going steady by this time. A marriage proposal was imminent, and the couple became engaged. Some quipped that an engagement was a "learner's permit." Sex was out of the question. It was not just a question of morality. Condoms were available, but they weren't foolproof. The diaphragm was the only reliable form of birth control in the 1940s, but it had to be prescribed and fitted by a medical doctor. No "respectable" woman got one unless she was about to be married. Most couples waited to have sex until after they were married, but there were occasional "shotgun weddings."

I never got past the second date with Ruth. Time ran out on my fledgling courtship in a most unexpected way.

ENLIST OR WAIT?

Late in the fall of 1943, our high school administered a test sponsored by the Army Specialized Training Reserve Program (ASTRP).[30] Those who had high scores would be encouraged to enlist so they could be sent to a college or university to study in areas where the Army needed specialists such as civil and electrical engineering, and chemistry. Most of the boys in the senior class took the test. Any form of advanced technical training bought valuable and perhaps lifesaving time in a war that was going slowly. Since my grades in mathematics and the sciences were average at best, I believed I had no chance of passing the test. Taking it seemed like a waste of my precious senior year time, but my parents insisted. I was an obedient son. I took the test.

I was amazed when only two of us passed it. Neither of us had good grades in mathematics and the sciences. I was doing really badly in geometry. Working out theorems that thousands of students had solved over the years seemed like an exercise in futility. Our experiments in chemistry seemed to have no practical use. My friend who also passed the test was close to flunking out. How did we pass the test while dozens of others failed? Years later I learned that regurgitating facts and numbers were not signs of ability and that an unruly and undisciplined mind was still in its formative stage. Even then, it had the ability to make bold leaps during objective testing.

Several parents of honor roll students were furious. They didn't blame their sons. They blamed the test. A few demanded that the tests be rescored. That request was ignored. What was done was done. The Army was

---

30   This is sometimes also referred to as the Enlisted Reserve Corps, the Army Specialized Training Reserve Program (ASTRP), and the Army Specialized Training Program (ASTP). The different titles were based on the age of the student, the year they enlisted, and the curricula and courses offered by the Army during each twelve-week cycle. The cadets were selected by the army and assigned to the institution. Expenses of the training were paid by the War Department.

immovable. Several parents registered a complaint with the Army; but
they were ignored. Others wrote to
their congressman. They, too, were
ignored. Nothing was changed. Two
rather average students had passed
the test and were eligible for technical
training at an unidentified college or
university.

My parents were proud of my
unexpected achievement. I suspect
they were amazed. Their son had
outperformed the school's top students. I, too, was amazed. While I
was adjusting rather well into my life
as a high school senior, I still had an
inferiority complex when it came to
my academic courses. Passing that

Senior picture, 1943.
Pottsville High School

test gave me my first glimmer that I possessed above average intelligence.

We were faced with a quandary. Should I be allowed to drop out of high
school and enlist in the reserves to take advantage of this opportunity or
wait to be drafted when I turned eighteen in June? Could the Army be
trusted once I had enlisted? We were aware that the war was going slowly
in the fall of 1943. No quick victory in sight. My parents thought that
any time I spent taking college courses would delay my being assigned
to a combat unit. They also thought that if I had a technological skill, I
wouldn't end up in the front lines. After long and agonizing discussions,
they decided to allow me to enlist. I was elated and apprehensive. I was
thrilled by my success, but I feared that I would be a fish out of water when
the Army assigned me for higher education. What if I failed?

I took a train from Pottsville to Allentown on March 20, 1944. After
I boarded the train, I noticed that a group of nattily dressed Black men
were playing cards at the end of the car. One of these men was the legendary bandleader, Duke Ellington.[31] The rest were his famous band. As

31   Edward Kennedy "Duke" Ellington (1899-1974) was a popular American composer, pianist, and leader of a jazz orchestra from 1923 until his death. Throughout his
fifty-year career he was one of the most celebrated musicians and innovative artists of
the time. He and his orchestra appeared in venues from the Cotton Club to Carnegie

I screwed up my courage, I fumbled to find a scrap of paper. I walked to Mr. Ellington and shyly asked him for his autograph. He graciously signed it with a flourish. I didn't have the audacity or presence of mind to ask the other band members for autographs. That was the first but not the last time I asked a celebrity for an autograph. I recently gave that precious slip of paper to my wife Linda. She is a pianist and a composer, and the Duke was, too.[32] He not only wrote pop songs, he also wrote symphonic works. So does my wife.

I reported to the Allentown recruiting center and began my processing into the Army. After I presented my parents' notarized permission slip and filled out several forms, I underwent an eye test. I knew that my left eye was 20-200 without glasses. Technically, I was blind in that eye when I wasn't wearing glasses. I read the chart quickly while I wore my glasses. Then they ordered me to take them off. My right eye without correction was 20-40. There was no problem there. I panicked. I knew that I would not be able to read the top letter with my left eye. In my young mind, rejection from military service was a form of disgrace. I didn't want to return home as a 4-F after going this far. I quickly decided that I would cheat on the test. I don't see this as an act of bravery or patriotism. I knew some would gladly fail the test. I was tempted, but I feared ridicule of those who had failed the test more than I feared being in the Army. I quickly memorized the five top rows of letters. Would that be enough? It was all I had time to do. When they covered my right eye, I recited the letters. My left eye was rated 20-100. That was enough to pass the test. While my need to wear glasses disqualified me from flight crews in the Air Force, jumping with the Paratroopers, and enduring the rigors of Ranger combat, I was qualified to fight in frontline Infantry outfits.

Hall and was known throughout the world. He appeared in movies, television, radio, and on dozens of recordings. Throughout his career his music crossed over many styles and genres, from pop to orchestra to sacred. He wrote more than one thousand compositions; many became popular hits and jazz standards. He received many honors and awards during his lifetime, including a posthumous Pulitzer Prize Special Award for music in 1999. Duke Ellington died of complications from lung cancer and pneumonia on May 24, 1974, a few weeks after his 75th birthday. After his death his son, Mercer, took over leadership of the orchestra until his own death in 1996. Ellington's compositions continue to be performed and his influence remains strong to this day.

32   Linda will be the first to tell you that she is nowhere in the same league as Duke Ellington.

A physical examination followed. We were ordered to go into a locker room, strip, and stow our clothing in a metal locker. There was no need to worry about theft. An armed guard stood by the door. We emerged quite naked into a brightly lit room. I never felt more naked. While I had taken naked showers after gym classes and gone skinny-dipping at the YMCA and in creeks around town, this was different.

First, I was weighed and measured. At that time, I wasn't quite five feet eight inches tall, and I weighed a scrawny 145 pounds. My feet were examined carefully. Athlete's foot could be cured, but flat feet immediately disqualified an enlistee. The physical was an impersonal probing of private parts. I moved along a line of doctors, each of whom gravely examined a single part of our bodies.

"Skin it back!" was the command for what was called a "short arm inspection." This exam was used to determine if anyone had contracted a venereal disease.

A command to examine for hemorrhoids was, "Assume the position and spread your cheeks!"

Then, after a careful perusal of one's rectum, a finger in a rubber glove probed me to determine if I had any prostate problems.

The most painful was the examination for hernias. That command was, "Turn your head and cough!" Then the doctor would grasp the groin by a testicle. It hurt. It was repeated on the other side of my groin.

We quickly moved down the line. The doctors had no time for niceties. They were working on an assembly line that had to examine dozens upon dozens of men daily. Our exams were brutal and quick. The sanitary conditions the medics worked under would seem appalling now. I felt thoroughly humiliated when I got to the end of the line, but I passed this part of the physical with flying colors.

A blood test followed. It, too, was painful. The non-com[33] who drew blood did it clumsily. I bit my lower lip. I was determined to hide any sign of pain. I succeeded. After my physical was complete, there was the series of shots. These, too, were administered quickly and with no concern for comfort. The upper part of our arms and one buttock ached later that evening and into the next day. In the days to come, I learned that every

---

33 A non-commissioned officer, also known as a non-com or NCO, is a military officer who obtained their position through the enlisted ranks rather than by earning a commission. The Army non-coms usually include corporal, sergeant, and warrant officers. Non-coms are often considered to be "the backbone of the armed services."

time I moved to a new post I would again have to endure such a physical exam. There was even one on the day I was discharged from the Army.

Finally, they determined I had no physical problems. I was fit to serve. As the afternoon ended, I was inducted into the United States Army's Enlisted Reserve Corps, or ERC as it was called.

At the same time, I became a high school dropout. I suspect I am one of the few PhDs who never finished high school. Yes, I possess a high school diploma, but it was a gift to all of us who left school before graduation. Those who died in action were given posthumous diplomas. Many who hadn't finished their senior course work had an uphill fight when they enrolled in colleges and universities after the war.

∗   ∗   ∗

After our move to Pottsville, I remained in contact with my New Kensington friends by mail. The news wasn't always good. The two Holste brothers, Robert and David, who were the sons of the Arnold High School principal, died in combat. While they went to a rival school, they were friends and ran around with the rest of us. The youngest, David, was a good friend of mine. It was hard to think he was gone. He was not alone. As the war raged more and more Gold Star banners were posted in windows throughout town. Silver Star banners were displayed for those who were in the service. The Silver banner my parents proudly hung in their window survives among my World War II souvenirs. It's faded from the sun and a little tattered. My Mother even bought a wooden plaque commemorating that her son served in the Army. It, too, survives and hangs on my office wall.

I returned home from Allentown and waited for my assignment. For a while, I continued attending classes. My grades in Mr. Gaskin's geometry class got worse. They were bad enough to threaten my graduation if I remained in school until the end of the year. I did well in my other classes, and my cartoons were still popular. I enjoyed my social life, but I felt suspended. I could be called up and leaving any day. Everything seemed temporary. I continued dating Ruth, but I avoided pushing our still tentative relationship any further. Perhaps we would pick up where we had been after the war. Perhaps not. The idea of marriage never entered our discussions. At most, she said she would miss me. I didn't want to marry before I entered military service.

I was notified by mail that I was assigned to take basic engineering classes at the prestigious Virginia Military Institute in Lexington.[34] The term would begin on Monday May 8, 1944. Mom and Dad were thrilled. VMI was nicknamed the West Point of the South. This state-supported military college opened in 1839 and is the oldest institution of its kind in the United States. It has a long, distinguished history. Its graduates were automatically commissioned Second Lieutenants in the Virginia National Guard. From there it was an easy step to a commission in the Army. One of the early superintendents at VMI was General Thomas "Stonewall" Jackson. Notable alumni included General George C. Marshall, the top U.S. Army general during World War II; and General George S. Patton, Jr.,[35] whose father and grandfather had also attended VMI. Little did I know that in less than a year I would be a combat rifleman in Patton's Third Army.

My father was especially pleased. I would be studying engineering. As for me, I was fearful. What had I gotten myself into? My classes at VMI would be more rigorous than the high school classes that were causing me problems. Would I disappoint my parents by flunking out? If I failed it would humiliate them, especially after the furor over the grading of the ASTRP test. I resolved to do my best.

I was given two weeks to put my affairs in order. Dad took some vacation time so that we could visit New Kensington and my grandparents in Ohio. He had put aside some gas rationing stamps for a summer vacation trip. They were precious, but they would now be put to better use. I had a chance to attend a day of classes during our brief stopover in New Kensington. I would share a day of their high school life. It was a good day. It gave me the opportunity to visit with old friends and teachers. All were impressed with my assignment to VMI.

---

34   More than 2,100 Army Specialized Training Program (ASTP) members studied at VMI during WWII.

35   General George Smith Patton, Jr. (November 11, 1885 – December 21, 1945), attended Virginia Military Institute from 1903-04. While studying at VMI he was nominated for West Point by a senator from California. Patton left VMI to attend West Point in 1904. He had a rocky start and was forced to repeat his first year after failing mathematics. He graduated from West Point on June 11, 1909, with a ranking of 46 out of the graduating class 103 and was commissioned as a second lieutenant in the Cavalry Branch of the United States Army.

One of the classes I sat in on was an advanced science course taught by a teacher I will call Frederick Markham.[36] He was a stubby little man who lectured with a croaking bullfrog voice. He was more than a little boring. He was called Freddie behind his back. I was informed that the senior girls played a game with him in his classes. In 1944 women's skirts became shorter. They approached the scantiness of miniskirts. Freddie seemed to be the epitome of a quiet, conventional man; but the girls had discovered that when they sat in the front row and crossed and uncrossed their legs, Freddie became a befuddled and stammering mess when he was presented with a brief flash of panties. In honor of my visit three or four of my old dance partners sat in the front row. Poor Freddie! When shapely young legs crossed and uncrossed again and again, almost in unison, his face turned red, and he stammered and stuttered. He tried to avert his gaze, but he could not keep his eyes away from the exhibition in front of him. He barely managed to finish the class. I was told after class ended that one of my classmates had worn no panties! The girls left it up to me to guess which one of them it was. Indeed, public school teaching for male teachers had its fringe benefits during the war years. Looking back, it seemed to me, in a way, that the girls of my class were giving Freddie a glimpse of his lost youth. Their ribaldry reminded me that they had moved from being girls to becoming young women.

The shortening of hem lengths is said to be a signal of a nation at war. Perhaps it is a sign of the biological need to replace young men lost in battle. Shorter skirts did not appear again until the 1960s when the mini and then the micro-mini came into fashion. These short skirts coordinated with the Vietnam War. The mini was especially daring. By then I was a university teacher, and on occasion I was treated to my own vistas of delight.

*   *   *

After my whirlwind visit to my boyhood past in New Kensington, I had brief visits with my grandparents in Ohio. The Coleman side said nothing about my being called up, but my Grandfather Phillips told me he thought that old men should fight the wars they caused. I know that Grandpa Phillips would have gladly taken my place. I also knew that

---

36   Not his real name, nor his real discipline.

Grandfather Coleman was frightened by the prospect that the Coleman name could end on a faraway battlefield. But he was a Coleman and, as such, he said nothing. I sensed his worry and love, but in that branch of the family the unsaid had to be sensed rather than spoken.

I regret that he did not live long enough to experience the lives of his two great-grandsons or the births of his two great-great-grandsons. He died in 1952, two years before my first son was born. He would be so pleased to know that the Coleman name has survived into the 21st century. That would have meant a lot to him – and to my father who died in 1979.

*   *   *

When we returned home, a packet of railroad and bus tickets and food vouchers waited for me. I was about to join the more than 16,000,000 men and women who served in our armed services. That was one tenth of our country's population. Most of the rest of the country joined the war effort. Women joined the workforce by the hundreds of thousands. Factories and shipyards ran day and night. The Great Depression had ended. War profiteering began. Patriotism was blended with profits. When the unions demanded a share of the wealth, factory owners called them unpatriotic. FDR tried his best to control this, but controls of the market were biased in favor of wartime needs. Our Armed Forces needed weapons, airplanes, tanks, ships, and ammunition. Many of those on the home front profited from the war. Those who served in the Armed Forces toiled for a pittance. They even had to pay for G.I. insurance that would provide some benefits to their survivors.

AN AGE OF INNOCENCE ENDS

Into my heart on air that kills
From yon far country blows:
What are those blue remembered hills,
What spires, what farms are those?
That is the land of lost content,
I see it shining plain,
The happy highways where I went
And cannot come again.[37]

This poem from A. E. Housman's *A Shropshire Lad* still haunts me, but it was especially painful as I packed to leave home after my trip back to my family roots. The hills of Pennsylvania and Ohio were still winter barren. Spring would come, but by then I would be elsewhere. I didn't know then that the "yon far country" would be the hills of the Rhineland. A phase of my life came to a close during my trip to my ancestral homeland. A time of innocence, of adolescent pain and joy, and a great deal of wonder came to an end as I prepared to leave home for the first time.

In looking back, my boyhood was better than it seemed at the time. Memory mercifully suppresses the unpleasant while it preserves the pleasant. Small unhappinesses fade into insignificance over time. Joys remain. In looking back, those negatives, those slights, and those frustrations became important foundation stones of my adult life. In many ways my future was already set and firmly in place as I prepared to enter the Army. Yes, some of those stones had to be moved about and some had to be removed, but I was on my way. I had no idea then what my future life would be. All I felt was a sense of loss, of apprehension, of doubt in myself and my abilities. That ASTRP test had set me on my way to a new and certainly harder test.

*   *   *

---

37   "An Age of Innocence Ends" is from *A Shropshire Lad*, a collection of sixty-three poems by the English poet Alfred Edward Housman. It was published in 1896.

One word best describes my memory of my boyhood – wonder. I remember the lingering and lonely whistle of the midnight train floating across the great Allegheny River. I remember that river's deep green beauty, its steady power as we paddled our canoe, and the mystery of its depths. I remember the baroque paddlewheel steamboats pulling barge after barge of coal, moving down that river from upstream mines, pausing to go through a lock, then sailing on. They are certainly one of the most beautiful objects created by our country.

I remember the immense train engines drawing more than one hundred cars past our house in Parnassus. I remember taking a passenger train with my friends for outings at the Kennywood amusement park. Once there I remember persuading a girl to ride in the flat-bottomed boats that passed through the tunnel of love or to ride with me on the roller coasters. I remember seeing girls' skirts flying high as they passed over an air jet while they exited the fun house. It was a glorious spring day topped by the return ride home on the train.

I remember going to the Allegheny County Airport to see the old Ford Tri-motors take off and land. I remember biplanes and monoplanes. I remember going to air shows, and I especially remember going up on the heights above New Kensington to watch the mail planes sweep in, hook a bag of mail, and soar on to their next pickup.

I remember carnivals and circuses and, especially, the wonder of watching a circus come into town at dawn and the setting up of its main tent.

Mail plane pickup

I remember going to Pirates baseball games at old Forbes Field in Pittsburgh. There I saw great players now in the Hall of Fame. Closer to home, I remember watching legendary players in the Negro League playing our Corbins. I remember sneaking in to play on their field.

I remember playing at sports with my friends. I remember our church league softball games even though I was relegated to right field. I loved the feel and sound of my bat hitting a ball solidly. That is a true harbinger of spring. I do remember being one of the last chosen in a pickup game; but that, in time, goaded me to excel where I could excel. I wasn't very good at basketball but playing dirty alley basketball with my friends was a boyhood joy. I loved playing tackle football without pads and the hard contact as I took down an opponent. I remember coming home battered, bruised, and even bleeding, so tired I could barely stand, but exhilarated from the joy of totally sensing my young body after I had pushed it beyond its limits. We played then for the joy of playing. Yes, we wanted to win; but the game was what it was all about. And we did it far away from the eyes of cheering and jeering adults. For a while, at least, we were in an exclusive boy's world.

Some of my memories are fragmentary. I remember the excitement of discovering a book that would sweep me away from the world I lived in, the joy and sadness of jazz and pop songs, the power and complexity of classical music, the mystery and beauty of great paintings, the thrill of theatrical performances during those open houses at Carnegie Tech, marveling at the enormity of dinosaur bones at the natural history museum, inventing with my Erector and chemistry sets, drawing cartoons, and writing poetry. I didn't know then, but I was filling my mind for the years ahead. I still am.

Most of all I remember the girls I danced with and dated. I remember the time I first put an arm around a girl's waist, of dancing close, our bodies moving together to music we loved. I remember the mystery and beauty of those young, evolving bodies. I remember playing jukeboxes as I savored a hot fudge sundae, walking and shooting the shit with friends, delivering newspapers, working at a grocery store, glitter balls piercing a dark dance floor, asking girls to dance, and hoping they would. I remember shedding my adolescence as I moved toward manhood. Looking back, I remember that, in spite of it happening during the Great Depression and then while our nation was at war, my boyhood was a wondrous time.

*   *   *

As I filled my suitcase, I packed away seventeen years of my life. My emotions were mixed. I was excited that I would be far away from parental supervision; but I did not realize that I would be facing something much more severe, the rigors of being a soldier. There was sadness, too. A phase of my life was over. I was leaving my "blue-remembered hills." As I closed my suitcase, my boyhood ended.

> In the time of your life, live – so that in that
> wondrous time you shall not add to the misery
> and sorrow of the world but shall smile to the
> infinite variety and mystery of it.[38]

---

38 *The Time of Your Life* by William Saroyan is a five-act play set in a San Francisco. The production opened on Broadway in 1939 and was co-directed by Eddie Dowling, who played the part of Joe, and Saroyan. The cast included a young Gene Kelly, in the role of Harry, who danced to his own choreography. It was the first drama to win both the Pulitzer Prize for Drama and the New York Drama Critics Circle Award. It had three Broadway revivals in 1940, 1969, and 1972, and was adapted for film in 1948 with James Cagney as Joe. In 1958 it was presented on live television in the *Playhouse 90* series, starring Jackie Gleason, Jack Klugman, and Dick York.

PART II

A YOUNG MAN GOES TO WAR

A CRY TO ARMS

Jackboots pound out their beat
As war drums throb
And trumpets blare
Amidst screams of adulation
From an unthinking mob.
Moloch claims his sacrifice
As we give up our young
To his insane demands.[1]

---

1   "A Cry to Arms" by William S.E. Coleman. Copyright © 2003. All Rights Reserved.

6

A Long Night's Journey into a New Day

I HAVE A fragmented memory of my trip to Lexington, Virginia. After tearful goodbyes with my parents, I boarded a night train in Pottsville to begin my 400-mile, life changing journey. It wasn't an express. That would have cost extra. I walked down the narrow platform past the massive steam engine. We would be backing out of the station. Jets of steam hissed and swirled around me as I lugged my heavy suitcase down the long platform toward my assigned car. Black porters dressed in white jackets waited to assist passengers as they mounted the steep steps into the passenger cars. They looked trim and elegant.

One kindly older man greeted me with a broad smile and helped me as I mounted the high steps into the passenger car. He handed up my suitcase to me. I thanked and tipped him, then turned and walked into the car. It was almost full. My ticket was for a seat in coach class. That didn't matter. Even in wartime, train cars were quite comfortable and well kept. Passengers from the West had taken most of the seats, but I found one on the aisle. There was no offer of a window seat. That was reserved for soldiers in uniforms, women, and the elderly. I was a boy in civilian clothes. Finally, the train pulled out of the station. I leaned over my seatmate and waved to my parents. Mother was crying. My father put a protective arm around her shoulders as he waved. His face was grim with Coleman stoicism. His only son was going to war, a war he would have fought for me.

My Army food vouchers allowed me to enjoy sit-down meals in the dining car. I could not resist this luxury, so once we were underway, I made my way to the dining car. I was greeted with a vista of two lines of tables. All held crisp white linen tablecloths and napkins, gold outlined china, and gleaming silverware. I was directed to a table by a distinguished Black maître d'. He, too, was immaculately dressed in white. Once he saw my Army voucher for dinner, I was treated with deference and respect.

I had never enjoyed such dining elegance, and it would be a long time until I did again. I was used to simply presented American meals at roadside restaurants during trips with my family. Dad always made sure we made inexpensive menu choices. We were lucky if there was a tablecloth. It was "Eat up and let's get on our way." Of course, there was never time for dessert. That would have cost extra.

The elaborately engraved menus presented too many choices. Some, to my consternation, were in French. That confounded me. This was my first encounter with a multiple course dinner. Worse still, everything was *a la carte*. Adults could have an aperitif before dinner, a glass of wine during, and an after-dinner drink. I couldn't. The legal age for having alcoholic drinks was twenty-one. It was the same for voting. I had been raised to be a teetotaler so attempting to order a drink never occurred to me. Not being able to vote bothered me even then. I was old enough to fight and die for my country, but I had no say in how it was run.

My voucher allowed me to have a luxurious dinner that included a dessert. A kind, white-haired waiter helped me with the complexities of my order. As I waited for my dinner to be served, I sat alone, deep in thought as I watched the scenery rush by. After a while another waiter returned and, with dramatic flourishes, served each course of the best meal in my young life. I felt thoroughly grown up. I could hardly wait for breakfast.

After dinner I returned to my seat in coach class. I tried to read a short story in one of my paperback books, but my mind wandered. I turned my attention to the rush of passing scenery as twilight faded into darkness. As night approached, I was assigned an upper bunk in a sleeping car. Once I climbed up the ladder into my bed, I struggled to discreetly change into pajamas behind a closed curtain. I slid under the covers and attempted to sleep. I was restless at first. Too many first impressions had entered my mind, but the rhythmic click of the train's wheels finally lulled me into a deep sleep. I was jolted awake each time passengers were picked up. I nodded off, only to awaken again as I heard the lonely wail of the train's whistle penetrating into the night. It was a sound I had grown to love when it wafted across the Allegheny River as the midnight passenger train from Erie sped toward Pittsburgh. After a couple of hours there was a stop in Philadelphia that was long enough for our cars to shift to a Washington, D.C. bound train.

I awoke early and enjoyed a lavish breakfast in the dining car. Again, there were many choices. My waiter advised me how I could gain full advantage of my travel voucher. After my breakfast, I wandered back to the observation car and watched the tracks recede behind us. There was a bar, but I settled for an ice-cold Coke. I sipped it as I watched the world retreat into the distance. It was hypnotic. Time seemed to be retreating as I plunged into a future indefinite. For a while I was lost in time. My mind focused on those retreating tracks and nothing else.

After a while, I returned to my seat. There I read from a paperback collection of American short stories. It was one of the dozen or so books I carried with me. I had no guidance in selecting them. I bought some on bookracks in drug stores. I bought two or three at a newsstand in the New Kensington train station. It was run by a pasty-faced, creepy man. Once, as I looked at his rack of paperbacks, he handed me one and said with a leer, "This one's a hot book." Of course, I bought it. It turned out to be a collection of short stories written by Somerset Maugham. It wasn't sexy. It was elegantly written.

None of the short story writers in my paperback collection were studied in my high school literature classes. John Steinbeck was never mentioned in spite of the popularity of his 1939 novel about the Great Depression, *The Grapes of Wrath*. I loved his short story "Nothing So Monstrous," and was shocked by "Johnny Bear." Another overlooked writer was Erskine Caldwell. The candor of his novels and short stories, and especially *Tobacco Road* and *God's Little Acre,* scandalized their readers. His short stories realistically captured grim moments in the lives of Georgia sharecroppers. James Farrell was another contemporary and controversial author. Many libraries banned his *Studs Lonigan* novel trilogy. Ernest Hemingway was another academic outcast. I encountered him first with "The Snows of Kilimanjaro" and "The Short Happy Life of Francis Macomber." Both compacted the material for a novel into a short story.

These writers wrote honest and realistic stories that were rooted in the present. Most school boards then – and many now – would have been outraged if they were included in a high school anthology. Few made it into college and university collections in the 1940s. When they did, only the most innocuous were chosen. These stories and others written by William Faulkner, William Saroyan, Thomas Wolfe, John O'Hara, and others thrust me into an adult world that was alien to my small-town churchgoing upbringing. They also gave me a sense of the stylistic differences between great writers and, perhaps, an inkling of how I might create my own writing style. I wanted to know more about these thoroughly American writers, but I had no systematic understanding of how they fitted into the overall picture of American literature. That understanding would come sooner than I thought it would, and from a most unlikely teacher.

*   *   *

One more leg of my trip remained after I arrived in Washington. Now I had to make an overnight bus trip to Lexington. It was unseasonably warm as I lugged my suitcase out of the train station. I asked the way to the Greyhound Bus Station and was told it was quite a distance away. Fortunately, Dad had given me some money to cover any unexpected expenses, so I took a taxi. That, too, was a first for me.

Buses were pulling in and out of the terminal as I got out of my taxicab and paid my fare. The buses were roaring, smelly behemoths. Each had a square, massive grill flanked by large headlights. Their wheels were enormous, and their tires were solid rubber. I felt very small amidst all those multi-wheeled monsters. Inside, the terminal teemed with a wild variety of people waiting for their buses. Amidst them were soldiers. Some were in transit for a leave, others were returning to duty, and some had been crippled by battle wounds. One soldier was an amputee who had lost a leg in combat. As I walked towards the ticket counter, I passed another soldier who had lost most of his face. It was horribly scarred and distorted. I averted my eyes and shuddered in horror. What if this happened to me? I must admit that I've always had a difficult time looking at the wounded and mutilated. Even now I look away from those torn apart by war on television news programs. That aversion goes back to that tragic young man who had no face. The only difference is that now I curse those who thrust us into unneeded and endless wars in the Middle East.

I had a long wait for my bus. I bought a newspaper, but I soon finished it. I turned to my book of stories. An hour passed, then another. Each time the garbled public address system announced a departure, I edged forward in my seat in anticipation even though I knew it wasn't time for my bus to leave. Seated across from me was a pretty young woman who was close to my age. She was well dressed and quite attractive. Once she smiled at me. I smiled back. That ended our non-verbal communication. For the moment.

Finally, my bus was called. I was well back in the boarding line. The steps into the bus were high and awkward to manage even though my suitcase was checked and stowed in the bottom of the bus. I looked back the dark, narrow aisle. Only one seat remained. It was next to the pretty young woman. She smiled as I placed my hand luggage on the rack above us. I sat down beside her. The padded bench seat was narrow so her soft thigh pressed warmly against mine. It was a pleasant intimacy. We waited in awkward silence for the bus to pull out. Then the front doors closed, and the driver backed out of his slot, turned, and pulled out into the street. The bus's motor roared as we picked up speed. It bounced roughly on the potholed street. We were on our way.

The young women asked where I was going as the driver maneuvered through the complex network of circles that characterize Washington street design. I told her I was under Army orders to report to Virginia Military Institute. She seemed impressed. I was charmed by her Southern drawl as we spoke over the roar of the bus's engine. Her voice was as sweet as warm syrup. It was a new sound for me. Northern women tended to place their voices higher, and rural northern women placed theirs even higher. More often than not they were piercingly nasal shrieks.

Most intercity roads had two lanes in the 1940s. Only a few had a third passing lane. Virginia's highway system was worn and badly maintained. Our bus's progress was even slower after we passed the city limits. The driver constantly shifted gears so that he could reach an optimum speed. It was going to be a long overnight journey. The roar of the motor was always with us.

The young women and I jounced against each other as we chatted away. It was an unavoidable intimacy. Like many Southern women, my travel companion's manner was flirtatious. Tennessee Williams, a writer I didn't know then, caught that penchant in his plays; and Margaret Mitchell in *Gone with the Wind* created the ultimate Southern woman in Scarlet O'Hara. Later in life I learned that subtle suggestion of future intimacies was a game many Southern women played with the male of the species.

We relapsed into silence after we exhausted our few common subjects. As twilight came, she drifted off into a deep sleep. For a while I watched the lovely Virginia scenery pass by. Early vestiges of spring were evident. Then I nodded off. Later, I edged into consciousness to find the young woman's head on my shoulder. I didn't move. Then I dropped into a deep, dreamless sleep.

RACIST REALITIES INTERRUPT

We were jolted awake when the bus lurched to a stop. The driver told us that we had a half hour to eat a late dinner in a decrepit roadside restaurant. It was there I encountered "White Only" facilities for the first time – water fountains, rest rooms, and the waiting room. I was horrified to see that the "Black Only" area had no water fountain, only a rusty spigot for drinking.

I had been in classes with Blacks since junior high. We shared the same bathrooms, showered together after gym classes, drank from the same water fountains, and ate at the same tables in restaurants. We lived in harmony, even though we rarely mixed socially. Segregation of any kind seemed barbaric to me. Here I saw it at its fullest.

As I entered the "White Only" restroom, I thought of my friend Doug Waters and what he would have encountered here. If he had dared to dance with a white girl, as he did more than once at Saturday night dances in New Kensington, he would have been lynched. At a less dramatic level, we couldn't have sat together on that bus; and we could not have eaten together in that shabby little restaurant. I should have turned around and gotten back on the bus, but I was hungry. I was sickened to find myself in a segregated world. Worse still, I would be in it for as long as I remained at VMI. I still resent spending my money in that sleazy bus stop.

As I stared at a tattered menu, my seat companion walked up to my table. "Mind if I join you?" she asked in a particularly dulcet tone.

"My pleasure."

She smiled sweetly, sat opposite me, and picked up a menu.

"I've stopped here before. They have good home cooking. Nothing fancy. Just things like you get at home."

I looked at my wristwatch. Ten minutes of our thirty-minute stop had passed.

"We better order," I said.

My dinner was basic and hearty. Hers was light. We chatted about nothing of consequence as we hastily finished our dinner. I said nothing about my revulsion against segregation. I assumed it was an aspect of her Virginia life that she accepted. Somehow the possibility that she harbored racial prejudices made her a little less attractive to me.

Once we were on board the bus our conversation about little or nothing continued. I have always had trouble with small talk. I find it tiring to think of mundane things to say. Fortunately, we quickly became drowsy.

"I'm sleepy," she said.

"Me, too," I replied.

"We can be more comfy if you put your arm around me," she said as she leaned against me.

Of course, I complied with her request. We settled in. I found her warm body next to me comforting. Later, out of a deep sleep, we kissed. It was a warm, soft-mouthed, gentle kiss. We held each other. Finally, we drifted back to sleep. Nothing was said. What could I say?

She got off the bus at a small town stop just before Lexington. As she moved into the aisle, she leaned over and lightly kissed me on the lips. "Take care of yourself, soldier boy. You better come home, y'hear?"

We never communicated again. I didn't ask for her mailing address. Perhaps I should have. I'm certain of one thing, though. I will always remember that kiss and those words, "You better come home, y'hear." But I don't remember her name.

Even now I wonder if she was a racist. What if we had corresponded and met again after the war? What if I had fallen in love with her before I found out she was a strident racist? Could I have walked away from a woman I loved over a deeply held principle? I'll never know, but I hope I would have had the strength of character to walk away. Of course, it's possible that she could have become one of the early heroes of the Civil Rights era. I'll never know. She was just one of many unfinished stories in my long life. There were many more to come. All those "what ifs" echo in my mind. In the main, most were lucky escapes. Life takes strange and unexpected twists and turns, some bad, some good.

We pulled into Lexington shortly after dawn. I got off the bus. The sleepy southern town was barely awake. As I came out of the station, I looked for a taxi. There were none in sight. I went to the ticket window and asked for directions. I was assured it was a short walk to the campus. I had no idea when I would eat again, so I went back into the bus station and had breakfast at its lunch counter. There was a scrawled sign in the window, "No Coloreds Allowed."

After I finished eating, I picked up my suitcase and trudged up a long-sloping hill toward my new home, the looming towers of the Virginia Military Institute, the almost legendary West Point of the South. I arrived on May 4, 1944.

HITTING THE GROUND RUNNING

When my wife Linda and I visited VMI in 2002, little had changed. The grounds remain impressive in their austerity. When I arrived there in 1944 there was only one barracks. It resembled a large fortress. Tiers of rooms looked in on a quadrangle through a huge double window.[1] A small archway that opens dramatically onto the quadrangle is the only entrance to the Barracks. On its left side is a booth where cadets are checked in and out. This single entrance faces a vast parade ground. At its front is a heroic statue of General Stonewall Jackson that is flanked by antique cannons. Housing for the faculty and military staff are at the far end. One of the Union cannonballs that hit the barracks during the Civil War rests on a cement pedestal at the right corner of the ground. On the south side of the parade, Letcher Avenue leads towards Washington and Lee University (then known as Washington and Lee College), a half mile to the southwest. Washington and Lee remains a well-respected liberal arts university. It manages to do so without VMI's rigid military discipline.

A well-stocked library, a classroom building, an indoor swimming pool, and a chapel are on the opposite side of the street. Down the hill past the left side of the barracks are more classroom buildings and a dining hall. Farther down on the right was a huge indoor dirt-floored field house that was used for cavalry training. We didn't know it at the time, but we were going to receive the last cavalry training given by the Army.[2] Nearby was a rifle range.

---

1 The Old Barracks sits on the site of the old arsenal, which received the most damage when Union forces shelled and burned the VMI in 1864. The Old Barracks is a fine example of early Gothic Revival architecture and has been designated a National Historic Landmark. Following the WWII, a new wing – the New Barracks – was completed and opened in 1949. A third barracks wing was completed in 2009.

2 Horse mounted troops were originally known as the Dragoons – the name is derived from a "dragon," a handgun version of a blunderbuss used by the dragoons in the French army in the 18th century – and employed during the Revolutionary War.

As I struggled up the hill, I noticed that a handful of other enlistees had been on the bus with me. Together we presented our orders and were sworn in. I was allowed a few minutes to leave my suitcase in my room – Room 318 – in the Barracks. There I met my roommate, Ben Neufeld. We had no time to get acquainted, but I found out that he was Jewish and from New York. He seemed as awed by this first day as I was.

That first day was a whirlwind of activity. First, we were issued textbooks and desk supplies at the bookstore. These were deposited in our rooms. Then we marched to the post quartermaster's store. There we received bedding, towels, washcloths, dental and toilet supplies, two sets of the standard summer khaki uniform, and dark green fatigues. We also received a khaki dress jacket. Ties, a billed dress hat, a soft day cap, leggings, olive drab underwear, brown socks, and ankle-high GI boots were included with the dress uniforms. We were also issued baggy fatigues for exercise and work

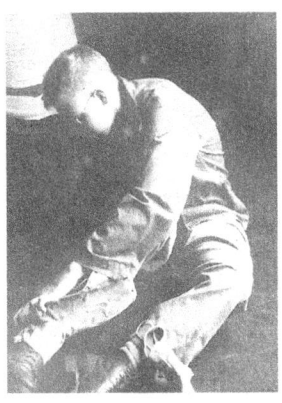

Bill lacing his leggings.

details. They were loose and ill fitting. The huge pockets at hip level were made so they would expand. They looked sloppy, but they were very comfortable. The fatigues were designed for work, not fashion, and topped with a floppy billed cap. We weren't issued the two-buckled combat boots

---

The Congress of the United States formed the first U.S. Cavalry unit in 1792. In 1808 Congress authorized a standing regiment of light dragoons consisting of eight troops. This was expanded to two battalions of volunteer cavalry in 1813. These horse mounted troops, also known as the cavalry branch, were an integral part of westward expansion, the war with Mexico, the Civil War, the American Indian wars, the Spanish-American War, and WWI. The last horse cavalry charge by a U.S. Army cavalry unit took place against the Japanese forces during the fighting in the Bataan Peninsula, Philippines, in the village of Morong on January 16, 1942, by the 26th Cavalry Regiment of the Philippine Scouts. The last horse-mounted charge of any Army organization while engaged was in Austria in 1945.

Cavalry instruction ended in October 1946, and in March 1947 the Army made the final disposition of tactical cavalry horses and ended all training and educational programs dealing with mounted troops. The U.S. Cavalry was absorbed into the Armor branch as part of the Army Reorganization Act of 1950. During the Vietnam War the designation of Air Cavalry was introduced regarding the helicopter-borne forces; and mechanized and motorized ground units received the designation of Armored Cavalry. Today, the 1st Cavalry Division is the only active division in the U.S. Army with a cavalry designation. It maintains a detachment of horse-mounted troops used for ceremonial purposes.

favored by the Army. Instead, we had to learn how to put on leggings, a vestige of the First World War – and even earlier. These had to be threaded through buttonhooks, a time-consuming process.

The last item of clothing we were given was the Army Specialized Training Program (ASTP) patch that we were to sew on the right shoulder of our uniform. This handsome emblem combined a lamp of knowledge and an upright sword. Some wag dubbed it the "Bedpan and the Spreader." The implications of that term escaped my young and innocent mind. Another wit translated ASTP to "ass trap." The patch differentiated us from the VMI civilian cadets when we went into town. That seemed to be an advantage for us. Lexington had grown weary of the arrogant cadets.

Finally, we were issued an aged 30mm bolt-action Springfield rifle, a telescopic sight, a bayonet and its sheath, a web ammunition belt that included a trench knife, an entrenching tool, a fiber helmet liner, a canteen, a mess kit, and other accessories. I was disappointed with my rifle. I had hoped that we would be issued the recent M1. It allowed you to fire again and again by just pulling the trigger as it released a clip of eight bullets. Inserting a new clip was a simple and quick operation. By now the Springfield, because of its long-range accuracy, was used by snipers. I looked forward to target practice. When I was a Boy Scout, I had done some target practice with a similar bolt-action rifle. At that time, civilian possession of semi-automatic weapons was illegal in the United States.

All of this equipment was furnished at no charge to us, but we were responsible for the upkeep and maintenance of our new possessions. Since we were in the Reserves, we received no pay; but we were clothed, fed, housed, educated, and trained.[3] I was on my own when it came to spending money. I brought some of my savings from my work at the Acme Grocery Store with me, and my parents sent me money every week. I soon discovered that I had little time to spend it.

Before the day ended, we were instructed how to properly wear our uniforms. The Army – and VMI's – dress code forbade any individual touches. A tie had to be worn at all times, and it had to be tucked into our shirt just below the third button. Our daily khakis uniform was topped

---

3 According to the Virginia Military Institute archives, "These men were less than 18 years of age and came to VMI from their homes. Their expenses at VMI were paid by the Army, but they received no Army pay; were restricted as to uniforms issued by the Army, etc. Thirteen who were less than 18 years of age at the end of the second period were transferred to another college. The foregoing refers to the term which ended February 5, 1944. After May 1, 1944, many members of the Enlisted Reserve Corps were admitted."

with a cap whose piping indicated we were trainees. We placed our metal ASTP insignia badge on it. The rulebook said our caps had to be three fingers above our right eyebrow and angled upwards over our left. I spent a lot of mirror time angling my cap in a jaunty, carefree manner that also met Army regulations. Getting that extra fraction of an inch was my stab at retaining my individuality in the conformist world I had entered. No civilian clothing was allowed. We weren't even allowed to wear civvies when we had a pass into town.

After dinner we were free to do what we wanted to do. Some went into town to see a movie. Ben and I chose to put our austere room in order. No posters, pictures, or decorations were allowed, and the furniture had to remain in place. Our room was just like all the others in the barracks. The only departure from the norm was how we arranged the desk accessories

Bill outside his dormitory room at VMI.

we brought from home. There were cots on opposite sides of the room. We each had a wooden footlocker as well as a small closet. I used my footlocker to store my civilian clothing and other personal items. Each of us had a set of drawers. Here we placed our underwear, socks, and pajamas. We soon learned that they had to be folded or rolled in a precise manner. There was a small wall bookshelf on each side of the room. This was for textbooks. Books brought from home had to be hidden out of sight. A large desk dominated the center of the room. There we would sit opposite each other as we did our homework. We were not allowed to have a personal radio or record player. We were allowed to subscribe to a newspaper. These would be delivered to the quadrangle's guard post. I eagerly picked mine up every morning. However, I did have to go into town for a Sunday newspaper.

As Ben and I put our living quarters in military order, he introduced me to the bagels, lox, and other Kosher delicacies he brought from home. They were complete novelties to me, and they were delicious. I, in turn, introduced him to my Mother's orange cookies and other sweets she had packed for me. Ben was just one of a large contingent of students from the New York City area. The rest of us were scattered across the eastern United States. Many religious and ethnic groups were represented, but there were no Blacks and Hispanics.

I was pleased to discover that two of my New Kensington friends, Calvin Manley and Vernon Wills, had passed the test and were across the quadrangle from me. It was good to see familiar faces. I had grown up with both of them, and Vernon had been a particularly good friend. I would have preferred either as a roommate since it would have given me a sense of home, but we had no choice in that. Like me, neither Vernon nor Calvin had been academically distinguished students in high school; but both had passed the ASTRP test. We were amused that the academic stars at Ken Hi hadn't made the cut. We had little time to talk. There was too much to do that first day.

7

Beginning a Life at VMI

W E WERE AWAKENED each morning by a bugler sounding "Reveille." This rude awakening was the first of many bugle calls we learned to identify. After we got up, we made our beds. The top blanket had to be so tight that a coin would bounce if it was dropped on the coverlet. If the coin did not bounce, we received a demerit. Too many demerits resulted in penalties such as restriction to barracks or special work details. We immediately made sure our room was ready for inspection before we went to a communal latrine-shower. There we took care of our morning needs and showered. Most of us had just begun to shave so that went quickly. We returned to our rooms, checked them again for orderliness, and made sure our uniforms were correctly worn.

A bugle sounded "Assembly" and we, along with the VMI cadets, grabbed our books and notebooks, rushed to the square in front of the barracks, and formed pre-assigned ranks. During World War I – and perhaps before – some wag added ribald lyrics to the call:

> *There's a soldier in the grass*
> *With a bullet up his ass.*
> *Take it out! Take it out! Take it out!"*

After we were called to attention, we answered a roll call of our names with a lusty "Yo!" A latecomer received a demerit. Anyone who was absent had some serious explaining to do. Then the bugler sounded "To the

Colors," and we saluted the flag as it was raised. Orders were barked out and we turned and marched out onto the street and down to the mess hall. This was a spacious room filled with tables set with military precision. The tablecloths were starched and white, the silver gleamed, and the dinnerware was fine white china. It almost matched the grandeur of my dining on the train. We had assigned tables. The chaplain said a prayer, and we recited the Pledge of Allegiance as we saluted an immense flag on the wall. Immediately after we sat down, lines of Black waiters served us. No time was wasted. Breakfast and our other meals were on the clock. The most positive thing I can say about VMI is that the food was excellent.

We were better off than the first-year civilian cadets. They were called "Rats." Their regimen was more severe than ours. They had to march in a double brace;[4] and when they ate, they had to eat a "square meal." To do this, they sat at a brace on the edge of their chairs and ate their food with a square military gesture. First, they picked up their food on a fork or spoon. Then they lifted it vertically, stopped, and brought it horizontally to their mouth. Once the food was in their mouth, they reversed this process and repeated the sequence until they had finished their meal. This hazing was accepted as the norm for incoming cadets. They also had to carry out orders from upperclassmen. These included mundane duties, so in a way VMI freshmen were slaves. Their first year of college must have been a miserable experience. Fortunately, those of us in the Military were not subject to being a Rat. We ate our meals like normal human beings, and we were exempt from serving the will of upper classmen.

In 1938 Warner Brothers released *Brother Rat*, a broad farce based upon a Broadway stage play written by two VMI graduates, John Monks, Jr. and Fred Finklehoffe. Its stars included Eddie Albert, Wayne Morris, Jane Wyman, Ronald Reagan, and Priscilla Lane. VMI was so proud of the movie that we were shown a well-worn copy as part of our indoctrination. It didn't relate to the realities of life at VMI. The high jinks of the movie cadets, while amusing, would have amassed them a mountain of demerits and, in at least one instance, immediate dismissal.

---

4   A double brace is marching in double time – 180 steps per minute – while in the brace position. A military brace is a body posture position while standing or sitting at attention. It is used primarily at military schools. A way to describe it would be to have a person lie down on the floor on their back and try to touch the floor with the back of their neck. This movement forces the chin down. The brace is an attempt to imitate that position while sitting or standing. Now imagine trying to eat all of your meals in a military brace position.

After a hearty breakfast we exited the dining hall, formed ranks, and marched back to the assembly area in front of the barracks. Roll was taken again, and we were given a short break to take care of any toilet needs and to get our book and notebook for our next class. The bugler sounded "Assembly" and we returned to our ranks. Once again roll was taken. Then we marched onto the street toward the classroom building. After we came to a marching halt, we were ordered to enter the building and go up the stairs in twos to our first class. If our professor was a military officer, we stood at attention by our assigned seats and awaited his entrance. If he was a civilian, we sat and remained seated when he entered. Class began immediately.

When a military professor entered, we snapped to attention. He was always in full uniform. He formally greeted us, "Good morning, gentlemen."

We replied in unison, "Good morning, sir."

He replied, "You may be seated."

We obediently sat down. He checked his seating chart to see that we all were there, and class began.

After the class ended, we exited the building in the customary double column, assembled on the street, marched back up the street, roll was taken again, and we were dismissed for our break. We returned, roll was taken, and we were marched down the hill to our next class. It was usually in the same building as the last class. All this was repeated after lunch. These rituals struck me as absurd. Many of my new friends agreed with me, but we knew that any objection to our military discipline would result in disciplinary action. Authority at VMI could not be questioned.

We endured the daily boredom of close-order drill on the huge drill field. Officers or non-coms in the resident cadre commanded these. Commands were rapid fire. "Attention!" "Right face!" "Left face!" "About face!" "Parade rest!" "At ease!" Once this was mastered, we began to march. "Forward harch!" "Column right, harch!" "Column left, harch!" "To the rear, harch!" "Column, wheel!" "In place, harch!" "Halt." "Parade rest!" "At ease." Commands during marching had to be given and executed on the correct foot. At first our responses to the marching orders were ragged. More than once we ended up in a hopeless jumble with everyone going in different directions. Soon we were able to march with precision on the field, but we never looked as sharp as the civilian cadets.

Once we mastered the basics of marching, our rifles became part of our drill. More commands were added. "Right shoulder arms!" "Present arms." This was part of the inspection of how we maintained our weapons. The non-com or officer grabbed it firmly from our hands. We soon learned to let it go easily. Otherwise, the rifle butt would swing back and hit us in the crotch. That could be painful.

After dinner the bugler sounded "Retreat." Again, we assembled in our assigned ranks. Of course, roll was taken. Then the bugler sounded "To the Colors," and we saluted the flag as it was lowered. The flag was folded into a triangle and put away for the night. We returned to our rooms or checked out to the library until it was time for lights out at ten. Our day ended with the beautifully sad "Taps." By then I was very tired. Sleep came quickly. Usually, I slept so deeply that there was little room for dreams.

TRADITION, TRADITION, TRADITION

VMI was – and probably still is – deeply rooted in the part it played during the Civil War. One of its Superintendents, General Stonewall Jackson, was one of the most brilliant tacticians in the Confederacy. Cadets were conscripted to fight in the May 15, 1864 Battle of New Market. The Cadets were held in reserve until late in the battle. When they entered it they suffered severe casualties, but they played a part in driving Union Major General Franz Sigel and his army out of the Shenandoah Valley. Their heroism is commemorated by a huge painting in the Chapel and a statue called "Virginia Mourning Its Dead." We observed the mournful annual New Market Day ceremony held by the faculty and cadets.

Many VMI alumni have played an important part in our nation's military history. The two most famous are General George Marshall and General George Patton. Of these two, Patton had the least distinguished academic record. Perhaps he was irritated by the rigid military discipline. If so, I understand why. Getting used to VMI's oil and water mix of academics and military training and discipline wasn't easy. It went against the grain of everything I learned in high school. Our high school history classes taught us that Americans were individualists, and that American soldiers had initiative. We were also taught how inventive American soldiers defeated the rigid tactics of the British Redcoats by adapting to the freer Native American way of fighting. The Revolutionary soldiers quickly learned that firing a musket while hiding behind a tree wasn't cowardly, it was practical, and a survival tactic. Marching shoulder to shoulder against an enemy, as the British did, was foolhardy. It was especially true when they wore vivid red coats. British officers wanted to keep their battle organized, neat, and orderly. I was reminded of this when I coped with VMI's lockstep life.

Most of us resented our regimented life, but we obeyed and conformed. We soon learned we were referred to as G.I.'s, the name for a common soldier.[5] We learned other terms, too. One graphic description referred to those who overly applied strict military discipline, making life worse than it needed to be. Officers or non-coms that were too rigid or insisted on behavior according to the book were called "chickenshit."[6] Those who eagerly accepted their orders in hope of favoritism or advancement were called "brown-nosers" or "ass-kissers." A more polite way of saying this was that the person was "bucking for" promotion.

General Charles E. Kilbourne, the Superintendent and Commanding Officer of VMI, frequently met with us. He was an imposing elderly man who had fought with distinction in the Spanish-American War, the Boxer Rebellion, and World War I. He proudly wore the three top military decorations that were awarded for bravery in combat. He was a Southern gentleman and proud of it. I still remember his rich, baritone Southern accent. He held forth on VMI's long history and the value of its traditions. He proudly proclaimed that attending VMI was just as prestigious as going to West Point. During his meetings with us, he constantly reminded us that if we graduated from VMI, we would be commissioned as lieutenants

---

5 The letters G.I. were originally used by the military to refer to equipment, such as metal trashcans, made from galvanized iron. During the WWI, the German artillery shells used against American soldiers were often sardonically referred to as "G.I. cans." The terms "Government Issue" and "General Issue," used to describe general items and equipment of soldiers and airmen, were also connected to the adoption of the term "G.I." When the Selective Service System (a.k.a. "the draft") was enacted in 1940, and especially by the time America entered WWII, the common usage of the term "G.I." was expanded to include the soldiers and airmen, along with their equipment. At the end of the war General Dwight D. Eisenhower said, "The truly heroic figure of this war is G.I. Joe and his counterpart in the air, the navy, and the Merchant Marine of every one of the United Nations."

6 According to Paul Fussell's book *Wartime*, "Chickenshit is so called – instead of horse – or bull – or elephant shit – because it is small-minded and ignoble and takes the trivial seriously."

and on our way to a military career. That struck me as ridiculous. Boys who were barely ready to shave were not officer material.

General Kilbourne wasn't shy about expressing his conservative political views. I don't think he realized how objectionable they were to many Northerners. During one of his lectures he discussed the virtues of the poll tax, a fee that was designed to prevent Blacks – and the poor – from voting. It wasn't a very subtle way of limiting the vote to the affluent and landed gentry. After a long peroration of rising Southern rhetoric, the General concluded with these very words, "Any man who's too shiftless to earn the money to pay a poll tax doesn't deserve a vote."

We received this declaration with stunned silence. He had just said that wealth and property had primacy over universal voting rights. Of course, this living relic ignored the rampant poverty among Blacks and sharecroppers in the South. They worked hard, but at best they earned subsistence wages. Needless to say, his lectures didn't dent my political views. Most of us Northerners considered General Kilbourne an absurd vestige of an Old South that thrived by owning slaves. Sadly, his ideas haven't died. Stratagems to prevent the voting rights of minorities and the poor are now being installed in state after state. This, combined with grotesque geographic gerrymandering, is taking away the vote from minorities. Not all of these states are Southern. I find it disturbing that the class system of my boyhood is being formalized by law. The use of a law to disenfranchise a segment of our society is, to me, un-American.

I resented Kilbourne's obsession with the glory of the Old South and his lectures about the Confederacy's military glory. He ignored the fact the South had lost the Civil War. He listed VMI traditions that he expected us to observe. One of his commands irritated us Northerners more than the others. We were told that we must salute the statue of Stonewall Jackson that stood at the front of the parade ground. We did, but in retaliation we also saluted the Union cannonball that sat on a cement podium on the corner of the field. It had hit the barracks during the Civil War. To us it was a symbol of the Union victory over the South.

When our insolence was reported to General Kilbourne, he called an emergency meeting of ASTRP members and berated our satirical action. I remember his exact words when he concluded, "Gentlemen, you should not salute a cannonball. It's an inanimate object."

We stifled our amusement. Stonewall Jackson's statue was an equally inanimate object. We ignored his admonition and continued saluting the cannonball. I must admit we saluted less obviously. In looking back, this incident reflected the persistence of the bitter rivalry that emerged during the Civil War and continued in the years after it was over. Even now, the Confederate flag is displayed in many southern government buildings.[7] There are even occasional discussions of a new Secession.

When I debated at the Judge Adjutant General's Graduate Law School on the University of Virginia's campus in 2003, I couldn't resist including a visit to VMI.[8] I wanted my wife Linda to see where my higher education began. The drive from Charlottesville is a pleasant half-day trip through hills and valleys. We stopped at Thomas Jefferson's home at Monticello. It's a model of a design for the orderly life of an orderly mind.

As we toured the campus of VMI, I was pleased to see the Union cannonball still sits on its pedestal, but now it's wrapped in years of decaying toilet paper. Linda took a picture of me saluting it. Then she insisted that I pose saluting Stonewall Jackson's statue. I did so reluctantly. The campus still retains its 19th century character in spite of a number of new buildings. A new barracks has been added, but much of the campus remains as it was. A nice young man spoke to us as we wandered around the campus. When he found out that I had attended VMI during the war, he gave us an impromptu tour. Thanks to him, Linda and I were allowed to walk inside the Old Barracks quadrangle. I saw the room I shared with Ben so many years ago. Room 318 is exactly as it was in 1944. Tradition dies slowly.

---

7 More recently, and much to my horror, I discovered that the Confederate flag was also displayed on the desk of one of Iowa's members of Congress, the Republican Representative Steve King, a virulent conservative. What makes this even more incomprehensible and reprehensible is that Iowa was a free state during the Civil War. King, from northwestern Iowa, caused much furor in the press with his often racist and unabashedly bigoted statements, even in Congress. (Update: In 2020 King lost his bid for re-election to someone equally conservative, but who appears to be more prudent about expressing his views to the general media.)

8 It was my second debate at JAG. In both I debated an Army representative, a retired Lieutenant Colonel, as to whether the encounter at Wounded Knee, South Dakota on December 29, 1890, was a battle or a massacre. I argued that it was a massacre. My opponent prepared his argument by using secondary and older sources. There is ample evidence to support my view and very little to support his. My argument can be found at greater length in *Voices of Wounded Knee* (University of Nebraska Press, Lincoln, NE and London, England, 2000), the non-fiction book my wife and I coauthored using research we had collected over a period of three decades. From the reaction I received following the debates, everyone who attended remarked that I won both debates.

ACADEMICS

During our first meeting with General Kilbourne, we were given the opportunity to sign the VMI Code of Honor. If we did, we pledged to never cheat on tests or plagiarize papers. We also agreed to report anyone who cheated. Those who signed would not be monitored during tests since everyone was a monitor. The General proudly stated that anyone who agreed to the VMI honor system would be greeted as an honorable man anywhere in the country.

I had never cheated in school, so I signed. Many of the New Yorkers in our class did not. They believed reporting cheaters went against their street creed and that it was a form of squealing. The rest of us did not. Our teachers resented that they had to move the New York objectors to another classroom and proctor them while they took even the shortest quiz. I soon found that taking tests became more traumatic than the tests themselves. I was afraid to turn my head in any direction, and I sat low in my seat so that I wouldn't be accused of looking over the shoulder of the student in front of me. I asked myself, could someone report me who was eager to ingratiate themselves to our superiors? What if someone I had offended falsely accused me? Relaxing during tests is important. I could not. I began to envy the New Yorkers.

VMI required our professors to grade us at least three times a week. Some were short quizzes, some were full-blown tests. The results of our quizzes and evaluations were posted weekly on a bulletin board outside our classrooms. This allowed us to see how well we were doing in our classes – and how well our classmates were doing.

If you had a bad week in a class, you'd better have a good one in the next. As for me, I soon was stuck somewhere in the middle. This added to the pressure I was under. If I passed the twelve-week term, I might be asked to stay for another. Each week I spent at VMI meant one less week that I might be in combat. The competition intensified with each posting. Getting good grades, to put it simply, became a matter of life and death.

Most of the experienced professors at VMI had gone off to war. We were left with a cobbled-together faculty. Most were in the military. Mr. Atkins, who taught algebra, was one of our few civilian instructors. He was one of our better teachers. I particularly remember a young lieutenant who taught physics. He was handsome and ramrod straight. He looked the role of a young officer on the rise. He had just graduated and was teaching until he was called to active duty. His lectures were a confused jumble. Mercifully, I have forgotten his name. There were other professors, but most have faded from my memory.

I struggled to survive in my math and science classes. Even as I approached eighteen, my mind was disorganized. I lacked focus, especially when I was not interested in my work. It took me several years to learn how to use my mind. I have always done well on standardized tests, but that did not transfer to a great deal of my learning. This was especially true when my teachers were less than adequate.

Only one professor stands out. I owe so much to him as a teacher and a writer. He was a courtly older gentleman who had served with the British in Lahore, Punjab.[9] His deep tan and parchment-like skin suggested long service near that place of romance and danger shown in so many movies, the Khyber Pass. Sadly, I do not remember his name, so I will call him Sir.[10] He taught a course in military English. In it we learned to write precisely formatted communiqués in terse, formal prose. He was well aware that the subject matter of his course was dull, so he studded his lectures with entertaining digressions about frontier warfare in India and, most importantly to me, his taste in modern American literature.

Some of us stopped at his desk after a class in which he had spent time talking about his favorite modern American writers. Much to our surprise, he suggested that we meet with him in a classroom in the library one evening a week. To do this he sent through an authorization for us to sign out of the barracks for an hour. We eagerly accepted his offer. His lectures on recent American writers were brilliant and inspiring. He asked us to read a story by one author and be ready to discuss it at our next meeting. He always allowed time for questions and discussions. There were no tests or quizzes. We were taking this short course for enjoyment – and our personal growth.

Some of the writers discussed were Ernest Hemingway, John Steinbeck, James Farrell, Theodore Dreiser, John O'Hara, Dorothy Parker, Edna St.

---

9 The province of Punjab became part of the British Indian Empire in 1849. Lahore was the cultural and economic center of western Punjab. Lahore played an important role in the independence movements of both India and Pakistan. In 1940 the All India Muslim League passed the Lahore Resolution, demanding the creation of Pakistan as a separate homeland for the Muslims of India. Pakistan achieved independence on August 14, 1947, and Lahore was made the capital of the Punjab province.

10 After some research, I was able to find out his name, and a bit of his history. Dr. Frederick Mowbray Velte (1893 – 1962).

Vincent Millay, and F. Scott Fitzgerald. These writers dealt with reality, psychology, and politics. I had read some of their stories in my well-worn paperback collection, but now they fitted into a historical and cultural context. Our discussions gave their work deeper meaning. Together they reflected life in early 20th century America.

VMI library.

Sir's compelling lectures sent me rushing off to the library. I read stories in the stacks when my class assignments were too time consuming, but I also checked out several books. My fascination with American literature was detrimental to my studies, but I couldn't resist entering this new world. I didn't have time to read novels, so my reading was devoted to short stories. All were different from the 19th century works I read in high school. This is not to put down those earlier works. Sir mentioned them, saying they were the foundation stones upon which modern American literature has been built. It could not exist without the works of Edgar Allan Poe, Washington Irving, Nathaniel Hawthorne, Herman Melville, Bret Hart, and especially Mark Twain and Stephen Crane.

One of the books I discovered in the library stacks was Ernest Hemingway's *The Fifth Column and the First Forty-Nine Stories. The Fifth Column* is Hemingway's only play. It isn't very good, but the short stories excited me. It began with his first published short story, "Up in Michigan," and concluded with his latest short works, "The Short Happy Life of Francis Macomber," "The Snows of Kilimanjaro," "The Capital of the World," and "Old Man at the Bridge." "Up in Michigan" contained the first graphic description of a sexual encounter that I had ever read. Until then I had no idea that writers could venture into this territory. "The Killers" was understated and tragic. The later stories contained enough material for a novel in just a few pages. Hemingway's clean, precise style economically created a new world for me.

Sir pulled no punches in his discussions. I never realized that Shakespeare's plays had been bowdlerized in the editions we read in high school until Sir mentioned it. If something earthy could not be cut, it was left unexplained by our teacher or by a footnote. This prudishness extended into the bestselling novels of our time. In them when the moment of sexual intercourse began, everything became hazy and impressionistic.

As we approached the end of the term, Sir invited our study group to his home at the far end of the drill field. It was an elegant and very British evening. It was then we discovered he had a stunningly beautiful daughter named Lois. All of us coveted a date with her, but Sir was our professor. I managed to speak with her. While she was nearly my age, she seemed much more sophisticated than I was at the time. My boyish clumsiness with young women took over. It was an awkward experience, but it was also a lovely evening.

I owe so much to Sir. He inspired me to read beyond class requirements. His lectures allowed me to become an autodidact and even a writer. His informal weekly meetings convinced me that I was not cut out to be an engineer of any sort. Instead, my interests veered between the polarities of literature and history. They determined what majors I would take when I entered college after the war. Better still, he inspired me to become a teacher.

Playing Soldier

In addition to our heavy class load and close-order drill training, we received a truncated version of basic training. There was a physical education class that included the usual jumping jacks, pushups, and chin-ups. There were regular swimming classes. Prior to this, I only managed to paddle around a swimming pool. I finally learned how to swim properly. One very solid boy in our class never managed. His body mass was so dense that he sunk to the bottom of the pool and had to be rescued. He also was excused from going to swimming lessons after his humiliating first day.

I enjoyed target practice at the outdoor firing range near campus. Our bolt-action .30 caliber Springfield rifles were extremely accurate. I'd done target shooting when I was on camporees with the Boy Scouts, so I had some experience before I hit the range for the first time. Fortunately, I shot right-handed, so I used my good right eye to focus on the target. I was quite successful, even at long distances. If I had shot this well later on during Infantry basic training, I would have qualified as a sharpshooter.

The red bullseye on our targets was an abstraction to me. I never let it go through my mind that I would be shooting at the head of a real human being. Subconsciously, I made target practice a game. In a way, it was. Shooting a bolt-action rifle was not the best kind of training for learning how to fire the gas-operated, semi-automatic M1 Garand rifle used in Infantry combat. Pulling the trigger eight times could empty its eight-bullet "en-bloc" clip. Then another clip could be inserted as you continued to fire. In combat, accuracy was less important than laying down a sheet of rifle fire that pinned down the enemy.

Next, we learned the six basic movements of bayonet fighting. All were designed to disable the enemy. Our training began by sparring with each other. For safety, this was done in slow motion. We then progressed to attacking dummies attached to wires. The best bayonet fighters among us were big, strong, and fast.

We were told that it's difficult to penetrate a muscular human body with a pointed weapon. Even a strong thrust wouldn't enter a body more than an inch or two. You didn't kill with a bayonet. You disabled the enemy by wounding him with thrusts and slashes. The bayonet fighting shown in movies had no relation to the reality of the real thing. The butts of our rifles were also a useful weapon. Needless to say, I hoped to hell I would never be involved in a bayonet charge. At that time, I weighed slightly more than 150 pounds and had little upper body strength. I had quick reactions, but they were of little use unless I fought against a person my own size.

Fighting with any sharp weapon frightened me. Most of us agreed on that. I gained some comfort when older combat veterans who trained us said the Germans disliked bayonet fighting as much as we did. They also warned us that the Italians and Japanese excelled in fighting with bayonets and knives. None of us wanted to fight in Italy or the Pacific. None of us looked forward to combat of any sort. When I was in Infantry combat, I only heard the chilling command "Fix bayonets!" a few times.

One of our physical training instructors was Johnny Beazley, a famous St. Louis Cardinal pitcher. He was a compact, handsome, and personable

young man who had been on his way to being
one of the best pitchers in the major leagues
when the war interrupted his career. In 1942,
during his first full year in the majors, he
won twenty-one games and lost just six. He
won two complete games against the Yankees during the 1942 World Series. After the
season he enlisted and was sent to pitch for
an Army team. During a game he felt pain in
his arm, but his commanding officer ordered
him to pitch through the pain. The injury that
resulted was devastating. In those days there
was no reconstructive surgery for pitching

*At VMI with Springfield .30
caliber bolt action rifle and
attached bayonet.*

arms. When he returned to civilian life in 1946 his record was seven
wins and five losses. He never recovered his old form, winning only nine
games for the rest of his career. He left baseball in 1949. In just three
years he lost his edge.

We were thrilled to have such a famous instructor. He taught us basic
jujitsu and other forms of hand-to-hand combat. It was a dangerous process that had to be approached with care. We learned how to break an
arm with one simple move. Another move enabled us to throw a bigger
person to the ground. We learned how to do this in slow motion. We were
taught that when we were in close hand-to-hand combat there were no
Marquess of Queensbury rules. This included blinding the enemy with
the thrust of two extended fingers. Our instruction became lethal when
we learned how to kill an enemy with our bare hands. Beazley's classes
made warfare more real to me than any of our other training. After each
class we were told that we must never use these techniques if we got into
the boyish fistfights that sometimes broke out in our barracks. As for me,
I put what I had learned aside when the war ended. These techniques of
killing remain in my memory bank. I wish they didn't.

Our most exotic – and retro – form of military training was conducted
by a small cadre of aged U. S. Army cavalrymen. Some of these grizzled
fighting men fought in the Spanish-American War; all had fought in the
First World War. They presided over extensive stables of fine riding horses.
We were taught how to groom and saddle up our mounts. Then we learned
the basics of riding in a spacious indoor riding arena. That progressed
to open jumping. Galloping single file as we approached hurdles was a

frightening experience. I ended up astride the neck of my mount after my first jump. I slowly learned how to stay in the saddle.

My prized graduation wristwatch fell off during a jump and was trampled into a flat metal disk. My parents replaced it with a watch that I wore for many years. Now it sits in a box on our dresser. It's dreadfully corroded. That was the result of our being put through a gas chamber as part of my Infantry basic training. I will describe that in detail later.

The climax of our cavalry training came when we rode several miles outside of Lexington for an overnight bivouac. We didn't have to march. We rode all the way. It was great fun. We all felt like we were 19th century cavalrymen, especially when we were ordered to prod our horses into a

canter. We made sure our horses were fed and secured before we put up our pup tents. They had to be carefully ditched. We were instructed to preserve the sod so that we could replace it when we left the camp.

VMI's cooks brought our dinner out on a truck. We turned in early, but not until we enjoyed time around the campfires. I slept well. It was a quiet spring night. I found the occasional snorting and movement of my horse comforting. When I awoke in the morning my body ached from sleeping on the hard ground. Some of that ache was restored by a hearty breakfast. We had to leave the campground just as we found it when we rode away.

Bill on the 25 mile march and bivouac at VMI.

I can proudly say I received some of the last cavalry training given by the United States Army. Of course, I never got to use that experience when I was in Infantry combat. When I visited VMI with my wife in 2002, there was no sign of cavalry training. I discovered that it was no longer a curriculum item. Now that enormous riding arena is an indoor rifle range.

Our training also included two long marches to that bivouac area. This was to build our endurance. If we graduated and were commissioned second lieutenants, we had to look fresher than our command at the end of a long march. We were required to march with our rifles, all our basic equipment, and our backpacks. These were filled with one-half of a pup tent, pegs to secure our tent, a sleeping bag, a change of clothing, and toiletries. It was a heavy load. My legs were weary after the long march. A couple of men fell out near the end. I did not. Fortunately, my legs were strong from my years as a newsboy.

Once there, we set up our tents. We knew the rules since we had done the same with our cavalry outing. We enjoyed a hearty supper. It was much like a Boy Scout outing. The only thing that was different was that with the scouts we rode back and forth to our campsite in a car caravan.

Some of the more outgoing New Yorkers volunteered to present an evening's entertainment. Among them was Melvin Kaminsky, a loud, rather brash kid from Brooklyn. Later he would become known as Mel Brooks.[11] His gravelly voice hasn't changed over the years. Their entertainments

were pure Catskill shtick. Many of the jokes were rooted in their New York culture, so they meant little to us. To be blunt, they weren't very good, but they passed the time before we crawled into our sleeping bags for the night.

The army non-coms who commanded us didn't have to wear packs. Their tents and sleeping bags were taken to the campground by trucks. Some of us complained about this privilege when we returned to campus. Our captain agreed with us. They had to wear packs when we marched to our final bivouac. They resented this deeply.

Bill returning from the overnight bivouac.

As we waited to begin our last march, I walked by one of our sergeants. He looked grim. He was wearing his backpack, too. I couldn't resist telling him he looked very "G.I." He was furious. When we returned from the bivouac, he put me on report as being insubordinate. When I reported to our captain's

---

11 Melvin Kaminsky/Mel Brooks wasn't the only person to go through VMI as part of the ASTP program during WWII who would later become famous. Brooks/Kaminsky and Bill were part of the 5th ASTP cycle at VMI. Earlier, during the 2nd ASTP cycle, Eugene Louis Vidal (1925-2012), known professionally as Gore Vidal was a cadet. Vidal came from a prominent political and military family. After Vidal's training period at VMI, he joined the Army Transportation Corps as an officer and was sent to the Aleutian Islands. Following the war he became an award-winning writer, novelist, essayist, playwright, screenwriter, actor, and provocateur.

office, the sergeant stood to one side. He recited what I had said word for word. The captain asked me, "What did you mean by this statement?"

I replied, "I meant that he was giving me a good example of how to be a soldier."

The captain had a hard time keeping a straight face when he told me I should be more respectful to my non-commissioned officers. After this near escape from severe military discipline, I learned not to make any kind of joke around a non-com or an officer even though some of them were living jokes.

YOUTHFUL HIGH SPIRITS

Practical jokes abounded during my twelve weeks at VMI. They provided a boyish escape from our otherwise intense, disciplined life. Pranks started with short-sheeting beds and progressed from there. Short sheeting was accomplished by folding up the top sheet, so that it appeared that there were two sheets. When the victim got into bed, he was stopped short of stretching out his legs. Then he had to get up and remake his bed. The exceptionally strong boy who was so adept at bayonet fighting got into bed one night and thrust his feet down with such vigor that he tore two holes in his sheet. Fortunately, the ripped sheet was mixed into the weekly laundry.

Early on, some guys mixed peroxide into a dark-haired boy's hair tonic. He woke up the next morning with brindle-colored hair. The jokers didn't know that the *Articles of War*, the Army's code of conduct, forbids soldiers from drastically changing their appearance unless they get the permission of their commanding officer. Dying one's hair in those days was unheard of. The victim cleverly managed to keep his cap on most of the time, but the change in his hair color was finally noticed. Finally, he was called in to explain his hair. He very cleverly covered for his friends when he told our captain that repeated exposure to the sun discolored his hair.

Some boys on the third floor filled a large barracks bag with water. It took four boys to lean out and pour the water through the window into the room below. Suddenly a mini waterfall cascaded out of the lower room, spilling over the balcony to the courtyard below. Some of the boys in the courtyard were drenched.

One reoccurring prank was to pilfer silverware from the dinner table and stick it in a back pocket of the pants of the soldier in front of you when we marched in formation to the assembly area. When we reached the parade ground, the victim had to choose between keeping the stolen silverware and trying to return it at the next mess call. Sometimes the victim realized he had a piece of silverware in his pocket and passed it to the pocket of a person in front of him. Often there was a chain reaction with the final victim becoming the goat of the joke. It was a risky game. Discovery by one of our non-coms would have meant a demerit – or worse. I must confess this is the only prank that I participated in.

Some boys managed to find pills that changed the color of urine. These were prescription medicines used by doctors for urinary tests, but somehow the jokers managed to get a variety of them. They inserted them into the bottom of soft chocolate drops. Then they lured their friends into eating them. The next day they followed their friends to the toilet to see their amazed expressions when they peed green, blue, purple, and other colors. One boy peed red and fainted.

Two of the more affluent boys bought several boxes of *Rinso* laundry flakes in town and hid them in the bushes. Somehow, they managed to get out of the closely guarded barracks late at night, broke into the swimming pool, and dumped their cache into it. When the first swimming class dove in the next morning, it was soon covered with foam and bubbles. Even though there was much less than a foot of suds in the water, the prank was considered a success. It took two days to drain the pool and get it back in working order.

The commandant was furious, but the culprits were never caught. Most of us knew who did the deed, but we weren't telling. We considered pranks – however costly – outside the limits of VMI's honor code. Later we heard the two pranksters were contemplating filling the pool with packages of Jell-O. The term ended before they realized that ambition. I've always wondered if it would have worked.

The most sadistic practical joke I became aware of would now be considered a type of hazing. I didn't find it funny, even for the time. It happened when two enlistees persuaded a VMI cadet to join them in lighting their farts. Before each lit up, they ceremoniously applied a wet washcloth to their behinds. They told the gullible cadet they did this to make sure the areas surrounding the rectum were damp. This, they claimed, prevented the lighting of body hair. Each joker lit up his own gas jet and sent out a short flame. The third boy, encouraged by the success of his new friends, applied a washcloth to his hind parts. He didn't know that his friends, if we can call them that, had dipped his washcloth in natural alcohol stolen from the chemistry lab. The unsuspecting boy lit up, farted loudly, and screamed in pain as his anal hair caught fire. He ran headfirst out of the room and almost catapulted over the second-floor balcony. His friends caught his feet just in time.

We all heard a scream that was followed by eloquent cursing. It was followed by raucous laughter. Everyone ran out onto the balconies. We were opposite the atrocity, so we saw a cadet, his bare butt smoldering, dangling over the balcony railing. We didn't hear what exactly had happened until the next morning. The cadet was humiliated and rather sore. Since the cadets were segregated from us none of us had the opportunity of seeing his hairless and red ass in the morning shower, but we heard about it from other cadets. From this time onward the VMI cadets steered clear from the smart-assed Army students. The victimized cadet was too embarrassed to report the incident, so the screaming and cursing was passed off as a barracks disturbance.

It was an accepted tradition that when a cadet had a birthday, his squad serenaded him with "Happy Birthday" during an evening meal. After the meal was finished and everyone marched to the assembly area and dismissed, his squad would grab the birthday boy and pull him over one of the cannons near the Chapel. Then each member of the squad smacked him once with the web belts we wore. Web belts applied with will to one's buttocks were painful. I suffered this indignity when one of my friends ratted to my squad that it was my birthday. It wasn't a pleasant experience.

A Pennsylvania Dutch boy, whom I will call Fritz Eichelberger, was a member of our unit. He was chubby, genial, and a likeable fellow. He spoke with a quaint accent that was rather charming. His birthday was early in our twelve-week term. He received his whipping amiably and with no complaints. To show pain would have been unmanly. Much to Fritz's amazement we sang a second "Happy Birthday" to him few days later. I remember Fritz exclaiming in his thick Pennsylvania Dutch accent, "Yee-sus Kee-rist, dis isn't mine birthday!"

We were relentless in performing the birthday ritual.

When we sang a third greeting to him a few days later, Fritz took off running when our unit was dismissed from the assembly. All of us pursued him as he took refuge in the chapel. We all roared into the chapel at a full

sprint. We came to a skidding stop when we saw our amazed commandant, General Kilbourne, walking up the center aisle. Fritz skidded to a
stop face to face with the general. He braced to attention and snapped off
a salute which the general returned. Our squad had no other alternative
than to do the same.

The general asked in his mellifluous accent, "May I ask why you gentlemen rushed in here?"

Fritz had the quickness of mind to reply, "We're here, sir, for our
evening prayers."

"You come in here every evening for your devotions?"

"Yes, sir!"

We all nodded in agreement.

"I find it heart-warming to see such religious zeal among you young
men. May I join you in your devotions?"

We had no other alternative then to file into pews while the general
knelt in the center aisle and led us in prayer. He had believed us![12] It was
all we could do to keep straight faces. Fritz had no more birthday sere-
nades. In fact, he became something of a hero.

MY FIRST STAGE APPEARANCE

There was a United Service Organization (USO) training unit at nearby
Washington and Lee College. After their training, they dispersed throughout our many theatres of war. Once there, their job was to raise the
morale of our troops, either with their performances or by helping troops
perform for themselves. All USO members had extensive experience in
professional theatre and film.

Two older trainees, who had produced and staged the famous *Straw Hat
Revue* on Broadway, offered to stage a revue using ASTRP students as part
of their training. At that time, revues were very popular. They continued
to be part of Broadway seasons until a few years after the war. Now they

---

12 Or so we thought. Looking back, decades later, and after having spent a lifetime
in education, I can see that the general saw through us and knew exactly what he was
doing. He probably figured that the easier and greater punishment would be to have
us sit through a prayer service. And, in hindsight, it worked since we never serenaded
Fritz again.

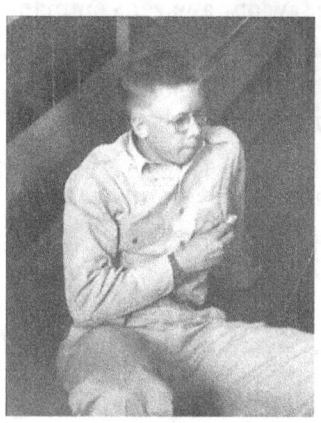

Bill at rehearsal for
Ercsapoppin

are non-existent. A vestige of them appeared on television variety shows in the 1950s and 60s. The best of these were the old Sid Caesar shows. Years later, Carol Burnett almost matched Caesar on her good nights.

Revues usually had a theme and included short skits, comic bits, and music and dance numbers. They did not require long rehearsals, so the project fitted into our tight schedules.

I'm not sure how I got the courage to sign up to audition for the show. I was amazed when I was cast as part of a trio who sang a ribald version of the popular Cole Porter song, "Begin the Beguine." This was my first appearance on stage outside of some elementary school plays. Needless to say, I was struck with stage fright at my first rehearsal. I still remember some of the lyrics:

When we begin to clean the latrine,
To take up our mops,
And shine all the seats in splendor.

I was fortunate that my first stage appearance was in a trio. I could hide my stage fright in the relative safety of our group. I still have stage fright when I make a public appearance of any sort. Now I can mask and control that fear. In spite of this, I sensed that wonderful flow of adrenaline when the audience applause swept up from the house.

Our revue was called *Ercsapoppin,* a reference to our status in the Enlisted Reserve Corps. The title was also inspired by the 1941 Broadway revue *Hellzapoppin,* a collection of old gags and routines. Melvin Kaminsky – Mel Brooks – was one of the principal comedians in our show. He and two other New Yorkers did rapid-fire insults, some of them in response to hecklers planted in the audience.

You're a bum!
Sir, I'll have you know I am a member of the cinema.
Then you're a cinema bum!

and

Sir, I'm Frank Sinatra's brother.
Yeah, not-so-hotra.

One of the putdowns for a planted heckler was, "I don't know what I'd do without you, but I'd rather." Another was, "Did your mother have any children?"

The real treat was seeing the producers do their old routines during rehearsals. It was a glimpse of Broadway and vaudeville in its former glory. Our directors were very funny men. I remember many of those routines and their shtick. Some were almost absurdly abstract. Each comedian would enter from opposite wings, one with his umbrella up, the other with his down. They approached each other, stopped, and looked at the other's umbrella. The first comedian then put his umbrella down, while the other put his up. They continued to walk across the stage in opposite directions. All this was done with utmost seriousness. They never let the audience know they were performing a gag. I instinctively studied their impeccable timing and filed away the bits they performed and taught to other members of the cast. Over the years I've used them in comedies and musicals I directed. Some jokes never wear out.

The chapel was packed for the two-night run. Townspeople wended up the hill to fill out the house. Everyone was very complimentary. At the time, I passed it off as a once-in-a-lifetime experience. As far as I was concerned, I had little inclination to appear on stage again. Nevertheless, it was my first step into live performance, and a tentative step to my lifelong profession – theatre. Bigger steps would come years later.

Short Passes into a Lazy Southern Town

Lexington had its charms. The streets were clean, and the houses were well kept. No one rushed about. It seemed to be a place of gentility and civility. Everything had a slow, almost leisurely pace that even included the way language was spoken. The lazy cadence of southern speech has its charms, especially in the mouths of women. Vowels were elongated sensuously, and consonants dropped away at the end of words. Many spoke with a rich eloquence that was colored by similes and metaphors.

The speech I heard moved like warm molasses across a dark glass, albeit a dark glass that hid a seething sea of racial hatred.

Racial epithets had their own hierarchy. Older women spoke with all their gentility of "nigras." Middle class men and women together called them "colored." Men apart resorted to the "N-word" with great frequency. I soon learned that the educated middle class of the South saw itself as a chosen people, an elite who had the God-given right to keep Blacks in their place. They even looked down on the "White trash"[13] as a class beneath their contempt.

Once I heard a Southern "gentleman" justify the act of lynching that had largely faded into the past. He looked on the passing of that hideous practice without regret. After all, he said, Southern womanhood had to be protected from the bestial lust of a subhuman race. The hatred that fueled that hideous practice lingered; and their religious leaders and politicians confirmed it. Today this tide from the South's dark past colors our politics and characterizes views held by many members of the Republican Party. It has also bled into the North. There, the Radical Right and more than a few members of the more discrete Center cloak their ugly inner bigotries and angers in religion and morality. It has been used as a tool to influence public opinion and poison the mainstream and fringe media. This vestige of our past gorges as nauseous bile in the throat of our political system.

Classes and training exercises at VMI met every day except Sunday. Wednesday and Saturday classes ended at noon, providing us with precious time for ourselves. On Wednesdays we had to be back for dinner and study hours. There was barely enough time to see a matinee movie. If the movie ran long, we left. We didn't dare miss the pre-dinner roll call.

On Saturday evenings we didn't have to return to the barracks until ten o'clock. We were also free all day Sunday. Since Lexington was in the Bible Belt, there were no Sunday movies. There was little else to do in town. You can't spend all your time in a drugstore soda fountain. While I had grown weary of being dragged to church by my parents on Sunday and Wednesday evenings back home, now I broke down and attended a small Methodist church on occasional Sunday mornings instead of going to Chapel at VMI. It whiled away an hour and reminded me of home.

---

13 "White trash" is an American racial slur used to derogatorily describe poor white people, especially in the South. Similar descriptions in other parts of the country include "cracker," "hillbilly," and "redneck."

AYOUNG MAN GOES TO WAR

We quickly learned to use our free time judiciously since the fast pace of our classes kept us on our toes. Study time was critical to our future at VMI. We didn't want to see our posted grades go down, and we wanted to remain qualified for another term, or even terms. The war was plodding along slowly in the spring of 1944. There was progress in the Pacific, but our advancement up Italy's boot was slow and bloody. The Russians were driving the Germans back from their huge initial gains. There were rumors of an impending invasion of France. If that happened, we all believed the war would end quickly. We were so wrong.

I saw more examples of segregation each time I went into town. Lexington was divided into two parts. One was home to the mildly affluent White middle class; the other, for the Blacks, was impoverished. We were advised not to venture into that area. The middle of the town was strictly segregated. This included public water fountains. Movie theatres relegated the Blacks to the balconies. In most, they had to enter by outside stairs.

One Saturday night, some of us lost track of the time. When we realized that we were past curfew, we approached the barracks carefully. There was only one way to enter, a narrow gate. On the left side was a windowed office that served as a guard post. We decided to approach the gate out of view. Then we got down on our hands and knees and crawled one by one into the quadrangle. Once there, we turned left so the two sentries never saw us. This was my first experience with infiltration. We were not caught.

Sometime during the middle of my twelve-week term, I began dating Elizabeth, a pretty blonde I noticed during a Sunday evening service at the Methodist church. I walked beside her after we left the church. She was a shy and gentle person who had little to say. When we arrived at her home and walked up on the front porch, I asked her to go out on a movie date. I was pleasantly surprised when she said she'd like that very much. I was even more surprised when I found out she was the daughter of VMI's First Sergeant. He was in charge of operations for all cadets and was the highest-ranking non-commissioned officer.

Our dating consisted of an early Saturday night movie and then church together on Sunday. Afterwards we sat on her front porch swing. There we tentatively kissed and embraced when her parents were safely inside. There was little passion in our meetings. Our dating was chaste and correct. We never spoke of a future together even though that was implied in every male-female encounter of that time. As a lowly Private I had nothing to offer a young woman. It was a pleasant interlude I remember fondly.

My parents, who drove down to visit me, were pleased that I had found a good Methodist girl to date. They were impressed that she bore one of our family names, Hess, and my Grandmother Coleman's first name. Elizabeth and I wrote for a while after I left VMI, but our correspondence drifted away. I hope she has had a good life.

Pop, Bill, Peggy, and Mom at VMI.

Other students sought less ladylike "dates." These could be seen strolling along the streets of Lexington. Some of these women charged a goodly sum, some were enthusiastic amateurs. The more predatory boys attended revival services held by the evangelical Baptist churches. I never went to one, but others told me that as the services became more and more emotional, people would weep, confess their sins, and come forward to accept Jesus. The more enthusiastic participants spoke in tongues. A few even rolled around on the floor in ecstasy. I discovered that the reasons my friends attended these services was less than spiritual. Instead, they found the hysteria of the service sexually excited many of the young women and that they were quite willing to allow a soldier to walk them home. I suspect the number of virgins in local Baptist congregations was severely reduced that spring.

D-Day

Late in the morning of June 6, our classes were interrupted. This was unprecedented. Classes were sacrosanct. They were never interrupted or cancelled. We left our classroom and marched to the assembly area in front of the barracks. We wondered what had happened. General Kilbourne appeared and curtly announced that the Normandy invasion was underway. I felt a chill pass through our ranks. Thousands of young Americans were dying as we stood there listening to this news.

Then the Commandant read General Dwight D. Eisenhower's D-Day Order to our troops:

You will bring about the destruction of the German war machine, the elimination of Nazi tyranny over the oppressed peoples of Europe, and security for ourselves in a free world.

Your task will not be an easy one. Your enemy is well trained, well equipped, and battle-hardened. He will fight savagely.

But this is the year 1944. Much has happened since the Nazi triumphs of 1940-41.

The United Nations have inflicted upon the Germans great defeat in open battle man to man. Our air offensive has seriously reduced their strength in the air and their capacity to wage war on the ground.

Our home fronts have given us an overwhelming superiority in weapons and munitions of war and placed at our disposal great reserves of trained fighting men.

The tide has turned.

The free men of the world are marching together to victory. I have full confidence in your courage, devotion to duty, and skill in battle.

We will accept nothing less than full victory.

Good luck, and let us all beseech the blessings of Almighty God upon this great and noble undertaking.

After a moment of stunned silence, the general led us in a silent prayer for the men storming onto those bloody beaches. The fate of the world hung on their ability to land, hold on, and then advance into France. While I was beginning to lose my belief in prayer, I prayed that day. If the invasion failed, how long would it be until we could muster another attempt? We hoped this was the beginning of the last stage of the war. Surely, once we were established on French soil, the Germans, now extended on fronts in Russia and Italy, would collapse.

While we had been on the attack for several months, we were now entering enemy-controlled Europe. Those brave men who charged onto the beaches of Normandy deserve our deepest appreciation. Few human beings have ever suffered such an ordeal. No day of combat has been more intense. 10,274 died on the beaches of Normandy and thousands more were wounded. Steven Ambrose, the historian, wrote, "Infantry combat is the most extreme experience a human can endure."

By the next day, we knew how bloody the invasion had been; but our soldiers held our beachheads and began to advance into the maze of the hedgerows. Soldiers often had to fight yard by yard to move forward. The numbers of gold stars in windows spread like a virulent disease across

The boy, now a man.

American residential streets. Thousands of families grieved, while thousands more held their breaths waiting and wondering if their loved ones were still alive. The casualties of D-Day and the advance through the French hedgerows were high. Just as bad – and worse – was yet to come as our armies moved across Europe toward Germany.

Following D-Day, there was little need for engineers of any sort, and the Army no longer was interested in training them. Our first semester was to be our last. Anything we learned in those three months became unimportant. We were done playing soldier. Now what the Army required was young bodies to feed the maw of an intensifying war. As soldiers fell, replacements were needed. We all knew we would be among those replacements. After we completed our twelve-week term we became cannon fodder. The god of war needed new flesh for his feast upon the young.

On June 7, the day after D-Day, I turned eighteen. In the Army's eyes I was now a man. Shortly after that the term ended. Before I was assigned to active duty, I was given a short leave. My mind wandered as I headed for home. My experience at VMI convinced me that I could never be happy in a military environment. I was not designed for a strictly disciplined life. My young evolving mind was not capable of an academic life among the sciences. My mind was interested in too many things. It jumped from one thing to another on its own. I couldn't focus it or control its direction. I didn't realize then that it was seeking a creative outlet. That discovery would take time. I wasn't sure if I had a good mind. I wasn't sure of where it would take me in the years to come – if there were years to come.

Retracing the steps that brought me to this point, I began my trip back to Pottsville – first by bus, and then by train. As VMI faded into the past, my mind was racing ahead. I thought about the bigger journey looming in my future. Would I even have a future? Where would I be sent? I wondered if I would live long enough to find myself. Too many young men were dying, too many never got to realize their lives. Their hopes, their dreams, and their potential to make a positive impact on the world were lost before they ever had a chance to try.

Casualties had mounted since D-Day. I was swept with melancholy and a sense of loneliness. I felt terribly alone. Even though fellow passengers surrounded me, I couldn't speak to any of them. They were strangers. Some, I am sure, feared for a loved one. Others might be grieving their own casualty of war. I had to keep my thoughts to myself. My apprehension was personal, something I had to deal with myself. A shudder passed through my body as a sense of fear swept through me.

I couldn't concentrate enough to read. As I watched the scenery sweep by, a myriad of questions flooded through my mind. I looked at my hands. No, I stared at them. I stared at their reality. It was as though I had never seen them before. I looked at my newly trimmed, carefully kept fingernails, at the bones and veins beneath my skin. I looked at the reality of my hands and asked myself, "What if they were blown away? What if I couldn't play the violin and the piano? What if I couldn't hold a knife and fork or feed myself? What if I wouldn't be able to hold a young woman close as I danced with her? What if I wouldn't be able to touch her soft skin?" Then I remembered that young soldier in the bus station on my way to VMI. "What if I was disfigured? What if young women turned away from me in revulsion, just as I had turned away from the soldier whose face was gone?"

My imagination raced out of control as we rode into darkness. Thoughts bombarded me. Questions overwhelmed me. My body shook in a massive shudder. "What if I was blinded by shrapnel? Would my wounds allow me to write, to draw cartoons, to read books? What if I had to spend the rest of my life in darkness?" Then came the darkest thought of all: "Was a partial life worth living?"

The answers to these questions came quickly. A sudden death was preferable. Then I pondered death itself. I'd gone to the funerals of older family members and my parents' friends. Only one of my classmates had died, and that was in junior high school. I didn't recognize him as he lay in his coffin. I wondered if his death had been painful or easy. I wondered if there was a Heaven and a Hell. Now I had my doubts, but the concept of oblivion eluded me. It still does. What if there is nothing? What if there's a sort of consciousness, of looking down on the world I left? Was Hell seeing what I had missed? Was Heaven leaving life behind, or was that Hell?

Then the shudder passed. It was replaced by a numbness, an acceptance of what was to come. That numbness gave me a sense of calm. I didn't know then that my mind, my imagination, and my emotions had begun to shut down. I was too young to ask others if they shared these thoughts. Men didn't do that then. We were alone with our emotions. Showing them was a sign of weakness. I didn't know then that this shutting down would be my savior during what was to come.

I longed to be home, even if it was only for a few days. I would be embraced by the love of my parents. For a brief time, I would be secure. I would go to sleep in my own room amidst my boyhood things, things thrown about in disarray, a disarray free from inspections or demerits. I longed to be able to play my own table radio, to hear news reports, to listen to the music I loved, and enjoy the comedy and suspense programs. I desperately wanted to turn back the clock. I wanted to be a boy again.

Every moment of the next few days would be precious. It would be a brief stop in a journey that would change my life, a journey that would define me as a human being and set me on my life course.

My journey home was too long. My time at home would be too short. For the first time in my life, I understood the full meaning of that wonderful word – home.

Spring, 1944. Bill at VMI with his parents
Ila and William Coleman.

PART III

THE REAL ARMY

Blood flows one way in life
and another way in song,
and one never knows
which flow is the right one.[1]

---

[1] From *Elegy for Kosovo* by Ismail Kadare.

THE MILITARY—

8

HOME AGAIN

M Y PARENTS MOVED to Orwigsburg during my time at VMI. It was a pleasant village near Pottsville. I took piano lessons there while I was in high school, so I already knew the area. Now Dad was closer to his work at the new Alcoa plant. This meant he could save some of his precious gasoline rationing coupons and use them for non-business purposes. That was how he and Mom were able to make the long drive to visit me at VMI.

They were waiting for me as I got off the train. Dad rushed down the platform and grabbed my suitcase. I insisted on carrying my Army issue duffle bag. Mom hugged me. There were tears in her eyes. It was a short drive to the house they now rented. Mom had carefully recreated my room on the second floor. Everything was as I had left it. Even though it was a different house, I felt like I was home.

My leave was too short. Dad took a few days of vacation so that we could drive the 300 miles to Ohio. There was no time for a stop in New Kensington. The Colemans were ever stoic, but I sensed Grandpa Coleman harbored a fear that the Coleman name might come to an end. We ate well and said little. The Phillips' were more open in their feelings. One evening Grandpa Phillips, who was seventy-five years old, sat with me on the enormous stone slab that lay before his small front porch. I remember him saying, "Old men ought to fight the wars they caused. We may be old, but we can stand and fight."

The war he imagined was hand-to-hand combat as it often was in the Civil War, or trench warfare like in World War I. The war now being fought in Europe veered from being bogged down to fast moving advances where fronts shifted quickly, and where even young legs struggled to

On leave with Coleman grandparents.

keep up with the tanks. I was touched by his willingness to fight in my place, but this giant of a man had bad knees and moved slowly. I knew one thing as we drove back home: my grandparents loved me beyond words. They took pride in my being a soldier, but they desperately hoped their grandson would come home when this war was over.

I had a chance to visit with some of my high school friends when we returned to Orwigsburg. Many were there, but quite a few were serving in the Armed Services and far away. One was Jack Malson. He joined the Navy early in his senior year and was serving on a ship in the Pacific Theatre. Harry Roadarmel was drafted, but he was classified 4-F. I discovered that he had begun dating Ruth, so that old flame was extinguished. At first, I was angered. He had been one of my three best friends. Later I forgave him. Fortunately, I had no deep attachment to Ruth, so her defection didn't bother me. When I left, I had no expectations. When I came home, I found that was for the best. Harry and Ruth married, had a family, and enjoyed a long life together. Both are gone now.

One evening Bob Hague, a classmate, held a party for me at his parents' home. It was a pleasant gathering. I was the only one there that wore a uniform. It was good to be dancing close to young women. That experience would soon be in the past. Every dance reminded me that I was leaving all that behind. I danced with many partners.

Each day was precious. I had no time for dates. My parents were too busy showing off their soldier boy to their friends. Of course, I was hustled off to church. Reverend Cox was long gone, so the sermon was more staid, more theological. It was very boring. We went to the evening service, too. As usual, it was badly attended. It, too, was boring. My parents' relentless insistence on my churchgoing contributed to my eventual breaking away from any organized religion. It also built my resistance to any form of religious ritual.

I would have preferred to stay home and listen to the *CBS Symphony* and *The Chamber Music Society of Lower Basin Street* on the radio. My leave passed quickly even though it was less than ideal. I had little choice in most of my activities. While Orwigsburg was close to Pottsville, I didn't drive. I depended on Dad to drive me to the social activities I had with my high school friends. In looking back, I believe my leave was rightly about Mom and Dad's feelings. Would they ever see me again after I was called up to active duty? Even so, I longed to behave like a teenager one last time.

That possibility ended when I was ordered to report to nearby Fort Indiantown Gap on August 14, 1944. There I would be inducted into the Army. It was another tearful parting. Dad and Mom drove me there early on the day. We had a little time before I reported. Mom had prepared a picnic lunch for us to eat. There was so much to talk about, but there was so little that could be said. After more farewells, I lugged my barracks bag into the gate of the induction center. I stopped, turned, and waved at Mom and Dad. I handed my paper to the guard. He smiled and looked at me, "Welcome to the Army, kid."

Dad had his arm around Mom as I entered the gate. I stopped, turned, and waved again. Mom was weeping. Dad was trying his best to be stoic and protective. I could tell by the look on his face that he was near tears, too. They had fought hard to bring me up, to shelter me from the Great Depression, and best of all, they allowed me to be a boy. They gave me that while they took so little for themselves. I turned and walked into a new world. I hoped they didn't see the tears in my eyes as I entered the compound.

After I presented my papers, I was sworn in. Then I was subjected to the indignities of a military medical examination. It was exactly like the one I experienced at Allentown a few months earlier. The big difference now was that there were hundreds of men in lines waiting to be probed, poked, and injected. I was measured again. I was still growing. I now weighed 173 pounds and topped five feet-nine. The food at VMI contributed to my weight gain, but the physical training added to my muscle mass.

A shot in the arm!

It was a very warm August day, and there was no air conditioning. The examination room reeked of sweat and other body odors. My sympathy went out to the doctors who conducted rectal exams. It was a miserable job for a man trained to be a doctor.

This time I had no problems with my eyes. My glasses corrected both of my eyes to an acceptable level.

I took the Army AGC intelligence and aptitude test. It approximated the IQ tests of the time, but the scoring was more severe. I felt good about it. I finished the test quicker than most of the men around me. We were not told our scores; but later, when I worked at a discharge center, I stole a glimpse of them in my files. I had done very well. Unfortunately, that didn't count as casualties mounted on all fronts.

The summer military clothing I brought from VMI was inventoried. Even more was issued. This included woolen winter dress. I moved into a barracks, there to wait for assignment. I discovered that my fellow inductees and I had little to talk about. I was beginning to become aware of how diverse draftees, and even enlistees, were. Most had not completed high school. Some were older and had been torn away from their families. It was a glum place. There was no patriotic talk about the need to defeat a terrible enemy. There was just a lot of quiet grumbling. As for me, I said nothing. I turned into myself. I felt terribly alone.

That evening after mess, I went to a movie at one of the theatres on the base. It was an Alan Ladd actioner, the 1942 *Lucky Jordan*. Somehow that odd detail stuck in my memory. As for the film, Ladd plays a gangster who needed reformation and earns it as he copes with Nazi spies. He gets the crap beat out of him in the first reel, and then he beats the crap out of the bad guys in the last. It was only an average movie, but it took my mind off what might come in the next few days. I awoke to *Reveille* the next morning and began to wait for my orders.

G.I. Issue

Assignment for training allegedly was based on one's education and qualifications, but the luck of the draw was also involved. My start at VMI had put me on course to become a Second Lieutenant. That ended on D-Day. Some men, after completing 18 weeks of basic Infantry training, were sent to Officers Candidate School at Fort Benning, Georgia. As an eighteen-year-old, I was not leadership material. I was immature for my age in attitude and physique. I looked 16, and I wasn't very strong. I put aside any ambitions of becoming a commissioned officer. I was certain of one thing. I was now a full-fledged soldier who probably was going to become an ordinary GI Joe.

I had an ominous premonition of where I would be assigned for basic training. It certainly wouldn't be to an Armored unit since I had never learned to drive. It was equally unlikely that I'd be trained for a clerical assignment since I didn't type. I wore glasses, so I wasn't eligible for the Paratroopers, Rangers, or the Air Force. Since I had taken advanced college courses in mathematics and science, I might be of some use in the Combat Engineers. The Artillery also might use those skills. I hoped for the Artillery. There I would be in back of front line combat. Sadly, I learned that I was only fit for the Infantry.

The war in the Pacific was stumbling along island by island. In Europe casualties soared after D-Day. The fighting in the hedgerows of France was brutal. Infantrymen were needed in huge quantities. Being assigned to an infantry outfit wasn't quite a death sentence, but it wasn't far from that. Everyone shared that view. The Infantry was the mainstay of the Army. Nobody wanted to be in it, but we had no choice. We went where we were sent. When the war began, the uneducated usually ended up in the Infantry. Now the Army needed thousands of young bodies, or to put it less politely, cannon fodder.

I wondered where I'd be sent when I completed basic training. Most of all, I hoped the war would end before I was tested by any sort of combat.

Since I lived in the East and trained at a base there, the odds were that I'd be sent to Europe. Even so, I feared that any surge in casualties in the Pacific would send me there. Nobody wanted to fight the Japanese. There were tales of their brutality during the Bataan Death March in the Philippines, and on other jungle islands. The Japanese didn't surrender, and

G.I. Shopping at PX.

they didn't hesitate to fight with bayonets. They fought to the death.

Older soldiers told us that the Germans, with the exception of Hitler's fanatical *Waffen SS*, were more sensible. If they were outgunned or outnumbered, they surrendered. They didn't like bayonet fighting. I hoped for the better of two bad choices if the war didn't end before my training was completed.

I had my first experience with a PX, an Army post exchange, as I waited. All items were tax free, and the markups were small. There was a soda fountain, a bar where 3.2 beers[1] were served, a jukebox, and a peep show that resembled a present-day television set. I didn't drink beer then, but I bellied up to the soda fountain. One of the most popular items on the peep show was a rather discreet strip tease. It played constantly. A young woman stripped down to her panties and an almost transparent bra. Total female nudity was in short supply in those days. Even the "girlie" magazines were discreet by today's standards. Frontal nudity did not appear in mass-market men's magazines until well into the 1960s.

G.I. Peep Show

---

1 "3.2 beer" refers to the alcohol content in the beer. An alcohol content of 3.2% (based on weight, rather than volume) is considered relatively low. Following the repeal of Prohibition, many states only allowed lower alcohol content beer to be sold in stores.

The jukebox had many of my favorite pop songs, but it also included country and western songs, many of which I had never heard. I enjoyed a country and western number, "I'm My Own Grandpa," which set up a cockeyed lineage of divorce and remarriage in which the singer became his own grandfather. It was very clever. Another was "The Tattooed Lady," a song filled with double entendres. I still have a copy of it on a 78-rpm record album. Some of these songs were more sophisticated than the country and western music I heard on WWVA (the Wheeling, West Virginia, radio station) during my boyhood.

One song in this genre was Slim Gaillard's "Kansas City Kitty." I loved its catchy lyrics:

> I left Frisco Kate
> Swinging on the Golden Gate
> When Kansas City Kitty
> Smiled at me.

The lyrics, like so many in classic country and western songs, often suggest the melody even without the music. As you speak the rhyme, you are compelled to reveal the melody. Many popular songwriters could learn from that. Another popular country and western hit of that time, "There'll Be Smoke on the Water When Our Army and Navy Sail on to Victory" also reveals its melody when you speak the first line of its lyrics.

HEADED SOUTH

No time was wasted at Indiantown Gap. I was on a troop train headed 800 miles south to Camp Wheeler, Georgia, later that week. Wheeler was a vast basic training camp located six miles outside of Macon. We carried all our equipment – except rifles – to a long troop train. The only Pullman car was reserved for officers. During the three-day journey the rest of us slept with our seats reclined as far as they would go. The toilets at each end of the car were clogged by the end of the second day. Our food was basic Army, nourishing but not very tasty. Cooks prepared our meals in a car at the front of the train. The food was then placed on carts and served to us as they moved to the back of the train.

There were few stops. We guessed that the Army feared that some would go AWOL – Absent Without Leave. It would have been foolish to do so. The penalties for going AWOL were severe. The punishment was even more severe for desertion. It could result in death by firing squad. As far as I could tell, no one departed for a hidden civilian life.

As I journeyed back to the South to begin basic training, across the Atlantic the Free French under General Charles de Gaulle led Allied forces into Paris on August 25. The liberated city was ecstatic with joy. The Germans withdrew to take up defensive lines. Allied advances slowed. The battle to invade Germany was beginning and casualties began to mount. I didn't know at the time that I would be part of the assault on the heart of Germany. At that moment all of Camp Wheeler's trainees were sent to Europe. As autumn began and casualties mounted, the need for Infantry replacements grew.

We traveled south through Maryland, then down through Virginia and the Southern Coastal states. Once we hit Georgia, for some reason, we continued south. We passed Macon, circled down into the Florida Panhandle, and then returned to our destination in Central Georgia.

Our troop train lumbered into Camp Wheeler's railhead. It stopped with a wheeze and an exhalation of clouds of steam. My memories of my arrival are vague. I do have an impression of troop trains arriving and discharging hundreds and even thousands of recent inductees. It was then I began to realize the epic size of the Second World War. We were only a fraction of the 16,000,000 human beings that would eventually serve in our Armed Forces.

CAMP WHEELER

Camp Wheeler was an Infantry Replacement Training Center named after Confederate General Joseph Wheeler. It was a vast complex of housing and training areas that sprawled over 21,480 acres of rolling hills dominated by pine trees rooted in sand. Here 17,000 trainees underwent an intense eighteen-week training cycle managed by a Regular Army Cadre of 3,000. Many cycles were underway at any given time so the equivalent of a division[2] of highly trained infantrymen was constantly flowing out of Wheeler.

We were relieved to disembark from the train. The cars had become nauseatingly repulsive. We picked up our barracks bags and were assembled to embark on the beginning of our training cycle. I heard distant rifle fire as we were marched to our assigned barracks. Once in a while there was an explosion of a grenade.

Rows of white, wooden barracks that were flanked by two narrow streets encompassed an assembly-parade ground, a company mess hall, a recreational building, a command center, and a supply center. Two of these barracks housed a training company. Another row held a training battalion. Battalion after battalion fanned out across the slightly rolling hills of Georgia. The coordination of the use of the many training areas that surrounded the inner complex of barracks must have been very complicated.

Each area was identical to the next. Each two-storied barracks housed sixty men, two non-coms, and one lieutenant. There was one latrine per barracks. This included stools, urinals, and showers. None had doors, perhaps for good reason.

As I entered my barracks, I knew I was in for some very serious training. What followed it depended on how the war would go in the weeks to come. There was no sign of a German or Japanese surrender.

Our bunks were lined up in a neat row on each side of the room. Each of us had a wooden footlocker, a shelf for possessions, and hangers for our uniforms. There was little room for personal possessions, so these had to be selected carefully. I limited mine to a few paperback books, stationery to write home, my sketchpads, and pens and pencils.

Nothing of great value was left in the open. We were even cautious about what we stored in our footlockers. Theft was not unusual. Since most of the men in the barracks hadn't finished grade school and some were barely literate, I left my books out. I was certain I'd have no trouble with book theft.

Recently drafted Southerners dominated my barracks. The few Northerners there tended to be older factory workers. Some were married.

---

2   A Division is a military unit, usually consisting of between 10,000 and 20,000 soldiers. During the World Wars the size of an Army division ranged between 10,000 and 30,000 soldiers. A division is made up of smaller units like regiments that are, in turn, made up of smaller units like battalions, companies, platoons, sections, squads, etc.

Some had children at home. Draft deferments became rare as the need of replacements grew. Scattered among this mix were eighteen-year-olds. Three of us had been at VMI together. I must admit that I was frightened by this new world. VMI now seemed like a protective cocoon.

I began my eighteen-week training cycle the day after my arrival. Here I would learn to master more than a dozen weapons used by Infantry rifle companies. Here my endurance would be tested to its fullest by long marches, some forced. Here I would learn that my basic training at VMI had been elementary – at best. Here I would become a soldier, an infantryman ready for front line combat. Here I would be transformed into a human being designed to kill other human beings.

I'd never been in close contact with uneducated Southerners before. Their racism was virulent and open. They differed from the educated Southerners I encountered at VMI who rationalized their racism or masked it in polite words. Of course, there were no Blacks in our program, but racism and ethnic insults flew about the barracks.

Most of these men were impressively profane. Before World War II there was less social swearing and use of profanity. I'd heard my share of swearing among older boys in high school, but these older men took profanity to a new level. I swore little at the time; and when I did, it was a "damn" and not much else. The words and phrases that rocketed around my barracks would still shock in our present-day use of free and open profanity.[3]

I soon discovered that the most accomplished cussers came from the Deep South. Their eloquent use of similes and metaphors was a form of folk poetry. Some were very funny. Their invective often traced their victim's family through several generations of unsavory family practices. I remember one that was limited to one generation, "I hope that when you come home from work tonight your Momma will crawl out from under your front porch and wag her tail at you." A Northerner condenses this same sentiment to, "You son of a bitch!"

---

3 During the war all of us peppered our speech with the 'f' word. At that time, it was socially taboo to use such language in mixed company and our speech was much more discreet. In fact, I never heard it used in a mixed social gathering until almost twenty years later. That was also near the time I first heard it on an American stage – I believe it was in Paddy Chayefsky's *Gideon*. That production also featured the first topless scene I saw on Broadway. As time and society moved forward, our social language became more candid and the idea of "mixed company" social rules became a thing of the past.

In the North cussing added one or two syllables to a sentence. It merely added a sound stress that was embedded in the flow of a sentence. Instead of simply saying, "That dog!" the person's anger was stressed by saying, "That damned dog!" If more emphasis was needed, the short sentence became, "That goddamned dog!" Northerners and Southerners freely used the "f" word in its many permutations. When a Southerner was enthusiastic, he often exclaimed, "San-n-fuckin'-tone!" A Northerner would say a more direct, "Fuckin' A!"

I believe American cursing is the underpinning of the rhythms of some of its best writing. Ernest Hemingway's stripped-down style is rooted in the simplicity of Northern cursing. It is rhythmic and prosaic. The rhetorical eloquence and imagistic poetry of Southern writers is deeply rooted in their profanity. Could there be a doctoral dissertation in a study of that geographical difference in American works of literature? On second thought, there probably has been more than one.

My most vicious exposure to the differences between Northern and Southern profanity occurred in our barracks one evening. A foul-mouthed GI from South Carolina was the loudest and most offensive. One of his favorite insults was, "The best part of you ran down your daddy's leg." Another was, "I hope you die with a hard-on!" I've forgotten his name, so I'll call him Joey-Bob.

A bed across from him belonged to a highly intelligent older man who had graduated as a metallurgist from the Rensselaer Polytechnic Institute, a prestigious university famed for developing engineers. I'll call him Jim. I have no idea how he ended up in Infantry basic training. He was a man of enormous strength. He had the muscular bulk of a weightlifter and was built like a compact bull. Usually, he quietly went about his business. We were unaware that he repressed a fiery temper that could erupt into violence.

One evening, Joey-Bob called Jim a "mother fucker" during an argument over a petty matter. Jim rose and exploded with rage. He shouted, "Nobody calls me that!" Then he grabbed his metal helmet and heaved it at Joey-Bob. It whizzed by me and others, narrowly missed Joey-Bob, and slammed into the wall. A terrified Joey-Bob fled the barracks. He steered clear of Jim from that day on. This was the first time I heard this epithet.

I was a shocked young man who had entered an alien world. What remaining innocence I still had was gone in a few days. Even so, my use of profanity remained limited. I never swore very much until the 1960s.

This was not out of religious strictures. I was uncomfortable swearing and doing so in mixed company never entered my mind. Of course, that has changed in recent years. Many women I know can singe my hair with their profanity.

My sexual instruction expanded quickly. Several of the men were embarrassingly graphic in describing their sexual exploits. Some carried pornographic pictures of their girlfriends and wives in their wallets. I had never seen photographic pornography before. It was a less than ideal portrait for human intercourse. Some married men discussed their marriages with affection and said how much they missed their wives. A handful spoke of their wives with physical revulsion.

Most of the Southerners were expert "bitchers." Those rough-hewn, weather-beaten men in my barracks had been yanked out of a hard, survival life to fight in a war that was far away. None of them expressed patriotic fervor. Instead, they "bitched" constantly about being in the Army and being forced to endure the rigors of Infantry basic training. Some of them even roared out a paraphrase of a ribald British folk song when we were on long marches:

> *I don't want to join the Army*
> *I don't want to go to war*
> *I don't want a bayonet up my arse hole*
> *I don't want my bollox shot away*
> *I'd rather stay at home*
> *In the good ol' USA*
> *And fuck my lady every day.*

They complained long and loud about our drill, our food, our living conditions, our leadership, and being in the Army. They saw no reason for fighting in a war that was across the Atlantic Ocean. I quickly grew tired of their loud complaining. I harbored my own discontents and being in the Army didn't enchant me, but I kept my thoughts to myself. I'd been a well-behaved boy while I was growing up. I accepted adult authority even though I had the beginnings of an inner rebellious spirit. I recognized being in the Army as a fact of life. I kept my mouth shut.

These draftees never read a newspaper. Few had radios in their homes since many lived far away from rural electrification. They came from a small, isolated world where they just managed to survive. They needed indoctrination before they were sent to a combat unit. They received an intense dose of it when we were shown Frank Capra's brilliant *Why We Fight* documentaries. These short films were powerful works of propaganda. They laid out the reasons we were at war simply and graphically. As for me, I wasn't brimming with patriotic clichés; but I believed this was a war that had to be fought. I accepted my training as a necessity and worked hard at it. I wanted to be prepared for what was to come in the months ahead.

Officers and Non-Coms

Our battalion had a tier of leaders that began with a colonel. He liked walking up and down the street between our barracks at night. He wore a long overcoat even in hot weather. During his walks he held a swagger stick behind his back as he pretended to be a thoughtful leader and, perhaps, an American Napoleon. I'm sure he did this to impress us, but I was not alone in thinking he cut a ridiculous figure.

Our company captain rarely emerged from his office. He left our discipline to two lieutenants, a first sergeant, and two barracks corporals. He only involved himself if there were major transgressions. Otherwise, he seemed to be busy in his office with paperwork and other administrative details. I was shocked when I was ordered to report to his office shortly after my arrival. I wondered what I had done to deserve this. I had received no reprimands. I had been a dutiful soldier as I tried to adjust to Army life. Even so, I was a little more than apprehensive.

After I entered his office, snapped to attention, and saluted him, he asked me, "Private Coleman, how old are you?"

I replied, "Eighteen, sir!"

"What's the date of your birth?"

I replied.

"You don't look eighteen," he said as he eyed me up and down.

"Do you have my records, sir?"

"I do."

"Do they give my age?"

"They do," he said as he examined a sheet.

He looked up at me and smiled, shook his head, and said, "They look younger every shipment. You may go back to duty, Private Coleman."

He threw me a casual salute and returned to his desk work. I saluted, did a snappy about face, and exited. It was not the last time I was asked about my age. It was checked every time I moved to a new unit. I looked very young for my age. The Army didn't want the responsibility of dealing with an underage soldier.

The running of our company was relegated to First Sergeant John LaChance, a regular Army "Lifer"[4] of French-Canadian descent. He must have been in his forties. He was a giant of a man who was more than six feet tall. He had a long, muscular torso and short, chunky legs. His forearms were as massive as many men's thighs. He looked like he could knock you through a wall if he thought you needed it. His size and roaring voice were intimidation enough.

He was amazingly foul-mouthed and threatening, but I felt that, in his heart, he wanted us to do well during our training. He held forth on a number of subjects at our formations. Some of these were instructional, some cautionary, some informational, some were comments on activities in other barracks, and some were on subjects the Army would rather not deal with.

One of LaChance's subjects of merriment occurred at the training battalion next to ours. It was made up of mentally challenged draftees who had slipped through induction. They required and received a specialized training program. Few went into combat. Some became company cooks, a few ended up in mess kit repair, and more than a few were assigned to Graves Registration, a unit that picked up the dead after battles, registered their dog tags, and placed their mutilated bodies in sleeping bags before they were sent off to burial.

Late one night we heard loud screaming and cursing coming from a nearby barracks. The next morning LaChance barely held back his laughter at roll call. After we had all shouted out, "Yo!" he explained what had happened the night before. Two men had a quarrel, and one had shit in the other's footlocker. A horrendous fight broke out. LaChance, rocking with laughter, proclaimed, "Men, I don't want any footlocker shittin' in my outfit."

He often lectured us on how to avoid venereal diseases. It was a problem that concerned the Army deeply since towns near military bases

---

4   A Lifer is a person who has chosen to spend their life in a particular career. This term is especially used in the military for those who serve continuous enlistments until their retirement.

were teeming with prostitutes and willing amateurs. He advised us to limit our sexual activity only to "the pros." Prostitutes who worked in whorehouses were less likely to transmit a venereal disease since local medical authorities checked them weekly. He advised us to avoid freelance streetwalkers and young amateurs seeking off-hour supplements to their day job. He cautioned us to use condoms if we had sex and told us they were free at medical stations. He told us that if we had sex we must stop at an in-town medical station run by MPs. There, soldiers would receive a prophylactic via a hypodermic needle inserted in the urethra.

His graphic descriptions of sexual encounters were given in nauseating detail. While I yearned to explore the mysteries of sex, I knew that resorting to prostitutes wasn't a good way to begin. I sublimated my sexual drive and went to the movies and read books. My determination to abstain was reinforced after I saw the official Army instructional film dealing with the varieties of sexually transmitted diseases soldiers could contract. It was required viewing for all soldiers. The results of these diseases were shown in graphic detail. At that time the most feared venereal disease was syphilis, the most common was gonorrhea. There were others, too. All were presented in vivid, frightening detail. Some men fled the theatre and threw up. Indeed, this film was hard to watch.

I was surprised when three of us who had gone to VMI were appointed as acting squad leaders. It was logical to select us since we had undergone a simplified form of basic training, so we accepted the appointments. It meant we had the responsibility of forming our squads into tidy ranks and giving them marching orders during close order drill. Of course, there were no new stripes or extra pay. Since we were only eighteen and much younger than many in our company, our appointment was not popular with many of the men.

The three of us were taken under the wing of Lieutenant Ernest Revere St. John. He was a dashing young man who had charisma to burn. He spoke with an aristocratic accent. Even his name, which was in iambic trimeter, echoed a deep American past. He took us aside and gave us private leadership lessons. He even taught us how to bear our bodies, so that we looked like we were in command. He was an excellent teacher. Since we had a semester of classes and basic military training at a prestigious college under our belts, he assured us we were prime contenders for the Officers Candidate School – or OCS as it was called – at nearby Fort Benning. It was there that most of the Army's line officers were trained.

Lieutenant St. John was immensely popular among all of the men despite his aristocratic bearing. Even the constantly complaining Southerners admired him. Unfortunately, he was with us for only a few weeks before he was sent overseas as a replacement. I am sure he distinguished himself in battle. He was an inspiring leader and placed his men above his personal safety. My wife Linda, after some research, discovered that he had risen to the rank of captain and lived a long life.

The corporal in charge of our training, a wiry little Southerner, was less admirable. He, too, was a Regular Army lifer who had found a cozy life away from the Great Depression. His face was red and streaked with purple veins, a result of years of excessive drinking. His features were pointy and prematurely wizened. His red face always looked like it was about to explode into a choleric rage. His cursing was epic. One of his favorite expressions was "Don't just stand there with your finger up your ass. Do something!" That was merely a baseline for his abusive language during our training exercises.

He referred to his acting squad leaders as "college-educated-sumsabitches." I quickly learned that many in my barracks mistrusted us because we had finished a single term of college. In the years to come I discovered that those with advanced college and university degrees are often the subjects of ridicule by the less educated and even the educated who harbor conservative views. We were called "chrome domes," "pointy-headed intellectuals," and worse. During the Nixon years, Vice President Spiro Agnew – before he resigned in disgrace – called us "nattering nabobs of negativism" in a speech written by William Safire.

Our corporal yearned to replace us with "good ol' boys." That moment came quickly. One day, during a ten-minute break during a training exercise, the three of us joined in some boyish horseplay and joking. The corporal saw his opening. We were "busted" back into the ranks. Since our rank was temporary, we suffered no other penalty or loss of pay. I felt more comfortable being one of the guys. There, within the ranks, I could learn the skills required of a future combat rifleman. In leading, there is little time to learn.

New acting non-coms were appointed. They were less educated and Southern. Since they wanted to ingratiate themselves to their superiors, they ran a tighter ship than we did. We immediately labeled them "brown-nosers" who were being chickenshit and bucking for a promotion. Lieutenant St. John's dream of our becoming officers evaporated. In my case, that was for the best. I knew I had no capacity or inclination to lead older men in combat even as a non-commissioned officer.

BARRACKS LIFE

There were sad cases among us. Some men were slow in taking instruction. Some were in bad physical condition. One was a tall lump of a country boy who had flat feet. He quickly wore down during our training program. He gamely marched in agony and never fell out. Eventually he was transferred out of the Infantry into a less active unit. There were a number of chronic bed-wetters in our battalion. Every barracks had at least a few drying mattresses, blankets, and sheets hanging on clotheslines during the day. If the bedwetters' condition didn't improve, they were discharged for medical reasons but only after receiving a psychological and thorough medical exam. In most instances it was a medical problem, but I suspect that more than a few peed their beds nightly so that they could get out of the army. Some members of the "Greatest Generation" were less than heroic.

Other men found Army life challenging in a different way. Most gay men remained closeted and took their sexual activity to town. Even there, they were in danger of being arrested by the military police or local authorities. If caught, gay men were given a blue discharge. Also known as a blue ticket, named for the color of the paper it was printed on, this was an administrative procedure given by commanders to men who were thought to be unfit for military service. While it was neither honorable nor dishonorable, it attached a stigma to the discharged soldier that ruined his life. The soldier was denied the benefits of the G.I. Bill and the Veterans Administration. Once back in civilian life, employers looked askance at men who had to show their discharge papers when they sought a job.

Two dozen or so men sleeping in a long room created many odd sounds at night. One man farted in his sleep. One night he let a very loud one go as he slumbered away. At the other end of the barracks someone intoned, "Speak, sweet lips."

Everyone burst out laughing.

Another man had a loud and very obnoxious snore. It destroyed our sleep. Having been a newsboy, I came up with a solution. I bought a newspaper at the PX. One night I rolled up the newspaper and quadrupled the fold, turning it into a hard object about the size of a baseball. I reared back in the darkness, aimed my missive at the offending snorer, and threw. It hit him on the head. Cursing, he jumped up in his bed and demanded to know who the son of a bitch was that knobbed him. I ducked under my covers, stifling my laughter. My fellow soldiers didn't hold back their laughter. We settled down, but the victim was so angry he never got back to sleep. He did not snore again that night. My comrades never informed on me. A few quietly congratulated me for allowing them to get an uninterrupted night's sleep. One or two asked me to do it the next night and in nights to come. To me, that was too risky. I didn't dare press my luck.

There were many pranks. Most of these were cruder and less ingenious than what I'd seen at VMI. Short sheeting, however, is universal in any barracks. The most common prank was placing a sleeping man's hand in a pan of warm water. He immediately wet his bed. Another time we filled a wine bottle with water. Then we fastened its cork to the sheet with a safety pin. When a soldier pulled down his covers and saw the wine bottle, he pulled on it and pulled the cork free. The water in the bottle wet his bed. The worst happened while a soldier napped above the covers on an afternoon break. He must have had an erotic dream since he had an enormous erection that peeked out of the gap in his GI shorts. Someone tickled it with a feather. You can guess the result.

One of the New Yorkers was named Ivan Jatkov. Another was named Herman Lipshitz. Before I shipped out, I looked up these names in the New York City Telephone Directory. Their names weren't uncommon there, but when La Chance roared out roll call, these poor fellows' names were greeted with barely suppressed laughter. I noticed that a smirk of amusement passed over La Chance's face. They were a morning amusement for our company.

An unfortunate young man in our platoon was susceptible to goosing. I don't remember his name, but I'll call him Jack. When someone jammed a finger in Jack's rear, he shouted whatever was on his mind. When goosed he had no inhibitions. He had a raging libido, and he verbalized it vividly.

When we were in formation, those in back of the poor man goosed Jack. He shouted out many unfortunate things, but the worst came when our entire company was drawn up for instructions from a lieutenant. The goose-ee screamed at the top of his voice, "Fuck you, Lieutenant!"

There was a long silence. Muffled guffaws rambled through the ranks. The lieutenant, who knew Jack's problem, was amused. Jack couldn't be prosecuted for his blurted obscenities and insults since he had a medical condition. Of course, there was a search for the men who provided the stimulus, but no one was ever caught.

I remember one Saturday evening when a group of us strolled together in Macon, Georgia. When a pretty woman walked toward us, one of my buddies goosed Jack. He shouted, "I love your tits!" To another he cried out, "Great ass!" He shouted to a well-dressed woman, "I want to fuck you!" She wasn't pleased. On another evening, a captain walked toward us. We all saluted. A friend goosed him, and Jack yelled as he saluted, "Up yours, Captain!"

Finally, our medics determined that poor, distraught Jack was physically unable to cope with the Army. He was discharged with honor. I imagine the poor man was relieved to escape his tormentors. Sometimes I wondered if Jack really was susceptible to goosing. Could it be he found a way to get out of the Army honorably? If so, he was a very fine actor.

Barracks Pranks in the Ranks.

9

A BASIC TRAINING DAY

OUR DAY STARTED before dawn. As the bugler sounded *Reveille*, our barracks corporal ran down the aisle between our bunks shouting, "Rise and shine! Rise and shine! Drop your cocks and grab your socks!" as he raked his baton along the metal frames of our beds. It was a rude awakening.

Latrine humor.

We rushed to the downstairs latrine. It was a race since there were sixty of us but only a limited number of facilities. We all managed to relieve ourselves, brush our teeth, shave, and shower so that everyone was able to begin the day squeaky clean. The Army was strict about cleanliness, so you didn't dare miss a shower. Sixty men living in close proximity can get very ripe. Those who neglected to shower in the morning and again after duty were punished with a GI-shower. If a soldier became too rancid, his comrades, at the insistence of our corporal, grabbed and stripped him, and threw him in the shower. Then they scrubbed him with lye soap using the hard-bristled brushes we used to scour our barracks floor. The soldier was red with abrasions from the cleaning. Few dropped back into their former bad habits.

We went to the mess hall for a hearty breakfast after our ablutions. Our food was basic – cereal, orange juice, eggs and bacon, ham, or sausage. I hadn't yet acquired a taste for coffee, so milk served as my breakfast drink. We needed all we could eat to replace the energy we burned up in our training. Breakfast was the first of three daily meals. A head cook admin-

Mess Hall Cooking

istered each company kitchen. He was given a fixed sum that allowed him to purchase food from a central supply store. He then set up menus. Some of the more experienced cooks added their own touches to their food preparation. Most prepared basic American cuisine that resembled what we ate at home. Seconds were encouraged. They were devoured.

Gravy with ham bits on toast was served at most lunches. It was nicknamed "shit on a shingle." A similar serving of scrambled eggs topped by small pieces of sausage was called "French-fried monkey vomit." While we weren't always enthused about our food, it filled our young bellies and gave us energy.

There was an ongoing rumor that our food was laced with saltpeter,[5] which was an anaphrodisiac that was believed to suppress erections. This, of course, is military folklore; but many men in my outfit believed they were not having erections as frequently as they did before they joined the Army. I suspect our lowered libido was more likely due to the intense physical activity that we went through during our long hours of training.

After breakfast we returned to our barracks and prepared for the day. The break was brief. We rushed out for roll call when the bugler sounded *Assembly.*

Once LaChance made sure we were present and accounted for, we marched off to a morning of training exercises. Most were specialized hour-long sessions. Some dealt with handling weapons, some with physical training, and some with close order drill. I resented the latter. I felt it was a waste of time at VMI, and I resented it taking time away from our

---

5 Potassium nitrate.

learning how to use weapons in combat. Some may argue that it taught us to react quickly to orders. Others say it trained us to work as a unit. I think they are wrong.

Instructional films were always a welcome break. In addition to producing the *Why We Fight* series, Hollywood directors, cameramen, writers, and editors worked with the Signal Corps to turn out efficient and interesting instructional documentaries. Lunch was followed by another *Assembly* call. Our afternoons were equally busy.

Smoking was permitted during our hourly five-minute breaks. The command was, "The smoking lamp is lit." Those who smoked were ordered to field strip their butts. To do this they peeled away the paper, rolled it into tight little balls, and scattered the leftover tobacco on the ground. We policed this and other refuse by moving across the area in a line. Our barracks and the areas around it were kept spotless. All this activity was supervised under the eagle-eye of our corporal. He was ruthless. He knew that if an officer inspected his barracks and found it out of order he would be reduced to Private and shipped overseas.

There were occasional night exercises, but after dinner we were usually free and on our own until curfew. Many went to a PX and drank 3.2 beer. More than a few staggered back to the barracks just before curfew. I wasn't among them. I didn't drink. No attention was paid to drunkenness after hours. A soldier's only duty was to be ready for the next day's training.

There were a number of small movie theatres spread across Camp Wheeler. If I remember correctly, admission was thirty-five cents. Each had a different movie that was cycled through all the theatres. They ranged from major releases to low-budget dreck. The quality of a film didn't matter. Sitting in a movie theatre was better than spending an evening in our barracks. If I wanted to see a movie more than once, I walked a little further and caught it at another theatre. Hollywood often released new films to army camps before they were put in national distribution.

I went to a lot of movies but after I had seen all the available ones, I stayed in the barracks and read. In addition to my stash of paperbacks, I could check out books from the libraries spread around the post. We could read newspapers, magazines, and books there. All had cubicles where we could listen to a wide range of music. No radios were allowed in the barracks. It was in those cubicles that I fed my interest in classical and jazz music that had been born out of listening to my radio while in high school.

We cleaned the barracks on a weekly basis. We collectively scrubbed the rough wooden floors on our hands and knees with hard-bristled scrub brushes and harsh lye soap. When we were done, the floorboards were white, and our hands were quite sore. Latrine duty was universally hated and reserved as a punishment for bad behavior. Toilets, urinals, and showers had to be scoured clean.

G.I. Mopping.

Sixty men can leave a lot of unpleasantness behind in a day, especially after a hurried morning's ablutions and voiding of bodily functions. If there had been no bad behavior, our vindictive corporal arbitrarily picked out a cleaning detail.

Our bunk areas were our responsibility. Our footlockers had to be placed at the end of our beds in a specified way. Our second pair of spit-shined shoes was placed beside it. Our combat boots were supposed to be flat to the ground. I had the misfortune of having high arches and tight tendons, so my toes angled upward. During my first inspection, the sergeant took one look at my carefully polished boots with the upward toes and exclaimed, "Who's the goddamned pixie?" Try as I might, I couldn't get my boots to lie flat.

There were regularly scheduled weekly inspections, but we had to be neat at all times since there were also unexpected snap inspections. During these checks our footlockers were also open for inspection. Our socks had to be carefully rolled and our underwear had to be precisely folded and stacked. Uniforms not in use had to be neatly hung, side-by-side, on the rack behind our bunks. Our personal possessions had to be neatly shelved. As at VMI, our bunks had to be so tightly made that a dropped coin would bounce. If it didn't then the inspector tore our bed apart and made us do it again. Any sloppiness was rewarded with unpleasant duties.

There was a strict ten o'clock curfew except for men on a pass into town. Lights went out as the bugler played that most beautiful of all calls, *Taps*. Its plaintive melody echoes through my head as I write this. It was at once an echo of the home I left behind and a soothing comfort after a hard day of training. It and my weariness made going to sleep easy – except when that guy began snoring. If it got too raucous or went on too long, I nobbed him good and hard. He'd rouse, curse, and then roll over on his side. My young body needed rest. No more snoring. Then my aching body could drift into a deep and dreamless sleep. The next day would be more of the same.

Messy Mess Halls and Boyish Pranks

Mess halls were one-storied, rectangular, prefabricated, wooden build-ings. At one end was a double serving line, at the other a double line for scraping away food scraps from our plates. The long room was dominated by rows of long tables and benches that were similar to those seen in outdoor picnic areas.

The mess hall was a welcome reward after our day of training. If we were too far away from our barracks, our meals were delivered to us. The food was always warm and filling. Army food was hearty and basic. I'm not sure how our food's nutritional merits would be evaluated now. We ate a lot, but nobody got fat. Most of us supplemented our diets at the PX. I consumed my share of ice cream sundaes, root beer floats, and milkshakes there.

Mess duty, also known as the Kitchen Police or KP, was cycled in alphabetical order on a rotating basis. We were assigned to peel potatoes, wash dishes and cookery, carry out garbage, and other menial duties. The only advantage to KP was that we had access to extra servings of food after the kitchen was closed and before we began our after-meal cleaning. All of us figured out ways to escape the most menial and disgusting work. This, in Army slang, was called "gold-bricking." I am not without guilt when it came to evading unpleasant work duties. I quickly learned to keep my mouth shut while I did my assigned tasks. Complainers were often assigned the dirty work needed to keep our company kitchen sanitary and running.

Oops!!!

I drew my first mess duty on Thanksgiving. Drawing KP on a holiday was bad luck, but I ate very well. It was the best meal we had to that time. Even then, I was discouraged. My friends were free to go into Macon or see a movie on the post while I had to stay back and clean up after the meal.

Once, while I was cleaning off my plate at the end of a meal, I was talking to a friend and accidentally scraped some mashed potatoes and gravy onto a sergeant's trousers. He was in the opposite line. He didn't see what I had done until he was outside. I heard a loud curse. Fortunately, he didn't know who had done this to his clean uniform.

On other occasions, we furtively flicked spoonfuls of mashed potatoes and gravy toward other tables during dinner. Our aim, at best, was general; but the non-coms' table was a favorite target. The catapulted gob would drop wherever chance took it. Once it landed on a sergeant's head. Another time a corporal's clean uniform was soiled. The hardest thing was keeping a straight face when a corporal or a sergeant at another table was cursing about the wad of mashed potatoes and gravy in his lap. If any of us were seen laughing, we'd be blamed even if someone else did it.

When word spread about this gooey prank, guards were placed at each end of the mess hall. Their keen eyes watched as we ate, so our flipping ceased. The guards were withdrawn. In a few days we resumed our flicking attacks. Another cycle began. No one was caught.

PAYDAY AND THE GLORIES OF MACON, GEORGIA

Payday was once a month. We lined up outside the company office. Inside our captain sat behind a footlocker that was covered with a green cloth. On it was a ledger and stacks of bills and coins. We entered one by one and signed our name to the ledger to acknowledge that we had received our pay. The captain counted out what was due to us, and we were on our way. Pay for buck privates was fifty dollars a month, but there were deductions. Most of us took out a ten-thousand-dollar Army-sponsored life insurance policy. The premium was six dollars and fifty cents a month. It was cheap because it was term insurance. This was our only death benefit. It was a considerable amount of money then. A family survivor could buy a fine house or live three or four years at the equivalent of the average civilian salary. Of course, I signed my policy over to my parents.

There were several deductions that I don't remember. These may have been for income taxes and Social Security. In addition to these, I paid for laundry, dry cleaning, haircuts, and toiletries. I do remember that I was lucky if I netted thirty-five dollars. In those days that was quite a lot of money for a single person.[6] I never spent all the money I earned. Anything

---

6   According to an article By Malvern Hall Tillitt in Barron's *National Business and Financial Weekly* magazine dated April 24, 1944: "The lowest pay in the Army is the $50 a month; or $600 a year, received by the buck private, while in service within the bounds of the United States. The man may have given up a $3,600-a-year civilian job on entering military service. And, from the figures alone, he may apparently be taking a loss of $3,000 a year.

"On reduction of earnings to 'net income,' the comparison goes into reverse. This fact traces mainly to the major items of subsistence which are provided for men and noncommissioned officers in military service but for which the civilian must pay out of his pocket. In addition, civilians have much higher income taxes to reckon with.

"Of course, Army pay is not entirely velvet. Personnel below the commissioned ratings must take care of a number of minor needs and wants out of earnings. On the basis of itemized statements obtained in interviews with selectees in training and old-timers in service, and with privates, corporals, and sergeants, expenditures out of pocket run at about the same level for men and noncommissioned officers.

"Passing by the spendthrift and the tight-wad, and figuring by the month for ordinary spenders, these expenditures include two 50-cent haircuts by barber, $1.50 for laundry, $1.50 for tailor service (pressing and dry-cleaning), – $1.40 for movies, $3 for tobacco, 60 cents for soap, tooth paste, and razor blades, and $4 for other incidentals purchased at commissary or post exchange or outside camp limits. Miscellaneous outlays through the year – for civilian shoes and repairs, garrison cap, shoe polish, metal polish, and other articles – may run to $24, or an average of $2 a month.

that was left was put into a savings account. By the time the war ended I'd saved nearly fifteen hundred dollars.

Other privates were less frugal. Most went into nearby Macon on day and overnight passes. Macon, along with its combined statistical area, has grown into a city of nearly half a million in recent years, but during the war it was much smaller. Its main industry was catering to the thousands of GIs who took buses into town and sought out entertainment. The central part of downtown housed a myriad of bars. Its main street was studded with garish neon signs that declared the shop owners' love of all GIs. Most sold shoddy souvenirs and replicas of Army-issued uniforms. There were more than a few clip joints[7] where gambling was available. Wide-eyed country boys embraced the pleasures and pastimes of what, to them, seemed like a big city. They were overcharged and short-changed at every opportunity. Most came back to base dead broke after one weekend pass.

Prostitutes openly plied their wares. They worked either as streetwalkers or in brothels in the Red-Light District. The deeply religious and funda-mentalist city fathers denounced these houses of vice even as they allowed them to remain open for business. Macon, like many other cities near Army posts, turned a blind eye to any form of vice. Local corruption was immense. Anything that contributed to a town's economy was fair play.

Our Army medics accepted the realities of prostitution and set up Pro Stations in the Red-Light District. There soldiers on their way to a whorehouse received free condoms. After they had sex, they could receive a protective sulfa shot into their urethras. Most were poor country girls who had come into the big city to make a living and were snared into a life

---

"The enumerated expenditures out of pay, including miscellaneous expenses, add up to $15 a month, or $180 a year -- which leaves the buck private in service within the bounds of the United States with an annual remainder of $420. And this is the measure of his 'net' annual income, if he has no other revenues, for Federal income taxes do not apply to incomes of men in military service below $1,500 – and above that the serviceman also has his personal exemptions.

"These expenditures do not include the cost of sprees during excursions out of camp on leave, if any, or lavish entertainment of girl friends or losses at 'Georgia dominoes.' The buck private's net income, as here worked out, simply represents the yearly remainder of earnings during normal training camp life."

7 Also known as a fleshpot, a strip club, or a night club with adult entertainment, clip joints were notorious for making promises related to sexual activity that were unfulfilled, serving watered-down alcoholic drinks at premium prices, and throwing out customers when they refused to pay. These establishments were a holdover from the Prohibition Era, and often involved illegal activity.

that could only end badly. I avoided this area and the street prostitutes. I believed that paying a woman for sex was disgusting, especially after she had sex with several other men earlier in the day. I didn't want to lose my virginity with one of them. I remained celibate.

*   *   *

Macon was much like other cities I visited while I was stateside. Their contribution to the war effort was to fleece as much money as possible out of GIs' pockets. They were a microcosm of the profiteering that accompanies any war effort. My young mind reacted to this. "Why couldn't our well-trained military police be allowed to clamp down on the profiteering that ripped off a month of a buck private's salary in one evening?"

I didn't stop there. More questions flooded my mind. "If the government could draft young men, why couldn't it draft its industries? If there had to be a war effort – as there had to be during the Second World War – why wasn't it total?"

If that ever became government policy – and it never will – soldiers would come home to a level playing field. Perhaps, if there were no profits in fighting wars, we would have no wars. I was a very idealistic young man.

The Military Industrial Complex now claims, as it has for many decades, the lion's share of our national budget. Most of this budget is a secret to the voting public due to, as they claim, reasons of "National Security." This, of course, allows for vast possibilities of corruption with little accountability or consequences. Congressmen fear that eliminating often unneeded and outdated military equipment manufacturing would create mass unemployment in their states and districts. Everyone seems to forget that the tax money wasted on unused, obsolete, or ineffective weapons systems could put even more employees back to work on our crumbling domestic infrastructure. Internationally, we could also help eliminate the "need" for war if we provided meaningful aid and educational opportunities to the countries we now seem set on destroying. The sad reality – as former General and President Dwight Eisenhower tried to warn us – is that our Military Industrial Complex actually costs us jobs and deters the possibility of peace in the long run.[8] It also has a detrimental impact on our climate.

---

8 It always struck me as a bit ironic that President Eisenhower's warning was delivered in his *farewell* address on January 17, 1961, at the *end* of his two terms in office. I have always wondered why he didn't alert the nation to this threat during his eight years

Macon had four or five movie theatres. All had segregated seating. Two showed first run features, but I could see many of these films at Camp Wheeler for fifty cents or less. More cosmopolitan Atlanta was too far away for a weekend pass. It was a long bus trip away and was probably worse than Macon in its treatment of GIs. I was stuck with Macon. I went there rarely. Instead, I took advantage of the many cultural and entertainment resources at Camp Wheeler. Macon, to me, was a reprehensible city that profiteered from the gullible and reeked with open racism. After the war Camp Wheeler was destroyed and the land was returned to its owners. Macon had to make money in an honest way. It has grown in size since then. Perhaps there's a lesson in that?

---

as President and Commander-in-Chief when he had the full force of the "Bully Pulpit" and could have had a real impact on public perception, Congressional action, military and civilian budgets, and the increasing power of the Military Industrial Complex. Even though it was during the previous – Truman – administration following WWII that the Cold War was born, military budgets had quadrupled, and the political hysteria about the Communist threat in America gained momentum, it should be noted that during Ike's terms in office, plans for the systematic destruction of 1200 major urban centers in the Eastern Bloc and China by nuclear war was adopted and the general arms race continued to support the buildup of power of the same Military Industrial Complex he warned about.

Today military spending accounts for more than sixty percent of the U.S. discretionary budget, and the U.S. has been in a perpetual state of war for more than eighteen years even as the nation's infrastructure is crumbling, and public services continue to be decimated.

10

IN THE COMPANY WITH A COMPANY OF WEAPONS

AN INFANTRY COMPANY used at least sixteen different weapons. Two were reserved for officers, and three for specialists who had advanced training. All officers carried the 45 mm Colt M1911 pistol. Its large bullets were deadly, but its inaccuracy was legendary. The German mass-produced Walthur P-38 was a better weapon, and the Luger pistol was one of the best hand weapons ever made. I remember handling a captured Luger. It had a wonderful balance that leveled the weapon on a target. The heavy and badly balanced Colt only was effective at close range. We received only one day's training with it.

Higher-ranked officers and tankers carried the expensive and well-made Thompson submachine gun – the famed "Tommy Gun." Its .45-caliber bullets carried a lethal punch. One well-placed bullet could remove a limb. We never got to use it during our training. Once we were in combat, we coveted having one. It could have more than doubled our squad's firepower.

We received submachine gun training with the .45-caliber "Grease Gun" even though it was only carried by platoon-level non-coms. Its mass-produced metal tube-like structure gave it its nickname.[9] It was inaccurate, had limited range, and was hard to maintain. It wasn't a popular weapon. Its only virtue – if you can call it that – was its large, snub-nosed bullets. They packed a wallop at close range.

---

9 The weapon's appearance resembled the tool known as a "grease gun" used by automotive mechanics to lubricate car and truck joints.

The three heaviest weapons assigned to rifle companies were the .60 caliber Browning M1917 machine gun, the M1/M1A1 Flamethrower, and the 81mm MI mortar. They required specialized skills and advanced training. There was little time for that after I entered basic training. By then the Army needed a constant flow of front line infantrymen to replace the wounded and the dead. The use of heavy weapons had to be learned in combat.

The most versatile of these weapons was the .60-caliber Browning machine gun. It was a support weapon that could be operated from a fixed position or become mobile when it was mounted on a Jeep. It was effective against enemy personnel, lightly armored vehicles, and low-flying aircraft. Their armor-piercing bullets weren't effective against the heavily armored panzers unless their gunners lucked into hitting small vulnerable areas on these tanks.

The M1 Flamethrower was designed to burn out pillboxes and entrenched enemy soldiers. It required a team of two brave men who risked getting close enough to send a stream of fire into fixed fortifications. It was used in Europe when our soldiers attacked the Maginot Line's pillboxes. It was of little use once we broke out and became more mobile in our attack on Germany. It was mercilessly used against the Japanese during our island hopping. I was relieved that I didn't have to learn how to operate it. I'm not sure that I would have been able to release a burst of searing flame at other human beings. I still consider it a barbaric weapon. But aren't they all?

The huge 81mm M2 Mortar had the impact of an artillery shell. It was heavy and had to be set up and fired by a team of two men. It was a rear area weapon that softened up German positions when the Infantry went on the attack. Instruction in its use was reserved to advanced Infantry training. That training was not available when I was enduring Basic training.

We learned how to operate two support weapons. The first was the 60mm M2 Mortar. It was lighter and easier to set up than the 81mm. Firing either required skill and practice. Once you mastered how to use the mortar, it was devastatingly accurate. You shot over, then under. Once your target was bracketed, you hit your target with your third shot. It took two men to carry it and set it up. It was too heavy to carry during long marches, so the company Jeep carried it until we were under fire.

The other support weapon was the .30 caliber machine gun. It, too, required a two-man team: one to aim and fire, and the other to load and feed its long belts of bullets. I learned how to use it on a very noisy 1000-inch (83.3 feet) range. The targets were small. Since the .30 had a flat trajectory over a long distance, we had the equivalent experience of shooting at a distant target. Both weapons were subject to heavy enemy fire since they were a major element of a rifle company's firepower.

RIFLES FOR RIFLEMEN

The twelve-man combat Infantry squad was built around the firepower of the semi-automatic M1 Garand rifle. The Army put it into service in 1936 and issued it until 1963. It weighed a little less than ten pounds. It had a nice balance in my hands. It certainly was a more efficient weapon than the bolt-action rifle I used at VMI. I believe it was the best weapon issued to infantrymen during World War II. Its German *Wehrmacht* counterpart was the *Karabiner*, a mass-produced bolt-action rifle. It was accurate at long distances, but its hand bolt-action cut into its firepower.

The M1 had a gas-operated action that returned a new bullet from an eight-bullet clip after each shot. All you needed to do was open the bolt and insert an eight-bullet cartridge. You had to withdraw your thumb very quickly as the bolt slammed into place. I suffered a bruised thumb more than once when I didn't withdraw it quickly enough. Then you slammed the first bullet in the chamber, made sure the safety was off, aimed through the back and front sight, and you were ready to fire. Keeping a live bullet in the firing chamber at all times was forbidden – except in a combat situation. Every time you pulled the trigger an empty shell was ejected, and a new bullet went into the firing chamber. The clip was ejected when it was empty, and the bolt opened for a new one. A rifle squad could lay down a lethal sheet of fire when it was attacked or when it advanced on an enemy position.

While the M1 was a fine weapon, it had one serious drawback. If dirt or sand got into the bullet chamber or its firing mechanism, it jammed. It took time to pry out a jammed cartridge. That could be deadly in a fire-fight. While I despise the inventors of weapons of death and destruction,

I'm glad I had the M1 in my hands when I was in combat. It was the best semi-automatic rifle of its time.

A fundamental part of our training was learning how to field strip the M1, clean it, oil it, and reassemble it quickly. Its firing mechanism broke down into large elements that, in turn, could be broken down into smaller ones. Each part had to be cleaned and oiled before the rifle was reassembled. I became very fast in disassembling, cleaning, and reassembling my rifle. This was unusual since I often clutched when I was under extreme pressure to accomplish a physical task. One of our final tests was to complete a cleaning process under a blanket. That meant we could do it in the dark.

We began our training on a rifle range by zeroing in our weapons. This was a careful calibration of our rifle's sights, so they were more accurate. Once this was done, we were issued a clip of bullets to shoot at specified distances. We first shot with our sling wrapped tightly around our arm. To me this was awkward and uncomfortable. I preferred to shoot without a sling, but that was not allowed during our target practices. We increased shooting distances to a point where our target was very small. When we finished shooting on the firing range we were scored and issued a rating. We returned any unused ammunition. They wanted to make sure that no one would return to their barracks with live ammunition. We were never trusted to carry full clips until we entered a combat zone. Then we carried as much as we could fit into our web belts and as many canvas bandoleers as we could sling over our shoulders.

When we weren't shooting, we were assigned to individual target pits. These were nearly seven feet deep. Our job was to raise and lower large targets with pulleys. Once we were in the pit, we put up targets, took them down, marked them, and put them up again. If a rifleman missed the target, we waved a red flag that was nicknamed "Maggie's Drawers." We soon got used to the bullets whizzing over our heads as we scored the targets.

The pits smelled wretched, especially on warm days. Soldiers urinated there when nature called. A few did worse, but most who did dug holes and covered their refuse. It was a long, boring duty, relieved only by lunch and five-minute breaks. I always took a paperback book to pass the time between shots. Sometimes, when I was caught up in a story, I was slow putting up the target. I received a firm rebuke on a loud hailer.

The target pits were lined with wood, holding back the soft Georgian clay and sand. Over the months many soldiers had written graffiti on the walls. One I remember:

> A man's ambition is mighty small
> To write his name on an outhouse wall.
> Whoever writes these lines of wit
> Should wrap his shit in a little ball,
> And eat those little balls of shit.

Graffiti was widespread throughout Army bases. Above one urinal someone wrote, "Little bulls with short horns stand close." Another was, "Please do not throw cigarette butts in the urinal. It makes them soggy and hard to smoke." Some signs were defaced to make a new meaning. An inscription on a condom machine read "For Prevention of Disease." Letters were blanked out to make it read, "For vent of ease."

The most popular graffiti was a scribbled drawing of a bizarre looking man peering over a fence with the caption line, "Kilroy was here." It appeared everywhere. Some graffiti were scribbled on places that seemed impossible to reach. As the war progressed, Kilroy became a symbol of the American GI. He was everywhere there was trouble as he peered at the strange Army world.

When it was my turn to make the longest distance qualifying shots, there was a light fog and a steady drizzle. I could barely see the target. I qualified as a sharpshooter at VMI, but that didn't count since I was in the Reserves. Now, when the day ended, I was scored as a Marksman, the lowest rating needed to qualify for Infantry combat. If I had qualified higher, I might have been assigned to advanced sniper training. I'm not sure I could have handled the cold-blooded shooting of unaware enemy troops.

Once I was in combat, I realized that the rifle range was designed to train infantrymen for World War I. Men in trenches shot at each other at long range. As this war progressed in Europe, we were more mobile. Yes, we were bogged down from time to time; but not like they were when trench warfare was common, brutal, and prolonged. We often shot at each other on the run and at close range. I only remember shooting at Germans at a long range for a few days near the end of the war.

When we arrived near the front, we were issued an M1 that had been used by a soldier we replaced. There was no way of telling how many hands our rifles had passed through. Some who used it had been wounded. Some had been killed. A rifle had many stories to tell, but it only spoke when it was fired. These discarded rifles were picked up on the battlefield, checked, and reissued. There was no time or place to zero a rifle when you joined an outfit as a replacement. You made do with it.

Most of our instruction regarding the M1 was useless. Its only value was that we learned to clean, maintain, and shoot it; and learned to get its feel in our hands. It was a beautifully balanced weapon except when you attached a bayonet. Then it became nose heavy. I played with my M1 while I waited to shoot on the range. I even practiced a fast draw when I had it slung over my shoulder. I released it with a twist of my hand and flipped it to waist level, so that it was ready for a quick snap shot. I taught myself to do this until I could make the fast draw flip in a split second. Later on, in combat situations, it was clear that we needed more instruction in the practical use of our rifles. We could have used practice doing a fast draw.

The base of a rifle squad's firepower was the aged but formidable .30 caliber Browning Automatic Rifle – the BAR. It first saw action during World War I and remained in use until the 1960s. It weighed almost fifteen pounds. Its twenty-bullet cartridge added another pound to that weight.

If the BAR's trigger was held down, it would empty its twenty-bullet cartridge in one burst. A skilled BAR man fired bursts of four or five shots. If you fired more than that for any length of time, the barrel overheated. Even worse, the barrel could burn out. That could be disastrous in a firefight.

A two-man team was required to operate a BAR. One carried the BAR, but his assistant who carried the M1 could spell him off. Each member of the team wore a web belt that held at least a dozen cartridges. The assistant also had to carry bandoliers of ammunition clips for his M1. Each had other equipment to carry as well. The BAR team had the hardest job in a rifle squad. Carrying all that equipment required strong legs and great stamina. In time, I would learn that firsthand when I became a replacement for a fallen assistant BAR man.

We received several days of BAR training, target shooting on the firing range. In the right hands it was more accurate and had a longer range than the M1. There were no badges for shooting it. It was something every rifleman had to learn to use. If a BAR man fell, the assistant took over and a rifleman took his place.

We returned to the rifle range for the last time for target practice with the semi-automatic M1 Carbine. It had a shorter barrel for its .30 caliber bullets. Its main asset was its lightness. While it had a considerable range, it could not fire the distances the M1 Garand could. The M1 Carbine was reserved for low-ranking officers and platoon sergeants. It was fun to shoot. Better still, it was an important part of an infantry platoon's firepower when we advanced on the enemy.

OTHER FRONTLINE WEAPONS

The Rocket Launcher M1 – the bazooka - was another important element of a squad's firepower. It was a long-hinged tube that folded when it was carried. Technically it was called a rocket launcher. Its nickname is based upon an icon of the pop culture of the time. In the late thirties and early forties, Robin "Bob" Burns, a popular radio hillbilly comedian, invented a brass musical instrument made up of a long pipe with a funnel attached as a bell. He played it like a trombone. He called his droll sounding instrument a "bazooka."[10] A toy version immediately went on the market. A kazoo was attached to the mouthpiece. Santa Claus saw to it that I got one for Christmas.

The bazooka's armor piercing rocket shell was capable of stopping a German tank or penetrating a cement pillbox. It took two men to operate; one to hold it and aim, and one to wrap the wire from the inserted missile around an electrical terminal. It had a back flash that was dangerous to the assistant or men nearby. Its flash was visible to the enemy. After one shot, the enemy knew where you were. The Germans were always on the lookout for that long tube on the back of an infantryman. A bazooka man was a constant target for snipers.

The bazooka was the only weapon we had that could stop the German panzer tanks. Our tanks were thinly armored, and the 105 mm howitzer they carried did not pierce armor. The feared German anti-tank gun, the 8.8 cm Flak – also known as the deadly 88s – did.

---

10   The origin of the word bazooka stems from "bazoo," a slang word for "mouth," or "boastful talk;" and the Dutch word *bazuin*, meaning trumpet. The weapon's nickname came about because the shape of the Rocket Launcher M1 resembled the musical instrument.

In the right hands a bazooka could penetrate thick armor or tear off a tank tread. We were told that a direct hit exploded the shell into a molten mass that burned through a tank's armor and turned its interior into a fiery Hell. The bazooka required two brave infantrymen to stand and make themselves targets every time it was fired. We spent quite some time learning how to use the bazooka and coordinate as teams. It was time well spent.

Our tanks were effective against personnel and light armored vehicles, but useless when it came to standing toe-to-toe with the heavily armored panzers. The only advantage our tanks had was their maneuverability and speed. If we encountered enemy tanks, our tanks pulled back and allowed our bazooka teams to face the panzer attacks.

Detroit should have done a better job when it designed and manufactured our tanks. I believe that the cheapness of our military-industrial complex was responsible for this shortcoming in our basic mobile weapon. What did the loss of a few young lives matter when profits could be made? The term I've heard applied to this is "acceptable losses." To me, that concept is reprehensible, especially when heavier armor would have saved countless lives. Many years later this war profiteering was underlined when our war industry sent unarmored Humvees into combat in Iraq and Afghanistan. There our soldiers had to steal armor and weld it to the sides of their vehicles. It seems that patriotism disappears where profits are concerned.

Patton wisely learned to offset the vulnerability of his tanks with their speed. While he is famous for his armored divisions, most of his success was due to the bravery of bazooka teams in his rifle companies. I believe his reputation as a strategist arose from a need to compensate for the failings of American design and the ill-advised economies of our military-industrial complex. In time I would profit from Patton's genius – and perhaps his modicum of madness. His Third Army moved in daring dashes and end runs. He avoided head-to-head confrontations with the panzers. I can say that I am alive because of his daring tactics.

I disliked throwing the Mk2 Grenade – or, as it was popularly called, the "Iron Pineapple." It was a little larger than a baseball, but it weighed nearly one-and-a-half pounds. Its oval shaped body was corrugated so that it would fragment on explosion and send pieces of shrapnel in a fanning pattern. It was armed when you pulled on its circular loop and removed the pin that kept it from exploding. It remained armed as long as you held the handle in place. The handle flew away after you threw it, and its timing fuse was activated. It was a matter of a few seconds before it would explode. Your throw had to be looped high so that the grenade would explode just above or in an enemy position. If your trajectory was too low, the enemy had time to pick up your "live" grenade and throw it back. We were trained to use this most personal of all weapons from protective pits. I didn't have a good throwing arm so I'm glad I never had to throw one under fire.

Our grenade's German counterpart, the Model 24 *Stielhandgranate*, or the "Potato Masher" was designed to stun the enemy and exploded with little fragmentation. Tapping it on the helmet activated and armed it. That metal-on-metal sound was an indication that a grenade was coming.

We also received training in the use of the M7 Grenade Launcher. This attachment to the M1 greatly extended the range of the thrown hand grenade. Its tube was attached to the rifle barrel, and blanks were inserted into a cartridge. The rifle's base was firmly set into the ground before it was fired. The power of the blank's explosion could propel an armed grenade more than 300 yards. Each rifleman in a squad carried one of these devices. A squad's twelve men could send the equivalent of a light artillery barrage into enemy positions.

No American soldiers, with few exceptions, looked forward to fighting with knives and bayonets. Each of us carried a M3 Trench Knife, a weapon designed for hand-to-hand fighting. Its short blade was attached to a handle with finger holes that allowed it to be held firmly. We received no training in its use.

During all this activity, we received intensive training in bayonet fighting. I was a step ahead of my fellow soldiers since I had learned the basics of its use at VMI. Jim, the powerful and hot-tempered Rensselaer Polytechnic graduate, was a terror with a bayonet. Even though safety measures were in effect, no one wanted to be his drill partner. The day we attacked the training dummies that hung on wires remains etched in my memory. Jim impaled a dummy with a grunt of rage, ripped it to pieces, and tore it from its wires. If it had been a human body, it would have been completely dismembered. I shuddered. I knew that if I ever had to face that kind of strength and rage in combat, I'd have little chance of survival.

The Tough Get Going

Aside from using weapons, our training was rigorous and exhausting. There were obstacle courses that required several skills from climbing walls, to traveling, to hand-over-hand across small streams. I barely hung on to the rope as I edged hand-to-hand across a creek. Since I had little arm strength, this required great effort from me. Some men dropped into the creek. We even ran across logs floating in a stream. These were excellent physical training exercises since they strengthened our upper bodies.

One of the most difficult exercises I found was climbing up and down a net of rope ladders that hung against the mocked-up side of a ship. When several men were descending at the same time, the nets swayed in unpredictable patterns. They would have swayed even more if they had been attached to the side of a real ship in choppy waters. Descending safely was important because this was the only way troops entered landing craft. If your foot got caught in the webbing, you could end up hanging upside down. If you lost your grip and fell, your heavy equipment would plummet you down and sink you under water. There would be no time for rescue. You would drown. We fervently hoped that amphibious landings had ended at Normandy.

The most frightening training exercise was learning to use a gas mask. We were herded into a closed airtight chamber. We were told to hold our gas masks in our hands and not to panic or put them on until we received the command to do so. When they turned on the gas, we were ordered to put on our masks. Then, after they were secure, we were ordered to take them off, take a breath of the gas, and exit the chamber. We welcomed the fresh air outside since our lungs were searing. The gas they used remains a mystery, but my new stainless steel wristwatch became pitted with corrosion soon after that exercise. There were rumors of gas attacks in Italy, but the Germans rarely used chemical warfare during the Second World War.

I must admit that I enjoyed learning how to use all of these weapons, perhaps because many of the training exercises echoed our playing "Cowboys and Indians" when we were boys. There was a difference, of course. Now we were training to go into combat and use those weapons and tactics for real. Each passing day took us closer to actually being under fire. It was like I was in a relentless, inexorable machine that could destroy me. Then, one Sunday afternoon, my machine ground to a temporary halt.

An Unexpected Twist

My training cycle was almost complete when, shortly after Thanksgiving, I had an accident that put me in the hospital for a month. I decided to take a Sunday walk after church with some of my friends. I wore my low-cut civilian shoes. Why? My combat boots gave me ankle support, but I longed for the freedom of regular shoes. On my way back to the barracks, I accidentally stepped off the raised road and twisted my right ankle. Sprained ankles were nothing new to me. Mine have always been prone to sprains.

I felt a twinge of pain, but I managed to limp back to our company kitchen. As I ate dinner, I noticed an increase in the pain. By the time I finished eating, the muscles in my leg cramped and locked up under the bench I sat on. The pain by now was excruciating. It took two soldiers to pry my leg from under the bench and lift me away.

I couldn't stand. A Jeep took me to the base hospital. The pain grew worse. A doctor examined it and declared that I had a severe sprain.[11] At that time the cure for a sprained ankle was bed rest. I was unable to walk for most of a month, but I was soon able to get about on crutches. My training unit continued its course. When I recovered, I would finish my training with another unit.

There was a special ward in the hospital for men who returned from Europe with bad cases of trench foot. It was near my ward. At that time, the only possibility of a cure for trench foot was to elevate the legs and keep the feet bare. A foot begins to die when it's confined in a boot and there is no chance to change one's socks. Some soldiers had their feet amputated due to trench foot. The smell coming from the ward was horrendous. They say that an Army moves on its stomach. I say that it moves on its feet.

During my recuperation, I enjoyed the performances of USO troops that came to the base. Most of these small groups consisted of performers

---

11 After the war my parents took me to a doctor for further examination. We discovered that the initial diagnosis was wrong. After studying an x-ray, the doctor determined that my ankle had not been sprained, but it had been sub-dislocated. He said it could not be sprained again. His diagnosis was correct. I have sprained my left ankle several times, but I have never sprained my right. It has given me some pain over the years, it aches when the weather changes, and it is larger than my left ankle. Later on, during combat, a case of trench foot aggravated that pain. Since then, I have had little feeling in either foot. I can't test bath water with my feet, and they always feel like I'm wearing socks.

late in their careers. Some had come out of retirement to entertain the troops. I fondly remember one elderly low comedian who was quite funny. He had a rascally attitude and a wicked smile as he timed out mildly risqué patter. He probably had performed in burlesque. I'd seen vestiges of vaudeville in Pottsville, but I hadn't seen a burlesque show yet. There was a sad joy in these old men finding a new audience.[12] Their efforts were rewarded with gales of laughter and applause.

*　*　*

The Battle of the Bulge began on December 16, 1944, and lasted until January 25, 1945. My comrades during my first basic training unit had finished their cycle and shipped out just in time to be in the midst of the largest land engagement on the Western Front.

Hitler's objective was to split and weaken the Allied armies with a *Blitzkrieg* in the Ardennes. When the battle began, three German armies with more than a quarter of a million troops launched this "lightning attack" on a weakly-defended section of the Western Front. It caught the Allied troops by surprise. Less than 100,000 American forces bore the brunt of the attack and suffered the heaviest casualties of any operation during the war. In the first few days the 106th airborne was nearly anni-hilated, but they managed to hold on and buy time for the Allies to defend St. Vith long enough to throw a wrench into the German timetable. As the fighting intensified, the number of troops on both sides quickly grew.

Over the four-week duration of the battle, more than 1,000,000 soldiers fought on all sides. Out of the 500,000 U.S soldiers who fought there, 19,246 were killed, 62,489 were wounded, 23,554 were captured, and 3,058 were missing in action.[13] The Battle of the Bulge became the

---

12 My interest in comedy performance and its techniques were influenced by my exposures to these now-lost traditions. I was fortunate to see some of these greats, first in Pottsville, then while I was in the service. They influenced my stage direction and led me to write *Maxims for Comedians*, a handbook of comedy techniques that I used in my advanced acting classes.

13 A complete listing and breakdown of casualties (including all branches of service and theatres of war) from December 7, 1941 through December 31, 1946, as prepared by the Statistical and Accounting Branch Office of the Adjutant General Under Direction of Program Review and Analysis Division Office of the Comptroller of the Army, O.C.S. can be found at the government website: http://www.ibiblio.org/hyperwar/USA/ref/Casualties/Casualties-1.html#grade.

costliest and bloodiest action ever fought by the U.S. Army. I read somewhere that 19,000 deserted[14] and 45,000 were treated for trench foot.

I have often wondered how many of the men I trained with survived
that intense winter action. The casualties were so high that replacements
were flown across the Atlantic in transport planes.

Later I read that during the course of World War II, 70% of all Army
casualties were in the Infantry and that 16% of all infantrymen died in
battle.[15] The number of wounded exceeded 50% of the men who were on
the front lines. A few recovered and returned to action, some more than
once. Others were too badly wounded to fight again. On average, a combat
infantryman lasted one week on the front lines. By then he was either
wounded or killed. The trench foot attacked the few men that lasted longer.

As the Battle of the Bulge dragged on, I began to wonder if the tide had
turned against us during this massive German attack. Had the *Blitzkrieg*
that conquered so much of Europe found its second wind? No one knew
that the Ardennes Offensive was Germany's last-ditch effort to hold us
out of their Homeland, or that the enemy was, figuratively and literally,
running out of fuel. Of course, the biggest question that lurked in my
mind was, "When will the war end?" That end seemed far away in late
December. I didn't know then that my aching and swollen ankle had saved
my life by delaying my becoming a combat infantryman.

I must admit that I was content to be in the hospital, but I wasn't
malingering. When I tried to step on my right ankle, it ached and creaked.
It slowly improved, but it was far from ready for the rigors of more basic
training. It's true that I didn't look forward to being in combat. I wasn't
alone in that feeling. Patriotism has its limits when one's existence is at
stake. Mine waned as my ankle began to heal. I suspect I was not alone in
this desire for survival. Even so, I knew that my ankle would strengthen,
and I would soon be sent into a world of violence. The outward calm I tried
to project muted my anxiety. I decided that if I resumed my training and
went into combat, I would do my best. Everyone else did. Why not me?

---

14   For more information about this, see *The Deserters: A Hidden History of World
War II* by Charles Glass, published by Penguin Press, available in hardcover (2013), and
paperback (2014).

15   A more comprehensive breakdown of casualty statics will be found later in this
book. Figures are drawn from The Statistical and Accounting Branch Office of the Adjutant General Under Direction of Program Review and Analysis Division Office of the
Comptroller of the Army, O.C.S. can be found at the government website: http://www.
ibiblio.org/hyperwar/USA/ref/Casualties/Casualties-1.html#grade.

A New Outfit

Every Saturday evening young women from Macon were bused into camp to dance with soldiers. It was all very proper. When they arrived, they went directly into the dance hall. We weren't allowed to leave the building with the women even if they were willing. When the dancing ended, they immediately returned to their bus. I sat and watched the dancing during the first part of my hospitalization. Then, after four weeks, I couldn't resist asking a partner to slow dance. I danced very tentatively for a few minutes, but an eagle-eyed non-com saw me and decided I was ready to return to basic training. I was shipped out to another basic training unit the following day.

When I returned to duty, my ankle wasn't fully recovered so I spent most of my final training in pain. I soldiered it out. I lived with pain in that ankle from December 1944 until the end of the war. Now it aches with every change in the weather. I've sprained my left ankle again and again. The doctor in Pottsville was right. I've turned my right ankle many times over the years, but there was no swelling or intense pain. I've never had more than a prolonged ache.

The eighteen-week basic training cycles were shortened to fifteen as the need for replacements increased. Those who trained at Camp Wheeler were sent to Europe. Replacements who trained farther west went to the Pacific. I was relieved. Mixing jungle warfare with fighting the Japanese was alien to all the training I had received and would receive.

I repeated a week or so of my previous cycle before I moved on to new instructions in the art of Infantry warfare. I still enjoyed learning to handle the weapons, but now the increase in our physical conditioning tested my endurance. My legs were strong before I joined the Army, but now I was haunted by the constant creaking and grinding in my ankle during intense physical workouts and long marches. I feared it might give way and send me to the hospital again. I had no one to voice my concerns to, so I plodded away with the rest of the men in my new outfit.

A few Northerners were scattered through the new outfit, but it was predominated by Southerners who were even more Southern than those in my previous cycle. These were barely educated and even more foul-mouthed. Their ability to complain reached epic proportions. I had nothing in common with them. Instead, when I was off duty, I read as many books as possible that had been recommended by Sir at VMI. I didn't realize it then, but my future education was underway amidst noisy barracks life.

I made two friends in a barracks of sixty men. One was a Jewish boy from Philadelphia, the other a Scot from Barbados. I cannot remember their names, but I remember them well as comrades. The Jewish boy, whom I will call Norm, was well educated and cultured. We often went to the post library to listen to classical music. He had a quick sense of humor and liked wordplay. His tastes in reading and music were similar to mine.

The Scot, whom I will call Robbie, had a thick accent that was half Scottish burr and half the *patois* of the natives of his island. At first, he was hard to understand, but I quickly became used to his charming speech. He was darkly Celtic and quite handsome. While he was a British citizen, he had the misfortune of staying here long enough to be drafted. The wet cold, the clay and sand, and the pine needles got to him. While a Georgia winter was mild when compared to northern winters, the damp cold penetrated into our bones. Once or twice Robbie, who had grown up in a tropical climate, was on the verge of giving up. I wouldn't have blamed him, especially as he wasn't a United States citizen. But, to his credit, he never gave up.

The three of us went on passes into Macon to see movies. We didn't drink or go to the houses of prostitution. We were inseparable when we had time off. I'm sure the macho Southerners thought we were gay. Men sensitive to the arts and who read a lot were suspect in those days. I don't think that way of thinking has changed much over the years.

The three of us were excluded from conversations or invitations to go into town. We were outcasts. I didn't mind. Most of the men in my barracks would have been miserable companions on a pass into town. When I wasn't chumming with Robbie and Norm, I dove into my reading and myself. This wasn't difficult. As an only child, I'd managed to be self-sufficient, and I'd accepted the fact that my cultural interests didn't coincide with those of others. I soon found that living within myself amidst a crude collection of men was a benefit.

One Saturday evening I decided not to go into town. I had seen the post movie, so I spent the evening sitting on my bunk reading John Steinbeck's *Tortilla Flat*, a book I had bought in a remainder bin. It's a marvelous book that's filled with warm humanity, humor, and raffish characters. At times it made me laugh out loud. I was swept up in it.

At the end of the barracks four or five Southerners were playing poker. One said something about "the Goddamned Jews." Then he looked at me and said, "I'm sorry."

I asked why, and he replied, "You're Jewish, aren't you?"

I asked in return, "Whatever gave you that idea?"

He replied, "You read books, don't you?"

For three or four weeks I'd been Jewish! After that evening, they were much friendlier to me. Even so, I still preferred the company of Robbie and Norm.

Barracks Poker Game.

CHRISTMAS KP

As Christmas approached, the outcome of the Battle of the Bulge remained in doubt. My training cycle still had a month to go, but I feared that if the Bulge became bloodier, we'd be shipped out before our training was complete. Could fifteen weeks of training become twelve? In looking back, I think it is remarkable that the Army was able to train combat infantrymen that stood up to the best of the *Wehrmacht* and even the *Waffen SS* in fifteen weeks. Many of the men in my barracks openly expressed their lack of interest in fighting abroad. Soon they would have no choice.

I drew mess call on Christmas Day. I felt this was unfair since I had drawn Thanksgiving mess call in my previous company. I asked to see

KP break.

our Captain. He was sympathetic, but unrelenting. He couldn't make an exception. He was working down the roster alphabetically, and that was that. There was no way out of it. I returned to my barracks. The next morning, I dressed in my fatigues and reported for KP.

There was no possibility of a "White Christmas" in Georgia's damp and chill. By then, the Irving Berlin song made popular in the movie *Holiday Inn* was entrenched as a holiday standard. Even now when I hear it, I feel a twinge of sadness, of nostalgia. Years later when I saw the comedy *Private Lives*, Noel Coward nailed the importance of popular music in our lives with his line, "Extraordinary how potent cheap music is." How true! Many pop songs reverberate through our minds over the years. Some remind us of broken romances. Some of moments of joy. And some make us yearn for home.

As I went about my KP duties, Bing Crosby's classic version of "White Christmas" echoed in my brain. I'd experienced homesickness when I was at VMI, but it wasn't as intense as what I felt that Christmas day in 1944. I realized that this could be the last Christmas of my young life. I was almost in tears as I peeled potatoes. I thought of Mom and Dad back home. I wondered what they were feeling. The day began badly for me.

The holiday feast we helped prepare was classic Americana. It included slabs of turkey topped with gravy, tasty stuffing, cranberry sauce, vegetables, and finally, cherry pie topped with ice cream. We were allowed to take a break and join our comrades in devouring this reminder of life back home. This intensified my feelings, and my resentment. This was by far the worst Christmas of my young life.

After dinner, I was assigned to go outside to empty the garbage and clean the large metal trash bins at the rear of the mess hall. It was a bad way to finish a fine dinner. My resentment rose. I had done this at Thanksgiving when I was in the other cycle. I worked for a while and then left duty to go to the bathroom. I looked around and saw that no one was watching.

Instead of going to the bathroom, I kept on going until I was in Macon, Georgia. Once there I celebrated my own personal Christmas by seeing a movie. I've long since forgotten what movie it was. This was the only time I went AWOL – Absent Without Leave. If I had been caught, I would have been sentenced to a week or more in the guardhouse. To this point I had been a dutiful, well-behaved boy, but the injustice of two consecutive holiday KPs gnawed at me. I reacted by running away, by seeking a small sample of the freedom I gave up when I enlisted. I returned to the barracks late in the evening. So far, so good. No one had noticed my absence.

When I went through the breakfast line the next morning, the Mess Sergeant looked at me suspiciously and asked me where I'd been at the end of Christmas Day. I replied, "Out back." Of course, it wasn't the same "out back" where I emptied and scrubbed garbage detail, but I was honest in my reply. I had indeed been "out back," albeit miles away in Macon. Much to my relief, the Sergeant accepted my explanation. I continued through the line. It was then I realized that I could get lost in a mass of people if I kept quiet and drew no attention to myself. After this adventure, I learned how to become invisible when it came to getting assigned to unpleasant duties. My quiet manner and being of medium height helped accomplish this. I didn't stand out in a crowd. Unfortunately, I was approaching a time when I couldn't fade into a mass of soldiers and become a nonentity.

11

Basic Training Ends

O UR BARRACKS CORPORAL was named Schuler. He was a rugged but likeable man from Brooklyn who spoke with a distinct and sometimes amusing accent. His speech was studded with Brooklynisms. He spoke of being from "Green Pernt." During instruction he once said, "The cartridge measures from the pernt to the furst jernt of yer fingah."[16] He was a fair and a good man. We all liked him. Near the end of our training, he was called up for duty abroad. We regretted losing him. He would have been a fine leader of men in combat. I hope he survived the war and returned to a good life in his beloved Brooklyn.

Our company threw a very unofficial party for Corporal Schuler at a country club outside Macon. No officers were invited. Collectively, we chipped in and hired buses to take us there. Everyone got very, very drunk. I even ventured my first taste of beer. When someone passed out, he was placed on the ground outside the club. Soon there was a row of sleeping soldiers. One of the last was Schuler. The buses picked us all up before dawn, so we were in time for *Reveille*. Needless to say, we weren't at our best that day.

There were weekly long marches. These would prove to be practical training once we broke out of the Bulge and began to advance into Germany. We marched everywhere. When we marched to the sites of our training exercises, we kept a steady cadence. If anyone dropped out of step ahead of us, it was exhausting because each step required more

---

16 Translation: "The cartridge measures from the point to the first joint of your finger."

concentration. We marched longer distances during our last weeks of basic. The physical conditioning we gained from those long marches in full battle gear prepared us for even longer marches under more dangerous conditions.

Traditional marching chants helped our morale during our marches. In one our Corporal counted out our pace with, "You had a good home, but you left."

We answered, "You're right."

"You had a good home, but you left."

"You're right."

Then he said, "Jody was there when you left."

We answered, "You're right."

"Your baby was there when you left."

"You're right."

Then he would insert, "Sound off!"

We rhythmically replied, "One, two."

"Sound off."

"Three, four."

"Cadence count."

"One, two, three four. One, two…" There was silence for the next half count, then we shouted, "Three, four!" on the last beat. The syncopation of the silence enlivened our spirits.[17]

It was the simplest of our marching chants. You can see and hear an accurate version of it in the 1949 film *Battleground*. While it lacks the gore of today's movies, it's one of the more accurate of the World War II films.

Another chant was a simple ribald song that was sung with a marching rhythm. It began:

> *This is number one*
> *And the fun has just begun.*

It was followed by a raucous refrain:

> *Roll me over*
> *In the clover,*
> *Yankee soldier.*
> *Roll me over,*

---

17 In a musical rhythm, the march was in four (cut time). The syncopation in the cadence count would be (quarter note) "One," (quarter note) "Two, (eighth rest followed by eighth note) "Three," (quarter note) "Four."

Lay me down
And do it again.

Then we resumed the count as we progressed up the anonymous lady:

This is number two,
And my hand is on her shoe.

Other verses, separated by the refrain, followed:

This is number three
And my hand is on her knee.

This is number four
And I have her on the floor.

This is number five,
And we've just begun to jive.

This is number six,
And she's showing me new tricks.

Of course, there were many variations and many more verses. The driving rhythm of these chants helped us to endure long marches.

During one march, as we passed through a small Georgia town, those of us from the North bellowed out, "Marching Through Georgia,"[18] a song celebrating General Sherman's rampage through Georgia near the end of the Civil War. It had many verses, but this is a sample of the song that the Southerners found very offensive:

Bring the good old bugle, boys, we'll sing another song
Sing it with a spirit that will start the world along
Sing it as we used to sing it, 50,000 strong
While we were marching through Georgia.

Chorus:
Hurrah! Hurrah! We bring the jubilee!
Hurrah! Hurrah! The flag that makes you free!
So, we sang the chorus from Atlanta to the sea
While we were marching through Georgia.

---

18   "Marching Through Georgia" was written by Henry Clay Work in 1865.

When we returned from our march the Captain reprimanded us for singing this celebration of a Union victory. I'm not sure if it was because he thought our choice of song was in bad taste, or if he was concerned that some hot-headed Southerner might have taken a shot at us.

Our marching training climaxed with a 20-mile forced march wearing full field packs and weapons. We alternated between a brisk jog and a double-time march. As we marched my ankle began to grind and ache. My month-long stay in the hospital had also weakened my conditioning. Fortunately, my time as a newsboy gave me strong, overdeveloped legs. A few fell out of the march. Some were exhausted, others gave up, and one sat weeping by the side of the road. My ankle throbbed, but I was determined to finish with the rest. I focused on taking the next step. Then the next. I was among those who jogged into our company assembly area. We were dog-tired, but we pretended to be as fresh as when we started. We wanted other outfits to see how strong we were.

Finally, we received drills that reflected actual combat experience. I found crawling through the night infiltration course exciting. We were warned that live ammunition was going to be used. Machine guns were set to fire just above our heads as we crawled across a muddy terrain. Simulated shell explosions went off in fenced-off pits on either side of us. We crawled close to the ground as we advanced across the course. While we edged along, live tracer bullets whizzed over our heads. If a man panicked and stood up, he would be killed. No one died the night we crawled through the course, but I heard that once in a while somebody did.

After I crawled through the course for the first time, I volunteered for a second transit. By now I was used to the course, but I asked for a third transit. This time I moved across the course on my back. Now I could see the bright lines of tracer fire above me. I may have done it a couple more times. These repeated transits may seem foolhardy. To me it was a realistic choice. I wanted to gain all the experience under fire that I could before I entered combat.

Once we were adept with our rifles, we went through a village fighting course. It was set in a swampy bog. Mock buildings with working doors were spread throughout it. As we moved forward in a line, human-sized targets popped out at us. We had to shoot quickly since the target swung out of view in a flash. After we went through several variations of targets appearing, the results of our snap-shooting were evaluated. This training exercise was valuable. It gave us a sense of the reality of street fighting we would later experience. After it, I was able to fast draw and shoot from the hip with some accuracy.

The climax of our basic training was a long bivouac that lasted nearly a week. We returned from it with another twenty-mile forced march. We entered our company's assembly area chanting out "Sound Off!" Those who finished that grueling march were now full-fledged combat infantrymen. In the Army's mind we were now able to fight Germany's best. And, in a very short time, we did just that.

One Step Closer

Last leave before shipping out.

We were given one last leave before we were shipped overseas. I got home as quickly as I could. We made the long trip across Pennsylvania into eastern Ohio to see my grandparents. My parents said little about what might be ahead for me. The days passed too quickly. I remember little of that time except that my mom was very tearful.

I reported to Fort George G. Meade in Maryland. It was a staging area where we received new equipment, suffered more physical exams, received more shots, and waited to ship out to the next step toward going overseas – a POE, a Port of Embarkation. There was no more training. Our time was spent in waiting.

We had passes that allowed us to go nearby to Baltimore or Washington, D.C. Baltimore, a grim, ugly city, was closest and easiest to get to. On some of the passes I went to burlesque shows at the old Gayety Theatre. Five strippers were featured. They were backed by a scraggly chorus line, and at least two comics who performed ribald skits. A jazzy pit band punctuated the action. Its drummer provided erotic rhythms for the stripteases and rim shots for comedy lines and bits. The acts were announced by the rich voice of the Master of Ceremonies, who could also sing. He often played a part in the comedy skits.

Before the show began "Candy Butchers" worked the aisles with entertaining spiels as they sold boxes of candy and souvenirs. A shill often pretended to buy a box. When he opened it, he exclaimed he just found an expensive wristwatch. There would be a rush of buyers eager to take a chance on winning a watch. One sold books whose content would only be revealed when you held it to the light. I didn't buy any of these offerings, but a friend did. There were no dirty pictures. He had been taken.

The main draw was the star stripper. She was also the best looking of her colleagues. I remember two of the most famous, Ann Corio and Lily St. Cyr.

Unfortunately, I missed seeing fan dancer Sally Rand and the legendary Gypsy Rose Lee. Two lesser-known strippers joined the star headliner in a tour of the wheel[19] of burlesque houses in the Eastern United States. That meant that each week there were three new fresh faces with ample bodies for viewers to ogle. The remaining two headliners were house strippers. Sometimes a member of the chorus line was the fifth. Sometimes that slot was a competition between chorus line members. One aged and overweight regular was so unappealing that instead of "Take it off! Take it off," the audience screamed, "Put it on! Put it on!"

Three songs accompanied each strip. The first song was more elegant and romantic. I remember one beginning with "Sweet and Lovely." As the stripper performed a balletic dance, part of her flowing gown was shed. The second number grew more erotic. It was often performed to "Night and Day." By now the band was wailing and the drummer was throbbing beats for bumps and grinds. When it ended the dancer was down to her bra and panties. The lights were lowered, and the third number began. It was often danced to a song like "Night Train." The stripper's movements grew quite intense and arousing. When it ended, the dancer was down to scant panties or a "G-string," and pasties. She posed coyly and exited.

There was no full nudity then; but if a dancer had a wardrobe malfunction – sometimes intentional – and went too far, word got out. The management often encouraged this extra exposure. When word got out

---

19 Burlesque shows became popular in America during the last half of the 19th century in America and continued to flourish throughout the 1940s. Performers would tour their acts in burlesque circuit known as a "wheel." During WWII there were three wheels - the Columbia Wheel, the American Wheel, and the Mutual Wheel - that would supply theatres with a new show every week including cast, costumes, and scenery. The Minsky family was the most famous owners of burlesque theatres. Burlesque began to decline in popularity following the war and reached its "shabby demise" in the early 1970s.

that more female body parts were on view, attendance soared to see the "Whore Show." If the police entered the theatre, an alert stage manager switched on a red light in each wing. The dance ended abruptly, and the comedians entered and began a skit. The comedians improvised and extended the skit until the police left.

I found the comedians more entertaining than the strippers. The Straight Man – referred to as the Top Banana – was a well-dressed figure of sophistication, *savoir faire*, and dignity. He ended up in ridiculous situations with a low comedian who wore a garish outfit that featured baggy pants. Usually the duo was in pursuit of a Talking Woman. They never succeeded. If money was involved, she took them for all they were worth. The Low Comedian (a.k.a. the Comic), who always had a unique, slurring way of speaking, had a knack for misunderstanding words. If the Straight Man played a doctor in a skit, he would say, "I'm going to ascertain your predicament."

The Comic would back away in horror and say, "The hell you are."

If the Talking Woman – usually one of the strippers – undulated on stage and said, "I'm going to open my new pizzeria to the public tomorrow night," the Comic would fling a leer at the audience and say, "I'll be there."

I was very fortunate to see one of the greatest of all the burlesque comedians, Billy "Cheese and Crackers" Hagan. His signature exclamation was "cheese and crackers." It almost sounded like "Jesus Christ!" He, like all the best comics of the time, never resorted to foul language. Instead, the comics dealt in double entendres that placed the inferred vulgarities in their audience's mind.

One of Hagen's classic routines was the "Japanese Tea Party" in which he plays a servant who pours tea from a pot held at waist level to those seated on the floor. He held the pot in a way that, to the audience, the pouring from the spout gave the effect he was urinating. He'd release a stream of tea, sigh with pleasure, hit the cup accurately, and stop the stream before a drop was spilled. He was one of the great geniuses of low comedy.

Years later, while I was working on my doctorate at Pitt, I had the pleasure of meeting him. I also met some other great burlesque comedians as well since they visited my doctoral advisor, Ralph G. Allen,[20] when they

---

20   Ralph Allen (1934-2004) had a lifetime interest in burlesque, having first seen burlesque shows when he was a teenager. He received his undergraduate degree from Amherst College and his Doctorate from the Yale School of Drama in 1960. Years later he, along with Harry Rigby, conceived the musical comedy, *Sugar Babies*, based on his

Burlesque

were in town. Once I got to see the tiny Billy Foster do a very long set when the police entered the theatre in Buffalo. By then he was well into his eighties. Offstage these great artists were quiet and self-effacing men. Most never realized their greatness or the joy they gave so many people when they were in their prime.

On the bill with Billy Hagan was Rosa Chagnon, whose stage name was Baby Dumpling. Her claim to fame was that she combined stripping with tassel-twirling. She was a stout woman who quickly stripped to panties and a bra. She had tassels attached to each breast and on her buttocks. She could twirl these in many directions; and as a grand finale, she twirled them in different directions as her ample body gyrated about. She was also adept as a Talking Woman.

Many years later I met Rosa when she worked at the Student Union at Drake University. She was also active as a costumer for the Des Moines Community Playhouse. Rosa was a highly intelligent and great-hearted woman. One afternoon she and I sat over coffee as she described her burlesque days. I regret not taping her recollections.

Each show ended with a grand finale. Usually, it was a patriotic number performed by the entire cast. They were backed by truly cheesy scenery draped with American flags. For those who remained for the movie, there

collection of approximately 5,000 burlesque sketches. It opened on Broadway in 1979, and starred Mickey Rooney and Ann Miller. Following its three-year run (1,208 performances) on Broadway, it toured nationally for another three years with various stars including Eddie Bracken, Jaye P. Morgan, Joey Bishop, Carol Channing, Robert Morse, Juliette Prowse, Mimi Hines, Anita Morris, and Rip Taylor.

was an intermission. Once again, the Candy Butcher plied his wares. This time he used a different shill.

Between the burlesque shows, very bad no-budget B movies were shown. I remember one in which the famous stripper, Ann Corio, played a jungle girl. She wore a sarong that would now be considered discreet but was daring for its time. She was menaced by a man in a bad gorilla suit who was intent on sexually assaulting her. He always failed.

When I attended my first burlesque shows I didn't realize that I was learning comic acting techniques from some of the best comedians in the business. Many years later, when I directed college, university, and regional theatre productions, I would apply these timeless techniques.

MY FIRST PROFESSIONAL THEATRE

One evening I ventured into Washington, DC. It was a long train ride to our national capital. There I saw the folk play *Dark of the Moon*. It was on the road as it prepared to open on Broadway. I couldn't have made a better choice for my baptism in professional theatre. It opened my eyes to theatre as they had never been opened before. It fused folk songs (including the famous ballad, "Barbara Allen," that inspired the play), verse, choreography, and dialog into a total theatre experience that enchanted me.

The lead actress had been the voice of Snow White in Disney's *Snow White and the Seven Dwarfs*. Richard Hart was the lead. I only remember him in one starring movie role, *Green Dolphin Street*. I was struck by this highly theatrical evening and remember it fondly. Folk music and dancing were mixed with the dialog, and at times the actors seemed to dance their roles. It was my first view of what was called "Total Theatre."[21] The play was shocking at times, especially when its bewitched and pregnant heroine gave birth to a bat amidst a rousing revival service at a mountain church. A few theatergoers walked out in disgust after this scene. I was thrilled. I discovered that theatre was a performance medium that could deal with subject matter alien to the movies of that time.

---

21 The concept of Total Theatre began in the 19th Century and came into its own during the 1930's with artists like Jean-Louis Barrault and Antonin Artaud. The aim was to provide the audience with an overwhelming and unified experience where all elements work together.

Dark of the Moon had a brief Broadway run, but it became a staple in college and university theatre. Later I learned Howard Richardson and William Berney, both graduates of the University of Iowa, had written it. Few evenings in my lifetime of theatregoing had a more profound effect on me as an audience member and later as a playwright and theatre director. Theatre could be more than unhappy people sitting around a kitchen table or elegantly dressed men and women speaking finely crafted, witty lines. Theatre could embrace all its resources and create a total aesthetic experience.

*　*　*

My next step was Fort Dix, a Port of Embarkation (POE) camp outside New York City near Trenton, New Jersey. My equipment was checked again, and I endured more physical examinations. It was discovered that I had only been issued one pair of GI eyeglasses. I was told I couldn't ship out until I was issued a backup pair. I waited at least a week while my glasses were made. If it hadn't been for that delay I would have been in a bloody fight in Trier, Germany. In time I'd be a replacement for men who had fallen there.

I have often pondered my injured ankle, the wait for an extra pair of glasses, and the other delays that postponed my going into combat. Those days and weeks may have saved my life, or at least kept me from being wounded. They certainly spared me the Battle of the Bulge. I know it's mystic and places too much importance of my small being in our vast universe, but this chain of coincidences weighed upon me then. They still do. Is there some meaning in my long life, in my very existence on this small planet? No, I think it'd be presumptuous to think that I was singled out to live a long life. I was very fortunate, and I tried to do the best with the years granted to me.

Broadway!

We had passes from Fort Dix into New York. I was thrilled. I had never been to the Big Apple. I'd seen the movie, *Stage Door Canteen,* so I went there right after I got off the train. The real Stage Door Canteen had none of the glamour I'd seen in the movie. It was in a drab basement room whose low ceiling made it almost claustrophobic. I saw no famous people during my visits there. There was free food and dancing with young actresses. One griped about my New Kensington, Mrs. Leahy style of dancing. She said my swirling made her dizzy and quit dancing with me.

The best thing to come out of my experience at the Stage Door Canteen was that soldiers could get free tickets to Broadway shows there. I saw a George Abbott comedy, *Snafu,* a musical, *A Lady Says Yes* – and *Oklahoma!*

The title *Snafu* is an acronym for the Army phrase, "Situation Normal, All Fucked Up." The more socially acceptable civilian euphemism was "fouled up." The play was a formulaic American farce, but it was skillfully executed under the direction of America's finest comedy director, George Abbott. The play has been forgotten, but it gave me a glimpse of live screwball comedy. The legendary Abbott lived to be 107 years old and was working until he died of a stroke in 1995. During his long professional life – his career spanned nine decades – he created a broad style for American comedy. He caught the jazzy rhythms of American speech, and his pacing was relentless. Everything was done with crisp accuracy.

A Lady Says Yes, laced as a turkey by the critics, was fun in spite of itself. It starred the popular movie star Carole Landis in her stage debut. Other notable cast members included Jack Albertson, winner of an Academy Award for Best Supporting Actor in the 1968 film, *The Subject Was Roses,* and who later starred in the television sitcom *Chico and the Man* from 1974-78; and Jacqueline Susann, who became famous for authoring her 1966 book, *Valley of the Dolls.* Perhaps the most interesting member of the cast was Christine Ayres, who began her career in burlesque and became a star using the name, Charmaine.[22] At the time it was the only way you could see a stripper in New York since the colorful Mayor Fiorello H. La

---

22   Christine Ayres originally danced in burlesque under the stage name Charmaine. In 1943 & 44 she joined the *Zigfeld Follies* as principal dancer, with the billing, Christine Ayres. In *A Lady Says Yes,* she was billed as Christine Ayres, playing the character named Christine. According to her biography in the "Playbill" program for *A Lady Says Yes,* dated January 14, 1945:

Guardia had banned burlesque on April 30, 1937, for "corrupting the morals of the city." I have no memory of its plot, or even its premise. But I vividly remember that I had a front row seat that placed me directly in front of the orchestra pit and a very New York drummer. He kidded with me before the overture and whispered asides to me as the show progressed. When Christine/Charmaine did a fully clothed and very discreet bump and grind routine, he grinned and said, "Watch this."

He then launched into an arrhythmic, syncopated beat that threw her writhings off. The poor woman almost sprained her back adjusting to his drumming. I told him I was worried he might be fired. He replied with an evil grin, "What the hell? We're closing at the end of the week."[23]

Oklahoma! was another matter. It remained fresh even though it was late in its very long run. That first phrase of "Oh, What a Beautiful Morning" drifting into the house from offstage remains one of the great magical theatrical moments. The original Curley, Alfred Drake, was long gone, but his replacement was more than adequate. It was a great evening.

That musical whetted my interest in American folk plays. When I returned home after the war, I read Lynn Riggs' *Green Grow the Lilacs,* the basis of the book for *Oklahoma!* Riggs' play uses folk songs throughout. Rogers and Hammerstein expanded the score and replaced the folk songs with their own music. In a way, it was an act of hubris, but it worked. While I was enchanted by *Oklahoma!,* I'd like to also see a production of Riggs' minor masterpiece. Unfortunately, the vogue for folk plays has passed. There's a goldmine for folk plays buried in American folklore.

Christine Ayres (Christine) is the tall, sinuous reddish-blonde beauty who electrified Broadway audiences during 629 performances of the "Ziegfeld Follies." Born Christina Theresa Helen Sienkiewiez, of Polish parents in Detroit, infantile paralysis attacked her at the age of six and confined her to bed for six years. When she began to get her health back dancing was prescribed as an exercise. Her first job, at fourteen, was typing in a grubby local theatrical agency, whose proprietors soon decided the stately youngster would look better on a stage. Spotted first on amateur nights at a local burlesque house, for "expense money" of about $20 a week, it wasn't long before she was the main attraction, at the age of fifteen. She escaped the censors and juvenile authorities by changing her name to Charmaine, and there are few burlesque houses in the land where she has not headlined. Ambitious for a try at Broadway, she discovered it had to be done the hard way, via South America, where "Follies" producer John Murray Anderson saw her doing a rhumba and signed her. She was an immediate hit, and now has a speaking role in her second Broadway try.

23 The production lasted longer than the drummer thought it would. *A Lady Says Yes* opened January 10, 1945, at the Broadhurst Theatre, and closed after 87 performances on March 25, 1945.

In dress uniform before going overseas.

I didn't waste a minute of my three passes into New York City. I enjoyed the Christmas spectacular at Radio City Music Hall and took in a movie at the impressive Roxy Theatre (known as "The Cathedral of the Motion Picture") that included a big band. I went to the top of the Empire State Building, visited the Metropolitan Museum of Art, went by ferry to the Statue of Liberty, and visited other sights. I squeezed in a recent film in a 42nd Street "grind house" that showed movies day and night. That was long before 42nd Street became the center of New York pornography. In the mid-1990s the area was revitalized and is now known as "New 42nd Street."

Not everyone used their New York passes to attend cultural events. Some of the men went to barbershops and had their hair cut into Mohawks. They thought an American Indian look would terrify the Germans. It was an absurd idea. Were they going to take off their helmets at a moment of confrontation to scare the Germans into surrender? When they returned to the post, our officers took one look and made them shave off the rest of their hair. It was, and is, against military law to change your appearance without prior permission. It was still winter in Europe. The poor fellows were doomed to have the cold air circulating through the gaps in the webbing that held their helmets on their now-bald heads. Their scalps must have been very cold during their first weeks of combat. The rest of us were content to let our hair grow naturally. Most of us went to the post barbers. They cut our hair to a closely cropped crew cut. After the war, most veterans refused to have the crew cut even though it had become fashionable among civilian men.

A New Friend

While I waited for my glasses, I became friends with Tom Flynn. He was a bit older than me, married, and had two or three children. Flynn was totally Irish. He had Celtic good looks, a broad smile, brooding eyes, and a mystical sense of what was to come. One evening as we sat and talked, he told me how his two brothers had been lost in the war. One, a pilot, was missing in action. The other died in Infantry combat. There were no *Saving Private Ryan* accommodations then. Flynn was scheduled to go into combat in spite of his family's losses. As far as the Army felt, if an entire family died, they died.

I recently found a short story I wrote shortly after the war. It isn't a very good story, but it is a true account of my friendship with Tom. If it were ever published, a critic would say it was pat and made up, but sometimes life is more lurid than fiction. I will insert pieces of it through what follows.

I first met Thomas P. Flynn at Fort Dix. It was late in my stay there, and we were restricted to our barracks because we might ship out at a moment's notice. It was late afternoon when Flynn ambled into our barracks. He stopped to look around. He was stocky and black-haired. You could tell he was Irish by looking at his plain, honest face.

The bunk beside me was empty. He grinned at me as though we were best friends. He asked as he indicated a bunk next to mine, "Hello, kid. Is this bunk taken?"

"Not yet."

"Then it's mine."

He threw his two duffel bags down on the empty bunk and began to unpack.

"Don't bother," I said. "We may move out any minute."

Flynn shrugged his shoulders and sat down. "Just my luck to arrive in the nick of time."

I added, "It could be days."

He paused and asked, "I don't suppose I can make a phone call?"

"No phoning. That's what the man said."

"How long have you been here?"

"A week. I'm waiting for my second pair of glasses. They came today, so they can ship me out anytime they like."

As we quickly became friends, I learned that his full name was Thomas Patrick James Sean Michael Donal Flynn. He explained that it was an Irish tradition that a newborn male was named after all of his uncles. I soon found that Flynn could talk about the most ordinary things and make them interesting. That was fortunate because we had no idea just how long it would be before we took the train to the New York dock area.

I don't know how many games of double solitaire Flynn and I played, but it didn't help relieve the tension of waiting. Some men read and reread magazines that had passed from hand to hand and back again. Others played blackjack and poker. Bare light bulbs cast a cold and cheerless glare on men who'd be in combat in two weeks.

As we played, Flynn asked, "Are you married, kid?"

"I didn't have time for that. I enlisted when I was seventeen."

"You ought to get married, kid. It's the best thing that can happen to a man."

I asked the obvious, "Are you married?"

"Sure am. Married. Got three kids. All girls."

Flynn pulled out a black, frayed wallet from his back pocket and extracted a tattered picture. He handed it to me as though it was his most treasured possession. I looked at the picture. The kids had beaming grins spread across their very Irish faces. His wife was almost plain, but very pretty. She was the kind of woman who looks good without lipstick.

I meant it when I answered, "That's a real nice family, Flynn. It must be great to have a family like that."

His face melted into that wide and homey grin. "That's what I think, kid. You ought to get married. It's really great."

He took the picture back and looked at it once again. This his grin faded. It was then that I first saw a look I'll never forget. It was dark and tragic.

"What's wrong?"

"Nothing. I just wish I could see them one more time before we ship out. I'd settle for talking with them on the phone."

The tone of his voice echoed the look in his eyes. Briefly our eyes met. Then he turned away. He fumbled nervously for a cigarette. He lit it clumsily and exhaled a thin stream of smoke. I sensed that he wanted to say something that was hard to say.

Finally, he spoke, "I wish I wasn't going."

I gave the obvious answer, "None of want to go."

He paused for a moment before he spoke again. "Kid, I got a feeling that I'm not coming back." Tears welled up in his eyes as he said, "I don't think I'm ever going to see them again."

"Don't think like that."

"I can't help it. I got this deep-down feeling that I can't get away from."

"We all got feelings like that," I lied. "Everybody does. It's part of this waiting."

"No, kid, I'm not coming back. It's more than a feeling. It's something deep down that keeps whispering to me. I try to get away from it, but I can't. I know that I shouldn't think this way; but this damned feeling, this knowing, is always there."

It was then the Sergeant came in and announced in a stentorian voice, "Saddle up, men. We're moving out in half an hour."

Flynn shook his head and leaned back on his bunk. I said nothing. There was nothing to say.

Flynn was a good man and a wise friend to a young boy who faced a terrible unknown. While he had his own doubts, he encouraged me. He gave me a glimpse of mature family life, and he defined what a man could be. For a while he was a father figure to me. Many years later I tried to apply what he taught me when I became a father. I remember none of the details of our many conversations, but I remember his doom-filled eyes.

SHIPPING OUT

Finally, our time to sail came. The day we were shipped out, I wrote a letter to my parents. I wanted them to know I wouldn't be writing for a while. I had to be subtle as our mail was heavily censored. Officers read every piece of it. If something broke security, it was blacked out. To signal I was leaving, I quoted from a Longfellow poem, "The Day is Done:"

> And the night shall be filled with music,
> And the cares, that infest the day,
> Shall fold their tents, like the Arabs,
> And as silently steal away.[24]

I thought they'd figure out I was bound for Europe the night I posted my letter. The censoring officer didn't catch my literary message. Neither did my parents. After the war they asked me why I'd sent them that poem! So much for my attempt at breaking censorship.

On the evening of February 23rd, we boarded a train for the 70-mile ride to New York City's dock area – the NYPOE.[25] The train pulled up by a huge ship, the *RMS Aquitania*. It was a sister ship of the *RMS Lusitania* whose sinking and huge passenger loss in May 1915, contributed to our entry into World War I. We didn't know this as we boarded, and the British crew erroneously told us we were on the sister ship of the *Titanic*. We didn't find this reassuring.

As I peered out the train window, it seemed like I was going to embark onto an enormous movie set. The dark grey side of the ship loomed several stories high. I later learned that it had ten decks, some below water, some above. Empty now, it towered high. By morning, with 7,400 troops aboard, it would ride lower in the water. Its 901-foot length stretched far into the distance. This magnificent, four-stacked ship was a huge ark that had been refitted to carry only the male of the human species.

Lines of men carrying backpacks and huge barracks bags struggled up the several swaying gangplanks leading to the ship's interior. After a

---

24 Henry Wadsworth Longfellow (1807-1882) was one of the most popular American poets of his time. Some of his most famous poems include, "Paul Revere's Ride," "The Song of Hiawatha," and "The Courtship of Miles Standish."

25 A GI variant of the NYPOE – New York Port of Embarkation was TSPOE "Tough Shit Port of Embarkation."

All aboard!

short wait, we got off the train and marched into a great shed that fronted on a cement pier. It was awkward getting down the steep metal steps from the train. No Pullman porters waited to assist us. One or two men stumbled and fell. I managed to stay on my feet as I made the last huge step, but my ankle creaked ominously. It held up, but a sharp pain ran up my leg. I wondered how it would hold up in the days ahead. Would I be able to run under fire in full combat gear? This was only a small test of its strength. More were to come.

A military band picked up my spirits as we got off the train. Of course, their repertory included "Over There."[26] It seemed stirring and romantic to me at the time. I was an American soldier going off to war. That was the last touch of romance I'd have in the months to come. From here on it was grim realism. Any vestige of my boyhood idealism was about to be erased.

I struggled up the steep, swaying gangplank. The only thing missing from our heavy load of equipment was our rifle. We weren't trusted with these until we were close to the front lines. Once we stepped into the ship's

---

26 "Over There," was written in 1917 by George M. Cohan, the year that the United States entered World War I. It was the most popular song during WWI and remained popular during and after World War II. The lyrics to the chorus are *"Over there, over there, send the word, send the word over there that the Yanks are coming, the Yanks are coming, the drums rum-tumming everywhere. So prepare, say a prayer, send the word, send the word to beware – We'll be over, we're coming over, and we won't come back till it's over, over there."*

interior, the British crew ushered us below decks and down steep narrow stairs to a large, low-ceilinged room. Inside the room were multiple rows of bunks. They rose four tiers. The aisles between them were narrow. Our packs and barracks bags were dropped at one end of the compartment. Now we only carried toiletry essentials and whatever else we could stick in our pockets. I managed to keep two or three tattered paperback books with me. Among them were a book of poetry and a collection of short stories. I still have them. Flynn and I raced to grab low bunks. We were lucky to get bunks opposite each other on the bottom tier.

After a restless night in crammed quarters, we sailed shortly after dawn on February 24. I managed to get on deck to see us pass the Statue of Liberty as tugboats pushed us out to sea. There was no secrecy about our departure. It was apparent to the whole city that the *RMS Aquitania* was sailing into the broad Atlantic. All that strict censorship at Fort Dix went for nothing.

No convoy waited for us when we were released by the tugs. Convoys moved too slowly, and once we were moving, our ship was faster than any U-boat. At maximum speed, it was capable of reaching 24 knots (28 mph). We didn't even have a destroyer escort. It was safer that way. Once we were out of the harbor, our Captain set a zigzagging course at full speed. It was just us and a vast, turbulent winter sea.

We were alone in the Atlantic Ocean.

PART IV

INTO A THEATRE OF WAR

Now the Lord had prepared a great fish to swallow up Jonah.
And Jonah was in the belly of the fish three days and three nights.
Then Jonah prayed unto the Lord his God out of the fish's belly,
And said, I cried by reason of mine affliction unto the Lord,
and he heard me; out of the belly of hell cried I,
and thou heardest my voice.
For thou hadst cast me into the deep, in the midst of the seas; and
the floods compassed me about: all thy billows
and thy waves passed over me.
Then I said, I am cast out of thy sight; yet I will look again toward
thy holy temple. The waters compassed me about, even to the soul:
the depth closed me round about, the weeds
wrapped about my head.
I went down to the bottoms of the mountains;
the earth with her bars was about me for ever:
yet hast thou brought up my life from corruption,
O Lord my God.
When my swoul fainted within me I remembered the Lord:
and my prayer came in unto thee, into thine holy temple.
They that observe lying vanities forsake their own mercy.
But I will sacrifice unto thee with the voice of thanksgiving;
I will pay that that I have vowed. Salvation is of the Lord.
And the Lord spake unto the fish,
and it vomited out Jonah upon the dry land.[1]

---

1   Chapter 1 verse 17 and Chapter 2 of the "Book of Jonah," from the King James
edition of the *Bible*.

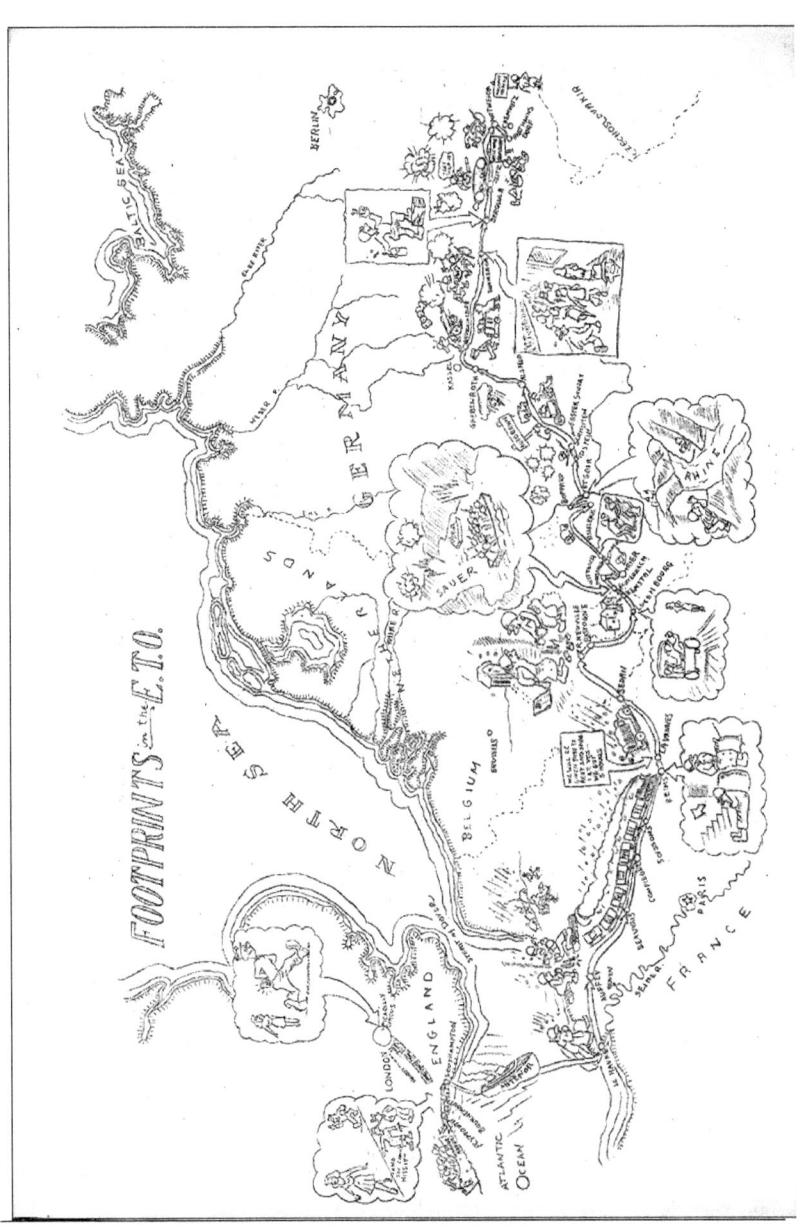

12

SEVEN DAYS AT SEA

I WAS TOLD that the RMS Aquitania could carry up to ten thousand replacements. One torpedo would have created more casualties than a major campaign and more than three times the number of casualties suffered at Pearl Harbor or those who later died on 9/11. The ability of those great ships to supply millions of replacements to all our fronts was one of the logistical miracles of the war.[2]

R.M.S. Aquitania

At the time, we only knew that we were alone in the open sea. It was not an encouraging thought. Going down in a huge ship in that endless, heaving sea was a frightening prospect. Later, as the stormy sea surged

---

2 By the end of the war the *RMS Aquitania* had sailed more than 500,000 miles and had carried nearly half a million soldiers. Following the war, she was used to transport war brides and their children to Canada. In 1949 she was taken out of service, retired, and, in 1950, became the last four-funneled passenger ship to be scrapped at Faslane in Scotland. Throughout a career that had spanned 36 years, the *Aquitania* had travelled 3 million miles in 450 voyages, carrying 1.2 million passengers, making her the longest-serving Express Liner of the 20th century. She was the only major liner to serve in both world wars.

about us, that prospect became even more frightening. Even if there had been enough lifeboats, we couldn't have survived those towering waves that washed above our bow.

In spite of the patriotic music played on the dock, our patriotic fervor waned as we settled into our cramped quarters. Few, if any among us, looked forward to combat. I don't remember anyone expressing a longing to get into battle and avenge the atrocities committed by the Nazis. No one made patriotic speeches. If you see that in a war movie, it's pure Hollywood. Some of the men were open about their fears. My father had raised me to ignore pain and fear, to "be a man." He taught me that my emotions were something that should be hidden inside me. While that repression of my emotions hasn't always been good for me and those around me, it served me well in the days and weeks to come.

In spite of our doubts and fears, we believed we were American soldiers who were a match to the best that could be thrown against us. Beyond that, it was something we had to do. There was no way out. To quit meant months and perhaps years in prison. Fighting wars was the curse of young men in centuries past, then in our own time, just as it will be in centuries to come. Now women join in. All are victims of the old men who create wars.

We were free to move about the ship. The sections for enlisted men were the same, but I was allowed a glimpse into the engine room at the bottom of the ship. There were no stokers, as the coal was fed mechanically. There the constant throb of the great engines drove us ahead. They were like an inexorable Greek Fate moving us toward an unknown destiny.

Some living areas of the pre-war ship had been preserved in their old glory, but these were off limits to us. That's where replacement officers were billeted. The British seamen told us they lived in spacious quarters and ate well. My resentment of the privileges enjoyed by our officers rose. I was not alone in my resentment. My only consolation was that when we went into combat our officers' privileges ended. The enemy shot at everybody.

I had never been on a ship before, let alone an ocean vessel. I spent quite a bit of time on deck during my first night at sea. It was a good time to stretch my legs and test my ankle. I liked the fresh smell of the salt sea air. I wondered at the foam-capped waves that surged about me. Above me a myriad of stars glittered across the sky. During those solitary hours on deck, I felt insignificant, but I was at one with Nature.

In the evening we were shown recent Hollywood movies in the several mess halls spread about the ship. The movies were projected onto sheets or walls. There were three breaks while the projected reel was rewound, and a new reel was threaded.

Two movies in particular seemed to track me across the sea to the Repo Depots[3] where we waited to be assigned to a combat unit. Then they emerged again after the war in Europe ended. I can't count how many times I saw *Bowery to Broadway*, a low budget 1944 Universal musical that starred Jack Oakie and Rosemary DeCamp. It was a typical backstage yarn set in vaudeville days. Oakie and DeCamp were delightful, and there was a stunning moment when a very young Donald O'Connor and perky Peggy Ryan performed a specialty number.

I was enchanted by the Warner Brothers biopic *Rhapsody in Blue*. I didn't know then that this biography of George Gershwin was highly fictionalized. I was swept away in its generous flow of pop and classical music. I knew Gershwin's pop songs, and I had listened to his *Rhapsody in Blue* at a friend's house, but I didn't know he'd written the opera *Porgy and Bess*, a piano concerto, and tone poems.

At this point *Rhapsody in Blue* hadn't been released in the United States. The Army often released their movies to the Armed Services before they opened to the public. It turned up again and again during the time I was in Europe. There were other less memorable movies, but even the worst was a welcome escape from being confined in tight quarters even though they were projected in even tighter quarters.

I became seasick on the second day of our voyage. Worse still, I contracted dysentery.[4] The English food was greasy and badly prepared. Our cooks were trained to be sanitary. The English cooks weren't. You could see a greasy mix of small pieces of meat gristle and vegetables in the

---

3   The slang term for the several replacement depots spread along the coast of France. They were also known as "Repple-Depples."

4   Dysentery is a disease of the intestine, and especially of the colon. It results in inflammation of the intestines, diarrhea, and abdominal pains. Various types of infectious pathogens cause dysentery, including bacteria, viruses, and parasites. Dysentery was most often caused by unsanitary conditions. According to the U.S. Army Medical Department Office of Medical History, the Army dealt with diarrheal disorders during World War II at a crude rate of 21 per annum per 1,000 average strength; or 13.6 per annum per 1,000 average strength for American troops in Europe during the interval from February 1942 to December 1945. The common causes were amebic, bacillary, and unclassified. In all forms, the cases of reported dysentery approximated 92,000 for the total Army in WWII.

serving barrels. I wasn't alone in my suffering. The dysentery, or "Hershey squirts" as some called it, quickly rendered the "heads" – the Navy term for toilets – disgusting. Our vomiting from seasickness made things even worse. The half-clogged toilets spewed their contents back at us.

The food we ate didn't help. I was puzzled why the cooks didn't requisition the excellent food served by the Army before the voyage. At the time I attributed this to British cheapness. Over the years, I realized that our allies were poor from the long war they had been fighting. They had no money to buy nutritious food since they were fighting just to stay alive. Now I blame our Army for not providing supplies of healthy food for our troops. However, I do blame that British crew and their unsanitary kitchen for giving me dysentery.

Flynn and I continued to talk about everything as our friendship grew. He never spoke of his premonitions again, but I sensed they were still there inside of him. He lived with a deep sadness, even as he became a much-needed father figure to me. He, too, suffered from dysentery and seasickness. We found that staying in our bunks muted the seasickness. It also helped to go on deck and breathe fresh air. However, that relief was only temporary. Seeing the waves and being caught up in the heaving of the ship sent me rushing back to the head.

Gambling was an escape for some men. Some played poker and other card games in their bunks. Throughout the day and night, crap games rattled endlessly amidst the flowing filth in the head. After I relieved myself several times a day, watching the casting of the dice gave me temporary amusement. The stakes were high. Money seemed unimportant now. I saw hundreds of dollars change hands on one roll of the dice. One soldier boasted that he could send a year's salary to his wife after one afternoon of play. I hope he did. He died in combat.

Cleanliness was impossible in those crowded quarters. The showers spewed saltwater. A sticky scum covered our skins after our showers. I longed for a freshwater shower. We finally had them at the Repo Depot in France. The daily showers there were most welcome. After that, I didn't have another shower or bath until the war ended.

Everything conspired to make our seven-day voyage miserable and interminably long. As I developed my sea legs, I went on deck as often as I could. The winter ocean churned with enormous greenish-blue waves topped by foaming white caps. Some were forty or fifty feet high. A few surged higher than our ship. I had no basis of comparison since the ship

rose and fell as it plowed relentlessly ahead. The enormity of
being in a mid-ocean storm was
a thing of awesome and savage
beauty. Being on deck was not
without risk, however. I could
easily have been washed overboard. If that happened, I would
have been a goner since the ship

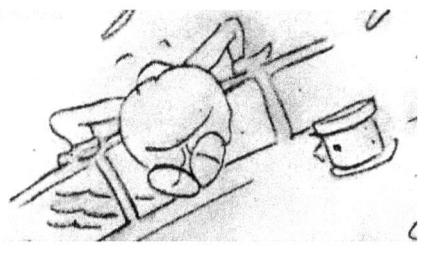

Seasick!

wouldn't stop. I also realized that if I were washed overboard, nobody
would know about it until I failed to report, or someone like Flynn would
try to find out where I was.

Regardless of the risk, I found comfort by being on deck. I was hypnotized by the raw power and height of that surging sea. For hours on end
I stood alone on the deck, watching those gigantic, ever-heaving waves.
Feeling insignificant amidst the awesome force of those waves placed me
in a perspective that I sensed when I was a boy, looking into a star-filled
night. I felt better out there. The cold wind and salt spray awakened me.
The piercing wind refreshed my senses, and the sea spray revived my
spirits. I savored the smell of the salt sea. It's a smell I recall even as I write
this. During these moments on deck my stomach calmed even though
the ship heaved and lurched as it plowed ahead; but when I went below,
it churned and cramped again, sending me rushing back to the head.

I was so ill by the fourth day that I wanted to die. That escape wasn't
forthcoming. I alternated writhing in my bunk with staggering on deck.
I needed the stability of lying prone, but I needed fresh air. Now when I
went on deck, that feeling of insignificance transformed into something
darker.

What did I matter amidst the rough grandeur of that stormy sea? I
seemed so small as I looked into a night sky filled with stars. There I saw
the constellations that fascinated me during my boyhood. I saw a vastness
that exceeded my imagination. What did my existence matter? Would
I even be remembered if I were to be thrown into Fate's wastebasket? I
knew that Dad and Mother – and my grandparents – would mourn my
passing; but when they were gone, I would be gone, too.

For a moment I felt the impulse to throw myself into that churning sea,
but that urge quickly subsided. I realized that life was too important, too
precious to be thrown away. I still had my misery, but I found a release to

endure what lay ahead of me. That moment of acceptance can be defined in a song lyric written many years later: "Freedom's just another word for nothing left to lose."[5] Although I didn't fully understand it at the time, I had experienced my first existential moment.

The sea calmed as we approached Ireland. Everyone rushed to the decks to see our first glimpse of land. A cheer went up when we spotted the distant, green hills of the Emerald Isle. We skirted them and sailed over to Scotland's Firth of Clyde on March 3, 1945. It was full of ships of all shapes and sizes. Flying above them were many tethered barrage balloons. They blocked low-flying *Luftwaffe* bombers that wanted to attack the ships below. That vast Firth was like a scene from a movie, but we didn't see it for long.

By late afternoon, Flynn and I were on a troop train. Eight of us were assigned to each train compartment. There were no bunks. We sat up as we roared south. As twilight gathered, I saw lines of people standing by the tracks, waving, wishing us well. Scotland was turning a refreshing green with the approach of spring, but I saw little of England since the rest of our trip was at night. It would be many years before I was able to visit Great Britain.

We passed through the rail yards of devastated London. As we did, I caught sight of the silhouettes of ruined buildings. Those shadows gave me my first glimpse of the horrors of war.

We arrived in the port city of Southampton near dawn. As we rode into the railroad yard by the docks, the morning light revealed a ravaged, war-torn city. It troubled me. I thought then – as I do now – that bombing civilians from a great height is a less than honorable way to fight a war. Yes, I realize that those men in bombers endured great physical danger and psychological tension. The mortality rate for those flyers was very high. I cannot begin to imagine being encased in that metal tube flying machine thousands of feet above the earth as flack and fighter planes attacked for miles on end. I admire those brave men, even as I despair at this 20th century innovation in killing people.

A flotilla of small troop ships at Southampton's docks waited to take us across the English Channel into the Fortress Europe. We entered the bowels of the troop ship. The bunk tiers in a hold were ten high. By nightfall we were on board and underway. It took all night to cross the

---

5   From the song, "Me and Bobby McGee" by Kris Kristofferson and Fred Foster.

narrow Channel. The men who climbed to those top bunks hoped they didn't roll out in rough weather or in their sleep. Again, Flynn and I were fortunate to claim lower bunks.

My seasickness abated, but I still suffered from diarrhea. We also knew that we were in another deathtrap. A single U-Boat could sink our ship. Fortunately, the channel was narrow at this point, and it was a short voyage.

AN INNOCENT ABROAD

As we sailed into the Le Havre harbor just before dawn, we saddled up to debark. My huge pack was filled with clothing and field equipment. Over it was a rolled-up sleeping bag. This was affectionately called a "fart sack." The rest of the roll included a blanket and a poncho that formed half a pup tent. In addition, I carried my barracks bag. It was a heavy load.

This was Le Havre

After I struggled down the narrow gangplank, I stepped onto French soil. Now I was in the ETO – the European Theatre of Operations. La Havre was surrounded by the 15th Replacement Depot. This reception area for troops arriving in Europe distributed infantrymen to the several American armies spread in a line across Europe. The 15th Depot was divided into Cigarette Camps,[6] named after popular American cigarette brands.

---

6   It is estimated that nearly three million American troops either entered or exited Europe through Le Havre between 1944 - 46. The camps were named after popular cigarette brands for security and psychological reasons. Camp names included Herbert Tareyton, Lucky Strike, Philip Morris, Pall Mall, Old Gold, Chesterfield, Home Run, Twenty Grand, and Wings (https://www.skylighters.org/special/cigcamps/cigintro.html). Lucky Strike was also a popular brand of cigarettes included in the C-rations provided to U.S. combat troops. A slogan heard on radio commercials in 1945 was LSMFT "Lucky Strike means fine tobaccos."

Camp Tareyton

We immediately began the march to the closest, Camp Herbert Tareyton, located in the Forest of Montgeon. As we did, we passed through devastated Le Havre, the most damaged city in France. This was the first daylight view I had of the horrors of war. What I saw was appalling. It had had been pummeled into rubble. The Germans occupied the city from 1940. Before they left, they sank ships and destroyed much of the port. The greatest destruction, however, came in 1944 when Le Havre suffered 132 bombings by the allies. The British Royal Air Force (RAF) carpet bombed the city into rubble and killed thousands in *Operation Astonia* on September 5 & 6, 1944, before finally liberating the city on September 12.

The road to the camp was made of loose giant pebbles that were the size of baseballs. They rolled under my feet as the more than hundred pounds I carried bore down on me. Adding to my torment was the dysentery I contracted on the *Aquitania*. My aching ankle creaked with the stress of each step I took, and I could hear those bones grinding and popping as I placed one foot in front of the other. I feared my ankle would give way completely. I longed to step off the road and walk in the grass beside it, but we were told we must never step off. The Germans had planted hundreds of land mines throughout the area. My ankle held up, but the pain of walking over those moving pebbles brought tears to my eyes. As I marched, I despaired at the prospect of enduring this pain while I was in combat. I would have been justified to report my pain, but I felt that doing so would be asking for a special favor. I said nothing. I toughed it out.

Camp Tareyton was located in the city limits, with a capacity of 16,400 men. When we arrived, we moved into large wooden-floored squad tents. Each had two rows of cots, each footed by a locker. A potbellied stove warmed us at night. Our footlockers had to be locked since gamblers who were having bad streaks were desperate for money or goods they could barter. Fortunately, I carried the little money I had in a money belt that my father gave me before I shipped out. My small hoard of paperback books didn't interest the looters.

I went to a movie the first night I was in camp. I was treated to *Bowery to Broadway* for the second – but not the last – time. It seemed to appear every time a movie was shown to troops. It passed away two hours and diverted my mind from what was to come next. A burley, shaggy bear of a man told dirty jokes as the projectionist rewound and changed reels. Some of his jokes were classics I still tell my friends. His ribald intermission riffs were more entertaining than the film. On another night I saw *Rhapsody in Blue* for the second – and not the last – time. While I knew the plot, I enjoyed the film's feast of music. Both movies followed me during my time in Europe.

At Tareyton, we waited for our assignment to a combat outfit. While the few days there passed slowly, I wasn't alone in thinking that each day in the Repple-Depple was a day I would not spend on the frontlines. There was no area for drills in the crowded camp, but there was plenty of time to write letters home and to read the Armed Services editions of popular books that were passed from hand to hand. Others devoted their time to gambling.

There were new and old copies of *Yank Magazine*. *Yank* was a weekly magazine published by the United States military. It was written and illustrated by enlisted men. Two of its best artists were Howard Brodie, a front line artist, and George Baker.

Brodie's realistic paintings and drawings are a valuable record of what men experienced in combat. I loved his roughhewn black and white sketches. They were technically accurate, but they also managed to bore into the harrowing experience of Infantry combat. Somehow, he managed to catch the haunted eyes of men who had been in combat too long. Later he would illustrate John Hersey's *Into the Valley*. It is a book I still treasure.

Yank had another wonderful cartoon character. The comic strip *Sad Sack*, drawn by George Baker, was lighter and designed to give us a needed daily laugh. Baker's title character became a symbol of a not quite average GI. Some of his strips were ribald. His most daring showed Sad Sack having a wet dream. There was quite a furor when copies reached stateside. General Marshal defended him by saying his strips raised the morale of our troops.

Baker's criticism of the Army was gentler and more oblique in *Sad Sack*. Even so, he annoyed some officers since the Sad Sack (of shit, if you knew Army profanity) was a constant loser. Baker did not use his strip to push issues. I still have worn books of Baker and Brodie's work. All made me aspire to become a professional cartoonist. I have realized many dreams in my life, but that one never materialized.

In addition to *Yank*, the daily *The Stars and Stripes*, an American military newspaper that has been around since the Civil War, kept us in contact with what was happening in the war. It featured the realistic – but satirical – cartoons of its principal cartoonist, the great Bill Mauldin. His work often had a vicious sense of humor. His continuing GI Joe characters, Willy and Joe, represented us all. They reflected our weariness and disenchantment. He caught his Willy and Joe in combat and rear area situations that were familiar to anyone who had been in combat.

I believe that *The Stars and Stripes* had some autonomy and freedom. Even so, Mauldin later wrote about censorship battles he encountered from officers who were intent on preserving our morale by putting a happy face on the war.[7] He persisted and presented a dark side of the war with his bitter humor. After the war he became an editorial cartoonist, winning two Pulitzer Prizes for his work.

Milton Caniff, a civilian cartoonist who created the popular *Terry and the Pirates*, contributed to our morale with *Male Call*, a slightly sexy comic strip that wasn't designed for civilian eyes. He offered it free to military newspapers. Its beautiful star was Miss Lace. She often appeared in revealing lingerie as she "interacted" with soldiers from a nearby base. She remained chaste throughout her many adventures. She was a very sexy woman for that time.

Our armies broke out of the Bulge as March approached. The fighting was less bloody than it had been at the depths of the *Wehrmacht's* massive winter counteroffensive, but there was more fighting ahead. Some would be intense. While the morale of the German army was shaken, their troops fought on even though defeat seemed inevitable. Ideology became unimportant. Now they were defending their homeland and their women and children.

As Hitler withdrew his forces across the Rhine and organized a defense of Germany, he ordered the destruction of all the Rhine bridges. We were cheered when *The Stars and Stripes* reported that the 9th Armored Division had discovered that the Ludendorff Bridge at Remagen remained standing. The Allied forces captured it and established a bridgehead on the other side of the Rhine on March 7. This was near the time I joined

---

7   In a matter of months, I would be encountering similar officer censorship of some of the cartoons I drew when I worked on our battalion history after the war.

my Infantry squad. The Allies managed to get six divisions across the bridge before it collapsed on March 17. While six divisions were a small penetration, it meant that the heartland of Germany was under attack.

We all harbored the hope that the *Wehrmacht* would collapse and that the war would end quickly. We didn't realize that millions of men, tanks, trucks, and tons of equipment had to be sent across the Rhine before a full attack on Germany could begin. Mustering that huge a force took time.

Shortly after we received this good news, a Ranger recruiter met with us. He told us that if we volunteered to join this elite unit, we would receive advanced training. All of us mulled this offer. Would we be sent back home to receive this training? Would it be here? In either case it meant a delay in going into combat in a war that was going well. That was tempting. After the meeting one of the cadre told us that training for the Rangers was simple. Green recruits were sent into an intense battle situation. Those who came out alive were Rangers. Then they were sent into more intense battle situations. Very few volunteered. I was not among them.

As we waited for our travel orders, we were given evening passes into Le Havre. We were warned to travel together and never be alone in the blacked-out city. Side streets were to be avoided even when we were in a group. The French still resented the carpet bombing of their open city. Occasionally a lone American was killed.

I only took one pass into Le Havre. There was little to do there for a young man with no vices. I steered clear of the Army-supervised houses of prostitution where a long line of men sheepishly waited to be serviced. When they were finished with their brief encounter, they visited a "pro" station by the outside door and received the usual injection into their urethra. We were assured that Army doctors regularly examined the women. No one stopped to think that there were many customers between these examinations.

I've always found the idea of prostitution repugnant. Other comrades did not share that feeling. Many viewed this as their last chance to have sex before they died in battle. Our Army was indirectly involved in the operation of these houses of prostitution, but its involvement was keeping them free from venereal diseases.

On the other hand, the German and French armies openly ran brothels for their troops. While prostitution was accepted in Europe before the war, it became an important way of earning a living during and after the war. Soon I would see husbands selling their wives, and boys peddling their teenage sisters. War drives people trying to survive into performing desperate measures. Years later I found this line from the movie *Chinatown*, written by Robert Towne, to be true:

> *You see, Mr. Gittes, most people never have to face the*
> *fact that at the right time and right place, they're capa-*
> *ble of anything.*

I spent at least a week at Camp Tareyton, waiting to be assigned to a combat unit. My lack of activity during this time gave my ankle time to strengthen, but it remained weak. I didn't shake my dysentery.

The days and weeks that followed are a mix of specific images, blurs, and impressions.

13

To The Front

They went with songs to the battle, they were young,
Straight of limb, true of eye, steady and aglow.
They were staunch to the end against odds uncounted;
They fell with their faces to the foe.
They shall grow not old, as we that are left grow old:
Age shall not weary them, nor the years condemn.
At the going down of the sun and in the morning
We will remember them.[8]

M Y JOURNEY TO the front began when we were marched to a rail-head and placed into the legendary "forty and eight" boxcar. Only 20.5 feet long and 8.5 feet wide, these French, narrow gauge rail cars were designed to carry either 40 men or 8 horses. In either case straw was heaped on the floor. We slept in our sleeping bags with a blanket folded inside. Our pillows were our packs. No one was in charge of each car, so we had to make our own arrangements for storing our duffle bags and claiming our sleeping areas.[9]

---

[8] Two stanzas of the "Ode of Remembrance" from the poem *For the Fallen* by British poet (Robert) Laurence Binyon (1869-1943). Originally published in the London *Times* on September 21, 1914.

[9] The American Legion started an auxiliary called the "The Forty and Eights" after the end of WWI. To qualify, you have to swear you had ridden in one of those small, narrow-gauge boxcars. I never joined it or the American Legion, or the other major veteran's organization, the Veterans of Foreign Wars (VFW). These groups were run by former officers, and many of them hadn't seen a day of combat. Most were ardent flag wavers and conservative in their politics.

One liberal group, the AMVETS (also known as American Veterans), was formed at the end of the Second World War and, in 1947, it became the first WWII organization

Most of the European railroads had been bombed. We passed over rough tracks and rickety bridges that had been hastily repaired by our engineers. Some bridges swayed as we crossed and seemed on the verge of collapse. Our progress was slow. Often it was at a walking pace. Our only stops were for us to relieve ourselves away from civilian eyes.

Forty and Eight

Somehow, I acquired a small but detailed map that allowed me to trace my journey toward the front lines. I could compare our progress with maps of the front published in *The Stars and Stripes*. Our daily progress told me that it would be several days before I joined a combat unit. I had mixed feelings. I hoped the war would end before I was in combat, but I also wanted be part of what General Eisenhower had called "A Great Crusade." Most of all I wanted to live and go home. Is there a more beautiful word in the English language than "home?"

Even though it was early March, the harsh European winter was turning into spring. Most of the time we kept our boxcar's heavy sliding door open. A few of us rode with our legs dangling; others stayed inside playing cards and shooting craps. I stayed clear of these games of chance. I didn't want to lose the little money I had.

---

chartered by Congress. The AMVETS supported former Vice President Henry A. Wallace's left leaning bid for the Presidency in 1948. As a result, this pacifistic organization came under heavy fire during the Red-baiting Joseph McCarthy era, and never became the force that the American Legion and VFW were. If I had joined any veterans' group, it would have been the AMVETS. After my time in the Army, I was in no mood to join anything with military ties or influences. I did enlist in the Army Reserves when I was discharged, but there was a good reason for my doing that.

I tried to read, but the sway of the car hinted that I could regain the seasickness that I had managed to shed at the Repo Depot.

We were hungry for news of how things were going at the front. We jumped off the train at stops and grabbed copies of *Yank* and *The Stars and Stripes*. They were passed around and avidly read. The Allied Armies were securing more bridgeheads across the Rhine, but there were no major breakouts. We didn't know that General George Patton's Third Army was held in check despite Patton's desire to make a bold thrust into the heart of Germany. Later I learned that his boldness was checked, in part, due to the caution of British Field Marshal Bernard Montgomery's preference for antiquated battle tactics.[10]

While I devoured any news I could find in these two publications, the view outside the train was more interesting. There I saw the ravages of war and its impact on people who were swept up in it. We passed through towns that had been devastated by the battles that swept back and forth through them. They looked like lines of steamrollers had ground them into rubble. As I looked out, I thought that I would be contributing to the ruin of German towns and villages in a few days.

Lines upon lines of French civilians of all ages stood by the tracks. Some were there to cheer us on, but most harbored the hope we would toss them food, soap, chocolate, and cigarettes. American soldiers had the reputation of being generous and good-hearted. Most of us threw gifts to the children. Amidst them were black marketers who grabbed what they could so that they could sell it later.

Some soldiers sold their items for francs and barter goods. French money was available, but no one wanted it.[11] Our government guaranteed the Occupation francs. The French wanted neither. Money had little value in a world of shortages. People wanted tangible goods like food, soap, silk stockings; anything they could sell on the black market.

The few goods we possessed were worth a lot. Our K-Rations contained a pack of four cigarettes and a small bar of chocolate. A bar of soap went for a dollar or more. A carton of cigarettes was pure gold. We

---

10 An account of the intense rivalry between Patton and Montgomery can be found in Ladislas Farago's 1964 biography *Patton: Ordeal and Triumph*. It can be argued that the war in Europe would have ended much quicker if Patton had been given his way. The book remains in print and is available in paperback and on Kindle.

11 I brought home a few French franc bills. They were beautifully colored and designed. It's a pity they have been replaced by the euro.

were allowed to buy a carton a week for a nickel a pack. These could be sold for the equivalent of two dollars a pack on the black market. A few men brought along silk and nylon stockings. These were worth twenty dollars or a night of sex if our train had stopped long enough. A few men parlayed two or three packs of cigarettes or a bar of sweet-smelling soap for a quick trick behind bushes when we stopped for a piss call.

I had little to give, but I gave what I had to the children. I couldn't profit from those victims of a long war, and I wanted those children to remember that Yanks were good people.

After one of our encounters with civilians, a barely literate Southerner exclaimed, "Damn, what fine schools these people must have! Look at them kids. Some of them are only five or six years old, and they all speak French!"

He was quite sincere in his observation. In a way, his exclamation summed up the American attitude toward the rest of the world. All too often we assume that everyone is like us. Even at eighteen, I recognized the unintended humor of what he said.

Above us we saw and heard the relentless drone of a wide ribbon of Allied bombers headed north toward German cities, now being hammered by thousand-bomber daylight raids. Goering's *Luftwaffe's* fighter planes had been decimated in the Battle of Britain, and our air raids hampered Germany's ability to build more. The few that were left were no match for our escorting fighter squadrons. The tide of war was shifting rapidly in our favor, but the *Wehrmacht* and the diehard *Waffen SS* still fought back.

My trip towards Germany was like a journey through a long tunnel. What we saw was only a fraction of the Allied war effort. The true scope of the epic war that was sweeping across Europe was narrowed to those of us who rode in that boxcar. I have used the word epic for the first time, but I will use it again and again.

As we rode north, I read from my book of poetry. I found my greatest comfort in "Ozymandias" by Percy Bysshe Shelley:

> I met a traveler from an antique land,
> Who said: "Two vast and trunkless legs of stone
> Stand in the desert. . . . Near them, on the sand,
> Half sunk a shattered visage lies, whose frown,
> And wrinkled lip, and sneer of cold command,
> Tell that its sculptor well those passions read
> Which yet survive, stamped on these lifeless things,

The hand that mocked them, and the heart that fed;
And on the pedestal, these words appear:
My name is Ozymandias, King of Kings;
Look on my Works, ye Mighty, and despair!
Nothing beside remains. Round the decay
Of that colossal Wreck, boundless and bare
The lone and level sands stretch far away."

That poem spoke to me. Its sense of the eternal versus the temporal deeply moved me. The unimportance of tyrants in the larger sweep of history put all that I saw in perspective. I read Shelly's poem over and over again in the weeks to come.

The *Bible* offered me less comfort, but I read "The Twenty-third Psalm" again and again:

The Lord is my shepherd; I shall not want.
He maketh me to lie down in green pastures:
he leadeth me beside the still waters.
He restoreth my soul: he leadeth me in the paths of
righteousness for his name's sake.
Yea, though I walk through the valley of the shadow of death,
I will fear no evil: for thou art with me;
thy rod and thy staff they comfort me.
Thou preparest a table before me in the presence of mine enemies:
thou anointest my head with oil; my cup runneth over.
Surely goodness and mercy shall follow me all the days of my life:
and I will dwell in the house of the Lord forever.

That Psalm's gorgeous sonority meant more to me than its inner meaning. It did nothing to replace my waning religious beliefs. The fourth verse certainly applied to my growing fears. Did I have the courage to walk through the valleys of death that lay ahead of me? I felt dreadfully alone. I dove deep inside myself. There I sought numbness, and emotional neutrality.

As our train continued its snail's pace towards Germany, I hungered for more to read. I needed diversion, not consolation. I scrounged for discarded Armed Forces Editions of recent novels. Those of us who enjoyed reading passed them around. I traded for my first James M. Cain novel, *The Postman Always Rings Twice*. I liked Cain's terse, hard-boiled writing style. I hunted for more of his novels. Years later, when I read literary criticism, Edmund Wilson placed him with Dashiell Hammet and Raymond Chandler as one of "The Boys in the Backroom." The hard-biting prose, terse dialog, and film noir plots of these writers seemed less affected to me than that of Ernest Hemingway.

Onaway

Onaway insignia

My tortuous rail journey took most of a week. When we disembarked from the train, we were told that we were now members of the 417th Infantry Regiment in the 76th Division of General George S. Patton's Third Army. Nicknamed the Onaway Division,[12] the 76th was the Third's youngest Infantry division. Many considered this the best assignment in the European Theatre of Operations (ETO).

The Third's casualty rate was the lowest, partly because Patton had been kept on the shelf, and partly because of his daring tactics. Those who went to the Seventh and Ninth armies were not as fortunate. The Ninth was attached to Montgomery's forces. He tended to attack head on or hold his positions. His troops suffered more shelling and mortar fire. It was from these weapons the Infantry suffered the greatest casualties. The same was true of the Seventh and First armies to the east of us.

When we joined the 417th Infantry Regiment we shed most of the equipment we carried from the New York POE and Le Havre and kept only what we needed for combat. What we left behind was labeled with

---

12   "Onaway" is the alert cry of the Chippewa Indians, in whose hunting grounds the 76th Infantry Division trained while at Camp Mc Coy, WI. Prior to this they were known as the "Liberty Bell Division." The Division insignia is an escutcheon which has a red field and a blue chief, separated by an olive drab line. A three-pronged white device is superimposed on the blue chief. The white device was a medieval English heraldic symbol meaning "First Son," based on the Division description from World War I, "The First Sons of the Nation."

our names and placed in storage. I did not see those belongings again until after the war ended.

The 76th Division was relatively new. It had gone into combat late in the Battle of the Bulge and had distinguished itself in its first action by breaching the Siegfried Line after crossing the Sauer River near Echternact. Some of us who traveled from Le Havre were assigned to the 417th Infantry Regiment's First Battalion. Others went to other front line units of the division. All the Infantry outfits had been decimated and needed replacements.

We first were assigned to Infantry battalions. Flynn and I stayed together when we got into a "Deuce and a Half," the 2½-ton 6X6 U.S. Army cargo truck. We sat opposite each other on benches. Our packs were stowed on the floor and at the back of the truck's cab. We were part of a convoy that would take us to the First Infantry Battalion headquarters. There we'd be assigned to a front line company.

With each passing mile my apprehension rose. I think apprehension is the best word to describe my feelings. For some unexplainable reason I was not afraid, but I did have specific fears. They all dealt with dismemberment and the loss of sight or hearing. I asked myself which I would choose if I had to make a choice. My love of music made me want to preserve my hearing above all else. These thoughts I kept to myself. To offset them a numb sense of stoicism rose within me.

I wrote a memory of my journey to the front while I was in college. It's more accurate than what I can dredge up from the decades-old memories:

THE JOURNEY

Ahead of us there was thunder in the night. Strange rumblings echoed from a horizon rimmed with fire. It was artillery fire. Was it ours, or was it theirs?

We were afraid of what lay before of us, what lurked behind that blazing horizon. I was afraid. I never admitted that to the other men. No one admitted it. That was something we kept to ourselves.

Ahead in some valley plain, or on some wooded hill, or some town street shattered by shellfire, inside a building or when we came around a corner or opened a door, death waited for some of us. For others it would be screaming pain. For the rest there was survival, a survival filled with terrible memories. I looked about. Some of us would not return, others would, some with shattered bodies, some with hideous memories. I asked myself, "Will it be me?" I put that thought aside. Instead, I concentrated on trying to sleep, to close myself off, not to think. I shifted my mind into neutral.

Even in riding, there was waiting. There is that old Army expression, "Hurry up and wait."

Our journey seemed endless as the long line of trucks rolled ahead. The convoy moved along at a snail's pace.

Ahead, the shellfire grew louder.

It was cold and wet. We were miserable in spite of the fact we were covered by a tarp. For a moment I felt like I was in a covered wagon. It would be worse when we had to walk. I hated to think of that. My only consolation was that each moment that passed drew us closer to the end of the war.

Ominous rumblings echoed from a twilight horizon rimmed with red explosions of artillery fire. Was it our fire, or the enemy's? As we came closer to the front, we tried to talk as we jounced about. We never talked about what was to come, and we never spoke of our inner fears. Instead we talked about home and our lives before the army.

The roar of the truck's engine drowned our attempts at conversation. We couldn't talk much. Maybe a few words. What was there to talk about? Would we be afraid? Would we be wounded? Would we die? These were questions men don't ask each other.

Our two-and-a-half-ton truck was packed with men and equipment. It had been worse when we had our duffle bags, but these were left at regimental headquarters. For two hours some sat on the cold, steel bed of the truck, some on the board benches on each side of the truck bed, all shaken by every jounce as we were jostled.

As we lurched forward to the front lines, a growing crescendo of artillery reverberated in the gathering night. We were frightened. Tonight, tomorrow we would experience Infantry combat.

The convoy moved forward. Closer. Closer. And the shelling grew louder and louder.

I turned to Flynn and shouted, "Aren't we ever going to get there?"

"What's the hurry, Kid? Enjoy the ride," he said as he flashed a smile, but there was that haunted look in his eyes. I knew he was still living with his premonitions.

Flynn always called me Kid. He was older, twenty-six, twenty-seven maybe. I was eighteen-and-a-half. I wished he wouldn't call me Kid. I wasn't a boy amidst men. As I sat there, I thought, *I'll show these old guys when we get there. I'll show them.* I asked myself, what will combat be like? I didn't want to die. I certainly didn't want to be maimed. My life had barely begun. I'd necked in parlors with girlfriends, but I'd never been with a woman. And what about my parents? They had expended so much of their adult lives in raising me, an only child. Their lives centered on me. What would happen to them if I became another Gold Star on their block?

A tall, lean Texan, sitting against the truck cabin, muttered, "I wish to hell I could have a smoke."

There was no smoking while we were in the truck, but some of the guys had a quick smoke as they took a leak during our hourly piss calls. They carefully saved what was left of the butt for the stop. Any moment of smoking was precious to them. I didn't smoke. I tried it once in high school after a dance. It made me sick.

Another guy said, "Hammer on the cab and say you gotta take a leak."

"Hey, Sarge," the Texan yelled at the driver, "I gotta take a piss."

A hoarse voice growled from inside the cab, "Piss off the back. There's no stopping until the point truck says so."

We all took turns as we lurched ahead into the twilight.

Finally, the trucks ground to a halt, and the driver shouted, "Piss call!"

It was good to take a leak on solid ground. The air was filled with the smell of urine and cigarettes.

"Saddle up!" someone called.

We clambered back into the bed of the truck and claimed our places. There was jostling and bitching as we settled in, each where he sat before.

Each of us was alone within ourselves, alone amidst the twenty men in the back of this grinding truck.

Flynn tried to stretch out. "Watch where you're putting your goddamned feet," a guy opposite him muttered out of a half-sleep.

"Sorry."

Flynn pulled his feet back and mumbled, "My goddamn foot is asleep."

"So what? My ass just died," the Texan said.

"This is a crock, a large steaming crock of shit," a Southerner added.

"Was that what I smelt?" the Texan asked.

It was amiable bitching.

By now we could hear small arms fire.

The convoy stopped.

"Dismount!"

The command echoed up and down the long line of trucks. We had stopped in the middle of a small town in Luxembourg.

"Where the fuck are we?" someone asked in the truck in front of us.

"Beats the shit outa me," a hoarse voice replied.

A buck sergeant we didn't know joined us and said, "Ease up, we're sleeping indoors tonight. Column of two, each side of the road!"

We picked up our gear.

"Forward, harch!"

There was a long line ahead of us. It was barely lit by a quarter moon. As we trudged forward towards a small hotel, the sounds of a distant battle rose ahead of us.

I asked myself, "Will I still be alive tomorrow?"

*   *   *

During one stop for the night, we stayed in an old hotel in Luxem-bourg.[13] It had a winding staircase. It was a simple building with no decorations. The rooms were just as austere. Our boots echoed as we climbed to our high-ceilinged rooms.

Four of us were assigned to a bed. What we thought were loose mat-tresses on top of the beds were called eiderdowns. I understand that the French and British call them duvets. They were down-filled coverlets that Germans used instead of blankets. Once under one, you became almost too warm. Our billet for the night had no heating, so these covers were badly needed. In fact, they were much warmer than the single Army woolen blanket we carried in our packs.

As I drifted off to sleep, I heard distant shellfire. I tried to ignore those ominous rumblings. Soon I would be sleeping in a newly dug foxhole, or as I later had to, on the bare ground. I finally managed to get a decent night's sleep. In the morning we went to a nearby mess tent and had a substantial breakfast. Then we got in our trucks and moved forward toward that relentless shellfire.

* * *

In the winter of 1967, I passed through Luxembourg again. By chance, I stayed at the same hotel we stayed in that night. It was an eerie feeling climbing those same winding stairs and again hearing the sound of footsteps echoing in that stairwell. The rooms were the same. Perhaps the eiderdown covers were the same as I had slept under more than two decades before. This time there was no distant shellfire, but there were uneasy dreams throughout an unsettled night.

* * *

As we moved forward, we passed through shattered Metz and on to Trier.[14] Just before we came to Trier we crossed into Germany. Others had broken the Siegfried Line. The damage about us was recent. Metz was flattened, and Trier was devastated. That night we again heard the

---

13   The distance from Le Havre, France, to Luxembourg is approximately 325 miles (calculated using the roads that existed during World War II).

14   The distance from Le Havre to Trier is approximately 380 miles.

thunder of artillery and saw red flashes of distant shellfire ahead in the dark night sky.

Human bodies were being shattered just ahead of us. I spent a restless night. Now I was even closer to the front. What lay ahead? Would I live through the next day? Or would my body be maimed? These were the questions that raced through my mind. At such a time it is better not to have much imagination. None of us spoke our fears. That would have been less than manly.

My private apprehensions went deeper. The dysentery I contracted in the *Aquitania* persisted. Even while riding in a truck it gnawed away at my energy. My ankle was yet to be tested. At best I could move at half my normal speed, and I had never been very fast afoot. I kept these fears to myself.

Years later, Linda and I visited Trier. There were remnants of a Roman amphitheater and arena on the edge of the city. By now all the war damage was gone. It was a prosperous city, a brief tourist stop. As we wandered the Roman ruins, I thought of battles reaching back nearly two millennia. I was glad I missed the fight for Trier. Thanks to a pair of eyeglasses, I had been spared that bloody chore.

The shellfire remained a constant reminder of the dangers in store for us. Now the fiery red night sky was like a continuing sunset. It seemed to me that Hell was straight ahead and there was no escaping it. Our men were dying out there in that shellfire. We also knew Germans were dying, too.

During the day, formation upon formation of bombers flew over us. They were headed to the center of Germany. I can still hear that relentless dull roar of their engines. Closer still were our low flying fighter planes zooming ahead of us as they strafed and dive-bombed German positions. It was open season on humanity.

Soon we would be hunters and the hunted simultaneously. I remained apprehensive, but I don't remember being afraid. In looking back, I don't understand my stoic acceptance of what lay ahead of me. I later heard other veterans talk about "the numbness" that came over them in combat. Perhaps it was a merciful psychological mechanism protecting me. It certainly was not courage.

I had been more afraid about what was to come at the POE and on the *Aquitania*. All that sound of shelling ahead of me and the roaring air activity was a great spectacle to an eighteen-year-old boy. For the moment life was more like a movie than the reality it became. For the moment no one was shooting at me. War was a spectacle.

Close Order Drill

Our last stop before we were assigned to our outfits was at the headquarters of the 417th Infantry Regiment's First Battalion. Our equipment was re-checked, and we were issued our weapons, ammunition, and grenades. My M1 was well worn. I wondered how many hands it had passed through. I felt some security in being able to hold it in my hands and sense its balance.

Our teeth were quickly examined. The dentist discovered I had eight cavities. In looking back, I wonder why this had not been discovered before I went overseas.

It was Army policy that men going into combat had to have their teeth in good condition. This meant another delay. I didn't mind. By now, any delay was welcome. The downside of this was that any friends I made at the POE, during the ocean crossing, and at Camp Tareyton moved on ahead of me. Flynn and I had remained together while we passed from army to division Repo Depots. It had been a great comfort to have my new friend on this journey. However, when we reached our battalion command post, we were separated. Flynn was assigned to Baker Company. I would be sent to Charley Company. Now I really was on my own. I felt alone in a sea of soldiers.

I stayed behind for two days of dental work. There was no novocaine. A corporal was assigned to power the primitive drill with a foot pedal. Once in a while he would become bored, his pedaling slowed, and the drilling would become more labored. The pain was excruciating.

The dentist did not help alleviate my pain. He was a foul-mouthed man in his thirties who was obsessed with sex. I believe he thought he could avert my attention from my pain by telling me about his sexual adventures with German and French women in graphic detail. His stereotyping of these women could have caused another war. He preferred *Fräuleins* for their personal hygiene, but *mademoiselles* in his view were far ahead when it came to oral sex. German women, he opined, were perpetually horny since their husbands had been away from home for years. He claimed that they usually did the deed for free. The more practical French women tended to seek payment either in money or luxury items such as soap, silk stockings (where would we get these?), chocolate bars, and cigarettes.

The dentist believed that the cigarettes were for their lovers and husbands. Of course, he believed that French men sent their wives out to supplement the family income. His own wife at home fell far behind on his merit scale. She had reserved sexual activity until after their marriage and insisted on the missionary position. Worse still, according to his graphic descriptions, her personal hygiene was quite deficient.

He finally finished filling my teeth with a flourish and announced, "I'm seriously considering divorcing my wife and moving to Europe after this damned war is over."

Since I grew up in a world where pornography was not easily available, his graphic stories exceeded anything I had heard – or could even begin to imagine –before. After two days of writhing in pain as he described his acrobatic sexual adventures, I was ready to face the worst the Germans had to offer. Or at least I thought I was.

The weather was dry and warmer during our second and final ride to the front. The truck ride forward again reminded me of what was ahead. The debris of battle became newer with each passing mile. At one point, on either side of a road were bloated cattle killed amidst a battle. They were caught in the middle of a war that was not theirs, and they died. The animals were the real innocents.

Later that day we passed a cluster of dead German soldiers who had been burned alive with a flamethrower. In that moment the war became immediate to me. Their blackened bodies were twisted together in a hideous sculpture; their moment of death was frozen in time. That sight has been seared into my memory all my long life. It still wrenches my guts. Worse still, I will never forget the smell of decaying, burned flesh. Someone would have to pry them apart and bag their bodies. Goya[15] caught the horrors of war so deftly, but this manmade three-dimensional object seated so close to the road exceeded that great artist's vision of man's inhumanity to man.

---

15   Francisco Goya (1746-1828) was considered one of the most important Spanish painters of the late 18th and early 19th centuries. He was known as a printmaker, a portraitist, and a muralist. His *Disasters of War* series of prints, as well as many of his other paintings and drawings, remain powerful artistic statements on the human condition and humankind's inhumanity to its own peoples.

I never again saw the aftermath of what happened to human beings killed by flamethrowers. This terrible weapon was used extensively in the Pacific but rarely in Germany. I suspect that this cruel horror was reserved mainly for the Japanese. After all, I suppose our leaders reasoned, the Germans were from the same race as us. I wonder if we would have used the atom bomb against a German city if it had been available while the war raged in Europe. I doubt it.

By now we knew that we were very close to the front since our Graves Registration units had not picked up those German bodies. Ahead in the distance we heard the persistent shellfire. Battles were being fought within the range of our hearing. Soon we would be in one of these battles. I shook away any thoughts of death and worried about being maimed or in terrible pain. Or being burned alive.

When we moved forward, we passed those unfortunate Graves Registration men as they scoured a battlefield for bodies. Their faces were empty, and their complexions were almost as gray green as the dead they collected and bagged. Their grisly job was an extension of the "policing" an area after a day of training. Then we moved along a line, picking up cigarette butts and scraps of paper and debris. Now the debris was the dead. Now the smell of the recently dead spread across this dying land.

One gruesome detail of Graves Registration duty was making sure the bodies were identified. They took off a dead soldier's dog tags which had indentations on each side. The tag was placed in the soldier's mouth and the jaw was kicked shut, forcing the dog tag between the teeth. Then they placed the body in a sleeping bag, zipped it up, and threw it on a truck. How haunted these slow thinking men must have been in the years after the war. What terrible dreams they must have had. No, what terrible dreams they must still have. None of us would have left combat for this less dangerous job.

Those who were relegated to Graves Registration included soldiers who tested low on the AGC test and Blacks. Combat infantry squads were not integrated until after the Rhine was crossed. Even then, that blending of troops was minimal. I never served with a Black man during my days in the Army. Many Blacks drove the trucks for the Red Ball Express, units that brought supplies to the front.

There was one Black infantry unit in Italy that served with great courage and distinction. Their combat record was only matched by a Japanese unit. Native Americans, however, served in many combat units on all fronts during the war. Through some crazed form of logic, they were not seen as racially different from whites.

As we moved toward the front, I saw no American bodies. They were immediately removed from the battlefields we passed through. Being a victor had its perquisites. The picking up of German bodies came last. Later I learned that many German families never found out the fate of their sons. This was especially true on the Russian front.

In time I grew immune to the sight of torn and mangled bodies. Dead bodies around us became part of our day. Within a few days we walked past our fallen comrades and paid no attention to them. The human mind and its memory mechanisms can be merciful.

14

Patton's Third Army

A LITTLE HISTORY might be useful here. The 76th Infantry Division – nicknamed Onaway – landed in England on December 21, 1944, received additional training, and arrived in Le Havre, France on January 12, 1945. After relieving the besieged 101st Airborne at Bastogne and halting the German advance during the Battle of the Bulge, the Third Army was assigned to the VIII Corps on January 18, 1945. Its strength was listed at 350,296 men, with a total of 34,000 under strength. Most of the shortage was in infantry divisions, particularly rifle companies.[16] It immediately went into action and distinguished itself in a night crossing of the flood-swollen Sauer River near Echternach, on February 7. After crossing the swiftly flowing river, the 76th stormed 1,600 yards into the pillbox-infested Siegfried Line. For this it received a Presidential Unit Citation.

Our informal Battalion history, *Always First*,[17] which I helped write and illustrate after the war ended, reports in more detail on the events that happened with the 76th prior to my arrival at the front lines:

---

16 The Third Army strength numbers for January 19, 1945, as cited in *Patton's Third Army, A Daily Combat Diary*, Copyright © 1992 by Charles M. Province. Published by Hippocrene Books, Inc., p. 157.

17 *Always First*, Published by the 1st Battalion, 417th Infantry. 76th Infantry Division under the supervision of Major Verne E. Pate. Assistant supervisor and editor 1st Lt. John Milliken. Assistant editor T/Sgt. Clyde H. Horning, Co. C. Cartoons drawn by Pfc. Arthur Buck, Co. D, Pfc. William S. E. Coleman, Co. C, Pfc. Eugene R. Cox, Co. C and Pvt. Donald M. Geil, Hq. Co.

At Merchamps we set up a perimeter defense. Here we had our first taste of combat although it wasn't on the front lines. We stood on guard in the snow and participated in patrol activity. This was the sector of the deepest German penetration in what is known as The Battle of the Bulge. On the 25th of January we boarded trucks for Luxembourg. Arriving in Luxembourg we were established in a defensive position, with patrols going to Echternach and across the Sauer River into the Siegfried Line. It was our initial contact with the German Army.

In the cold blackness of the early morning hours on February 7th, men of the First Battalion, undergoing thus baptism of fire, embarked in small boats at Echternach, Luxembourg, to cross the swollen Sauer River and plunged into the vaunted German Westwall. In pitch dark, with the river swollen to a raging torrent, they made the crossing, under a hail of Nazi small arms, mortar and artillery fire. Men, flung into the icy waters when their boats were sunk, struggled toward the far shore. Reaching the east bank, the dough-boys stormed up the steep, slippery cliffs of Germany and plunged 1600 yards into the Siegfried Line to take and hold high ground. We became the only Battalion in all the Sauer and Our rivers crossings to reach its objective in strength on the first day.

Our Regiment was attached to the 5th Infantry Division so that unit was credited with our success, but off from all except radio contact and knowing we were evacuated, the men dug in, beat back Jerry tank counterattacks and then fought for additional ground and German pillboxes. Supplies were dropped from artillery liaison planes while engineers battled to construct bridges across the swollen river to supplement our dwindling stores.

Casualties were quite heavy, and our Battalion Medics cannot be praised too highly for their magnificent performance of duty under the most trying conditions. Story on story could be told of their heroic deeds.

The Siegfried Line at the point of our entrance was perhaps the most heavily fortified and deepest of defensive installations encountered by any of the allied Zones. Concrete forts, offering mutual fire support, were so thick that on a mathematical basis, one might be found in each 40 square yards of the ground we traversed.

On the 16th of February, our Regiment was relieved by the 385th Infantry and we moved back to the town of Berbourg, Luxembourg to reorganize, rest, and re-outfit for future action.

While at Berbourg we were issued passes to the city of Luxembourg and spent the balance of the time resting and discussing that never-to-be-forgotten river crossing. While we were relaxing, the Medics were still busy taking care of the wounded. Sunday, February 25th the entire Battalion attended a memorial service for our fellow comrades who gave their lives at the Sauer River crossing.

Sunday evening, we packed up and left Berbourg for Ferschweiler, Germany, when we detrucked and marched to Hosthum; at this point we set up a defense in the woods while preparations were made for the attack. In the evening of the 26th we moved to an assembly area near Wolsfelderberg, and in the early morning hours launched a dawn attack toward Wolfsfeld. Companies A and B cleared Wolfsfeld and Badenborn.

The next day companies A and C, with the aid of companies B and D, cleared Ittel-Kyll and moved to the high ground beyond. The Battalion closed in on Kordel and cleared it on the 2nd of March after which the Battalion went into reserve and a defensive position south of Kardel. We were relieved of our defensive position on line by 1st Battalion, 385th Infantry, and withdrew to Butzweiler and billeted. Approximately at 0230, March 5, the Battalion moved by motor convoy to Trier where we undertook offensive action to gain high ground at the bench of the Moselle River and wipe out enemy pockets of resistance.

During the early morning hours of March 5th the Battalion marched over the hill from Trier into Eitelsbach. Most of the hills were covered with vineyards instead of trees and hidden in their vineyard-covered hills were snipers that had full view of all action taking place. The town was cleared of all snipers, then C. Co. moved into Mertesdorf clearing it of all snipers. The Battalion was temporarily held up here due to snipers and direct fire weapons.

By March 5 it was estimated that the Third Army was facing about 45,000 German soldiers and about 50 tanks. My sub-dislocated ankle and the wait for an extra pair of glasses spared me from being in those intense battles.

At 0200, March 10, 1945 an attack was launched to take the high ground and clear out all snipers, as indicated on sketch. Companies reached their objectives and were dug in by dawn when the Germans counterattacked with tanks and infantry in force, capturing part of Company B and causing the remainder to withdraw. Thus leaving C Company vulnerable to the entire counterattack, who later was forced to withdraw most of the company to Mertesdorf. Prior to withdrawing, Co. D mortar men in Mertesdorf went into action and fired 340 rounds in 7 minutes to stop the counterattack.

At 0200, March 12, 1945, Co. A left their position and moved through Mertesdorf to launch another attack on the hill from which Co. C was found to withdraw, and this time we drove the Germans out and held our objective. Late that afternoon the 43rd Squadron, 3rd Cavalry moved into our position thus returning us. As we were having the hill, Jerry started to throw everything he had back on the hill, but this time we were gone and the 43rd Squadron was getting the counterattack. We then moved by motor convoy to Rodt.

On the 15th of March we entrucked and left Rodt for Rivenich when the Battalion relieved the 2nd Cavalry on the 16th of March.

Here we set up a defensive position, with patrols moving to the South side of the Moselle River.

On the 17th of March the Battalion received an order that the "Articles of War" had to be read and explained to all EM. As always, the men put up a big howl – Why they had to listen to the "Articles of War" when the enemy was throwing intermittent artillery fire at us. But as good soldiers they sat down and listened to them being read and explained. We left Rivenich at 0900, 20th of March for Wiebelsheim where we remained in reserve waiting for the Division order to move.

I vividly remember this reading of *The Articles of the War*. These *Articles* had to be read to all soldiers regularly. They were our law, and the Army wanted us to know that law. If we disobeyed any one of these commandments, we were severely punished. Nothing was said about the Geneva Conventions, but we knew the protocol for the treatment of prisoners and that we should not shoot at German medics.

The *Wehrmacht* knew them too. They rarely shot at our medics either. If they did, I would like to think it was a mistake or they had not seen the white cross on our medics' helmets. Now these *Articles* are called *Rules of Engagement*.

Few Americans were taken prisoner during my time in combat. Mass surrenders of Americans ended with the Battle of the Bulge. We were only at risk during patrols. The real danger was being captured by a *Waffen SS* division. The *Wehrmacht* was more humane in its treatment of prisoners. This wasn't true in the Pacific. The death rate for the Allied prisoners of Japan was 27 percent, far greater than the rate for British and American soldiers in German captivity, which was about 4 percent. Nevertheless, we feared being captured.

After the battle at Trier, the 76th took up positions near where the Moselle and Rhine rivers meet to ensure the security of the main lines of communication, and to remain on the defensive.[18] When I arrived at

---

18   Ibid. The information is from *Patton's Third Army, A Daily Combat Diary. p. 199*

the front, Patton was poised to cross the Rhine. Again, he was held in reserve in order to let British Field Marshal Montgomery and his Twenty-First Army Group seize the bridgehead over the Rhine River north of the Ruhr.[19] The weather continued to be a problem as well.

*   *   *

---

19   The cautious and political Eisenhower feared how Americans at home would react to letting Patton go on the attack, even though many historians believe that the war would have ended before Christmas if Patton had been unleashed simultaneously with D-Day.

15

CHARLEY COMPANY

"You were so scared that you were brave."

Survivor of Omaha Beach

CHARLEY COMPANY WAS a rifle company. There was no one ahead of a rifle company except Germans. That meant we were on the front lines. When I joined C Company on or about March 15, the squad was bivouacked in Rivenich, a small German village a short distance from where the Moselle River joined the Rhine. Our truckload of replacements dismounted and was assigned to different platoons of Charley Company of the First Battalion of the 417th Infantry Regiment of the 76th Infantry Division, then assigned to Patton's Third Army.

I trudged into the Second Platoon's billet at nightfall. For the moment we lived in an old farmhouse as our outfit ran patrols. Digging in for the night would come later.

I was one of three replacements assigned to the First Squad of the Second Platoon. Nick Fox, a Texan, was appropriately tall and lean, and brimming with energy and enthusiasm. He was a good soldier and cheerful company even when things were at their darkest. The other, Larry Freeman, was a rangy, rawboned Georgian who looked a little like the actor Chuck Connors.

The three of us brought the squad back to full strength. Now we were twelve. We knew we were replacing men who had had been badly wounded or died. No one spoke of those who were no longer with the squad. It was as though they had never existed.

We reported to Charley's commander, Captain Walker. I never knew his first name. He was immensely popular with his men, and we liked and admired him. When we advanced as a company, he was always near the point. I believe he had been with C Company since the 76th went on line, but I am not sure. He had grown prematurely bald in his few weeks of combat. Some say it was the result of an allergy to the wool knit cap we all wore under our helmets. I suspect that his hair loss was more from the pressure of leadership under fire.

After he had interviewed Fox and Larry, he asked me the usual question, "When were you born, Private Coleman?"

He crosschecked my reply with my record folder. I'd heard his reply too many times during basic and before I shipped out, "They're getting younger by the day."

When I joined my outfit, we had no platoon lieutenant. The last one died in an earlier action. The Second Platoon's acting commander, Staff Sergeant Piatt, escorted us to the billet of the First Squad. He was a small, handsome man whose face resembled Henry Fonda's sensitive look. He had acquired a noticeable limp during earlier combat. I don't know if this was due to an injury, a wound, or just plain weariness. He was very capable and a great deal of fun when he got going.

Piatt was our platoon's acting Lieutenant. He should have received a battlefield commission, but he did not. He held a first sergeant's rank. In time, I found out that most platoon lieutenants were superfluous. The platoon was usually run, and run well, by a first sergeant and those immediately below him.

We functioned very well without an officer. Our non-coms attained their positions because they survived the bloody days before I joined the squad. They survived, and then they led – and they led well. Even though they were close to us, they led us when the chips were down. They did not need the separation that officers demanded. Because of that remoteness, many officers did not lead as well as the non-coms.

Our officers had commandeered several of the quaint old farmhouses in a fairytale village nestled in a thick Rhineland pine forest. Each squad had its own house. There was no electricity in this backwoods village, so kerosene lanterns lit our night hours. Their glimmering, yellow light added a sense of coziness to our billet.

Our farmhouse combined a barn with living quarters. There was a festering manure pile at the back of our house. It generated heat in winter.

This ingenious, if rather noxious, arrangement reflected the German efficiency. The kitchen was less than sanitary. Chickens roamed about its dirt floor. The owners, who lived elsewhere at night, returned in the morning to check and feed their livestock. They never mentioned that some of their chickens were missing.

We were cordially greeted when we entered the main room of our billet. Four men were out on a night patrol. One was AWOL in Paris. The rest played cards, shot craps, and cleaned their weapons. I was amazed. The room looked as if it had been designed by Walt Disney for *Snow White and the Seven Dwarfs*.

The first to greet us was our Squad Leader, Buck Sergeant Mike Lipesky. He had a broad Slavic face that often broke into an infectious smile. He was near my height, but he carried more weight than I did at that time. I was about 5'9" and weighed about 150 pounds.

Mike was gentle and quiet, but he exuded confidence. He led by example, with quiet assurance and great patience, not by command or edict. Later I learned that while he was only a few months older than me, he had already led the Squad in some very serious action. We couldn't have had a better Squad Leader. Soon we became friends. After the war we wrote for a while. Then our friendship drifted away as did all my wartime friendships. I hope Mike had a good life. I often think of him.

Mike quickly got down to business. Larry and I were assigned to dig in together. Larry and Fox became riflemen since their marksmanship rating was higher than mine. I was appointed Assistant Browning Automatic Rifleman (BAR). My job was to carry extra ammunition cartridges. Reed, our BAR man, was approaching thirty and had a family back home. He was quiet in manner, but he gave me solid basic instruction in how we would work as a team. I always had to be close to him as he set up a base of fire. That way, I could toss him more ammunition if he ran out. Sometimes, on longer marches, Reed took my rifle; and I carried the twenty-pound BAR.

I have long forgotten the names of some of our squad members, but I do remember Lawrence Stallins, a lean, grizzled man in his late thirties. He had a talent to complain, but it was always tinged with wit. Being a good old boy from North Carolina, his speech was a lazy drawl.

There was another older man who was part of our bazooka team. I don't remember his name. He moved more slowly with each passing day and developed a pronounced limp. Obviously, he was in continual pain, but he persisted. He never gave up. He said little. I soon found that as my body wore down during combat I said less and less. I focused on making the next step, on surviving.

Jimmy McElhanney[20] had been a garbage man in Philadelphia. Everyone called him "Mac." I was warned that you didn't want to cross Mac or make him angry. He was a dangerous and violent man. He was proud of his collection of gold German wedding rings and gold teeth he had kicked out of the mouths of dead Germans. I have a pair of *Wehrmacht* field glasses that I bought from him when he needed money to stay in a crap game.

Custis Bibb Rootes, a.k.a. "Rooter," was a different case. Rooter[21] had grown up on a small farm in South Carolina. He was addicted to gambling, and especially craps. Soon we discovered he had devised a way of sliding the dice in a way that increased his odds of winning. Otherwise, he was not very bright. In combat, he was virtually useless. Near the end of the war, we found he had never fired his rifle. He didn't want to have the bother of cleaning it! When we were on occupation duty, he got into deep trouble with venereal disease. He was, and perhaps still is, an aggravating and fascinating human being.

Another younger man, Donnie[22] – I forget his last name – was in the midst of an emotional breakdown. The rigors of combat had shattered his spirit. He sat by himself and shivered from time to time. Two days after we crossed the Rhine, he broke. He was thrown on the back of a jeep until the end of the day's march. Shaking and crying, he laid on a stack of backpacks and other supplies. Then he was sent to a rear area hospital for treatment. When he returned, he was assigned to company headquarters as a runner. He was despised by the other men. Perhaps some feared his battle fatigue was contagious. Many saw a psychological breakdown under combat pressure as a sign of weakness. Hidden within all of us was a fear that it might happen to us. I felt sorry for him even though I thought a mental breakdown was something one could control and stop. Several other soldiers in the company treated him cruelly.

Before long I became acquainted with the term "million-dollar wound." It was a wound that would not impair you, but one bad enough to get you

---

20 Many of the names in this book have been modified or changed.

21 Not his real name.

22 *Idem.*

sent home. There was talk of self-inflicted wounds. I suspect at least one of the men no longer in the squad had taken this route out of the war. There was no disapproval, just a discussion of how it was one way out of the continuing battle all infantrymen faced. I would soon find out what would drive men to such thoughts. Years later such a wound became key to the plot of my war play, *Pillars in the Night*.

Larry Freeman, who came to the front with me, quickly became my best friend. It was a friendship that continued after the war. We corresponded as we started college. Finally, one of us dropped the ball and the correspondence drifted away. The son of a sharecropper, he grew up in poverty. Unlike many of the Southerners I encountered in the Army, he had finished high school and was very intelligent. When we moved out, I dug in with him. Reed continued digging in with another member of the squad. When we marched or went on the attack, I stayed close to Reed.

Two or three of the men in my squad were colorless. They quietly did their duty and said little.

These were some of the members of my squad. I may have some mixed in with men in other squads of our platoon since we were usually billeted as a group. Those I remember had vivid personalities and a unique view of life. All our backgrounds differed. I have faded group pictures of several of our squad members. I can name all but two.

The twelfth man was AWOL in Paris. He'd been the Assistant Squad Leader. No one spoke of his absence with rebuke. Instead, they spoke of Carlos Bustamante with respect.

Our company kitchen was still catching up with us, so we dined on one of the least popular GI foods, K-rations. I dutifully cleaned my M1 after dinner. Soon it was time to turn in. I joined three others in a wide bed. While we had no heat, the duvets kept us warm. Again, I heard distant shelling. Mike Lipesky assured me that it came from a battle on the other side of the Rhine.

"Miles away, Kid, miles away. And it's going their way."

After breakfast, Mike took Fox, Larry, and me on a daylight patrol. This was to give us a sense of what was to come, and to build our confidence.

We carried our M1s, ammunition belts, and trench knives. A half-dozen grenades hung from the buttonholes in our fatigues. Our bedding and other equipment were left behind. On patrol you traveled light.

Mike's first instruction was simple and clear, "I don't care if you have a clear shot, I don't want any sniping. Our job isn't to let them know where we are or if we've ever been there. Our job is to collect information and pull out. If they see us and start shooting, bug out and meet us in the village."

We stayed off the dirt roads and trudged through thick pine needle droppings. A blue-green daylight filtered through the dense tree cover. My body was at full alert. I held my M1 at the ready. There was a bullet in its chamber, and its safety was off. I couldn't relax even though there were no Germans in sight. Might they be lurking in the next cluster of trees or bushes? Or had they retreated across the Rhine?

Finally, we arrived at the bluffs that loomed over where the Moselle River flowed into the Rhine. We remained within tree cover as we peered across the Rhine. There the Germans were moving heavy equipment into the hills. Were they withdrawing, or were they setting up new defensive positions in the hills? Mike would report what he had seen to Battalion Headquarters, and Intelligence would evaluate the information we gathered.

By late afternoon I was comfortably reading *Double Indemnity*, a popular James M. Cain novel, by kerosene lantern. My first day of Infantry combat had been a long hike, looking at German maneuvers, and returning. I was relieved. I hadn't received my baptism by fire in a pitched battle.

Shortly after I nodded off, our missing squad member, the legendary Carlos Bustamante, arrived. He had been to Paris on leave and had overstayed a few days, resulting in being listed as AWOL. For that he lost his Corporal rank, but Mike made sure he was still our assistant squad leader. Buster, as we called him, was a darkly handsome Texan Mexican in his mid-twenties. He spoke with a slight accent. He had led a hard life as an impoverished Texas border Hispanic. He freely admitted he'd spent some of his teenage years in a reformatory for committing petty crimes in the depths of the Great Depression. I often wonder what became of him in the postwar years. I'd like to think that he had a long, good life.

Buster immediately regaled us with stories of his sexual encounters with French women. I can remember him saying more than once, "Those French *mademoiselles*, they fuck like minks."

One woman in particular had taken a special liking to Buster and invited him to stay with her for a few days. Buster, of course, decided to abandon sightseeing and concentrate on international relations of a more primal sort. He had no intention of deserting. He just wanted to enjoy a few more of the sensual aspects of Parisian life until his money and barter goods ran out. Then he dutifully returned to our squad. Captain

Walker recognized Buster's importance. Within a week Buster's Corporal stripes were restored.

I soon learned that Mike and Buster were excellent teachers. They taught us the ins and outs of Infantry combat during breaks. Usually, they were small details that a greenhorn could overlook. Mike was a man of few words; but when he used them, they counted. More importantly, he taught by example.

Buster, in addition to leading most night patrols, was our main teacher. His teaching methods were more dramatic than Mike's. Buster prepared us for intense combat with his stories and opinions. He was not trained or required to do this. He did it as though it was second nature to him. In the days and weeks to come I put his teachings to good use. Everything he said was valid. One of the reasons I survived combat was because of Buster's instructions.

I remember a few of his lessons. His first was that the closer you got to the enemy the safer you were. Germans, like Americans, hated fighting with bayonets or knives. The drafted *Wehrmacht* troops were sensible. If they were outgunned or outnumbered, they surrendered. The *Waffen SS* were not as reasonable. They were not as tough as legends have them, but they were committed ideologically. Buster told us they should be killed without mercy. He taught us to move, to zig and zag when under fire. He told us that there were few casualties from rifle fire because it was difficult to move and fire with accuracy. It was equally difficult to be shot if one kept moving in unpredictable patterns. He also taught us that when we heard the distant cough of a mortar firing, we had three or four seconds to find cover. I put this to good use in street fighting. He also told us that the Germans smelled bad, so if we were on night patrol, we needed to sniff for their smell. Later I found that this intense body odor was due, in part, to a diet dominated by cabbage.

Mike Lipesky added other details. He was more concerned with how our squad acted as a unit. Indeed, when we were under fire, we acted as a single unit. We were all that an Infantry squad should be. Mike was a great leader. He and Buster whipped us into shape with a minimum of words.

I remember one evening when he was discussing the problems of getting wounded during a battle. Each platoon had a medic whose job was to crawl under fire to a wounded soldier crying for help, give him a shot of morphine (which we all carried), bind his wounds, and drag him to a safe position.

Buster's opinion differed from our untested perceptions. He enacted the moment as he rolled around in mock pain: "Don't just lie there screaming, 'Medic!' 'Medic!' Give yourself a shot, bind the wound, shut up, and wait until it's calmed down. Davy over there," he said as he pointed to our medic, "he's got forty guys to look after. Some are dying. Some are bleeding to death. And what do you have? A scratch on your ass."

Then he sat up, arms wide, and shouted, "If you yell, you're giving away a position. Keep your goddamn mouth shut, take aim, and kill another Kraut."

We were all laughing by the time Buster had finished his performance. Davy, standing to one side, was clapping his hands in approval.

Some of this information sounds simple; but when one is under fire, it's not easy to remember what one was taught. It has been said that if an infantryman can survive a week of front line combat, he has a good chance of living through the rest of the war. After that week, the only thing that can kill him is a mindless shell or a lucky shot.

Bill, (top left) with members of his Infantry Squad

OUR OWN SMALL WORLD

During my first days with my squad, I became aware that was I not in a large army, even though there were hundreds of thousands of men strung along the center of Europe. I was a member of a company made up of three rifle platoons and within those platoons were three squads. My squad was the center of my world for the time we were together as a unit. We were dedicated to helping each other and surviving. The other eleven men in my squad were very different from each other. One, at least, was a reprehensible and even cowardly human being. The rest were good men who were devoted to each other. That sense of camaraderie remains one of the remarkable experiences in my life.

As I write this, the word "machismo" and the entire concept that lies behind that word is in disrepute. I have found that simple minded in recent years. Being macho can be a bad thing, but that ability to face danger and fight back is also something of immense value. When the chips were down, we moved as one. It was like we had one mind. Some of that came out of our training. Most came from an instinctive sharing, a collective will to survive and live another day.

The men in the front-line Infantry were remarkable human beings. They paid a great price. Not the least was that horrible memory of killing another human being. That memory goes with one to the grave – and perhaps far beyond. I feel that sense of guilt. I pass it off lightly when I talk about it. I have to. "That way madness lies."

We were well indoctrinated before we were shipped overseas. This was done in large part with Frank Capra's *Why We Fight* documentaries. Once we were on the line, all that indoctrination was thrown overboard. Our main goal was to survive. If that meant moving ahead, we did. If it meant surrendering, some did. I am proud to say that I never took one step backward while I was in combat. The same can be said for all the men in my squad – with one small and understandable exception. I will describe that moment later.

The men who fought with me did so because they were trapped in an enormous machine. In the war movies of that time, one soldier always ended up making a ringing patriotic declaration of why we fought. We never once talked about the meaning and intent of what we were doing. During those rare moments when we could hide in a cellar or a village just back of the lines, our conversations dealt with our past lives and the lives we hoped to live when we came home. These conversations were a vacation from the realties about us.

I was the only one in my squad who had enlisted. All the rest had been drafted. I never mentioned my enlistment to my fellow soldiers. I was afraid that they would think I was some kind of nut. They all knew I had a semester of college under my belt, but that was all I told them. I was the only one in the squad who had progressed that far in school. Most had never finished high school. Some left after grade school.

Why did we fight? We were trapped within a great war machine, and we had no other choice. Once we were within that cruel mechanism, our main intent was to protect each other as we were commanded to advance. We did not fight for our country. We fought for our friends.

FOOD

I read somewhere that during World War II, a front line Infantry soldier required 96 bullets and six pounds of food each day. Our company kitchen was far behind us, so our GI food was K-rations. Each of its three meals was packed in a cardboard package that was slightly larger than a Cracker Jack box.[23] Each included a canned entrée and a beverage mix. Biscuits and cheese supplemented this. Those of us with dysentery traded for the cheese. It slowed our agony, but it didn't cure it.

This was rounded up with an afternoon chocolate bar, chewing gum, a packet of toilet paper, and a packet of four cigarettes.[24] Since I didn't smoke, I traded the cigarettes for other items. The three meals provided us with about 3,000 calories.

Despite our daily supplies of K-rations, our young bodies needed more food. I knew I was weakening, but there was no cure. Dysentery was not the sort of thing that sent you to a rear area hospital or aid station. I was not alone. Several others had contracted this affliction on the *Aquitania*.

---

23 Three of the companies that mass-produced military rations during World War II were The Cracker Jack company based in Chicago, Illinois; the H. J. Heinz Company, based in Pittsburgh, Pennsylvania; and Patten Food Products.

24 The Army's promotion of low cost and even free cigarettes can be credited with establishing a generation of heavy smokers.

The only thing that kept all of us going was our youthful resilience and our dogged determination to be a part of our squad.

We were constantly foraging. The crafty farmers in our village hid most of their food. We immediately set out to find it. We also stole chickens, eggs, and canned goods from the Germans when we could find them, but they were in limited supply. We quickly found that their coffee was *ersatz* – synthetic – and tasted awful. The Germans, cut off from so many of the world's goods, created artificial substitutes for almost everything.

Looting was discouraged, but no one was prosecuted for stealing food. In fact, no one was prosecuted for stealing souvenirs. My only regret is that I did not steal more. Stealing anything within the Army or looting from the enemy was called "liberating." That we did at every opportunity. However, I knew that I would have to carry any liberated loot with me. Nothing could be stored away with the hope of picking it up on our way back after the war ended. This was not an option. We had to eat what we stole.

Some men rummaged for beer, wine, and schnapps. Schnapps was greatly prized. I took sips of it, but it burned my mouth. I liked wine better, but it was not an obsession with me as it was with the other men. Those of us who didn't drink went on the prowl for food. I especially enjoyed the heavy dark bread the Germans made. I still enjoy it to this day. There was homemade cheese and long circles of hard salami. One of the Southerners nicknamed this "horse cock."

We quickly discovered that the best and easiest way to obtain sources of extra food were the supply trucks of an artillery unit stationed near us. This unit was posted on the edge of town in order to send continuous barrages of fire into the German lines ahead of us. Their C-rations were superior to ours. They came in large cardboard boxes and contained food for an entire squad. It was much better than our K-rations.

One night when hunger struck, some of us went on our own patrol. We cut our way through the thick canvas back cover of an artillerymen's truck and quietly relieved them of three or four boxes of C-rations. We had a great feast that night. Later we discarded the empty boxes further down the street. The squad that lived there was accused of the theft. Nobody was disciplined. The following morning empty ration boxes were dumped in front of our billet. Another squad had also enjoyed a feast. This time we were blamed. We denied any involvement just as the other squad had. The next night another squad received empty boxes.

The commanding officer of the artillery unit paid a visit to our company commander, Captain Walker. More denials.

Stealing from those who were better supplied did not disturb our consciences. We believed it was wrong to feed the artillerymen and tankers better than us. After all, they rode where they were going, whereas we would be marching most of the time. Our instincts told us that our midnight thievery was necessary. It added to our energy reserves, something that we were going to need in abundance when we moved out to cross the Rhine. Very soon we would learn that our instincts were so right!

Captain Walker called us out in company formation. Assembling us was not a great idea. Occasionally, the enemy lobbed in a random artillery shell. Fortunately, they were badly aimed. Our captain's message, in brief, was, "This stealing shit must cease." Of course, it did not cease. As he spoke, we noticed a semblance of a smile pass across his stern face. Had he been stealing from the artillery too? We listened gravely and resumed our late night thefts shortly after the sun set. No flashlights were needed. The shelling ahead of us dimly lighted our efforts.

We asked ourselves, what were they going to do if they caught us? Send us back to a rear area stockade? That would be a reward. By now we realized there was not much they could do to a front line infantryman for minor transgressions. Discipline was largely in our hands. The best officers knew this. They needed us more than we needed them. Our platoon was truly exempt from close supervision. Since we had not received a replacement lieutenant, First Sergeant Piatt continued to serve as our acting platoon commander. He joined us in our nightly thievery.

The angry artillerymen resorted to posting a nightly guard even as we stood guard to protect them with guard outposts on the edge of the village. That ended our foraging until they tired of standing guard on their own equipment. We resumed foraging again. Again, the empty boxes were discarded in front of another billet. There were loud complaints and dire warnings again. All of us assumed an air of boyish innocence. We were never caught.

Amidst all this, we ran day and night patrols of a more legitimate nature. They were for reconnaissance. We were ordered not to engage any German troops. The information we brought back was more important.

GERMAN WEAPONRY

The German 88s were feared by all infantrymen. They were versatile artillery pieces that could be used against aircraft, tanks, and ground troops. While our tanks had more speed and agility, German 88 shells easily pierced our tanks' armor.

Older members of our squad spoke of the terror of an intense artillery bombardment. There were tales of shells with a man's name on it. The fluttering sound of a shell coming in on our position was nicknamed "incoming mail." The few times I was shelled were moments of sheer, helpless terror. You hoped you were dug in deep enough and that there were no direct hits.

The men spoke of another fearsome weapon, "The Screaming Mimis." This was a battery of rocket launchers that released a barrage all at once. I only encountered it once. It was designed to obliterate a wide area of dug-in soldiers. Its incoming sound was truly terrifying. Thus, its nickname.

German non-coms carried the Walther P-38 pistol. It was inferior to the Luger issued to German officers. We all wanted to capture a Luger and make it part of our own personal weaponry. I handled a few. They are remarkable. When you lower them into a firing position, they seem to level themselves. The .45 pistols issued to our officers were notoriously inaccurate even at close range. Both German pistols were better.

The German grenades were inferior to ours. Our grenades fragmented on explosion into small pieces of shrapnel. They were lethal. The German grenades were concussion weapons. They might deafen you; or if they landed too close, kill you; but they were not as effective as ours. None of us liked using grenades. If you threw them too low, the enemy would have time to lob them back at you.

The German bolt-action rifles were not in the same class as our Garrand M1s. The only advantage they had was in long-range accuracy. The Germans had nothing like our aged BARs. These remarkable automatic rifles were the base of our squad firepower.

The German machine guns were mixed in their merit. They fired at an incredibly fast rate. The ripping sound of their firing was terrifying, but they burned up too much ammunition too quickly. They were nicknamed burp guns because of the sound they made. Our .30 caliber machine guns were much more effective when they were used in the right hands.

Our .50 caliber machine guns were even better. Most were mounted on jeeps and tanks.

Our mortars were equal on all accounts, but the Germans had nothing like our bazookas. These were tricky to use, but they were the only thing we had that would stop a German tank. Our tanks wouldn't, our artillery couldn't, but a two-soldier bazooka team could. I curse the American auto industry for making such ineffective, badly armored, and badly armed tanks. Those two bazooka men had to stand and fire at an enemy tank. Each shot was a tremendous act of courage. Once they fired, the flare of the rocket gave away their location. They had to cut and run quickly. One shot at a time was all they got. Two shots were an invitation to enemy fire.

BECOMING A FIGHTING UNIT

We left Rivenich at 0900, 20th of March for Wiebelsheim where we remained in reserve waiting for the Division order to move. Of course, we didn't lay around idly waiting, we sent out motorized and foot patrols to reconnoiter the roads and bridges, so when the order came to move, we would know the condition of roads and bridges. On the 23rd of March the Battalion was ordered to carry Gas Masks at all times. Again, the men put up a big howl, why must we carry those blank blank things, they are only in the way.[25]

Mike and Buster worked together in perfect harmony. Their mutual respect was obvious to all of us. We couldn't have done better than these two squad leaders. All of us trusted these two men completely. We would follow them anywhere. They never let us down, and they never made a bad decision when we were under fire.

There was a saying that if an infantryman could survive his first week of combat, the odds for his living longer improved. I received my real Infantry training by going on as many patrols as I could. There must have been more than a dozen. This paid off in the weeks to come.

An Infantry patrol numbered three to five men, with no more than five. Patrols were selected in three ways. Some were drawn alphabetically from the Company Rolls. They were made up of men who didn't know each other. Others were assigned at Platoon and Squad levels. Some of

25 *Always First.*

these patrols were assigned, others were made up of volunteers. The more dangerous called for volunteers first. I am proud to say that I volunteered often for patrol duty. Whenever Buster asked for volunteers, my hand shot up in the air. I knew I would be safer with him.

The countryside around us was hilly and forested. It was a sample of the terrain we would encounter in a few days when we crossed the Rhine. I learned survival tricks firsthand on those patrols. There were tense moments and close calls, but Buster saw to it that no one was killed or injured. Part of this was because of his daring.

We quickly learned to move swiftly and silently at night. In the day we moved from cover to cover. I hate to admit it, but I rather enjoyed going on patrol, especially if Buster led it. He seemed to live a charmed life. I wanted to hide in the shelter of his boldness. I was flattered when he asked me to be part of his night – and day – patrols. He often did that. As he mentored me, he, too, used the nickname of "Kid." Of all the men in the squad I looked the youngest. Buster became one of my best friends. I valued that friendship. I felt that I had been admitted to a very exclusive club.

As a patrol leader Buster was a genius. He was aggressive on patrol, and even more so in day-to-day front line action. He was a prime example of Patton's ideas about fighting a war; but unlike our General safely back at his headquarters, Buster's daring was his leading us deep into enemy lines. I vividly remember going on his patrols. The enemy never expected us to be as far behind their lines as we were under Buster's courageous leadership. We often went as far as five or six miles behind enemy lines. Our main fear was being cut off and captured.

Our night patrols were three or four hours of unrelieved tension. We never knew what lay ahead as we moved forward in the darkness. Nothing much happened in those first patrols, but they were valuable learning experiences for me. They also tested the grinding and pain in my right ankle. That pain, plus the dysentery, was always with me.

Day patrols provided different tensions. You were exposed even as you moved from cover to cover. Sometimes while on patrol, we ventured to the bluffs overlooking the Rhine. We were close to where the Moselle joined the Rhine. I remember passing through those thick Rhineland forests. There was a pine smell in the air, and the light of day filtered down in a bluish haze. If no enemy had been lurking ahead, it would have been a mystical and special place. However, each step was filled with danger. We soon found that most of the regular German troops had withdrawn across the Rhine. Even so, we could not relax on patrol. There were snipers and rear guards. I was always tense during daytime patrols. I felt vulnerable. A single German soldier could end my life with one well-aimed shot. I much preferred being shrouded in night than exposed on a daylight patrol.

Standing Guard.

If we encountered a sniper, we took cover and headed in another direction. German snipers hid themselves well, so we did not take the time to hunt them down. Our business was to collect information.

In those first days I was on the line it was much like we were going to work. There were usual duties, policing our quarters, and standing perimeter guard. Otherwise, we were on our own. We were on the front lines, but most of the time there was little danger, especially compared to what other divisions were going through as they advanced to their positions along the Rhine. By now the Germans were on the other side of the river.

There were no big battles or even firefights. We would go out on patrol, wander about behind the German lines and return. Our patrol leader would file a report about what we had seen or not seen. After each patrol we returned to our snug billet. We knew that our perimeter would delay any attack. Once we came in from a patrol, we resumed our foraging for food. We also slept as many hours as possible. The rest of the time we spent talking about our lives back home and a variety of other subjects. Those who had experienced combat instructed us in tactics not taught in basic training. I was fortunate that my first days on line mainly involved patrol action. I had time to learn the skills I needed in the weeks ahead.

As we edged into combat, we learned informal and sometimes profane terms. To attack quickly and withdraw was "to fart and depart." To move quickly we were ordered to move "on the double" or "to haul ass." Another command for an advance was "hubba-hubba-hubba!" That term was also a male expression when he saw an especially beautiful young woman. To move out on attack we were often ordered to "rock and roll." Years later this became a musical term.

The older men regaled us with tales of the sex lives they enjoyed back home. These graphic tales generated great frustration among those of us who were eighteen-year-old virgins. Many of the young German women were attractive, and many were more than willing to have sex with their conquerors, but the Army had a non-fraternization policy. We were forbidden to speak to any German, male or female, or to have any social or physical contact with enemy women. That policy continued into the Occupation when the war ended. Sex-starved GIs defied it again and again with the more lusty young women. However, while we were in that small German village, we saw few attractive young women.

I suspect wary parents had spirited their young daughters off to an even smaller village that was free of American troops. After all, enemy troops were known to rape and pillage. They were not aware that most American troops had little interest in rape. Seduction, yes. However, we were not beneath liberating souvenirs from German houses. Among mine are German epaulets and an Iron Cross. In addition, I have wads of the inflation money circulated in Germany during the German depression following the end of World War I, a depression that gave Hitler an issue to create his Nazi government.

During these first days I thought that if this is war, it isn't that bad; but the shellfire and air strikes I heard far ahead of us told me it was going to get much worse. The Germans were being softened for the attack to come. I wondered how battered they would be when we crossed the Rhine. The older men told us that worse was yet to come. They were right.

There are stories that older infantrymen dumped dangerous patrols and actions on the replacements. Some say this drawing back from danger by combat veterans explains why some of them survived so long in combat. That may be true in other outfits, but the older men survived in ours because they were combat wise. Most taught us how to survive in a firefight or shelling. Never once did the older members of my squad dump undesired duty on Larry, Fox, and me. Instead, they sheltered us and taught us how to survive. We felt we were an integral part of a fighting unit in a handful of days.

Some say, and rightly so, that an Infantry squad becomes a family that's determined to protect its members from a hostile world. I say we became a country of twelve very different men who were fighting for each other's survival. We became the country we were fighting for. We were our main cause. All else seemed distant and far away, but our twelve men were a living breathing reality. We depended on each other. I am alive because of these fine, brave men.

A week or so after I arrived at the front, our platoon was assigned Lt. Stanley Terebinski. Even though he joined us only a few days after we had arrived, we were now more experienced in the wiles of Infantry combat than he was. You learn fast in combat, or you die quickly. Each day of survival added at least two more days of survival to the normal week of survival allotted to front line infantrymen.

Terry, as we called him when he was not around, had been a night-club magician and knew all the tricks of a card sharp. He performed his magic tricks for us, but he would not play cards with his own men even though there were poker and blackjack games when we were off the line. He did his gambling in other platoons, and with officers he did not know. When he was not gambling with another outfit, he entertained us with his intricate card tricks.

Terry had just finished OCS – Officer Candidate School – at Fort Benning. When he arrived, he realized that Piatt was running our platoon very well. Terry wisely let the experienced Piatt make the major combat decisions. He wasn't much of a leader, but he did not get in our way. We liked Terry for this.

Too many replacement lieutenants tried to take command in combat situations they did not understand. Many endangered their troops. More than a few were killed by their own men out of desperation for their own safety. In Vietnam this practice was called "fragging." I was told that most of the officers who suffered this fate were West Point graduates. Why? I suspect that they were trained by officers who had fought in World War I and were teaching outdated Infantry tactics. OCS-trained officers had been taught by recent veterans of combat. I believe that most front line infantrymen agree that OCS officers were invariably better front line leaders than the West Pointers who dominate the Army's high command.

I never encountered a West Pointer while I was in combat. Infantry outfits consumed platoon officers more quickly than West Point could supply graduates. Later I learned that West Point graduates wanted a brief time in front line combat to make themselves eligible to pick up a Combat Infantryman Badge – a medal reserved for men in the rank of colonel and below. These upwardly mobile young officers often hoped for a medal, too. Some medals could easily be generated by having another young officer write up a fictional act of bravery. Awards would later give their careers a boost.

Patrols weren't recorded in our battalion log, so I can't be specific about how many patrols I went on. However, I vividly remember my last daylight patrol before we crossed the Rhine. Buster led it. Not a word was spoken as we moved through the thick Rhineland forest. The daylight that filtered through the heavy cover had an eerie green-blue tint. It could have been a setting for a fairytale. The thick mat of pine needles made walking difficult, but we were silent as we moved through the tall trees around us.

Finally, we came out of the forest onto high bluffs and saw where the Moselle joined the Rhine below us. The stately Rhine snaked through high hills. It was broader than the Allegheny River back home, but the view was very much like the one I grew up with in New Kensington. The only difference was that predominance of pine trees.

We crawled to the edge of a high bluff. Across the broad river we saw a quaint German river town. German troops moved along the river road opposite us. They seemed to be mustering forces against our crossing. Later we found they were preparing to withdraw deeper into Germany. There they intended to mount a defense against our final assault on Germany.

We could have fired across the river at the enemy, but we were ordered to observe, not to attack. Nobody broke that discipline. I did put a few Germans in the sights of my rifle. With one squeeze of my trigger, I could have killed an enemy. Buster saw me doing this and gestured for me to not shoot. His silent command was unnecessary. I had no intention of being a sniper or starting a firefight. After a moment of silent observation, Buster waved for us to regroup and return to our billet. We were relieved. It had been another routine patrol.

After almost two weeks of day and night patrols and round-the-clock perimeter guard, we were more than ready to move out. That's not to say we wanted to go into battle. We wanted a change. Waiting is a deadly thing on the front lines. No one knows what's coming next. Complete rest and relaxation is impossible.

*　*　*

Bill's Combat Infantryman Badge

It was near this time that I received my Combat Infantryman Badge.[26] Of all the awards I have received, I value it the most. Once we survived seven days of combat, we not only received the Combat Infantryman Badge but a promotion to Private First Class. The Badge paid $10 a month; the PFC rating $5. The raise was a moot point by then, given that I hadn't been paid since I was at Le Havre. Not everyone lived long enough to receive the award. In more intense action, the life of a front line infantryman was less than seven days. While our experiences so far hadn't been as bloody or dangerous as what many combat veterans had experienced in the same amount of time, we had honorably and honestly met the criteria. Very shortly we would continue to earn our award many times over.

The decoration was an extension of the Expert Infantryman Badge; this was a long, silver rectangle. Amidst a field of blue sat a silver rifle, the Springfield Arsenal Musket, Model 1795. An elliptic oak-leaf wreath, symbolizing steadfast character, strength, and loyalty was added to this decoration to indicate that an infantryman saw front line combat. I have two in my jewelry box. One was shaped to be worn as a wristband. The other remained as it was issued. Many of us wore that wristband for many years after the war. I rarely wore it. I put aside my military paraphernalia as soon as I came home.

---

26   The Combat Infantryman Badge was created in November 1943 to enhance the morale and prestige of service in the Infantry. It is awarded to infantrymen and Special Forces soldiers in the rank of colonel and below, who fought in active ground combat in units of brigade size or smaller. A Soldier must meet the following three requirements to be awarded the Combat Infantryman Badge:

1. Be an infantryman satisfactorily performing Infantry duties.

2. Be assigned to an Infantry unit during such time as the unit is engaged in active ground combat.

3. Actively engage the enemy in ground combat.

When you see a general on television wearing a Combat Infantryman Badge, it is almost certain he does not deserve to wear it. It was designed for infantrymen who survived seven days of front line Infantry combat. No one over the rank of colonel – and he had to have headed a front line company – was privileged to wear this decoration. This was an award for dogfaces – as we infantrymen were called.

In later years I resented seeing high-ranked generals wear this decoration. Few higher-ranking officers, if any, had the opportunity of commanding a front line combat group. They were too busy politicking their way upward into the upper ranks. Most never saw any kind of front line combat. The few that did, did so briefly. Combat awards were a necessity for promotion in the higher ranks of the Army. Army officers need wars to advance their careers. The trick is not to die in one. Few did.

I value my Combat Infantryman Badge above my Bronze Stars. It indicates I served in the company of brave men who faced the enemy head on and sometimes face-to-face. That elegant silver and blue badge means I served with the bravest of the brave. I am honored to have been a part of the select few who served in front line action and truly earned that badge.

16

Each Unit is an Island

"It takes 15,000 casualties to train a major-general."[27]

An Infantry outfit at the company level was a law unto itself. There was little outside of combat that frightened us. No one higher than a colonel made it to the front lines, and we saw few of those. There may have been a few exceptions, but those happened mainly when a unit was surrounded or under intense penetrating attack. I am sure that high-ranking officers found themselves in front line combat during the Battle of the Bulge. They certainly did at Normandy during that bloody landing.

Our company commander, Captain Walker, was a fine man and a great leader. He was always with us. In full company advances he led the way right behind the first scouts. Our battalion commanders stayed well behind the lines. Once in a while they would venture forward for morale purposes, but usually they kept their place in the rear echelon. They were never with us when we were advancing on an enemy objective. Only our Captain Walker stood beside us at the front. Even so, our battalion

---

27   Ferdinand Foch (1851 - 1828) was a French general and military theorist who served as the Supreme Allied Commander during World War I. He oversaw the Marne, Flanders, and Artois campaigns of 1914-1916 and, in 1918, became the Allied Commander-in-Chief of the French, British, American, and Italian forces. On November 11, 1918 Foch accepted the German request for an armistice. He considered the Treaty of Versailles to be too lenient on Germany, and as it was being signed, he declared: "This is not a peace. It is an armistice for twenty years." He did not live to see his prophecy come true twenty years and 65 days later when World War II began. Other quotes that Foch is known for include, "None but a coward dares to boast that he has never known fear," "Don't tell me that this problem is difficult. If it wasn't difficult, it wouldn't be a problem," "Accepting the idea of a defeat is being defeated...," and "In war, he who has doubts is lost: one should never doubt."

commander, Colonel Clarence A. Mette Jr. and Major Vernon Pate, his adjutant, had more decorations than the bravest among the enlisted men. How they earned these medals in rear areas remains a mystery to me.

We were aware of their absence from the front. In a way we resented it, but in another way, we were relieved. We styled our dress and use of weapons to fit our needs. We paid no attention to military rules unless they suited us. We did our work, which was to defeat the enemy and survive to fight the next day. While we did this, we hoped they ordered tactics that would work. If they did not, we improvised as good soldiers have done over many centuries.

There was an Infantry snobbery regarding what was rear echelon. The officers and non-coms at battalion level considered themselves as front line soldiers. To us, they were rear echelon. The artillery that supported us was also considered rear echelon. Since mortar men were within our rifle company they were considered to be "close" to the front lines. That is, they were about 100 yards behind us. All officers above the rank of captain were considered rear echelon. Since captains were heads of rifle companies they were not. Our captain advanced within our rifle company's attack formation. Anyone behind us was considered privileged.

PATTON

"You're going to be up to your neck in blood and guts."[28]

I never saw George Patton in person, but his presence was always with us. His Third Army was a glamour army that moved quickly and daringly. One of his famous sayings was, "We herd sheep, we drive cattle, we lead people. Lead me, follow me, or get out of my way." He also said:

> "Some goddamn fool once said that flanks have got to be secure. Since then, sonofabitches all over the globe have been guarding their flanks. I don't agree with that. My flanks are something for the enemy to worry

---

28   Patton's warning to his officers on what they should expect in combat made such an impression that he got the nickname, "Old Blood and Guts." This, in turn, resulted in a common GI saying about Patton: "our blood, his guts."

about, not me. Before he finds out where my flanks are, I'll be cutting
the bastard's throat."[29]

His brilliant tactics were like the German blitzkrieg. His attacks were
mobile and hard-hitting. Since we rarely had head-on engagements with the
Germans, our casualties were lower than those in other armies. Instead of
creating a front and moving in a mass attack, he thrust through German
defenses and circled around them, striking and enveloping them like a
cobra. Often when the Germans were isolated, they surrendered. His
columns slipped away from the hard punching battle of opposing artillery fire. If attacked, his tanks thrust ahead through openings provided
by Infantry attacks.

While much is made of the way he used his armor, he used his infantry
just as well. The twelve-man Infantry squad is a well-designed combat unit.
It can unleash a sheet of fire on an advancing attack, and that fire held
the enemy down as we moved forward. The closer we got to the enemy,
the safer we were. The Germans shared our dislike of bayonet fighting.
More often than not, they surrendered before we got close enough to use
bayonets. Was this a lack of bravery on their part? No, many knew the war
was ending. They wanted to live just as much as we did. Their manner of
ending it was to surrender, ours was to kill or capture them.

Other generals were more cautious. Montgomery, who was widely
despised in spite of his reputation in Africa, dug his troops in and spent
weeks preparing to advance. As his front line soldiers waited, they became
easy targets for shellfire. Their casualties were much higher than ours, and
they gained far less ground. They also suffered greater casualties. They
might have faced greater opposition or fought in different geographic
situations, but I think we had our own problems, too.

When you are on the attack you do not encounter as much shell and
mortar fire. The German panzers were our main danger during these
final weeks of fighting. They were fearsome and well designed, but those
of us on foot were even more mobile. Their gun turret could not swivel
fast enough to aim at us. Even so, moving amidst those behemoths was
a terrifying experience even though we knew we were relatively safe.

Our tanks, while thinly armored, moved quickly. It was the Infantry's
job to keep up with them. Without us, they did not have the protection

---

29   Said in a conference with his officers on August 1, 1944. This quote can be found
in *General Patton: A Soldiers Life* by Stanley P. Hirshon, (2002), page 502.

of our bazooka teams. Even with these brave men, our tanks pulled back until the panzers were stopped.

Once in a long time a panzer would plow into our lines and attempt a breakthrough. A few brave men jumped on them, opened their hatches, dumped a grenade inside, slammed the hatch shut, and jumped away before the explosion inside. For the men inside the tank, it was a horrible way to die.

Our basic training was more than adequate. It made each of us versatile and interchangeable. All of us were proficient in the use of a number of weapons. As replacements we were plugged into a decimated squad and became combat-ready immediately. Infantry squads also were self-teaching units. Dangerous assignments were equally shared. Somehow the bold spirits of our squad leaders filtered down to us.

Patton said that "The object of war is not to die for your country but to make the other bastard die for his." I am alive and unscathed because I was in Patton's Third Army. Over the years I have read much about Patton. Many have thought that he was half mad, but aren't all geniuses half mad? Only through madness can they see the world from that slightly different perspective.

I also believe that genius is realizing the shortest distance between two points is a straight line. Patton understood that. The Third Army was used like a spear as it thrust into the enemy's most vital organs. Other generals occupied themselves with complicated strategies that were often bloody and disastrous. I am here writing this because of Patton and my squad leaders. He risked our lives sparingly, and my squad leaders made us wise in the ways of Infantry front line combat. For that, I thank Mike and Buster. I also thank George Patton, but I am glad I never met him. Unshaven and unwashed as we were, we would all have been sent to a brig for being unmilitary and out of uniform. It is just as well he never went near the front lines. There we were the experts.

THE FINAL PUSH BEGINS

As we held our ground and ran patrols in preparation for the big push across the Rhine to defeat the German forces, elsewhere things were beginning to happen. On the night of March 22, in a move inspired by William the Conqueror's entrance into England in 1066, General Patton ordered a division of the Third Army to secretly cross the Rhine at the German town of Oppenheim. They crossed by boat, encountered no resistance, captured 19,000 troops, and established a six-mile-deep bridgehead, all without artillery barrage or aerial bombardment. With this move, the Third Army accomplished the first crossing of the Rhine River by boat by an invading army since Napoleon Bonaparte.

Patton's crossing was contrary to the orders he had received from his commander General Omar Bradley who was mindful of the cautious preparations by British Field Marshal Bernard Montgomery to make the initial crossing. The next morning Patton telephoned Bradley and told him of his success.

"Brad don't tell anyone, but I'm across."

Bradley, taken by surprise, responded, "Well, I'll be damned. You mean across the Rhine?"

"Sure am," replied Patton, "I sneaked a division over last night. But there are so few Krauts around there they don't know it yet. So don't make any announcement – we'll keep it a secret until we see how it goes."

But by evening word had gotten out – to both the Germans and the British – and Patton called General Bradley again.

"Brad, for God's sake tell the world we're across… I want the world to know Third Army made it before Monty starts across," he shouted.

By the next day Patton's engineers had constructed a pontoon bridge over the Rhine. Patton arrived and began walking across the bridge. Half-way across he suddenly stopped, and said, "I have been looking forward to this for a long time." He then unzipped his fly and began to urinate into the river. This act of defiance was captured by an Army photographer.

When Patton reached the other side, he pretended to stumble, imitating William the Conqueror who had fallen on his face upon landing in England; but who then transformed his fall into a defiant gesture by grabbing handfuls of English soil and claiming that it portended his complete possession of the country. In a similar gesture, Patton clutched two handfuls of German earth, rose up and exclaimed, "Thus, William the Conqueror."

That evening Patton sent a message to General Eisenhower at the Supreme Headquarters. It said, "I have just pissed into the Rhine River. For God's sake, send some gasoline."[30]

Within three days Patton's troops were rapidly approaching Frankfurt, Germany. As the German defenses began to fall apart, they were able to capture more bridges intact and take more ground.

On March 23, General Patton issued a special order to soldiers and airmen of the Third U.S. Army and the XIX Tactical Air Command:[31]

In the period from January 20 to March 22, 1945, you have wrested 6,484 square miles of territory from the enemy. You have taken 3,072 cities, towns, and villages, including among the former: Trier, Koblenz, Bingen, Worms, Mainz, Kaiserslautern, and Ludwigshafen.[32]

You have captured 140,112 enemy soldiers, and have killed or wounded an additional 99,000, thereby eliminating practically all of the German 7th and 1st Armies. History records no greater achievement in so limited a time.

This great campaign was only made possible by your disciplined valor, unswerving devotion to duty, coupled with the unparalleled audacity and speed of your advance on the ground; while from the air, the peerless fighter-bombers kept up a relentless round-the-clock attack upon the disorganized enemy.

The world rings with your praises; better still, General Montgomery, General Eisenhower, and General Bradley have all personally commended you. The highest honor I have ever attained is that of having my name coupled with yours in these great events.

Please accept my heartfelt admiration and thanks for what you have done and remember that your assault crossing over the Rhine River at 2200 hours last night assures you of even greater glory to come.

---

30   There are many accounts of Patton's crossing of the Rhine and his famous urination into the river. Two accounts can be found online at
https://www.historyonthenet.com/pattons-entrance-into-germany-in-1945/, and
https://ww2db.com/battle_spec.php?battle_id=134

31   Numerous sources have accounts, descriptions, facts, and transcriptions of these events, speeches, orders, and quotes. This was referenced from *Patton's Third Army, A Chronology of the Third Army Advance,* August 1944 to May 1945, by Charles M. Province. Published by Hippocrene Books, New York, copyright © 1992.

32   For a more comprehensive list of towns, rivers, and battles, see *Patton's Third Army, A Daily Combat Diary.*

It is interesting to note that during this period of time the engineers built more bridges than at any other time in their 281 days of combat.[33] It was also around this time that the Third Army captured its 300,000th prisoner of war.

"Nearer My God to Thee"

Occasionally, the Germans lobbed an artillery shell nearby. On Sunday morning, March 25,[34] I decided to attend a church service that was being held in an open field on the edge of town. I knew that we would be crossing the Rhine any day now and decided that singing a few hymns, participating in responsive readings, and praying would comfort me. My nerves were jangled and edgy. The not knowing was getting to me.

A shell landed near the impromptu outdoor church. Although a bit nervous, we continued to assemble for the service. We sat on a gently sloping hillside. At the base of the hill were an altar, a pulpit, and a foot-pumped organ. Song sheets and responsive readings were handed out as a corporal played an old familiar hymn on the organ. I was relaxed in a few moments. What had been ponderous and boring at home was comforting now. This was just what I needed.

Then the service began. It was officiated by a fiery young Baptist chaplain. He took very little time for hymns and readings, but there was a very long prayer that was followed by an even longer sermon in which he stormed and ranted about the rampant immorality raging through our troops. He started with smoking, advanced to drinking hard liquor, and climaxed with fornication. He created visions of Hell in his tirade, a Hell that was waiting for us across the Rhine. There was no forgiveness or comfort as he heaped guilt upon guilt.

We all knew we would be crossing the Rhine, and we had no idea of what terrors lurked ahead of us. I am sure some of the men had sinned in

---

33   Ibid. *Patton's Third Army, A Daily Combat Diary*. p. 167

34   Interestingly enough, thirty years later on March 25, Bill again went to church. Only this time it was to marry Linda Robbins. Bill was probably nervous (Linda certainly was!), but in a different way than on that Sunday morning in 1945. Thankfully no shells were lobbed in the sanctuary either before or during the wedding service, and they were together in life for forty years.

the eyes of this evangelical firebrand. I did not smoke, drink, or fornicate. I was only eighteen, and I was frightened. In brief, I was an innocent. I expected more from a church service.

When the full impact of that Baptist's sermon struck me, it confirmed my earlier reactions to organized religion. That callow pastor's emphasis on small sins and transgressions rather than on the larger issues of human decency and bravery struck me as narrow and empty. It bothered me more that his concerns about human behavior were very much like the concerns expressed in the church pulpits of my boyhood. What bothered me even more was his lack of compassion and sensitivity to the fears we all harbored.

He could have told us that we were brave young men who were fighting to makes lives better for the millions of Europeans who were oppressed by Nazi Germany. He said nothing of that. Instead, he raged against sins of the flesh that few of us had the time or inclination to commit. It was at that moment I shed my religious upbringing. I grew up a little that Sunday morning. Another part of my boyhood ended that day.

Adding to my loss of what little religion was left in me was my knowledge of the mystical enormity of the universe. Those vast starlit skies contained infinite mysteries. I sensed a wonder at all those twinkling stars. I asked myself, how could there be a benevolent God in those limitless skies? That was a cosmic concern, and at eighteen I wasn't ready for cosmic concerns. A more immediate concern followed: How could God allow the violence, death, and suffering we saw all around us?

While I hadn't yet encountered the cosmic concerns of ancient Greek tragedy, I wondered if the Force that created that endless, cruel universe was malevolent. All these questions had no clear answers. That morning I began to form my own religious views. The anger I felt then transformed itself into ideas. Some of these ideas I found along the way in my reading and education, some I created on my own.

As I entered deeper into the violent world of Infantry combat, I began to believe that life is now and only now. If some greedy capitalist made my life miserable, he was stealing the only mortality I had, my present mortality. If I died because of a manmade war, I was robbed of the years ahead of me.

While there is the cliché saying, "There are no atheists in foxholes," none of the men I fought with seemed particularly religious. I never saw one praying before an attack. Some, but not all, went to the occasional religious services that were held in the field when we were not on the front lines. I soon found I was better off reading from my books of poetry and short stories. I found an understanding of human nature in those two well-worn books. They also gave me comfort.

For the moment I became an agnostic, but I sensed some greater power in the universe. I began to think then and I believe now that greater power doesn't give a damn about me. I am less than a grain of sand in the grand scheme of things. Therefore, it followed that I must seize life and make the best of it. I have tried to do that with mixed success during the long life I have led. I can say with some pride that I did not seize the moment for the security of great wealth. Instead, I sought out ways to make the world better. My career as a teacher began amidst all that ranting on a fine, sunny Sunday morning a few miles south of the Rhine River.

This is not to say that all chaplains were insensitive to the realities of war. One of each major faith was assigned to a Battalion. Many, I am sure, were good men. I just had the bad luck of the draw at a moment when I most needed spiritual help to comfort me. However, I am forever indebted to that young chaplain. I never went to another religious service while I was in the Army. In the years to come I have always been uneasy at a church service. Unknowingly, I began to move toward the Quakerism that later colored my life.

At that moment in time, I was far from pacifism. If surviving meant killing someone who was trying to kill me, so be it. I wanted to stay alive and return home. Winning a war was incidental to that. Anyone who got in the way of my returning home alive and in one piece was going to die. I had entered that ultimate jungle, the front lines in a vicious war.

BEING A BEAST OF BURDEN

While other divisions were gaining miles, capturing and clearing towns as they moved towards their positions for the Rhine crossing, we continued to be held in reserve. Our main concern was to make ourselves ready for what we'd encounter after we crossed the Rhine. There was no way we could have target practice, but I worked at handling my M1. I inserted cartridge after cartridge. The faster I got them into the chamber, the faster

I could fire my weapon. I practiced my fast draw again and again. After this, I disassembled and cleaned my M1.

In the living room of our quarters there was a sturdy oak door that led to the rest of the house. We used it as a target for practicing throwing trench knives. We became very skilled. Such a skill would be useful when the enemy was close or when we were on a patrol and wanted to kill silently. That beautiful door must still bear the scars of our knife throwing.

I managed to steal a second trench knife. I strapped this on my arm under my shirt with a web belt. I placed it so the hilt was near my wrist. With a quick flip of my wrist, I would release the knife into my hand and throw it or attack an enemy in hand-to-hand combat. I thought that if I was captured, I might be able to use it to escape. I practiced throwing that knife from the day I joined my squad.

I studied how the veterans of the squad prepared their uniforms and equipment for extended combat operations. Even though we left most of our possessions behind when we went on line, infantrymen carried a great deal of equipment. There was little room for personal effects. Since spring was near, we did not wear the heavy wool overcoats. Instead, we wore our wool uniforms and a heavy canvas field jacket. I still have my field jacket. It is well worn since my two sons often wore it. Each of its four expandable pockets were valuable repositories. Slits cut in the inner lining gave me more pockets. Now I could fill my jacket with necessaries.

All the other external pockets were filled quickly. I placed three K-rations in the interior slit pockets. That was a day's worth of meals. Toilet paper, dry socks, and handkerchiefs were stuffed everywhere. Having changes of socks helped prevent trench foot. They also served as padding in case of a fall. All of us carried a first aid kit that included a shot of morphine in case we were wounded and in great pain. Our kits also included a small brown glass bottle containing 50 Halazone[35] tablets that made almost any water we found safe to drink.

---

35 During WWI and WWII soldiers were issued Halazone (4 dichlorosulfamyl benzoic acid) tablets as part of their K and C-rations. These chlorine-based tablets rendered most water safe to drink by providing a portable water purification protection against such things as *Escherichia coli*. Two tablets, dissolved for seven minutes in a full one-quart canteen, would disinfect the water for up to three days. It proved less effective in tropical areas, so following WWII, Globaline iodine tablets were developed by researchers at Harvard University. Iodine-based purification tablets became the standard for military use, although Halazone tablets continued to be used by the military through the Vietnam War. The shelf life of Halazone is about two years.

Next, I put on my ammunition belt. A mess kit, a grenade launcher, a trench knife, a gas mask, and a bayonet were hung from it. Each of its pockets was filled with two loaded M1 ammunition clips. I hung hand grenades from every available buttonhole. On top of all this we slung several bandoleers of bullet cartridges crisscrossed over our shoulders, as many grenades as could attach to our belts and pockets, and a canteen seated inside a large metal cup.

We hated gas masks. While they weighed little, they added to our heavy burden. We also doubted that there would be any gas attacks. There had been no reports that the Germans had used gas anywhere except in Italy. Chemical warfare seemed to be a thing of the past now that fighting in trenches had become rare. I later learned that another reason for the hesitation was that during World War I gas warfare often backfired on the Germans due to the winds in Europe that often blew west to east. Hitler also did not order gas attacks, and most think it was because he had been gassed in WWI.

We quickly became cavalier with our gas masks. We cut our mask's rubber tubing up and used the segments to soundproof our dog tags. If not, they would clink during night action and patrols. After we ruined the tubing, the masks were useless, so we discarded them. A few days later when we were asked what had happened to them, we said we had lost them in action. We were issued new gas masks. In time, as we wore down from long marches and charges into German towns, we threw them away. I slung the hated gas mask over one shoulder. We carried so much that even a pound or so made a difference to us.

We carried a small pack. Inside it was a single blanket and a poncho. Attached to the back of the pack was an entrenching tool that was a combination pick and shovel. This was used for us to dig foxholes at the end of a day's march. Our sleeping bags were shaped like a small coffin, the kind they use to bury bodies at sea. There were nicknamed "fart sacks" by our Southerners. I do not remember if we carried them on our longest marches. The most useful thing we carried was a poncho. It could be half a pup tent, a raincoat, or a ground cloth.

All this added up to a considerable weight. I carried an extra burden. As assistant BAR man, I had to carry my own ammunition and even more for the BAR. I wore a suspendered web belt that carried 20 BAR cartridges. Each contained twenty .30 caliber bullets. These were fitted two deep into an ammunition belt which was supported by my shoulders,

Metal-sheathed
New Testament

not from my waist. My hips still carry the scars of carrying this belt since it rubbed against my sides as I marched.

I was weighted down with nearly fifty pounds of arms and equipment. I also carried one or two paperback books, some V-Mail[36] forms, and a notebook. I still have a paperback book of poetry I carried throughout combat. I also had a metal-sheathed New Testament that my parents had bought for me before I went overseas. Sold by the Know Your Bible Company out of Cincinnati, Ohio, the metal cover contained the words "May this keep you safe from harm." The inside cover read "The Shield and New Testament. The Heart-Shield Bible fits snugly in Uniform Pocket. The engraved gold-plated steel front cover protects his heart." There was space for my name and serial number on the inside cover. Later I found that it was dangerous to use it to cover one's heart. A bullet would drive the entire book into your body. Still, nearly every parent of an infantryman gave such a Bible to their son as a protection and a source of solace.

Mustering the energy to run took great effort. Somehow, we all managed to make charges when we had to. Those years of carrying 120 newspapers paid off. I was slow afoot, but I was durable on a long march, even with my creaking ankle.

I also carried the extra trench knife up my sleeve. I never had to use this hidden weapon in combat. My other trench knife was attached to my ammunition belt.

Finally, I prepared my helmet. Our helmets were made of two parts. There was a plastic helmet liner. In combat it was covered with a thick

---

36   V-mail was short for Victory Mail. In order to censor the letters and reduce the costs of transporting them for delivery, the military postal system copied the small (7 by 9 1/8 inches) v-mail letter sheets to film. Upon arrival at the destination the letters were printed back to paper at 60% size, resulting in a sheet that was 4 ½ inches by 5 3/16 inches. The V-mail system was based on the British Airgraph system. For more information, see The Smithsonian National Postal Museum website at: https://postalmuseum.si.edu/exhibits/past/the-art-of-cards-and-letters/mail-call/v-mail.html

metal outer shell. It was covered with netting for camouflage. While the outer shell could fend off the glancing blow of a rifle bullet or a small piece of shrapnel, it couldn't withstand a direct hit. Under the helmet we wore a wool knit cap. There was still a chill in the March air.

Since we did not fasten our helmet's chinstrap, we fitted the webbing of the helmet liner closely to our head so that it would not fall off when we ran or fell down. If the chinstrap was fastened and a shell exploded nearby, the concussion from the blast could break our neck. Most Hollywood movies of the time get that detail wrong. Again and again actors playing soldiers wore their chinstraps fastened.

Inside the helmet's webbing, I placed packets of government-issue toilet paper as padding. These small treasures were badly needed. The dysentery I contracted on the *Aquitania* still raged through my system. It persisted until the last few days of the war.

All this equipment was like a mass that hung over my body. My cartoons give an impression of the way we looked. We were not an impressive sight. As I grew to realize that the Germans feared us as soldiers, my sense of the ridiculous emerged. Little did they know how tired and worn down we were. Our advantage was that we had not had all those years of grinding warfare to cope with. We were all relatively new to battle.

Remember all this weight when I describe the long marches that lay ahead of us. Even when one was rested, running was an effort, and running was important. Running in rapid zigzag patterns protected an infantryman from rifle fire. Nothing protected us from machine gun fire. That was laid down in a pattern and not aimed at particular persons.

I practiced a fast draw with my rifle, drawing it off my shoulder and leveling it for firing in one quick movement. I managed to do this in a split second. I could fire with some accuracy from the hip. If I was caught by surprise, I could shoot an enemy before he could shoot me. If I missed him, he would probably turn and run. If worse came to worse, I had that knife up my sleeve.

Our bayonets were usually sheathed. When they were attached to our rifles, they weighed them down and made our fire less accurate. In my time in combat, we were ordered to fix bayonets only twice.

Most European bayonet fighting happened in Italy. It was a forced issue. Much of the fighting there was in mountains. It was brutal, a day-to-day slugging out for a few yards of ground. Nobody wanted to serve in Italy.

In the Pacific Theatre knife fighting was more common. The Japanese had no aversion to it. Our enemies there rarely surrendered. They preferred to fight to the death.

On the other hand, the German regular army, the *Wehrmacht,* was known for being sensible. The Germans, like us, disliked knife fighting of any kind. In close confrontations when a situation seemed hopeless, they usually surrendered rather than fight hand to hand.

American soldiers behaved in the same practical manner. Surrender was preferable to certain death. We also knew that the *Wehrmacht* treated prisoners reasonably well. There was no deliberate starvation or torture as there was in the Pacific. After basic training, when we found out we were going to Europe, we were relieved.

The exceptions in the German army were the *SS* Divisions.[37] They were less likely to surrender. However, their fanaticism made them less than ideal soldiers. They were more predictable. In truth, when they were put into a dangerous situation, they lacked the courage of the common, conscripted soldiers of the *Wehrmacht.* Still, the *Waffen SS* were dangerous. They feared what we might do to them if they were captured. However, they often failed to observe the Geneva Conventions when it came to their treatment of prisoners. None of us wanted to surrender to them. From what we were told, death was preferable.

On the other hand, many in the *Wehrmacht* greeted capture as their way out of a war that had drained their spirit. I am glad that I did not have to face German soldiers while they were enjoying their first surge of success.

But for now, for better or worse, I was ready to go into extended combat. I can't accurately say how much weight I carried, but it was more than seventy-five pounds, or half my body weight.

---

37 *SS* stood for *Schutzstaffel,* meaning protective echelon or squadron. Headed by Heinrich Himmler, the SS were the political soldiers of the Nazi Party. They were known for their security, surveillance, and terror within Germany and German occupied Europe. The double S was stylized to look like two parallel lightning bolts. They were the organization most responsible for the murder of more than six million Jews and millions of other victims of the Holocaust.

PART V

INTO THE HEART OF GERMANY

What do you do in the Infantry?
You march, you march, you march.[1]

---

1 "What Do You Do in the Infantry," by Frank Loesser, was the official song of the Infantry. It was recorded by many artists of the time including Glenn Miller, Bing Crosby, and The Sportsmen.

17

CROSSING THE RHINE

On the 27th of March we entrucked and left Wiebelsheim by motor convoy to cross the Rhine River on a Pontoon Bridge. We crossed the river at 0200, 28th of March. Traveled South on the East Bank of the river to St. Goarshausen when the convoy left the river and traveled east to Nastätten when we detrucked. From here we traveled on foot using the approach march through Egenroth, Huppert closing in on Hohenstein where we spent the night.[2]

THIS IS WHAT was written in *Always First*. It is terse and lacking details. By this time the bridge at Remagen had been crossed.[3] We were not the first to cross the Rhine, nor would we be the last. Within a few days most of the soldiers in the European Theatre of Operation – ETO – had crossed the Rhine and were racing into the heart of Germany. That night, when we crossed that broad river, we began the last battle for the conquest of the Third Reich. What was to come was an epic that exceeded even the most sweeping visions of Homer.

---

2 *Always First*

3 To learn more about the Allied invasion of Germany and the capture of the Ludendorff Bridge by the 9th Armored Division of the U.S. First Army, I recommend *The Bridget at Remagen: The Amazing Story of March 7, 1945*. Written by Ken Hechler in 1957, the book was adapted into a highly fictionalized screenplay by Richard Yares and William Roberts for the 1969 movie, *The Bridge at Remagen* starring George Segal, Ben Gazarra, Robert Vaughn, E.G. Marshall, and Bradford Dillman. It was directed by John Guillermin with a musical score by Elmer Bernstein. There is also an excellent article online at Wikipedia about the Battle of Remagen.

We crossed on a bright moonlit night.[4] As we were some distance away from the river we were loaded on trucks and rode to the river. Ahead of us was a pontoon bridge. It can be seen in the remarkable color documentaries taken by Hollywood film director George Stevens during the last weeks of the war.

My memories of this time are largely in black and white. I remember a few colors, such as the blue green of the surging seas during our Atlantic crossing and the eerie green-blue in the thick forests as we trudged through the Rhineland. The daylight filtering through the forest was a sinister but beautiful sight. One never knew what was out in front, or what was behind the trees ahead of us. That added to the mystery of these woods that were lovely, dark, and deep – and oh, so dangerous.

There's a dash of brown and khaki in the images that fleet across my consciousness, and that odd dusty green of German uniforms. Lastly, there are flashes of the brilliant red of open wounds and recently shed blood. That quickly turned to black. Over the years I learned that many other veterans share a similar color memory of the war. It is like I lived in an old movie.

As we crossed that swaying, surging pontoon bridge, a shell was lobbed into the river upstream. There was that familiar whistling sound, an explosion, and a geyser of water a hundred or so yards to our right as our trucks slowly made their way across that uneasy bridge. There was no stopping, no turning back. No one took cover. It was as though it had never happened. That one shell burst was the only sign of resistance during our brief night crossing. Why only one? That remains a mystery to me to this very day. A full barrage would have destroyed that bridge and sent us plunging into the swift Rhine waters.

On the other side we dismounted, formed two columns – one on each side of a paved road – and began what was the longest Infantry foot march in any American war.[5] None of us imagined the physical ordeal ahead of

---

4 There was a full moon on the night of March 28, 1945.

5 According to modern US Army doctrine, the average rate of march for trained Infantry under favorable weather conditions is 2-1/2 mph over roads and 1 mph cross-country. A normal foot march covers 20 miles per day. The normal pace is 30 inches (76 cm), 106 steps per minute, for a rate of 4 kph. In a 24-hour period, with 5-8 hours of marching, the normal distance traveled is 20-32 kilometers. More than 32 km is a forced march. An Infantry division on the march averages 12-15 miles per day, an armored division 100 miles per day. *U.S. Dept of Army. Staff Officers' Field Manual: Organization, Technical,*

us. My bad ankle worried me even more. I was terrified because I knew that those grinding ankle bones could give way with the next step.

All fear of the enemy disappeared as I concentrated on taking the next step, then the next, and then all those that followed. Battle seemed simple beside the pain and exhaustion I felt as we moved deeper into Germany. I had every right to drop out, but I refused to do that.

The need to put my head down and survive without complaining made many of my combat experiences a blur of impressions. Some things stand out with great clarity, some appear in my memory as an impressionistic haze, and some do not exist.

Now the American Army entered the center of Germany in force. At this time neither tanks nor tank destroyers accompanied us. We had jeeps in our column, most carrying one .50 caliber machine gun. These were effective against aircraft and troops. They were completely ineffectual against German tanks. Only our bazookas were of use during panzer attacks.

As we marched ahead in two columns, we kept about 10 feet between us. This meant that one shell would only get two or three of us. In many war movies men are shown advancing in tight clusters. That was counter to all rifle squad strategy.

For the moment the weather was warm, and there was a mist of rain that I found refreshing. We had a five-minute break every hour. I quickly learned to sleep most of those five minutes. On one of our first breaks, I remember that I laid down on the pavement in a small village, resting my helmeted head on the curb. I managed a full five-minute snooze before we were ordered back on our feet. Even now, I can drop off in a few seconds if I feel the need of a nap. I must admit that now my naps last longer than five minutes.

I cannot remember whether we started the march at dawn or in the night. That first day of marching is a blur in my memory bank.

We moved out the next morning on foot through Breithardt, Steckenroth, Oberlibbach, Oberauroff, Idstein, and finally Wüstems.

---

and Logistical Data, Part I. FM 101-10, Oct 1961. pp. 123-124. https://www.ibiblio.org/pub/academic/history/marshall/military/mil_hist_inst/m/march2.asc

"Prior to crossing the Rhine the entire US Third Army shifted its axis of advance in order to counter the unexpected German offensive in the Ardennes. A quarter-million men and 25,000 vehicles travelled distances of 50-150 miles through ice and snow and were able to launch a corps-level attack in three days." FM 21-18, pp. 4 & 6.

During the day's activity approximately 20 miles [probably 30 to 35 miles of marching along winding roads] and captured 8 towns or villages, the largest being Idstein approximate population 10,000.[6]

I cannot remember us taking a town of 10,000; but the record shows we did. We advanced to the east with no resistance for about 35 miles in our first day. This was the furthest any of us had marched in a single day. In training we had 20-mile marches. My ankle, while sending my brain tinges of pain, functioned well, but I still suffered from dysentery. Sometimes I dropped out to relieve myself. Then I jogged to take my place in the ever-advancing column. Others shared my problem.

Our two columns wended their way along rough roads. We passed through dense forests and small towns. Most of the towns were eager to surrender. Ordinary German civilians were war weary. Their soldiers were, too; but they still fought when they had to. Resistance was token or non-existent. The mass of German troops withdrew deep into Germany, but a few remained behind for delaying actions.

We dug foxholes after our first day and settled in for a short night's sleep. Larry and I dug in together. This was the first time I spent a night in a foxhole. The recommended size of a GI foxhole was approximately three feet wide and six feet long. It bore a close resemblance to a shortened grave, but not as deep. Ideally it was four to five feet deep. These dimensions meant that a tank could run over us, and the treads would not touch us. If we kept our heads below ground level, we were protected from gunfire, nearby shell bursts, and all but direct hits. We rarely had time to dig to an optimum depth. Our rapid advance prevented such permanency.[7]

During our three-day march, I discovered that I was able to sleep while marching. Once I tumbled off the road and into a ditch. The man marching in front of me slept much more than I did. His marching became erratic, and he fell out of step. This irregularity exhausted me. Marching in step with the person in front of me preserved my waning energy. I kept

---

6 *Always First.*

7 In a speech to the Third Army on June 5, 1944, Patton said, "My men don't dig foxholes. I don't want them to. Foxholes only slow up an offensive. Keep moving. And don't give the enemy time to dig one either." In the same speech he also said that "I don't want to get any messages saying, 'I am holding my position.' We are not holding a Goddamned thing. Let the Germans do that. We are advancing constantly and we are not interested in holding onto anything, except the enemy's balls."

Foxhole dreams

trying to adapt to his stride. That was even more tiring. Worse still, these changes made my ankle ache even more.

As we marched ahead into the hills of the Rhineland, we saw our Republic P-47 Thunderbolts strafing in the valleys ahead of us. These barrel-chested pursuit planes were a large motor attached to the stubby body of a short-winged plane. They would sweep in over us, disappear behind the hills ahead of us, and make their strafing run. We could hear that ripping sound as their machine guns fired at ground targets. They would reappear as they swept upward to circle to attack again and again. They met no air resistance.

The few remaining German fighter planes were busy fighting our bombers as they plodded ahead to targets deeper and deeper inside Germany. It was comforting to realize the German forces ahead of us were being weakened by these incessant air attacks.

Behind us, artillery units added to the devastation. They lobbed shell after shell into the towns ahead of us. Their spotters were two-seat Piper Cubs. These light planes were flimsy and low powered. Back home they were used for recreation and private travel. None of their pilots were officers. They were warrant officers, a rather rare rank that stood between enlisted men and officers. When these planes flew high, we knew there were no German fighters coming in to strafe us. When they dropped to tree level, we knew an air attack was approaching.

Heinkel and Thunderbolt

At low altitudes, these slow-moving planes were hard to shoot down. Tracer bullets flew through their canvas covering. Their thin wooden frames and small engines made direct hits difficult. We marveled at the bravery of these pilots in their small planes. Little has been written about them. Helicopters now do their job.

We slogged ahead. We rarely met resistance. As we entered villages, German civilians often stood beside the road, their eyes vacant from the shelling and strafing. They stared at us, partly in fear but mostly in curiosity. Some saw us as a liberating army that was freeing them from years of tyranny. Others harbored resentment and anger. The Germans were quite skilled at masking their real feelings from us.

In the days to come I found the Germans supported anyone who might give them a better life. It was this sense of adaptation that allowed the Nazis to rise to power during the economic depression in the early 1930s. I believed then, and still believe, that the desire to retain their creature comforts was the basis of their efforts to ingratiate themselves to us. Patton once said that "the Hun is always either at your throat or at your feet." None of us believed the sincerity of their cheers and applause as we marched into towns. I am sure that most Germans were relieved that their war had ended. Maybe they would no longer be bombed. Perhaps now their prosperity would return, and Germany could become great again. Is my judgment too harsh? I don't think so.

It took me many years to even begin to understand what had happened in Germany. Now I believe that the same could happen here if the right pressures are brought to bear on average Americans. In fact, recent elections prove my fears. Collectively, the human race can be a vicious, greedy, short-sighted, self-centered lot. Human nature gravitates to those who promise quick and easy solutions.

That self-serving attitude was not the case for the men I served with during those dark days. We were surviving and protecting each other.

On the second day after our Rhine crossing, we marched 55 incredible miles and cleared more than 20 small towns. Early on that second day we attacked a town set against a high wooded hillside. We charged out of a wooded area onto a field that separated us from the town. To get there we had to run up a railroad embankment and across another field to reach the town's outer buildings.

My legs were weak from the long march and my dysentery. I ran across the field and up the embankment. As I crossed the rails, I realized that I was flying through the air and falling to the bottom of the other side of the embankment. It was like I was in slow motion. I felt like I was floating. For a moment I seemed to be suspended in time. I had heard that one did not feel anything when one was shot and that everything slowed down. During that eternal split second in the air, I was convinced I had been shot.

I landed in the field below with a thud. As I rolled over, I saw white sheets spilling from the windows in the town. They were surrendering. I was amazed to find I was all right. My heel had caught on the second railroad track and tripped me. My fall only bruised me.

When we entered the town square, an older man, carrying a white flag, offered the town's surrender. He was beautifully uniformed and bemedaled. We were convinced we had captured a high-ranking officer and took him into custody. Later it turned out he was the town dogcatcher! The Germans loved to wear colorful uniforms. They had one for almost every level of local officialdom.

We quickly moved out of the town. There was no respite from our advance. Later in the day a sniper took two shots at our advancing column. By now I knew the sound of a bullet that came close to you. It sounds like a hole being bored in the air. The hole is filled with a quiet fluttering sound. Of course, it's preceded by the crack of the firing, but when you hear that sound, you know you were narrowly missed. No one dropped for cover. We were too tired to make the effort. We knew that once we were on the ground, we would have to get up again. It was easier to risk being killed. Fortunately, that lonely sniper was a poor shot. He fired only two rounds. No one was hit. We kept on marching.

Later in the day a high-ranking officer – I suspect it was our regimental commander, a general – rode by us in a jeep. I remember his words,

"Damned good march, men. Damned good! We've set a new record for an American military outfit – fifty-five goddamned miles!"

We took no pride in his statement. The lazy son of a bitch was riding in a jeep while we were walking. How dare he use "we" in describing what we had done that endless day? To me, that was my bravest day while I was in combat. Being under fire seemed simple compared to that grueling day. I drove my body beyond its limitations. We all did.

As our long march neared its end and night fell, I was blind from fatigue. I mean that literally. I could barely see where I was going. Each step was an effort. My bad ankle shrieked with pain. We dropped to the ground in the middle of a forest.

Word came down the line that panzer tanks were roaming the area and that we should dig in. Larry and I tried, but the rocky soil made it impossible. We managed to scrape away a few inches of dirt. If there was a tank account, our shallow trench would offer no cover. By then we were too tired to care. We decided to sleep on the ground. If the panzers attacked, they would crush us to death. In our weariness, death would have been a welcome relief.

No tanks came.

The Third Day

In peace sons bury their fathers,
but war violates this order of nature,
and fathers bury their sons.[8]

We were up early the next morning. The older men were worse off than we eighteen-year-olds were. By now, I discovered that an older man had more endurance for a day, but his body took longer to recover. Attrition was beginning to wear all of us down. It was hitting the older men harder.

My ankle and the dysentery sapped my energy. I hid my weariness from the other men. My ability to hide injury and illness from my parents paid off during those hard days of marching.

As we moved into mid-morning and higher into the Rhineland forests, we were relieved we met no resistance. The German army had pulled back to set up lines of defense inland. Later we learned these were designed to defend Berlin. The *Wehrmacht* was planning its last stand. We feared it. I could see on my ragged map that if we continued in the direction we were going, we would end up on the outskirts of Berlin. It would be a bloodbath for the troops that attempted to take that great city. Thankfully, that bloody climax would be given to the Russian Army that was now surging across Poland. As far as we were concerned, they were welcome to the honor of taking Berlin.

We were somewhere north of Frankfurt and more than twenty miles inland. Our torturous route was a winding advance along rural roads that led us from small village to small village. Our real advance was a fraction of the more than one hundred miles we marched during those three grueling days.

By mid-afternoon we had advanced more than 25 miles. As we slogged down a narrow dirt country road amidst a thick pine forest, someone shouted, "There they are!"

Someone else shouted, "Get the sons of bitches!"

I turned and looked up the hill to my left. Helmeted grey-green figures filled the woods above us. Someone fired. I am not sure if it was them or

---

8 Herodotus of Halicarnassus (c. 484 BCE – c. 425 BCE), *The Histories*, Book 1, Chapter 87

RIFLEMAN

us. I saw a German soldier running away from me. He turned and fired at me. I fired, and he fell. He did not move. I had killed a human being.

My M1 jammed after that first shot, but I joined the charge. As I moved ahead, I pried the bullet casing out of the chamber with my fingernails and slid in a round of live ammo. I fired again. I managed to shoot a clip of eight bullets, one at a time. My fingernails were shredded.

I looked for Reed and discovered he had dropped down on the lower side of the road while the rest of us were advancing. At first, I thought he was retreating and acting in a cowardly way, but then I realized that he had taken up position to lay down a base of fire with his BAR. I should have stayed with him since I was carrying spare ammunition, but I did not want to retreat or take even one step back. Besides he had enough ammunition for a short encounter.

We charged a few yards and fell to our stomachs. Our weary legs gave out after each short charge. After we fell to the ground, we fired. My rifle jammed again. Again, I pried out the empty shell casing.

Once I got lucky and got off three or four shots before my rifle jammed again. I heard a German scream and saw him tumble to the ground. He did not move. I had killed another human being. At that moment I felt nothing. I advanced, firing as often as I could with my faulty rifle.

We took no time to ascertain the situation or the size of the force ahead of us. We attacked. It was a mindless reaction of well-trained young soldiers. It was not the reaction of experienced infantrymen. We were completely exposed. Fortunately, there was only a scattering of fire from the enemy hiding in the trees ahead of us.

The Germans, seeing this pattern of advance and fire, quickly surrendered. They thought we were disciplined fighters who ran, fell, fired, and ran again and again. In our exhaustion we had executed a textbook Infantry attack. The young men charged, while the older men laid down a fire-base behind us. I was with the young men. I remember no fear. I acted on my reflexes, built during basic training and fortified with my primitive instincts to do what was necessary to stay alive.

We took more than fifty prisoners in a matter of minutes. They were older men. A couple of them looked as old as my father who was forty-five. One even looked a little like my father. He was crying in

Super Duper Supermen Surrendering

fear. I realized that the Germans were terrified by the ferocity of our attack.

We took their arms and kept them in a circle until they could be marched to the rear. Mac took one prisoner out of the circle. We suddenly realized he intended to castrate the terrified man. Mac held his trench knife against the German's throat. He would ask the German to repeat an obscenity after him. Then he drew a little blood. The man was crying and shaking in fear. Mac found that funny. None of the other men did.

Then he said, "Now I'm going to cut your balls off."

His knife traced down the man's chest toward his crotch. Larry and I stepped in. We held our rifles on Mac and ordered him to back off. We stopped him from committing such an atrocity. He never forgave us for that.

We moved to the rim of the hill we had charged and took up positions there. Below was a small village that sat on both sides of a small river. From the distance it looked like an illustration for *Grimm's Fairy Tales*.

From the right and left of us, our mortars began to hammer the small town. Explosions puffed here and there, knocking down parts of buildings. Our artillery had not caught up with us, but we were tearing the town apart piece by piece. Machine gun nests along the rim of the hill fired into the village even though no human targets were visible.

In retaliation, machine gun and rifle fire streamed from the village. The sound of the German machine guns was terrifying. They fired two or three times faster than our 30mm machine guns. They had a ripping sound, and their sheet of fire was deadly. German rifle fire was less effective. They were equipped with bolt action rifles. They did not match the firepower of our M1s, but they were quite accurate. None of the fire reached us.

Baker Company was chosen to charge down the hill into the town. Flynn, my doom-haunted friend, was in that company. We sat under the cover of the trees above the village and watched our fellow soldiers advance. To reach the town they had to cross a broad, clear field. They had no cover. Some fell. Seeing our own men killed or wounded from a distance made it almost abstract. I believe that all of us were relieved we were not in that first wave.

Years later, while in college, I wrote a story about the action.

It was a fine bright day, a Sunday near the end of the war. Ahead of us, Baker Company posed to attack a village lurking in a deep valley below us. Then they moved out. Soldiers within the village fired at the advancing troops. Our mortars poured fire into the village, shattering its quaint houses. Then Baker moved closer. The battle was sharp and violent. It was one of those last fanatical gasps we were now encountering.

Some of our men fell.

Other men watched the action through field glasses that were passed back and forth. I couldn't. I had a terrible, ugly feeling that it was here in this small valley in Germany that my friend Flynn would meet his fate.

Over on the left, mortars coughed. Up on the ridge, our machine gunners poured streams of fire above our advancing men's heads and into the village. More of our men fell. Rifle fire crackled back and forth. Some of our men were pinned down, but others advanced into the village. Then the sounds of battle subsided into a hollow silence. Streams of smoke and fire rose from the village.

The battle was over. Baker Company had won.

We waited and waited. When the village was cleared, our Lieutenant received orders for us to move out. We knew the next town would be ours to take. We were relieved that twilight was settling over us. When we fought again, it would be another day. We knew we had one more night to live.

We moved in spread double-file along a rough road leading down into the now shattered and smoking village. It was a small town, isolated, and tucked amidst the vast wooded hills of the Moselle valley. Except for the dark clouds of smoke that stained the clear, darkening spring blue twilight, the town might have been ripped from a child's storybook.

As we walked ahead, we saw bodies on each side of us, scattered beside the road and across the broad field reaching down into the village, the inevitable aftermath of battle. They looked peaceful as they lay in the green grass. It seemed like they would arise from their rest and join us in our movement forward. Except for one thing: the familiar and dreadful claylike pallor that had come with death to their young faces. They were dead, but they did not seem dead. Death when you are young is an impossibility. One did not understand it, but we accepted it as part of our daily life. A few weeks ago I saw death for the first time. I cried. Now I looked at the dead and felt lucky.

Our column stopped momentarily as we waited for orders to enter the village. On the right side of the road were three more bodies. Someone had placed a piece of paper over the face of one fallen comrade. It fluttered in a slight breeze. I watched, fascinated. Then a firm gust blew it away. The face beneath was tranquil. Its motionless, staring eyes looked upward into the smoke-scarred blue twilight. Those eyes seemed to accept a destiny fulfilled. For a fleeting moment the image of a tattered photo of a pretty wife and three young children entered the mist of tears that clouded my eyes.

It was Flynn.

His intimations back at the POE had come true. I reached down and gently closed the eyes of my friend. For him the war was over. His children would never know what a remarkable man their father was.

Fallen comrade

This was my first close look at dead American soldiers. I had seen the dead before, but they were strangers from other platoons. In death they were all the same. Their faces were frozen, some peacefully, many with a final amazement. A few looked like they were sleeping. Their skin had a yellow-gray hue. I will never forget that color of death. It comes quickly to a human body.

We discovered that the ferocious defenders of the village were teenage boys – some barely into their teens – who were studying in a military school in that tiny town. They were left behind by the older soldiers and were told to delay us as long as possible. Their defense had been both gallant and bloody. These boys were quite possibly the best soldiers we faced during my days in combat. They bought most of an afternoon for the retreating *Wehrmacht* at a terrible cost. Most were killed in the assault. The few that were captured were tearful and trembling from fear.

The fight for the bridge in the town was later immortalized in a postwar German film, *Die Brücke (The Bridge)*. It's a powerful and tragic film. From my view from the hill, it was reasonably accurate. It was directed by Bernhard Wicki, a highly regarded director. I have always wondered if he was one of the boys that defended that town.[9]

---

9 It wasn't the same bridge or the same battle, although it was about the same time and the accounts are very similar. The West German film *Die Brücke (The Bridge)* was based on Gregor Dorfmeister's (a.k.a Manfred Gregor) 1958 anti-war novel of the same name. Dorfmeister (1929-2018) was a student in high school in Bad Tölz, Bavaria (about 32 miles south of Munich), and participated in the *Volkssturm* (people's army) defending two bridges against advancing American tanks. That event turned him into a pacifist. Following the war, he became a journalist, and supporter for disabled people. His second book, *Das Urteil (The Verdict)* was made into the movie *Town Without Pity* starring Kirk Douglas. Dorfmeister was awarded the Order of Merit of the Federal Republic of Germany in 1981. He died on February 4, 2018.

The 1959 movie *Die Brücke* was directed by Bernhard Wicki (1919-2000), an Austrian actor and film director. Wicki was imprisoned in the Sachsenhausen concentration camp in 1939 because of his membership in the *Bündischen Jugend* (German Youth Movement, not to be confused with the Hitler Youth). Wicki's directorial career included the 1962 epic WWII movie, *The Longest Day*, co-directed by Ken Annakin, Andrew Marton, Gerd Oswalk, and Darryl F. Zanuck; and *Morituri*, the 1965 WWII espionage thriller starring Marlon Brando and Yul Brynner.

WALKING WOUNDED

> At times he regarded the wounded soldiers in an envious way.
> He conceived persons with torn bodies to be peculiarly happy.
> He wished that he, too, had a wound, a red badge of courage.[10]

For a man who never experienced combat, Stephen Crane's *The Red Badge of Courage* is a remarkable accomplishment; but this quotation does not reflect those of us who returned unscathed. We did not envy those who had been wounded any more than we envied those who fell.

I did not fully realize how devastating a rifle wound could be until the end of the war. During combat the wounded were whisked away by our medics so we never had a close look at their wounds. Yes, I saw the dead, but I never took time to really look at them. That seemed like a desecration to me. I walked by them, averting my eyes or glancing at them quickly. That is, until I saw Flynn.

Once or twice at the end of the war when we were off line, we were taken to shower tents. There we could take a shower and revive ourselves. It was a rare treat. A couple dozen of us would take showers from several cold or lukewarm streams of water. If the water was hot, it was heavenly. Taking showers with us were men who had been wounded, recovered, and sent back to the front. It was a brutal education in wounds.

On the front of the body was a small scar where the bullet entered. On the man's back was a three or four-inch crater that was at least an inch deep. This was where the bullet exited. Other men had scars from shrapnel wounds. These wounds were rough and jagged. This array of scars was a sobering reminder of what could have happened to us. I am relieved that I never saw these scars before the war ended. Before that there was no time or opportunity for showers.

Hollywood movies of the time never showed the real nature of combat wounds. That did not occur until Sam Peckinpah's *The Wild Bunch*. Now blood packs and gruesome prosthetics are common in films. When I hear men and women eager for us to go to war, I wish I could cram the realities I witnessed – and others even worse that, thankfully, I did not witness firsthand – down their throats. Most men who send people into

---

10 From *The Red Badge of Courage* by Stephen Crane (1871-1900), an American poet, novelist, and short story writer. Crane wrote this novel, published in 1895, about a young private in the Union Army during the American Civil War.

war have no firsthand experience with the realities of combat. Yes, a few men enjoyed combat, but they were psychopaths. Most men who were in combat hate war.

Amidst us were men who had more than one Purple Heart. Each time they were healed they were sent back to their outfit. Later, when I was with the 30th Division, I met a man who had seven Purple Hearts. He was no longer able to speak coherently. He walked about barely aware of where he was. He was remote, and never spoke to the rest of us. He was a tall, gaunt man whose first name was Jess.

This return of the wounded to the front was another reason infantrymen resented the Air Force. Flight crews were allowed to return to the United States after twenty-five missions. I understand the stress they suffered in a contained space as they hit flak over their targets and on their way back and forth, but was that stress any different from men who fought on the ground?

18

Afterwards and Onward

In actual combat, dying is a lot easier than living.[11]

At 0700, 30th of March the Battalion started out on its next objective on foot. The objective was the towns of Finsternthal and Treisberg. At Finsternthal we met resistance, but this didn't stop the 1st Battalion, we moved in and took our objective. Company B went into the town with Company A on the left and a platoon of Company C on the high ground on the right, with the remainder of Company C in Battalion reserve. Company D was in direct support of Company B upon entering the town. Company B met heavy resistance, then company D's mortars went into action shelling every house in town, and the heavy machine guns fired into the woods beyond the town cutting off any possible route of escape for the enemy. The enemy was thus softened up and after a six hour battle the town was ours. From Finsternthal we moved to Treisberg where we dug in a perimeter defense on the high ground around the town.[12]

E ACH STEP NOW required great effort. One common Infantry ailment was the march fracture. After marching for days on end while carrying heavy equipment, the balls of our feet became bruised. It is quite painful. Each step sent a jolt of pain up our legs. We all had a touch of it. All of us gritted our teeth and soldiered on. The only cure was prolonged rest in bed. In a combat situation there wasn't time for that, so we endured the pain.

---

11 Quote attributed to a survivor of the Battle of the Bulge.

12 *Always First*

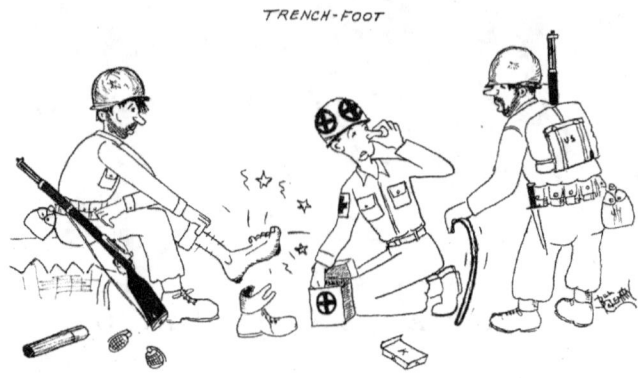

Adding to our weakened condition was the specter of trench foot.[13]
When feet are encased in wet socks in waterproof boots, blood circulation
is affected, and skin begins to deteriorate. The only cure for trench foot
was to be put to bed and elevate the feet. It was hoped that circulation
would slowly return, and the skin would heal. Some men had to have
their feet amputated.

Having changes of socks helped prevent trench foot. Even so, we all
suffered from this ailment. Once we crossed the Rhine, both of my feet
became discolored and slightly purple. Quite literally, they were dying. I
had no problem marching. I had less feeling in my feet, even though my
ankle still ached.

There was some discussion of taking us off the line, but none of us
complained. We knew that if one of us was sent back to a field hospital, the
squad would be short-handed until replacements arrived. We also knew
we were risking amputation if our feet continued to lose circulation. To
all of us, our relationship to our squad was more important.

---

13   Also known as Immersion Foot, trench foot occurs by prolonged exposure to
damp, cold, and unsanitary conditions. It was first noted in 1812 in Napoleon's Army,
and was a serious problem during World War I, affecting up to 20,000 British soldiers in
the winter of 1914-15. Trench foot occurs when the blood vessels constrict in an attempt
to stay warm by reducing blood flow to the feet. This can happen in temperatures ranging from freezing to 60 degrees (F). The reduction in blood flow results in nerve and
tissue damage. The damp environment can be caused by various factors ranging from
wet socks to excessive sweating. In as little as 13 hours trench foot can occur. Advanced
cases can result in gangrene and amputation. The medical term for trench foot is Non
Freezing Cold Injury (NFCI).

Fortunately, I carried those extra socks. They probably saved my feet. As we progressed into the heart of Germany, when I ran short of dry, clean socks I found a creek, washed a pair, and tied them on my ammunition belt until they dried as I marched on. If there was time, I soaked my feet in the cold water and dried them carefully. The discoloring stabilized.

One consequence of my trench foot is that, to this day, I still have little feeling in my feet; sometimes, I can't even feel a pin prick. My lower legs sometimes swell with edema after I sit too long. That needle-like numbness is especially noticeable when I get up in the morning. Even now, I cannot test bath water with my toes. The nerve damage means that I always feel like I'm wearing socks, even when my feet are bare.

No member of my squad requested to go to a rear area for medical attention even though we all suffered from trench foot. I couldn't do that to my comrades or to myself. In a company of more than 200 men, only Donnie collapsed during the march. When his nerves stabilized, he was assigned to company duty. We rarely saw him after that.

As night fell that evening after the battles on the hill and in the town, we took up defensive positions. I was ordered to go out on a night patrol with Buster. I did not mind that, but I was afraid that I might endanger the other patrol members if we got into a fire fight. I still was carrying a rifle that shot once and then jammed. I went to our Captain and complained. He said he had no rifle to give me. Buster wanted me to go with him, so I went on patrol with a faulty M1. Fortunately, we had no problems that night as we wandered behind enemy lines.

The next morning, I got a new rifle. On it was carved the name "Corky." It had belonged to someone who had fallen. This rifle worked. No, it was better than that. Corky was a marvelous rifle. I felt its balance in my hands. It felt like it had always been there. It leveled as though it knew where it was being aimed. My "quick draw" became even faster with daily practice, and my shooting improved drastically with it. I was reluctant to turn "Corky" in when we were disarmed just before we were shipped back to France. I wish I could have kept that remarkable weapon; not for target shooting, but as a tangible representation of my weeks in Infantry combat.

The crossing of the Rhine and the subsequent three-day march are barely mentioned in *Always First*. They should have been. I am convinced that few American front line units acted with more courage and determination.

The fact that we marched more than 115 miles in three days is incredible. What makes it all the more incredible was when you factor in our physical condition as we met this challenge.

To me the bravest thing I did during the war was being part of that long march. Each step was an effort, an act of will. Every step I took was tinged with a sharp pain in my ankle, especially when we were marching along rough dirt rural roads. Even though I was weakened with dysentery, I managed to keep pace with everyone in my squad. In looking back, I was part of an unsung American epic. To me that three-day march was my "Red Badge of Courage."

*   *   *

In early January 1975 I tried to drive the route of our march. With me were my ex-wife Phyllis, and my youngest son Eric. It was my second attempt at tracing the route of our march. The first was in the summer of 1967. Both times I managed to move a few miles into the hills of the Rhineland, but by then the roads had changed, woods had been cut down, and new buildings had sprung up. There were more towns now. Nothing was recognizable. I lost my way, drove back to the Rhine, and headed south.

LISTENING POST

The other day I found an aged file folder and a sheaf of my handwritten notes. The paper was yellow and faded. Fortunately, my handwriting then was much more legible than it is now. These notes were written in 1946 and 1947. Some were written immediately after I was discharged, some when I was in college. Two stories were marked by one of my English professors. Others were not. Three were about experiences I had during the war or right after it. There is a longish attempt at the beginning of a novel that later become the basis of my war play, *Pillars in the Night*. Even then I had aspirations of becoming a writer.

One account about being shelled had been erased from my memory until I read it again in the late fall of 2009. Even now it doesn't seem real to me, but I wrote it as a record of an actual event. The other, which I include below, snapped vividly back into my memory.

It was a dark night. We moved quietly through a thick, dark woods. The pine needles softened the sound of our feet. Ahead of us, the dark figure of our squad leader turned and motioned for us to move forward. We stopped at the edge of the woods. There we were hidden as the twelve of us took up positions in pairs. Then we took up our long vigil.

Usually our squad decided who went on patrols. Sometimes we volunteered, sometimes we decided by the flip of a coin. After our long advance, we were all tired, bone tired. No one volunteered, so Mike picked his five-man patrol. I was pleased when he picked me, but I was apprehensive. Tonight, we were on a most unusual mission. Our platoon had been selected to be the battalion's listening post.

We were told to set up a position at the edge of the woods and listen to what might be happening in the town in the deep valley below us. We were told to listen to any enemy movement.

If there were only noises of movement in the village below, we were told to quietly report this by walkie-talkie. If there was an enemy attempt to infiltrate our lines, we were told to report this as quietly as possible and to crawl in with the enemy until we could make a break for our line of defense. Our mission seemed doubly important when we were told that intelligence had reported that the remains of a famous *Panzer Grenadier* unit was being assembled in the village.

We didn't dare to dig foxholes. That would cause too much noise, so we lay on the soft, damp ground at the edge of the woods. As we settled in, a chill crept into our bodies. Even though it was quite dark, we felt naked and exposed.

In the town ahead we began to hear noises, a steady rumble and roar. It sounded like heavy tanks and half-tracks being deployed. Above it rose the rattle-rattle of lighter vehicles and a scattering of men's voices. Every sound seemed greatly amplified in the stillness of the night.

I looked to one side. I saw the shadowed outline of my buddy, fifteen yards away. While the town was dimly defined, the moonlight seemed like a spotlight on a stage, and we were the frightened and miserable performers standing before the most critical audience of all, the Germans.

Time passed too slowly. Our eyelids drooped. I laid on the operating rod of my M1. It was uncomfortable against me, but it kept me awake.

Dawn came slowly. Too slowly.

We looked down across the field as the town came into focus. We were shocked and outraged. The town was filled with American trucks and tanks. Our long night had been wasted. Truly the situation was quite normal. Everything was fouled up. As we trudged back to our platoon, we unanimously agreed that officers were the lowliest of creatures.

SPIRIT OF THE 76TH

THE LONG ADVANCE

Our company kitchen was far behind us, but our cooks struggled to deliver hot food to us. When they managed to catch up with us and serve us hot meals it was most welcome.

At this point my memory becomes very sketchy. I remember some moments in great detail, but at least one week that I was in front line combat remains a blank in my memory bank. As for that lost week, I have no idea what's missing. Perhaps it included searing experiences my mind repressed. It's more likely that sheer exhaustion blurred my consciousness to the point that my memory did not register those days.

I remembered riding through Mainz. The town was almost flat. We stopped and were allowed to attend a movie. The roof of the theatre had been bombed away. The destruction was devastating. Every town and many villages were severely damaged, first by our airplanes, and later by our artillery.

I remember receiving the command "Fix bayonets!" a few days after we crossed the Rhine. I vaguely recall that it was night and I wanted to sleep. The command sent a chill of fear through our systems. Remember at this time I weighed about 145 pounds. I had no bulk to put into a bayonet charge and in hand-to-hand fighting. All I had on my side were fast reflexes.

Foxhole shelling

To be perfectly honest, I do not remember what followed. I must have committed myself well since I was not an outcast the next day. I am glad that my memory fails me. I want no images in my memory bank of running a knife into another human being's body. I hope I did not.

All I remember is that I remained "The Kid," but I was treated as an important member of our squad now. I was one of the gang. If someone let the rest down, they became an irredeemable outcast, just as Donnie had. That night I must have passed some kind of test. I was accepted.

When I was a boy, I was always one of the last to be "picked up" in our games when sides were chosen. Now I belonged. Buster, especially, asked for me when he led out a patrol. I realized that I was a trusted member of our fighting team. In many ways this was my first real step to manhood. My boyhood had ended but my manhood was still developing.

We moved forward relentlessly. There was no rest. I remember digging in again and again. One night I slept – or was rendered unconscious – through a shelling. I awoke to find a shell hole inches away from the foxhole Larry and I dug the night before. It was like some monster had taken a bite out of the earth beside us as we slept. Larry and I dug to that depth only once during our weeks in combat. That was the night the shell came so close. If it had landed a few inches closer, I would have been dead. I believe it is at this point my memory becomes vague. Perhaps I suffered a concussion in that explosion. I am not sure. Some events were erased from my memory.

The first summer I was home after the war, I wrote about my experiences in combat. Recently I came across the following in a yellowing folder. Some of the material in that thick file found its way into my plays *Pillars in the Night* and *Odyssey's End*. Some may have been intended for a novel. I have slightly edited this section to smooth out its writing style, but it is essentially what I wrote shortly after I was discharged from the Army.

I pushed myself close to the earth, as close as I could. Mother Earth, accept me, take me into your bosom.

Every inch of my body was pressed against the soft accepting ground, but I couldn't be inside it.

I heard the screaming shell coming. My body became a tight knot of anticipation and fear.

And then the crash, the screaming splinters of metal shredding the air into ribbons of sound.

I waited, feeling no pain. I was alive, untouched.

Then another.

The earth again into me and me into the earth. Together we rose and fell. A whole battery of 88s opening up on us. No time to brace yourself.

Crash!

Another.

Another,

Another.

Another.

Hold on. Hold on, Oh, Jesus, Jesus, I'm afraid, afraid. Don't let me get killed.

Don't.

Don't.

Don't.

A whole battery of 88s opening up, throwing steel into the night around me.

More.

More. Oh, Christ, Jesus Christ.

More. Oh, Goddamn. "Save me. I am sick. Sick. Sick to death because I fear death."

The earth heaved. I was lifted into the air and slammed down. I couldn't breathe. Tears streamed down my cheeks, and I vomited. For a second I tasted the foulness, and I swallowed it again as I heard the shriek of another and another, and still another.

To one side, my left, there was screaming, a high piercing scream that rose above the sound of the shells exploding. A steady, unending, gasping scream of pain.

Jesus! Another. I held on. Fingers digging into the ground. Clutched fingers, torn nails, scraping on rocks and roots. *Oh, God! Stop it!*

Another.

The earth lifted and heaved as it was split and torn.

Then silence. Delicious, impossible silence, unreal and ghostly.

Except for the screaming! Some poor bastard screaming his guts out, "Medic! Medic!"

Lou on my left whispered hoarsely, "For Chrissake keep it down!"

Davy crawled toward the wounded man. I heard Davy say, "You wanna live?"

"Damn right I do!"

"Keep it down. Hold it in."

"Morphine. Please. Some morphine."

"You got it."

I remember nothing else of that night. I cannot place it in a sequence of my time in combat, but I believe it was the night a shell hit the side of my foxhole.

*   *   *

Once in a while the German planes would strafe us. I believe one particular strafing came the day after we were commanded to fix bayonets for the first time. We were moving along the slope of a hill when a two-motored German Heinkel bomber came over a hill and zoomed parallel to our position, firing and ready to drop bombs. We were in a wide, dish-shaped draw with a long ridge ahead of us. There was a lace work of tracer rifle and machine gun fire seeking to down the bomber as it passed over us. Before it flew out of sight it was hit. A stream of smoke came out of one of its engines; and, just out of our line of sight, it crashed beyond a hill.

When the Heinkel began its run, we were on a break and I had broken down my M1 to clean it. Before the plane finished its run, I had slammed my rifle together and got off a clip. My fingers have never been so nimble. I put my rifle together in a matter of two or three seconds. All that training in the care of our weapons had paid off. The final phase of our training had been to assemble a broken-down rifle in the dark.

No one knew who hit the bomber in a vital place, but I doubt that it was our 32 mm M1 fire. It was more likely one of the .60 caliber machine guns mounted on our jeeps. This was the first time – but not the last – our unit shot down a German plane.

Mortar loop the loop

FIGHTING IN THE STREETS

There was a day of street fighting that I remember vividly. We approached a medium sized town. Before we entered it, we had to cross a small river. In America we would have called it a creek. We discovered that the Germans had zeroed their mortars in on a crude plank bridge that we had to cross in order to get into the town.

By now, we were experienced enough to know the sound of a mortar cough when it was fired. A mortar crew consisted of two men. One aimed the weapon with calibrations on its base. The other armed the mortar shell and dropped it down the barrel. When the shell hit the bottom of the barrel it would explode with a hoarse cough. At that moment we had about three or four seconds to move and take cover. Once the shell exploded, we listened for another telltale cough. We moved again. No shell hit any of us. We were always under cover when the next shell landed.

We safely crossed the bridge without casualties and entered into the main part of the town. This was my first street fighting experience. I found it terrifying and more stressful than the fighting in the Rhineland forests. Each corner was a danger. Inside a building, the opening of a door became an act of will. Fortunately, the Germans kept withdrawing as we advanced from building to building. None stayed behind to fight a rearguard action. If you want a sense of that day, see the final scenes of Stephen Spielberg's 1998 epic war film, *Saving Private Ryan*.

While speaking of that film, I must note that its main accuracy is in the first moments of the invasion. Once they were on the beach, Hollywood took over. Riflemen do not shoot as accurately as they do in the sections when they get off the beach. In actual combat, wounds from rifle fire are far fewer than those received from machine guns. Most wounds occur during shellings and mortar fire. All that mowing down of German troops with single rifle shots is pure Hollywood.

Under the pressure of fire no one is accurate. The object is to pin down the enemy with a sheet of fire and put enough fear into him so that he will surrender. Yes, once in a while someone is shot; but rifle fire wasn't all that accurate. There was little time to take aim, and to fire when moving was inaccurate and a waste of ammunition.

Hollywood has always drawn its technical information from officer consultants rather than enlisted men. I suspect that few of these officers had seen combat. Instead, they assisted in staging battle scenes by the rule book. There were no rule books in combat. We improvised. By now, we were a team that worked together. We knew who we could count on and moved accordingly. Our squad had no real weak links except for one man. Luckily for him, we didn't find out the full story about Rooter until after the war was over.

*   *   *

Two movie directors, Robert Aldrich and Sam Fuller, were more accurate than most about the combat experience. Both had seen Infantry combat. Aldrich in his film *Attack!* and Samuel Fuller in *The Big Red One* catch much of the combat infantry experience on film. If anything is missing in their films, it is the gore now possible in PG-13 and R rated films. Before the movie ratings system was adopted, graphic violence was toned down.

A Midnight Clear also came close. It shows a small squad patrol action with relentless honesty. Many films were psychologically true to what happened to us, but most show us as selfless men and boys willing to give our lives for a noble cause. Believe me, the closer we all got to the front, the more our patriotism faded away. Then we moved into a survival mode. I believe that our ability to adapt and survive is what made the American fighting man great.

After *All Quiet on the Western Front,* one novel stands out as the finest about infantry combat. It is Van Van Praag's *Combat,* a grim and unrelenting book. It was well written and brutally honest. It's a pity the book is now forgotten. Huge parts of Norman Mailer's *The Naked and the Dead* are accurate. Some of Irwin Shaw's *The Young Lions* are to be commended.

As for plays, few stand up. Harry Brown's *The Sound of Hunting* catches the spirit of combat. Later it was made into a film that removed it from the confines of the cellar setting of the play. Arthur Laurent's *Home of the Brave* approached infantry combat in the Pacific from a psychological point of view. It, too, became a film. The scope of a war does not fit well on the confines of a stage.[14] Film is a better vehicle for telling such stories.

ON POINT

One sunny day I was assigned to be one of two scouts to serve as point men for our entire company. When an infantry company – some 200 men – advances, it moves ahead in the form of a large triangle. Each platoon marches as a triangle, too. The platoon has an advance man – a scout – and behind him two riflemen, and behind them a BAR and his assistant. That was usually me. The bazooka and its loader were further back in the ranks. Finally, there was a single man, a sort of rear guard.

One did not volunteer to be a company scout. You were assigned to this by luck of the draw. It was a duty no one wanted. Usually there were two scouts advancing approximately a hundred yards ahead of the whole company, and they were at least fifty yards apart. Each scout was quite alone and exposed. The Germans often let scouts through their lines so that the main body would be closer to enemy lines when firing began. As

---

14 I must mention my once produced play, *Pillars in the Night.* Some photos of Warren Smith's wonderful production of it remain in my files. Everyone connected with that production labored long and hard to make it as accurate as possible. I recently looked at the play. I think it stands up well. Even so, I am certain it will never see a stage again. Its cast is too large to begin with. Worse still, I fear there is no audience for it now.

Playing the counterpart of Buster in my play was John Aniston, Jennifer's father. He was the picture of Buster on stage and managed to get some of Buster's cockiness. One other member of the cast, Al Sarkis, recently called me, just to check in. Old friends do pop up from time to time.

Nobody loves me!

scouts, it was our job to draw fire that would warn the men behind us. Scouts were rarely killed, but they were often surrounded and captured. No one wanted to be a captive of the German Army.

The two of us moved forward, first across fields, then into forests. I held my rifle at waist level. I had a bullet in the chamber and the safety was off. As we moved forward, we knew that we could be moving into the middle of the German defenses. In such a thick forest we could have walked right by a German machine gun nest. Above us, snipers could be strapped high in the trees.

Each step was a frightening experience. We had no idea when we might venture into enemy lines. The advance through that Rhineland forest was especially tense. This could be the day we met heavy resistance. I thought to myself, "Of all days to be picked for this duty!"

We moved through the evergreens. They were close together. Even though it was a sunny day, we moved amidst an eerie blue-green light.

The other scout was more frightened than I. He often hesitated in his forward movement. To our rear the captain signaled us to keep moving. I felt no urge to hold back. Once I was as much as 30 yards in advance of my reluctant fellow scout. I never knew his name as he came from another platoon. Of the two of us, he was the more sensible young man.

It was a long day. The tension was always with me, but I kept moving. If we had encountered the German army, both of us on point would have been killed or captured. We were potentially sacrificial lambs. If we went down, the company would prepare for battle. Our job was to give them time for that preparation. The day was uneventful. The Germans had pulled back to strong positions. That night my nerves were frayed, and I was exhausted more than I usually was. I was very glad for the day to end.

Those days are a blur in my memory. I remember single events, places, or my own feelings. I vaguely remember digging in with Larry. I remember stealing more food from our armored escorts. I remember advances and charges. I remember warm meals catching up with us. I remember my friends and fragments of conversations. Perhaps we all were operating at what was barely a conscious level. Exhaustion gave me blessed escape from realities I do not remember. I must have functioned well since I remained part of our brotherhood, and I was always in demand to go on day and night patrols. If Buster approved of me, I did well.

In looking back, that long advance into the heart of Germany was an incredible physical feat for all of us even if there had been no fire and resistance. Each valley, each town, and each tree could hide a German ready to kill us. Add that tension to the incredible physical demands placed on us, and our constant state of exhaustion was understandable. Then add to that the fact that many of us were still suffering from dysentery and trench foot.

During that time, I was no longer the outsider I had been in my boyhood. I was one of many. I was accepted by my comrades. I wonder now how those brutish bully boys of my childhood would have handled such complete physical and emotional pressure under the stress of combat. In years to come, I always judged men and measured my friends very simply: Would they have stood with me in infantry combat? Would I want to share a foxhole with them? It is a gut judgment, but I still make it when I meet a new person, man or woman, by the instinctive feel I gained during the war. Invariably, the man I trusted in such a way was also a gentle, good man.

After the war, when I found myself under pressure in civilian life, I always reminded myself that I had seen worse. My lack of fear when it came to my lifework in theatre was colored by my experiences in combat.

Marching Fire

On the 31st of March the Battalion advancing towards Arnsbach and Hausen-Arnsbach entered Hunoldstal and captured it with little opposition. Moving on in an approach march formation, Companies C and D moved into Rod am Berg. Company A on the right flank and Company B on the left flank advanced simultaneously to form a pincers movement upon the dual towns of Arnsbach and Hausen-Arnsbach. The 901st Field Artillery supported, by fire, Company A in its attack in Hausen-Arnsbach, while Company D supported Company B in the attack on Arnsbach by heavy mortar and machine gun fire. The anti-tank platoon, tank destroyers, and tanks gave direct fire support from the high ground to the rear of Rod am Berg. The two companies advanced across the open plain under the curtain of supporting fire. Company B, using marching fire, closed in on Arnsbach meeting heavy resistance in house-to-house fighting. However, shortly after dark, both towns were reported clear of all enemy troops. Approximately 165 German troops were either captured or killed in the process of taking the two towns. Company B also liberated 1 officer and 28 EM from company L, 417th Infantry, who had been captured by the Germans in an earlier engagement. We also recaptured one American Light Tank, and one quarter-ton Jeep.

The next day, Easter Sunday, we were on the move again, with Company C taking the town Anspach, while Company A took Westenfeld. Still driving the enemy back, the Battalion moved into the towns of Obernhain, Wehrheim and Pfaffenwiesbach, where we were relieved by the 385th Infantry.[15]

As we swept deeper into Germany, we advanced to the edge of a wide valley fronting the town of Arnsbach[16] on the day before Easter Sunday. The First Battalion was spread wide and thin. Our Charley Company was at the middle of the deployment. Baker was on our right, and Able on our left. There we all made ready for the battle.

Beyond our battalion and to the right and left of us were the two other battalions in our 417th Infantry Regiment. We were poised to advance in a long line across that valley. It was the largest scaled attack I had been in. At least three thousand men were poised to attack the Germans in Arnsbach.

---

15 *Always First*

16 The spelling on this town is shown as Arnspach or Arnsbach, depending on the year and the map.

Regimental headquarters commanded that we use what they claimed was a new infantry tactic called marching fire. It was probably the dumbest strategy I encountered in my time in combat. We were ordered to march straight ahead toward the enemy at a slow fixed pace. As we advanced, we were ordered to fire our rifles from our hips and lay down a sheet of fire. The assumption was that we would force the enemy to take cover. They would be intimidated and surrender before we completed our attack.

We were ordered not to use our usual running zigzag patterned advance. In that form of attack, we dropped to the ground and fired. Then we got to our feet, ran, and dropped again. It was obvious that if we advanced as a unit at a slow marching pace, we would be easy targets. One machine gun nest could decimate a platoon. There was nothing new about this. It was as though we were the British Redcoats marching to certain death during the Revolutionary War. Whoever thought up that damned tactic should have been ordered to lead us across that flat valley. No officer higher than a captain joined us in our attack.

As we waited to attack, my platoon was situated in front of our company's mortars. Briefly, at least, we were in what we considered our rear echelon. We were nervous. Even with our normal tactics, the broad valley ahead of us offered little cover. If the enemy was inside of Arnsbach many would fall during the slow advance.

To my left, across the valley where the hills began, a German Tiger tank lurked in a narrow draw. One of its treads had been shot off, and it was immobilized. Even so, its lethal 88 cannon laid out devastating fire into our long thin line. Our bazooka men were much too far away to fire at the tank, and our artillery was useless against it. Once or twice, we saw our 105 shells bounce off the Tiger tank's turret.

I saw German infantrymen in company strength setting up a defensive position around the immobile tank. Mac lent me his German field binoculars. (I later bought them from him and still have them). After I confirmed what my eyes had told me, I ran back to our mortars and pointed out what could be a launching point for a counterattack. Our mortar men quickly bracketed the draw with fire. They shot over and under as they bracketed their target. The third round exploded amidst the German soldiers. Now that the draw was bracketed, the mortar men poured round after round into the draw. Within minutes the German infantry lay wounded or dead. Dozens had fallen. Few moved. No medics came from out of the woods. If some were still dying, they died alone.

As I watched that deadly fire, I sat waiting, knowing that I had been responsible in part for the death and maiming of at least fifty German soldiers. I had no time to dwell on this sobering thought. I knew we were about to cross that valley under fire. I gathered my courage and concentrated on what lay ahead.

In looking back, I am amazed at how rational I was when I was under fire. I felt no fear, no sense of danger. Instead, I thought about what to do next. Yes, there was tension; but that came out of waiting, of being on lonely guard duty, and in now knowing what lay ahead. In the midst of fire, I was fearless. That was a "me" I had never met.

Why was I fearless? Perhaps it was because I was bone-weary as I marched ahead on a creaking ankle as I drove my dysentery-wracked body beyond conscious limits. Even so, I remained calmly rational. I am still trying to explain what might be called bravery to myself. After the war fear came to me in nightmares. At times I woke up screaming. In time, the dreams faded away but echoes of them linger in my mind on occasional mornings when I laze in a half sleep.

Shortly after the firing on the draw we advanced across the valley, firing from the hip. Before we started our long, exposed march, that cursed command came down the line, "Fix bayonets!"

Click! We did. Now our rifles, weighed down by our bayonets, were unbalanced and less accurate.

"Advance! March!"

An entire infantry regiment - more than three thousand men - moved forward across that valley in layered lines. *Always First,* the battalion history I worked on after the war ended, says only our B Company used marching fire. That is in error. I clearly remember walking across the vast field as I fired my M1.

In spite of being a single soldier amidst this mass of men, I felt exposed. Any moment a shell could come crashing in and wipe out our squad. Any second a sniper might choose me as his target of opportunity. Even so, I had no fear. My mind was numb, my body weary. I obeyed orders and advanced with my fellow soldiers. We said nothing to each other.

As I walked ahead, firing from the hip, I glanced to my right and my left. I shot off clip after clip as I shot ahead with no specific targets. Our Charley Company was on the left side of the attack. It was a frightening and epic moment. The tension was unbearable. Every vein of our being told us to charge at full speed.

Then, as we drew close to the town, I saw a man fall far to my right. Then another fell further down the line. Enemy fire intensified. Now it was a mix of rifle and machine gun fire. I heard that fearsome zzzzzz-tearing sound of the rapid-fire German machine guns. More men fell. Conditioned reflexes driven into our very being during basic training took over. We wanted to charge on the run.

I heard someone shout, "Fuck it, let's go!"

Together we joined the shout. We broke into a trot and then a full-fledged run. We roared as one as we launched our final charge toward the town. Our officers tried to restrain us, but we attacked. No more bullshit marching fire for us. We wanted to get inside that town's streets and the shelter of its buildings. Once there we could engage the enemy. We were not automatons controlled by some idiotic strategy devised at West Point. We were experienced infantrymen, brothers in arms, intent on winning by surviving. We were as one as we charged full bent toward that town.

How much of this did I understand at the time? None consciously, but deep inside me I felt I was as one with many. We were more than patriotism, more than country. We were human beings banded together. Indeed, we were a band of brothers. Our parentage was mixed, but we were one. I was as brave as the man next to me, and he was as brave as me. The politicians and diplomats may have brought us to this moment, but within the moment we were something unique, something that only young men experience at least once a generation. Our brotherhood of combat infantrymen did not exist for just that moment. We reach across centuries and join hands together with those who came before us over many centuries – and those who came after us in the years to come. It is tragic that so few have put that moment of togetherness into one coherent philosophy that would form a world government and allow us all to live in peace.

I have no memory of what happened when we got into that town. The attack began at dusk and went well into the night, lit by the waning gibbous moon. There was street fighting and advances from building to building, with us not knowing what would greet us when we crashed in a door. My brain filed the rest of that day and night away into some dark corner that I cannot access. *Always First!* says that our C Company finished taking Arnsbach the following day and continued our advance toward the east to Pfaffenwiesbach.

This is just one of my lost memories of my time in combat. Some have come back, but much remains lost. Perhaps that is merciful. Our battalion and division records report more battle action than I remember.

Once we moved out of that valley where we broke from our marching fire, many war-weary German soldiers surrendered with little provocation. There were so many they were dangerous to control. Fortunately, that was not the infantry's concern. Our job was to advance. For once the rear echelon troops faced some real danger.

* * *

Larry and Bill,
foxhole roommates.

19

Break Out

O NE DAY THE order came down that we were to steal anything with
wheels. We were told to keep up with the tanks. Some grabbed bicycles, many of us piled on horse-drawn wagons, and others stole German
cars. This was the first time I saw a Volkswagen Bug. It was noisy and
had little power.

With limited fuel, a steady, less precipitous advance continued. Our
tanks were moving ahead mile by mile, but now they could not burn up
gasoline as freely as they had in the first days of our advance. I have often
wondered what the course of world history would have been if Patton's
tanks had been free to probe even deeper into Germany at his own pace.
As an infantryman whose luck had been spent freely, I could have been
killed; but I have a sense that the more practical officers of the *Wehrmacht*
would have chosen to surrender to an American army.

Each day's advance was managed some way or another. One day we
were told to get on top of a tank destroyer and ride. It was a welcome relief.
A tank destroyer was a heavily armored treaded vehicle that looked very
much like a conventional tank. It was slower and heavier and was armed
with a Howitzer. I believe it was better than the 105s most of our tanks
carried. Our squad covered its top. We tried to be comfortable, but we
had to hang on precariously as the destroyer lurched ahead.

At the end of the day, we dug in. Some of the men stripped away some
of the tanker's possessions. One had taken a Thompson submachine gun,
a well-made automatic weapon reserved for officers and tankers. Later that
evening, an irate tanker went along our line of foxholes bitterly insisting
that the person who stole his weapon give it back. He was not successful.

Often when the Third Army broke out, Patton's fuel lines were shut off. It was a way to control his bold advances. No other army could keep up with us when we started moving. There was a danger we would get too far ahead and be cut off. If we were cut off, I suspect Patton would reverse field and plunge through the lines that had enveloped us. Patton was quoted as saying, "My men can eat their belts, but my tanks have gotta have gas."

Some believe that the bogged-down Montgomery insisted on these delays and fuel cutbacks. There is strong evidence to suggest that the British Field Marshal's slow advance to the north was what was delaying ending the war. Years later I read that he resented Patton's advance. He wanted the privilege of being part of the eventual German surrender. He may have hoped for the honor of capturing Berlin. We did not know this at the time, and we did not know how limited our fuel supplies were.

Montgomery, the hero of El Alamein, was not universally admired. Later histories of the war bear out those who saw him in a negative light. He even described himself as being "tiresome." He was difficult to work with, vain, and cautious. Patton was equally vain, but he did not have a definition for caution. Later, it came out that Montgomery and Patton were bitter rivals.

Those of us who had been assigned to the Third Army owe a lot to Patton. We were rarely bogged down into anything that even resembled the trench warfare of World War I. Montgomery, no doubt, was drawing his tactics from that earlier war. To give him some credit, the northern edge of our front was situated in the Lowlands. There were many rivers and bridges to cope with. To see how this added to his slow advance, see the 1977 epic war film, *A Bridge Too Far*.[17]

Higher ranking officers did more to slow Patton's progress than the German army did. If we had been given the fuel, I believe we would have

---

17   *A Bridge Too Far* is the 1977 war film based on the 1974 book of the same name by Cornelius Ryan, The film script was adapted by William Goldman. The movie was produced by Joseph E and Richard P. Levine and directed by actor and director Richard Attenborough. The story described the failure of the Operation Market Garden in September of 1944, when the Allies broke through German lines in the Netherlands and tried to secure nine bridges in order to cross the Rhine River. The goal was to finish the war by Christmas, 1944. The operation, led by Field Marshal Montgomery, was not a success, and the bridge at Arnhem was described as them having tried to go "a bridge too far." The city of Arnhem was finally liberated by the Canadian Corps on April 14, 1945, after two days of fighting. The bridge did not survive the war.

gone straight into Berlin. I also believe the Germans would have surrendered to us. I don't think they would have fought as they did against the Russians. To them, fighting the Russians gave them only two choices – victory or death. At the end of the war most Germans knew there was no chance of victory. In a short time, I would see evidence of the Germans' fear of the Russian army. It was a fate they brought upon themselves.

I put that verdict too simply. The Germans chose to turn their government over to a fascist regime that promised them many material rewards and a restoration of national honor. When I grew older, I realized that some cultures do not understand democracy – such as it is in our country now. At least some of us in America still harbor the idealism that formed our country. Sadly, that idealism is being eroded by opportunists seeking materialistic goals and short-term, short-sighted solutions. Germany gave in to a mad genius who promised prosperity, national identity, and cultural and racial purity. America currently seems hell-bent on following the same path.

Patton was a genius in his chosen trade. I am sure that if he had turned his mind to it, he could have been our Hitler, just as General Douglas MacArthur was trying to do when he was recalled from Korea by President Harry Truman. I have been privileged to know a handful of high-level geniuses in my lifetime. Each, to me, seemed to be almost a different species from those who were merely intelligent. The jump from high intelligence to genius covers an enormous gap. Most of those special geniuses saw through the pretense and hypocrisy that forms most political systems and which mask reality from the general public.

Mass Surrender Amidst Fleeing Refugees

On the 6th of April we were on the move again, and this time we traveled by motor convoy approximately 110 miles to Eschenstruth where we were in Regimental reserve. The next day with the entire Battalion mounted on our vehicles we moved as a task forced to Helsa, then we traveled along the main highway through the towns of Wickernrode, Grossalmerode, to Trubenhausen where we went back to foot travel again. We moved by this blistering means of transportation to Hundelshausen where we set up a defense on the high ground around the town for the night.[18]

To spearhead Patton's Third Army's deep thrust into Germany, the 76th teamed with the 6th Armored Division and began heading towards Berlin. Our advance was fast and relentless. There were pockets of resistance, but we swept through them with minimal casualties. It seemed that most Germans understood that the war was winding down, and theirs was a lost cause.

DPs and Refugees

We rode forward in trucks. The roads were clogged with a sea of humanity retreating from the center of Germany. Long columns of surrendered German soldiers escorted by a handful of guards headed to POW stockades far behind the battle lines. Their grey-green uniforms and caps were muted by dust. Their shoulders slumped with weariness, they shuffled as they walked, their eyes blank with remembered horrors of too many campaigns. We knew many of them had seen more horrors than we had. No, many had seen more horrors than we could imagine.

As our trucks nudged through the crowded road, some prisoners reached up and asked for rations. Some spoke English. We gave them nothing. Perhaps we should have, but a few days before these same men were shooting at us. Now they were begging within an arm's reach. We all hoped that the entire German Army was ready to surrender, but that was not the case. Many *Wehrmacht* units, afraid of retaliation from their Nazi commanders, fought on. The hated SS divisions were still ready to fight.

---

18 *Always First*

Moving with the German soldiers were Displaced Persons (DPs), fleeing so that they were behind our front lines. Amidst this sea of humanity
were thousands upon thousands of DPs.

They carried what little they possessed. Most of this had probably
been looted from the Germans who had used them. Some DPs pushed
carts, some carried their possessions on their backs. A few rode bicycles.
They were trying to make their way home – to France, Italy, Belgium,
the Netherlands, and Greece. We gave these people what we could spare.
Most of us tried to see that what we gave went to children first. In return,
they cheered us. We were their liberators. As I watched them pass by us,
I felt that our cause had been just.

We were amidst a trudging sea of epic desperation as our trucks and
tanks edged forward toward that final center of German resistance – Berlin.

I am sure the German soldiers feared what we might to do to them.
They outnumbered us. Fortunately, they were disarmed when they surrendered. The DPs knew they had hundreds of miles to cover before they
returned home. I never knew how they made that arduous journey. Did
they loot and steal as they made their odyssey? Somehow many survived
that epic journey home. Theirs is a story worth telling.[19]

The world about us was war weary. They had suffered interminable
bombing and shelling. They had suffered privation and grief. We were
boys, not fully aware of the carnage we created and encountered.

We had no time for empathy when we were under fire, no time to
feel sorry for our enemy; and they had no time for empathy toward us.
If the common soldiers on either side had that time, I think we would
have revolted and quit the war. Army discipline is designed not to let that
happen. Even its order of battle nullifies the possibility of sympathy. We
were conditioned to protect our own small unit, the squad. We became
one small country as we continued to advance. It was a deadly country
that was ready to kill other human beings at a moment's notice.

---

19 I highly recommend a wonderful Italian film, released in 1998, based on Primo
Levi's memoir, *Le Tregua (The Truce)*, about his return to Italy after the Red Army
liberated the concentration camp at Auschwitz. Although the camp was liberated on
January 27, 1945, Levi didn't reach Turin, his home, until October 19 of that year. His
route included Poland, Russia, Romania, Hungary, Austria, and Germany. *The Truce*
was directed by Francesco Rosi, written by Tonino Guerra, and starred John Turturro
and Rade Serbedzija. It is a powerful and moving film.

Pranks and Patrols

I continued to volunteer to go on patrol with Buster. One was especially memorable. We moved out in the dead of the night and passed quietly through a narrow railroad underpass. Again, we went deep behind German lines. At one point we managed to tear down some telephone lines. That was not part of our objective, but it seemed like a good idea at the time. By then, we knew that the Germans valued organization and efficiency. We believed the best way to demoralize them was to tear apart that tight organization in any way we could.

The patrol was uneventful. When we returned and approached the underpass we were challenged. We exchanged the words of the daily password and moved past a machine gun nest. In going out, we had been so quiet that we had walked right by that nest in an underpass that was less than twenty feet wide. Indeed, we moved quietly.

On one day patrol we again moved deep behind German lines. On the outskirts of a town, we found a small weaving factory. We entered its main building and passed through a large room filled with knitting and weaving machines. We tore apart the carefully threaded machines and misdirected the multiple lines of threads. Then we found its offices. In one office were banks upon banks of meticulously kept business files. We spent a half an hour changing the filed materials around from drawer to drawer, mixing them up as we did. It must have taken days and perhaps weeks for the factory to get back in order.

During my first weeks in combat, my dysentery persisted. One day, not out of fear but because I was trapped on a moving truck, I had an accident. That evening we moved into a German home for the night. I rummaged through bedroom dressers, desperately trying to find clean underwear. All I could find was a pair of long johns that was lavishly embroidered with flowers. I chose to wear it, hoping I would not be captured. Who knows what my fate would have been if it had been discovered I was wearing embroidered German long johns!

I carefully folded my soiled long johns and put it in the dresser drawer, just where my newly acquired underwear had been. In looking back, I pity the poor *Hausfrau* who discovered my dirtied long johns. What a way to remember the forces that had just defeated your beloved Fatherland! I replaced my flowered underwear as quickly as possible with army issue long johns.

When we were in convoy, we often had to relieve ourselves over the tailgates of the trucks. We only stopped for a five minute per hour break. That caused a lot of ribald merriment. The truck behind us would drop back as one of us dropped a load on the road. One of the privates riding with us was named Brown. He was a prematurely wizened country boy. One chant we developed was: "What color's shit? Brown, that's his name!"

Brown, not offended, cackled at our teasing.

*   *   *

As we pressed forward, one ever-present figure was Kilroy. Almost everywhere we went the cartoon sketch of a long-nose figure looking over a fence appeared on toilet walls and elsewhere. Below was scribbled, "Kilroy was here."

Kilroy was us. He was everywhere.

There were also chants and songs. I regret that I remember so few of them. Many were cleverly devised. All were a form of ribald folklore. In a way they reflected our irrepressible spirit. That spirit was essential to our survival – and sanity.

One song was a parody on "Mairzy Doats," a popular novelty song of the time. It went:

> *Mairzy Dotes and dozy dotes*
> *and Hitler's screaming mimis*
> *I'd dive for my foxhole, too, wouldn't you?*

BEING STRAFED

The next day, the 8th of April, we again mounted our vehicles and formed our Battalion task force and moved to Eigenrieden. Here we detrucked again and the Battalion spread out and clearing the woods and the towns of Dörna and Pfafferode. On the 10th of April we moved to Langensalza, staying there about eight hours and then moved on to Schwerstedt. We set up a perimeter defense and stayed there for the night. We moved out the next day entirely motorized, with the assignment of following the Sixth Armored Division. While en route to Buttstädt behind the 6th Armored, we were attacked by eight planes of the German *Luftwaffe*; four of them were shot down by a unit of 778th Anti-Aircraft which was attached to the Battalion. We closed in Buttstädt without further incident.

Approximately noon the following day the convoy was forming to move out when 2 enemy planes came over the town attacking the column. The Anti-Aircraft and Company D's machine guns opened up bringing both the planes down. Each unit was accredited with one apiece. The Battalion task force then moved to Poppel, where we detrucked and moved by foot to Neidschütz, in the meantime clearing approximately 20 towns and taking over 300 prisoners.[20]

One day we rode by trucks into a vast plain. No marching now, the advance was too rapid. At the center of that plain was an Autobahn, a German superhighway. Parallel to it were other roads. As we rode over the crest of a hill, a mind-boggling vista opened before us. The roads were filled with American trucks, jeeps, and armored vehicles. Above us

---

20 *Always First*

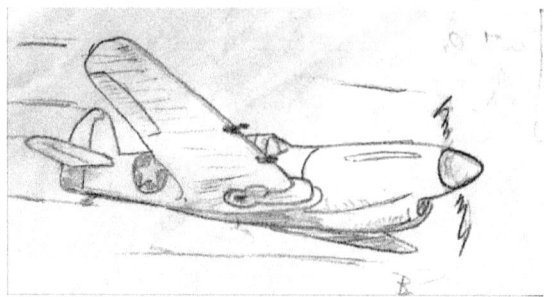

America P-51 Mustang

flew one of our daylight thousand-bomber raids. The bombers, in neat formations, reached from horizon to horizon, as did the men and their vehicles on the ground. How many men were in that advance? Thousands upon thousands, divisions, and perhaps most of an Army. I was thrilled at this awesome display of American power.

Then Focke-Wulf fighters appeared. They were newer in design than the better-known Messerschmitt ME-109s. The FW 190s were faster and better armed. Instead of attacking the bombers above them, they zoomed in to strafe our advancing columns. Every weapon we had opened up on them. Thousands upon thousands of tracers streaked through the day sky. Every few minutes one of the German planes went down in flames.

The fighters that soared above us were unpainted. In the haste to stop our advance they were flown straight out of a factory. The sun reflected off their shiny surfaces as they came in on their runs. The brave bastards flew into a hell of fire, a network of flaming bullets. Our own fighter planes stayed away. The fire sent up by the columns of advancing columns was too intense for them to enter. They wisely left the fighters to us, and rightly so.

All of us joined in the firing, even though rifle fire is ineffective against an air attack. We fired away clip after clip, but it was the .50 caliber machine guns that took the toll on the enemy fighters. Perhaps one of us hit one, but we could not trace our fire. Even though there was danger, this was a release from the tension of combat. We fired at will.

The scene was Homeric, a truly epic moment. In my boyhood I had been thrilled by the imagined vision of a thousand ships setting sail from Aulis for Troy. That was dwarfed by what I saw that day. That mighty power-filled plain was our route into the heart of Germany on our way to

Berlin. I carry that colossal panorama in my mind, and it reappears there with great regularity.

The power of America that day seemed insurmountable, and it was. When we began the war, trainees had to learn with wooden rifles. From 1941 until 1945 so much had changed. Now here we were, in the center of Germany, with forces that exceeded the imagination.

Our workers at home had built all that equipment, and our merchant marine transported it across the Atlantic. Then it was brought to the front by narrow gauge trains and the Red Ball Express, a truck convoy unit staffed primarily with African American soldiers. The logistics of what was done to get all that power to the center of Germany is mind boggling. That day I felt a surge of great pride in being part of what seemed like a great crusade to all of us. All the danger and horror of war faded for the moment as we surged forward with all that raw power. We were ending the war, and I was part of it.

Now our supply lines were so secure that no one told us to hold back and save ammunition as we fired at the strafing planes. Instead, we joined in the firing at the fighters. We shot bandoleer after bandoleer of bullets and got more. Here and there a German fighter plane went down in flames. As far as I could tell no vehicles in the columns were hit. The brave attack of the German pilots had been an act of futility. They were giving their lives for nothing. Why did they do it? Why didn't they quit and return to their bases?

Those who say the Germans were not loyal to their *Führer* are wrong. Many German soldiers fought as long as they had airplanes, tanks, and weapons – and the ammunition to fire them. Only then did they begin to surrender in large numbers. When they did, it was a flood, an inundation we were barely able to handle.

The strafing by newly built German fighters continued for several days. The machine gun bullets ripped along the ground, always missing. Maybe we were lucky during those days. Maybe the young pilots flying those planes were lacking in skill and training. Still, they bravely conducted daily sorties.

One day our truck had pulled up into a town square. Just as we were ready to dismount for a break, a Messerschmitt pursuit plane roared in on a strafing run. Most of the men jumped out of the truck bed and took cover. Two of us were mesmerized by the sight of this attacking plane coming in so low.

As the fighter's run approached us, we all began firing our rifles at the plane. Beside us a 75mm machine gun mounted on a company jeep chattered away, sending tracers through the air.

Then the plane seemed to stop as the streams of bullets centered on it. As it banked, I could see the pilot's amazed face as the bullets tore into his plane. He was that low. Then the plane veered, dropped straight down, and exploded into a nearby building.

I remained standing in the truck bed as this happened. I had no fear, but I was stunned by the proximity of this solitary fighter plane. I could not move. All I could do was stand and watch as the plane crashed, and its pilot died. That moment is seared into my memory. A moment that I did not forget.

Once in a while we saw V-2 bombs flying west toward England. A few German rocket fighter planes strafed us. They were much too fast to get into a dogfight and their ground fire was ineffective. They were virtually useless. One pass at one of our planes or a line of troops was all they could make. After that they would be miles away before they could circle back.

As this final rush of air attacks concluded, our colonel rode by us in his jeep. He shouted at us, "Men I want you to know we have fired more ammunition in the past three days than any other army unit in this goddamned war. Congratulations!"

No one knew for sure who had shot down the two German planes. We all were firing, and the matrix of tracer fire was a literal maze. Even though those planes were attacking us, no one was hit in those days of strafing. Even so, being strafed is an unnerving experience.

*   *   *

Years later, when I was working on my masters at Penn State in the early 1950s, I met a young German student at a party. I found out he had flown fighter planes for the German army. We discussed where we had been. He had been one of the pilots who had strafed us. We shook hands and congratulated each other for living through the war.

20

The End Draws Near

> Ours not to reason why.
> Ours but to do and die.[21]

W E RARELY DUG in as we swept forward. We usually rode in truck convoys or on top of armored vehicles. We were almost one with our tank battalions. Now Patton could be at his best. Our advance was bold and aggressive. There was no stopping now. We advanced and then advanced some more.

Because we rode so often, our ailing feet began to mend.

We began to feel we were invincible. The supermen were collapsing. Our morale soared. We now considered ourselves the best soldiers in the war. In a way, we were.

As we took town after town with little resistance, we shouted taunts to the watching German civilians. One of our favorites was, *"Deuschland unter alles!"* Translated into English, this means "Germany under all." It

---

21 A paraphrase adapted from Alfred, Lord Tennyson's epic poem, *The Charge of the Light Brigade*. The actual quote from the second verse is, "Theirs not to make reply, theirs not to reason why, theirs but to do and die. Into the valley of Death rode the six hundred."

was an inversion of the phrase from their national anthem which proclaimed, *"Deuschland über* (above) *alles."*

German POWs

By now the Germans were surrendering in huge numbers, but there
were still pockets of resistance. These
were usually fanatics, especially the
SS divisions who were determined to
fight to the end. The *SS* were also the
ones who committed atrocities against
captured troops. We were well aware
of the Malmedy Massacre during the
Bulge.

The conscripted German *Wehrmacht* had reached the bottom of their
manpower pool. Older men and young
boys were now in uniform. They were
commanded by battle weary veterans
who had seen action we could not imagine, some in Russia, some in France
and beyond. The common German soldier was ready to quit. Many chose
to opt out of the war they were clearly losing. They, like us, were caught
up in something they could not control. We had nothing but loathing
and hatred for the *SS*, but we respected the common German soldier.

In some towns the German civilians greeted us like rescuing heroes.
They cheered us as our armored columns rode through their villages and
towns. We did not trust their enthusiasm. Many, I felt, were cheering
their new masters.

Winston Churchill once commented that "the Hun is always either at
your throat or at your feet." We had gotten used to the Germans' ability
to shift sides for personal advantage, to inform against their neighbors,
and attempt to endear themselves to us. Others stood and watched, awed
by our forces and the sheer power of our arms.

The only Germans I even began to admire were the common soldiers
in the *Wehrmacht*. Most combat infantrymen would agree with that. The
common German soldiers were caught in a war they wanted to end. At
home, their compatriots behaved less admirably. Soon we would learn
how the human race would sink to the depths of depravity when even the
slightest economic pressure was applied by a ruling regime.

Slowly Germany contracted into a defense center as the noose tightened from the East and the West. American forces and Russian forces advanced toward Berlin. Only the German diehards fought on.

As the war wound down, all of us feared that we would die or be badly wounded before the war ended. More than a few of my comrades never made that day of final victory. I remembered that final scene in *All Quiet on the Western Front* when the young soldier reached for a butterfly and was shot.

My memories of that advance are merely an impression of always being on the move, sometimes on foot, but more often than not riding on tanks, tank destroyers, and trucks. As we rode, thousands of refugees fled from the action ahead of us. Troops escorted almost as many surrendered German troops. At times we pushed through a sea of humanity. At times there was action, usually isolated. Other times German fighter planes swept in to strafe us.

It is all a blur to me now.

SAD NEWS ON THE HOME FRONT

The 76th Division's log described our movement during the second week of April. As you read it remember that the CP – Command Post – was always well to the rear of our advance.

> On 8 April 1945, CT 417 was relieved by elements of the 3rd Cavalry and moved to Diedorf to take over the sector held by the 261st Infantry, establishing defensive positions and flushing the woods of enemy.
>
> On 10 April 1945, preparations were made to continue the attack to the East in the Division zone, with a temporary CP being opened at Thamsbrück and another CP being opened at Gebesee later in the day. To keep pace with the swiftly advancing troops, which had captured a score of towns and 250 prisoners (with some resistance being encountered from Volkssturm) the CP moved from Gebesee, paused at Sömmerda, and moved again to Vogelsberg.

On 12 April 1945, the CP was close at Vogelsberg, moving to Oster-
feld. Meanwhile, the 76th pushed its attack, capturing scores of towns
and hundreds of prisoners.[22]

As we surged deeper into Germany, the news came that President
Roosevelt had died.[23] All of us greeted this sad news with grief and dismay. Why did the man who led us have to die before he saw the end of
the war? Tears were shed even amidst continuing danger. We mourned
this great man. There was anxiety, too. None of us knew very much about
Harry Truman. Would he be up to the job?

Roosevelt changed our country greatly. He established Social Security,
created great public works projects, the TVA,[24] and even supported artists. This included the WPA[25] Theatre. Some of his New Deal programs
resembled socialism in their intent and were based on the "3 Rs:" *relief*
for the unemployed and poor, *recovery* of the economy back to normal
levels, and *reform* of the financial system to prevent a repeat of the Great
Depression. FDR sowed the seeds of a kinder treatment of the poor and
under-privileged and sought to give dignity and opportunity to all.

In the years that followed WWII, the Republicans ripped away controls and government supervision of essential services. Most of that social
progress has disappeared, and many in power have stated that their goal
is to erase all evidence of the New Deal. A great deal of damage has been
done in the past 35 years, and much of the progress and gains that made
our democracy stronger and our country great has been threatened or
destroyed. This is reflected in increasing poverty levels, food insecu-
rity, stagnant wages, homelessness, increased mental illness and sub-
stance addiction and abuse, underinsured health care, general instability,

---

22   The log of the 76th Infantry Division.

23   Franklin Delano Roosevelt, the longest serving President in U.S. history, was
pronounced dead at 3:30 pm on April 12, 1945, after suffering a massive cerebral hem-
orrhage a few hours earlier.

24   The Tennessee Valley Authority (TVA) was created on May 18, 1933, to modernize
the region's economy and society. It created public ownership of utilities and has become
one of the largest producers of electricity in the country.

25   The Federal Theatre Project was established in May 1935, to organize and produce
theatre events, providing work for unemployed theatre professionals during the Great
Depression throughout the nation. This program was established under the Works
Progress Administration (WPA) during Roosevelt's first term. The FTP functioned from
1935 to 1939 when its funding was terminated.

increased incarceration, social unrest, violence, divisiveness, declines in our educational system, and a crumbling infrastructure.

Even though the Republicans could muster no competitive rival during Roosevelt's terms, we were still a strong two-party system. Each party had its point of view. FDR created a government that was designed to serve the general public rather than huge banks, corporations, and special interest groups. Government was considered an ally, a force of good for the people. A life in politics was viewed as public service, and not to get rich and promote the wealthy. Regulations then were seen as a means to protect the population and level the playing field – unlike today when the "anything goes," "everyone for themselves," and "caveat emptor" rule.

Today, even the hard-fought progress in civil rights has been trimmed away. This continues to happen mainly by attacks on the voting rights of minorities and the disproportionate incarceration of people of color. Worse still, the thin line of separation between church and state has been all but erased.

I have always felt that fate was cruel in not allowing FDR to remain alive until the war was won. He fought the good fight. He stirred and rallied our sprits during the darkest days of the war. He was a great leader, a man who believed in social justice and economic security for all.

Conservatives accuse him of being a socialist. His best policies were just that. They were humane, Christian, and for the common good. Based on the idea that every human being has worth and deserves to be treated with dignity, and that the rising tide lifts all boats, FDR provided the country hope, relief, opportunities, and a chance for a better future. I have always been bemused that conservatives who advertise their Christianity do what they can to make the poor poorer and take away the basic rights of those who differ from them in race, religion, ethnicity, gender, and sexual identification. Roosevelt, with his New Deal, gave our country a glimpse of what it could be and should be. Perhaps one day his vision will be realized. FDR was one of a handful of great men who have lived on our continent. At the very least, he deserved a few more weeks of life.

Terrorists

There is no courage when there is no fear.[26]

On the 13th of April we moved from Neidschütz to Gladitz, with
all men riding on tanks. We were stopped here because of there not
being a bridge across the Weisse Elster River into Zeitz. While we
were stopped here Company D was credited with shooting down
another enemy plane. We finally had to cross the Weisse Elster River
by foot over the ruins of a blown bridge, in the hours of darkness.
This was necessary because the enemy had the crossing site under
direct 88 mm fire which prevented the Engineers from building a
bridge after we and 2nd Bn had cleared the town and thus prevented
the enemy from having observation on the river. The Engineers were
able to build a bridge and our vehicles were able to join us again.

We then moved, as a task force, to the town of Roda, when
Company V captured another 75 German prisoners and also released
500 French Officers, who were prisoners of the Germans. With
continuous pushing and driving we arrived at Erlau. We then set
up a defensive position. On the 16th of April the Anti-Aircraft unit
attached to the Battalion shot down a Focke-Wulf 109 and captured
the pilot.[27]

As the war wound down, the Germans mounted *Werwolf*,[28] a final underground resistance force to operate behind our lines. Their name was

---

26   Edward Vernon "Eddie" Rickenbacker (1880-1973) was an American fighter pilot
and a recipient of the Medal of Honor in 1930. He was the most successful American
fighter ace and received the most awards for valor by an American during WWI. His
awards included the Distinguished Service Cross, the Medal for Merit, the French Legion
of Honor and the Croix de guerre. After the war he was also a race car driver, automotive
designer, government consultant in military matters, and a pioneer in air transportation.
In 1935 he became the head of Eastern Air Lines and bought the company in 1938. He
was CEO until 1959 and remained as Chairman of the Board until 1963.

27   *Always First*

28   *Werwolf*, (in English, Werewolf) was named after the title of a 1910 novel by Hermann Löns (1866-1914), *Der Wehrwolf*. The story is about a peasant named Harm Wulf
who organizes his neighbors into a milita to pursue and execute marauding soldiers in
revenge of the Thirty Years War. The militia referred to themselves as *Wehrwölf*. While
Löns was killed in action during World War I (before the Nazis came into power), his
work became popular with the far right and was celebrated by the Nazis who used it for
propaganda purposes. It is also interesting to note that Hitler's first WWII Eastern Front
military headquarters was known as *Wolfsschanze*, or "Wolf's Lair."

well chosen. They preyed upon us, usually at night. During the day they assumed the guise of ordinary civilians. It was designed to frighten us, and it did.

One evening we got off our trucks and moved into a commandeered German house. Guard duty was set up. One of us had to walk that post for two hours, going back and forth between our billet and the billet that was company headquarters. The distance was about two hundred yards. Along the way was a deep cut in the land. There a guard was really open to an attack. I was one of those who drew guard duty.

I was awoken from a deep sleep for duty sometime after midnight. I went outside. The man I was relieving was from another platoon. He told me that they had found an American soldier garroted with a wire. His head was almost cut off. I had to guard that long dark post for two hours. Alone.

For a moment I considered the best way to walk that post. Then I slid a bullet into my rifle's chamber and took off my safety. With my finger on the trigger I began my progress to company headquarters. If I was attacked from behind, my finger would press on the trigger. Perhaps the shot would scare off any attacker. I walked through that deep cut alone. I have never been so frightened before or since. Each step forward was an act of will.

When I arrived at company headquarters, I collapsed against the front door. I took a few moments to muster my courage to walk my post again. That went on for two hours. They were the longest two hours of my young life. I was consumed with unspeakable terror, but I walked my post like a good soldier.

On my last round, I arrived at our billet and leaned against the door. I was exhausted from the tension and fear. The door opened behind me. I suddenly tensed and turned, rifle at ready. To my relief, it was my relief. I was very close to killing him. My nerves were raw. I went in and fell into a shared bed, dropping almost instantly into a very deep sleep. No one else died on that post that night. We were glad to be on our way the next morning. The Werewolves remained a presence, but unseen – at least by the men in my outfit.

Was walking that post during that long night an act of courage? At the time it happened, courage was the furthermost thing from my mind. I only wanted to finish my guard tour alive. I carefully thought out what I might do so that I would have the best chance of survival. If there had been a Werewolf waiting for me, I would have been very vulnerable. I weighed no more than 145 pounds and I was about 5 feet eight inches tall then. I was not even fully grown. He would not have known I was weak from dysentery and long marches, and with a gimpy ankle. Still, I believe that if I had died that evening, a Werewolf would have died with me.

In years to come, I drew upon my youthful fears. Occasionally during my adult life, an administrator or a colleague tried to intimidate me. One especially comes to mind, delivering an implied threat that I might suffer some undefined consequence if I did not mend my ways and write plays that were wholesome and free of sex and profanity. I watched his efforts with amusement. Before I walked out of that office, I told him firmly I would write and direct what I felt I needed to write and direct. How trivial his intimidation seemed after what I had seen as an eighteen-year-old infantryman! How could they intimidate someone who had walked along the fringes of a mortal hell?

The General and the Password

As we moved closer to Berlin, I was again on night guard duty. This time two of us were assigned to set up a roadblock on a country road leading into the German town where we were billeted. The road sat on a narrow embankment. On each side were low fields. My companion, Larry Freeman, and I decided the best way to block the road was for both of us to lay on opposite sides of the embankment. If a vehicle approached, one would move to the center of the road. It meant that person would be vulnerable to fire, so we alternated that assignment. The other would cover him. If a motor was revved up or a weapon appeared, we would both open fire.

Soon we saw the small dots of light on an approaching jeep.[29] Larry jumped into the middle of the road. It looked like one of our jeeps. The

---

29 During World War II, the use of radar – **RA**dio **D**etection **A**nd **R**anging – in battle was still relatively new. The ability to physically see an intended target was the most reliable and effective way to determine where it was and how to destroy it. In areas that were vulnerable to attack, blackout restrictions applied. Heavy curtains would be placed over windows so that the interior lights couldn't be seen from the outside in the hopes that this would reduce the chance of bombers being able to pinpoint the target and destroy the building. On cars and trucks, headlights and taillights would be blocked to the point that only a pinpoint of light to illuminate the road for the vehicle – enough

OH GENERAL — GENERAL — WHERE ARE YOU — ?

marking was for our outfit. The jeep stopped. Larry shouted the first word of the password, "Blue!" There was no response. I waited, my rifle at the ready. My safety was off, and I tightened my grip on the trigger. With a slight tug I could fire even if I was hit, or in my dying throes.

Inside the jeep was a driver and a general. Neither remembered the second word. This placed me in a quandary. If the password was not confirmed, I was obligated to shoot the people riding in the vehicle. I felt sure they were Americans, but orders were orders. More than a few infantrymen had died trusting men who seemed to be Americans. And who knows what havoc they might create in the village where our men slept that night.

While they stammered and tried to remember the second word, I quietly came up on the other side of the jeep and held my rifle to the general's head. He turned and saw me and my rifle. A look of terror filled his eyes as he looked into my rifle barrel. I knew he saw my hand on the trigger.

Larry said, "Blue!" again. There was more sputtering inside the jeep. Our standing order was to kill if there was no response after three times.

I was a split second away from killing a general and his driver when the general finally blurted out, "Moon!"

I lowered my rifle and replied, "Pass, sir."

He looked at us, very relieved, and said, "Damn good guard, men! Damn good guard!"

It was a simple-minded password, too easy to guess, but the general was under the gun and lost his poise and memory.

The next morning our company received a citation from the general for exemplary guard tactics. I still wonder what would have happened if I

---

light to see the road but not enough to make the vehicle an easy target for snipers or artillery strikes – could be seen.

had killed that general and his driver. It was my duty to do so in a combat zone. I am glad I never found out.

The Germans were notorious for infiltrating our lines. Many spoke perfect English, although it was mainly British English. Fortunately, only a few spoke with any of the many American accents. Still, they sent GI regulation uniformed soldiers behind our lines, some to spy, some for terrorist activities. If I had not forced the issue with the general and made sure he was American, and if the men in that jeep had been Germans, they could have infiltrated the village we were guarding. Worse still, they could have started to drive away, stopped, turned, and then killed us.

I hope that general and his driver wet their pants during that tense moment. I knew of no enlisted man who ever forgot the nightly password. I think the general thought he would be an exception. He certainly thought we would make an exception for him. I credit him with realizing we were doing our duty as outpost sentries.

The Final Days

In the 17th of April we left Erlau by motor convoy for Wittgensdorf. We again established a defensive line just to the west of Chemnitz. Here we sent out daily patrols with the mission of destroying all German soldiers and material encountered. This was also to give the enemy the idea that we had the intention of making a big push in the near future.[30]

As we approached Berlin, there was excitement and apprehension. We might be attacking Berlin. The thought was terrifying. At this time, back in Pennsylvania, my father read in the morning newspaper that the 76th was meeting strong resistance. Dad did not bring that paper home with him from work. He didn't want to alarm my mother.

During these last days we shifted from marching to riding in trucks and on tanks. Our trucks edged through a sea of humanity. Some were German troops seeking someone to take their surrender. The German soldiers were more exhausted than we were. The weight of American power was heavy upon them. When we captured them, their eyes were

---

30 *Always First*

set deeply in black sockets. Their gazes were empty, dark voids of fear and haunted memories. They were herded like cattle and marched to improvised compounds to our rear.

The Germans feared the Russians. They had good reason. Some of these disarmed prisoners had been on the Russian Front. The battles there had been bloody and unrelenting. The Russians, as they mustered their power, attacked in waves. They outnumbered their invaders, and they showed no mercy to the Germans who had raged into their Motherland. Why? The Germans had shown them no mercy. Thousands and perhaps hundreds of thousands of German troops were disarmed and sent back to Russia, there to work as slave labor. Some were repatriated after months and even years. Some died deep within Siberia, worked to death, just as Germans had worked their captives to death. Some may remain there to this day.

Many more of those who surged around us were Displaced Persons who were fleeing south and west. We had grown used to the columns of refugees traveling in wagons and on foot. They carried what they could handle.

Even the Slavic people were fleeing away from the advance from the north and east by the Russians. No one wanted to face Russian fury. By now it was an army of peasants, intent on revenge. Worse still, they had no food to offer the DPs they took under their wing. The British had less to offer than the Americans. Everyone wanted to surrender to us, but we did not have the means to help those who came to us for help.

The French, Belgians, Dutch, Italians, and Greeks were beginning a long trek home. They, like the Slavs, had been slave laborers. When we could, we threw them all the rations we could spare. We were in the midst of epic chaos. Somehow the maelstrom that whirled around us never drew us into total chaos.

We found that we, as Americans, were the only hope these milling masses had as they struggled to exist and begin their lives again. We were heroes, even though no one knew what we had done in liberating that surge of humanity. Only we were trusted.

As we swept north and east, the situation was almost chaotic. Pockets of Germans fought on. We dismounted from time to time to fight the few fanatics who still resisted. Most were SS units. They were well aware of the crimes they had committed, and their only hope of survival was some sort of negotiated end to the war. They received no mercy from the infantry.

All of this happened as great fleets of our bombers winged their way toward the German cities ahead of us. They hammered the *coup de grâce* into the heart of Germany.

Throughout our final days of advancing, an epic sense swept over me. I was part of something immense and profoundly titanic. A horrible war was ending. The size and scope of what I witnessed during those last days lingers in my memory. It beggars Homer. Amidst it all, liberated slave laborers were attempting to find their way back to their homes. Counter to them were Germans trying to get back to homes they fled as we advanced through Germany. Our convoys and columns of armored vehicles bulled through the tangle of humanity that clogged the main roads leading into the heart of Germany. We were outnumbered many times over.

*   *   *

In retrospect I wonder how many were aware of the Holocaust that had murdered six million Jews and hundreds of thousands, and even millions of European Roma (they were then known as "Gypsies"), homosexuals, and dissenters. These figures do not cover the terrible slaughters that took place in Russia, Poland, Holland, Belgium, Czechoslovakia, Yugoslavia, Greece, and other occupied countries. The Greeks alone suffered more than a million deaths. It was one third of their nation.

Years later Linda and I got to know survivors of the Nazi occupation in Greece. Some were in the resistance. One, Nikolas Tsetsio, was a hero. Our friend Stavros Romanos was tortured and left for dead in a mountain stream. Others told us of their lives during the occupation. Stavros attended the Greek National Theatre's acting school – along with Melina Mercouri – during that time. An anger still survives in the Greek soul. The Germans have never been forgiven. I doubt if they ever will.

How could a nation bear this horrible burden of guilt, a guilt that will be a stain on the national pride of Germany for generations to come? Exploring that deep sense of national guilt became a subject of my writing and research many years later. It is a guilt that is beyond human comprehensions. What must it be like to call yourself a German and to know your nation was responsible for killing millions upon millions of innocent people just because they were different from you?

It is a guilt shared by many nations. The United States is not exempt from this guilt, either. Our own leaders ignored reports of the indiscriminate slaughter within Germany.[31]

*   *   *

The *Wehrmacht* was collapsing. Some were goaded into continued action by SS Troopers; most defied their officers' orders. A few SS divisions remained intact. They feared capture, but they were on the verge of having to choose between Russian and Allied captors. The SS chose to fight to the bitter end. They realized that they were war criminals, and it had been announced that war criminals would be prosecuted.

Our task was to move through this sea of humanity and encounter the last resisting elements of the *Wehrmacht* - and the few SS divisions that remained. The war was winding down, but it was not over. All of us feared death now. None of us wanted to die in the waning days of the war – or to be gravely wounded. We wanted to survive all this alive and intact.

---

31 In recent years, information has come to light about when and how much the United States knew about the atrocities of the Holocaust during WWII. There has been criticism about what the US did and didn't do at the time it was occurring, but I will leave it to readers to further explore this matter on their own.

However, it should be noted the US doesn't have a great track record of its own in dealing with people it deemed inferior, or those who got in the way of the national interest, either. The United States was a nation built on the backs of the African-American slaves, and the treatment of the Native Americans was not only a murder of a people, it was the attempted murder of an entire culture. To learn more about one of the events in the history of the Native Americans and the expansion of the United States, I invite you to become acquainted *Voices of Wounded Knee* detailing the events leading up to and including the Massacre at Wounded Knee, South Dakota, in December, 1890, when 350 Lakotas were gunned down by the U.S Army 7th Calvary. This marked the end of the Indian Wars. Our book was published in 2000 by the University of Nebraska Press, and is available in bookstores and online.

21

GoodBye to the Third Army

On 16 April 1945, CT 417 crossed the Mulde River by motor, with a CP being established at Mittweida.

After mopping-up operations, the battalions strengthened their defensive positions and carried out aggressive patrolling.

On 17 April 1945, the CP was moved to Hartmannsdorf. Continuous reconnaissance and patrolling were maintained, and patrols numbering from 4 to 45 men were sent out with the general mission of killing or capturing enemy personnel and destroying equipment. On 20 April 1945, a prearranged raid was staged near the western edge of Chemnitz.

On 22 April 1945, the 417th Infantry passed from control of the Third United States Army to control of the First United States Army.

Preparations were made for a link-up between Russian forces and elements of the 1st Bn.

During the period, many enemy factories, warehouses, hospitals, and other captured enemy installations were guarded by units of CT 417.

At the close of the period, thousands of Allied Prisoners of War and thousands of slave laborers imported into Germany from foreign countries had been freed by CT 417 in its drive to the East.

The period ended with CT 417 in a defensive position, engaged in vigorous reconnaissance and patrolling, with those troops not engaged in operational or administrative duties engaged in training and care and maintenance of equipment.[32]

---

32 417th Regimental Report

On April 22 the 76th was transferred to the VIII Corps of the First Army. We lost our identity as a division with that transfer. The change was no demotion. The First was one of the best armies in Europe, but we were Third Army men. The Third Army abruptly swung east, veering away from Berlin.[33] We were not happy when Patton left us behind and moved on into Czechoslovakia. The Third swept on with little resistance. Our greatest regret was that we missed the wild celebrations of the newly freed Czechs. While the Germans had begun to greet us as liberators, we never had the thrill of freeing oppressed people.

It is interesting to note that between April 1 and April 21, Third Army troops had taken a total of 240,661 Prisoners of War. During the week of April 8 to April 14, a total of 4,331,087 gallons of V-80 gasoline was consumed. The amount averaged out to a total of 618,727 gallons per day.[34] We covered a lot of ground.

Our new outfit met some scattered resistance, but nothing major. The war was winding down. All we wanted now was to live on until it was officially over.

On April 22, the same day that the 76th was transferred to the First Army, the Russian troops entered the suburbs of Berlin. That same day, about 150 miles to the south, our battalion took up at a high position opposite Chemnitz, a large city. In it hid an SS division. On the other side was the Russian Army. We were relieved to learn that our job was to contain the SS troops until they decided to surrender. It was our hope they would be forced to surrender to the Russians who were approaching

---

33 According to historian Stephen E. Ambrose, author of many excellent books and articles about WWII, it is interesting to note that while many of the Allied generals were eager to capture Berlin, General Omar Bradley and Allied Commander Dwight D. Eisenhower were not. Part of this was due to the results of the Yalta conference where the Big Three agreed to divide Germany into zones of occupation and Berlin into sectors. Eisenhower knew that if the U.S. generals fought their way to Berlin, they would have to turn the territory over to Soviet forces at the end of the war. Eisenhower asked Bradley for an estimate on casualties in taking Berlin. Bradley said that it would be about 100,000 casualties, and that was "a pretty stiff price to pay for a prestige objective, especially when we've got to fall back and let the other fellow take over." To learn more about this, I recommend Ambrose's *Eisenhower and Berlin, 1945; The Decision to Halt at the Elbe* (W.W. Norton, 1967), and *Citizen Soldiers: The US. Army from the Normandy Beaches to the Bulge to the Surrender of Germany, June 7, 1944 – May 7, 1945* (Simon & Schuster, 1997).

34 These statistics, available in many sources, are referenced from *Patton's Third Army, A Chronology of the Third Army Advance*, August 1944 to May 1945, by Charles M. Province, copyright ©1992 and published by Hippocrene Books, Inc.

from the opposite side of the city. If the SS division fell to the Russians, there would be no mercy, no need for a war crimes trial.

At night we returned to our billets in still another quaint German village. Sometimes we were sent out on patrol. Again, I volunteered to go when Buster led a foray into the night.

There was a great deal of activity in the valley below us. Displaced Persons were fleeing to our lines to avoid the Russians. So were many Germans.

The Russians were feared for their bloodlust for revenge. There were tales of rapes and executions when the Russians took over a German town. We knew the Russian Army and people had suffered more than any other country during the war. Many years later I would read that suffering had been even greater than what we were told then. While it was said that 20 million Russians died during the war, it is more likely that figure approached 60 million. The Germans had every reason to fear them.

We heard many tales of the brute strength of the Russians. One friend told me he saw a Russian trying to start a jeep that had broken down. It would not start. The Russian, who was huge, lifted the jeep onto its side and examined it, trying to see what was not working.

Amidst all this SS troopers moved about the valley below us. They were frantically trying to find safer positions each time we located them. From our high position we sniped at them, picking off a few who did not move fast enough. That sniping seemed so abstract at the time. We never thought of the SS as human beings. They were targets. We knew of their treachery and savagery. That valley served as a shooting gallery. We had no regrets about our sniping. If they had been *Wehrmacht*, I think we would have shown mercy. Indeed, if they had been common German soldiers, they would have tried to negotiate a surrender.

We let DPs through our lines, but we turned our back to German civilians. We wanted to leave them to the feared Russians. We felt they deserved to face up to their crimes, or at least undergo some consequences from having profited by their use of the DPs as slave laborers.

We never saw any of these SS troopers face to face. I am not sure how we would have treated them as captives. We knew that these elite troops were brutal and never fought by the rules of warfare. Their most notorious atrocity occurred at Malmedy during the Bulge. There they lined up more than 100 American POWS, tied their hands behind their backs with wires, and executed them. From that time onward the Infantry declared open season on the *SS*. All the rules of the Geneva Convention were tossed aside when it came to the *SS*.

Those rules of war applied to the *Wehrmacht* troops who surrendered. We sent them back to a rear area. From there they were sent to holding compounds.

Many were repatriated, many more were sent back to the United States to serve as support workers performing common labor in military camps. Some months later, after I returned to the states, they were our servants. They did not get home until at least a year after the war, but eventually they were repatriated. In their last stages of incarceration, they were given passes to visit towns near the posts where they were stationed.

We ran occasional patrols during those last days. We ventured deep into that wide valley and then quickly withdrew. We rarely drew fire. If our officers had commanded us to move ahead into Chemnitz, we would have done so; but we would have done so with great reluctance. We knew the *SS* had no choice but to fight back.

During those final days we took few risks. The war all but over. Nothing could have been more tragic than dying on the last day of the last hour of the last minute of a war. A few men did. I mourn for them. They never tasted victory and what seemed to be a lasting peace.

I only saw one Russian soldier up close before the end of the war. He was a low-ranking officer who visited our company headquarters. He arrived in an American-built Jeep. He was a large man. His bearing was striking and very military. He went into our company headquarters, remained there for a while, came out, and drove off. That was the sum total of my experience with the Russian Army.

German POWs

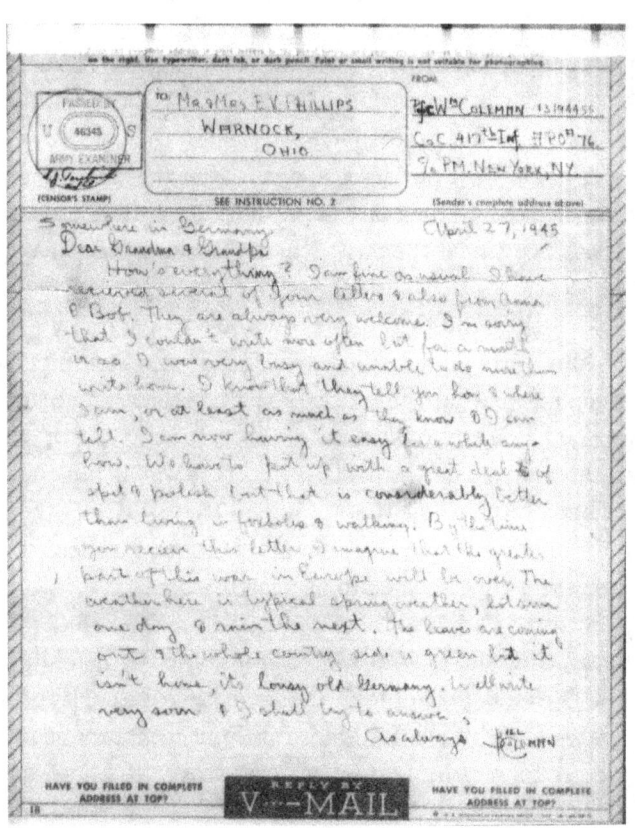

Somewhere in Germany   April 27, 1945

Dear Grandma & Grandpa

How's everything? I am fine as usual. I have received several of your letters & also from Anna & Bob. They are always very welcome. I'm sorry that I couldn't write more often but for a month or so I was very busy and unable to do more than write home. I know that they tell you how & where I am, or at least as much as they know & I can tell. I am now having it easy for a while anyhow. We have to put up with a great deal of of stuff & polish but that is considerably better than living in foxholes & walking. By the time you receive this letter I imagine that the greater part of this war in Europe will be over. The weather here is typical spring weather, hot one day & rain the next. The leaves are coming out & the whole country side is green but it isn't home, its lousy old Germany. I'll write very soon & I shall try to answer.

As always
Bill Coleman

To:
Mr. & Mrs. E.V. Phillips
Warnock, Ohio

From: Pfc Wm Coleman 13194455
Co C. 417th Inf. APO #76
c/o P.M. New York, NY

Somewhere in Germany   April 27, 1945

Dear Grandma & Grandpa

How's everything? I am fine as usual. I have received several of your letters & also from Anna & Bob. They are always very welcome. I'm sorry that I couldn't write more often but for a month or so I was very busy and unable to do more than write home. I know that they tell you how & where I am, or at least as much as they know & I can tell. I am now having it easy for awhile anyhow. We have to put up with a great deal ~~to~~ of spit & polish but that is considerably better than living in foxholes & walking. By the time you receive this letter, I imagine that the greater part of this war in Europe will be over. The weather here is typical spring weather, hot sun one day & rain the next. The leaves are coming out & the whole country side is green but it isn't home, it's lousy old Germany. Will write very soon & I shall try to answer.

As always
Bill Coleman

Victory in Europe

We pulled back to Regimental Reserve in Mühlau on the 24th of April. Here we trained and cleaned up our equipment. It was here, on the 5th day of May that we received Official notice that Unconditional Surrender of the German Armed forces would be effected at 0001, the 9th of May. No more firing unless in self-defense.[35]

None of us knew that Hitler committed suicide in a Berlin bunker on April 30, 1945. How he died remained a mystery for several years after the war. Many speculated he had escaped to South America. Finally, his skull was discovered in Russia. Indeed, he had died of a gunshot wound. Other members of his government were captured, and more than a few died by their own hand rather than face Allied justice. Many of his closest followers were never brought to justice. Victory was not a tidy thing.

Hitler's final days have been recreated on film several times. The best is the fine German film, *Downfall*.[36] It presents a chilling view of the fanaticism of his inner circle.

As the war drew to an end, I began to have time to think about what had happened to me in combat. In looking back, my life hinged on many factors. It began with that bad ankle in Basic. That had removed me from combat for a month. A month more would have placed me in the Bulge. Then there was the week I waited for new glasses at the POE. Finally, there were two more days with the dentist.

If I had a sense of destiny, I would believe that all these delays were intended to be and that, in some way, I was destined to survive combat. If those delays had not happened, the odds were that I would have been wounded or killed. I realize this sounds egotistical and more than a bit mystical. In looking back, I see no great reason for my existence on this

---

35 *Always First*

36 *Der Untergang (Downfall)* is a 2004 historical war drama film directed by Oliver Hirschbiegel and starring Bruno Ganz as Adolf Hitler. It depicts the final ten days of Hitler's rule in April 1945. It was nominated for the 2005 Academy Award for Best Foreign Language Film. It might be noted that since 2010, scenes from this film have become popular in internet video parodies, often showing Hitler reacting to present-day politics, sports, popular culture, and everyday life. Interestingly enough, these parodies appear to have gained the approval of the film's director who said that "The point of the film was to kick these terrible people off the throne that made them demons, making them real and their actions into reality. I think it's only fair if now it's taken as part of our history and used for whatever purposes people like."

planet. I have done good things in my life, and I have passed along ideas and concepts to a great many students. By now, most of what I conveyed has probably faded away.

Many days are fixed in my mind. Each has its own importance and meaning. One is May 7, 1945 – VE Day.[37] We were told to stay alert because hostilities didn't end until the next day. Even then, the Werewolves remained active. In time we learned that 405,399 Americans died during the war. Our casualties were low compared to those suffered by England and Russia. Now my thoughts were with those who died or those who were maimed. I was greatly relieved that it had not happened to me.

I had survived.

How horrible it would have been to die on that last day of the war.

---

37 VE Day is short for Victory in Europe Day, the day the war ended in the European Theatre of War.

A Summary of Statistics of Wounded and Injured in Action

From December 7, 1941 to December 31, 1946: [38]

Battle Casualties for all theatres and organizations: 936,259
  Battle casualties in Combat divisions (all theaters): 664,024
  Battle casualties in Infantry divisions (all theaters): 565,986

Deaths among battle casualties: 234,874
  Deaths among battle casualties in Combat divisions (all theaters): 140,175
  Deaths among battle casualties in Infantry divisions (all theaters): 118, 945

Killed in action: 189,696
    Killed in action in Combat divisions (all theaters): 117,891
    Killed in action in Infantry divisions (all theaters): 100,364

Wounded and injured in action: 592,170
    Died of wounds and injuries: 26,225
    Evacuated to U.S., Died of wounds and injuries: 84
    Returned to duty, discharged etc.: 182,665
    Returned to duty: 383,196

Captured and interned: 124,079
    Killed in action: 3,102
    Died of Wounds and injuries: 453
    Died from Other causes (non-battle): 9,098
    Returned to military control: 111,426

Missing in action: 30,314
    Declared dead: 6,058
    Died from Other causes (non-battle): 158
    Returned to duty: 24,098

---

38 More figures from the Statistical and Accounting Branch Office of the Adjutant General Under Direction of Program Review and Analysis Division Office of the Comptroller of the Army, O.C.S., can be found at the government website:
   http://www.ibiblio.org/hyperwar/USA/ref/Casualties/Casualties-1.html#grade.

Rec'd May 21st

Somewhere in Germany   Mon May 7, 1945

Dear Mom & Pop,

How's everything? No mail here today. The news is
very good & the complete end seems to be near. I
~~was jubilant a ~~
days ago but it looks like it will happen
very soon.

I heard Jack Benny last ~~ta~~ night. He
was in the usual form. We have been listening
to recorded music all day.

I can see that the war is doing a strange
thing to the languages of the world & especially
Europe. These slave laborers, (Russians, Poles,
Slavs, Cechs, French, Dutch Belgium, Italian, &
who knows what else), thrown together in the
same camps. There can be only one result, a very
polyglot language. In fact you can see the
influence even on English. Indeed there will be a

Somewhere in Germany

Mon. May 7, 1945

Dear Mom & Pop,

How's everything? No mail here today. The news is very good & the complete end seems to be near. I was a little too exuberant in my letter of two days ago, but it looks like it will happen very soon.

I heard Jack Benny last night. He was in the usual form. We have been listening to recorded music all day.

I can see that the war is doing a strange thing to the languages of the world & especially Europe. These slave laborers, (Russians, Poles, Slavs, Cechs (sic), French, Dutch, Belgium, Italian, & who knows what else,), thrown together in the same camps. There can be only one result a very polygot (sic) language. In fact you can see the influences even on English. Indeed there will be a very colorful English language when it is over.

A few weeks ago after our long march & when we finally mounted trucks after we had left the hills along the Rhine River & entered the Lowlands we saw how the Third (Army) rolls so fast. Up ahead is the tanks, tank destroyers, and half-tracks; the spearhead driving along the enemy roads. All along the roads is the wreckage of the retreating Germans. Helmets, rifles, gas masks, packs, cast aside the sign of a demoralized army. Strafed trucks, tanks, autos, & wagons lay alongside the way. The air corps had cut their equipment on wheels to pieces, even their foot soldiers on bicycles lay along the way. We followed the tanks at the speed of a truck on a cross country run back in the states. For once the Infantry had to ride. The *Luftwaffe* came out to strafe us & bomb us – we dismounted rather in a hurry. They were so low we fired rifle fire at them. The 50's on the trucks crackled against the steady & amazingly rapid firing German machine guns (1500 rounds a minute to our 500 rounds a minute!) Bluish smoke trailed from the engines – the plane crashed in the ground with a gigantic cloud of black smoke. One plane stunted directly over us drawing our fire so the others could escape & then fled himself. We resumed our journey.

The next day, as we went to mount our trucks once again they came over. They came so fast & low that we didn't even get to fire at them with our rifles. I saw one ME-109 swallow the trucks 50 cal. Tracers, start to disintegrate and then crash into the ground a block away at the most. Once again, the oily cloud of smoke rose over the wreckage. No trouble for the rest of the day. We mounted tank destroyers, clinging to its sides. We felt for sure that there would be a fight, but we just rode. We dug in for the night. There were more air attacks & I saw a couple more spectacular crashes from fairly close range. The Germans started a counterattack but the BAR man in the 1st squad threw a little too much lead to suit them & they never bothered us again. I believe they outnumbered us. A couple wandered right up to one of the fellows' foxhole in the dark & was captured. This occurred many times while we were dug in. The next morning we started to walk. We entered the outskirts of Zietz. There was a terrific battle on the outskirts on the right flank. Another infantry outfit seemed to be well in the town & had broken the main part of resistance. The dead of both sides still lay in the streets. We stopped for a few minutes partway inside of the town. Then hell broke loose, mortar shells tore into the building across the street across from us & into the square. In a second, we were inside the buildings. We liked it better there. Since then all we did was move. There were a few patrols, but now we're having it quite easy in this guard detail. Well until next time.

    As always, BC

G.I. Bath

BROTHERHOOD

All of us wondered how long it would be before we got home. The war raged in the Pacific, and as experienced infantrymen we feared that we would be sent into that bloody island-by-island struggle. What would happen next was something we discussed often. We felt that we had done our share in combat. We wanted to get out of the Army and go home.

Each of us had a different homecoming ahead of us. Some had girlfriends, some wives. Larry and I had a desire to go to college. The rest of the squad wanted to get back to work, raise a family, and settle into a thoroughly average life. Besides wanting to become a teacher, my own ambitions were vague. I wanted to marry and have a family, but I knew that was far in the future. I had no girl waiting for me when I jumped off the train in Pottsville.

Our company was stationed in a village in a rear area the day we learned the war was over. There was an enormous vat of water at least ten feet in diameter. It was poised over a blazing gas burner. We fired it up so we could have our first baths in weeks. We drew lots to decide who got to bathe first. Fortunately, my number was near the first. The water became dirtier with each wave of bathers. Finally, it was quite disgusting.

After we put on clean clothing, we drank wine. I got drunk for the first time in my life. There was a village pond. Some of us got in a flat-bottomed boat and embarked to the middle of the pond. The boat's bottom was rotten. We sank and found we were standing in knee deep in dark sludge. Our baths had gone for naught.

I am proud to say that during my weeks as a combat rifleman our squad never took one step backward. Reed did drop back in that foray in the Rhineland, but he did so to lay down a base of fire with his BAR. He did his job, and he did it well. We always moved forward, and we were always on the attack. I think that is why we all survived that time together. The twelve men who were in our squad when I joined it survived. That, in itself, was a miracle. Other squads in our company did not fare as well, but overall, our casualties as a company were light.

I believe that was due to Patton's strategy of keeping us moving forward. He rarely put us in a defensive position where we would suffer heavy mortar and artillery fire. I believe he was insane, but the military brilliance that emerged from that insanity preserved my life. There have been many biographies of this flamboyant but enigmatic man. I have not read them all, but I recommend Ladislas Faragó's biography, *Patton: Ordeal and Triumph*.[39] It is an enormous work, but it gets us as close to Patton as anyone will get.

---

39 Ladislas Faragó, also known as Faragó Lászlo (1906-1980) was a Hungarian military historian and journalist, known especially for his books concerning WWII. His most popular book, *Patton: Ordeal and Triumph,* published in 1963, formed the basis for the 1970 Academy Award-winning film *Patton* starring George C. Scott in the title role. In 1967 *The Broken Seal* was published. It later became one of the books that formed the basis for the 1970 Japanese American war drama, *Tora! Tora! Tora!. Aftermath: The Search for Martin Bormann*, published in 1974, detailed the Nazi presence in South America. His last book, published in 1981, was *The Last Days of Patton*. It was made into a television movie in 1986, again starring George C. Scott in the title role. Faragó, who was Jewish, was born in Hugary, and died in New York City at the age of 74.

PART VI

OCCUPATION DUTY BEGINS

It's a great responsibility surviving a war.
Lord Dunsany

Bill (middle row, left) and members of the rifle squad.

22

Keeping the Peace

On the 11th of May, the Battalion moved to its present area, with Company A in Greitz, Company B in Neumark, and Companies C, D, and Headquarters in Reichenbach. At the present time we are serving as occupation troops and what the future holds for us – only the War Department and the Good Lord above can say, and they aren't talking.[1]

M OST GERMANS EAGERLY gave up as the war was ending, but the Werewolves continued to resist. Their resistance to our occupation was short lived. Some among this group were women. They learned that in our military code of conduct – *Articles of War* – that rape of women, even the enemy, was punishable by death before a firing squad. I am sure that some women were raped, but I think it was not prevalent among front line soldiers. We were too close to our own humanity to commit atrocities, or at least most of us were.

Shortly after the war ended, two German women claimed they had been raped by men in our battalion. We were ordered to stand in ranks while the women walked by us. They had the option of pointing at a man or men who had raped them.

Our squad conferred before we marched to the lineup. None of us could have possibly committed the crime. We knew where all of us were when the rapes allegedly occurred. We arrived at a way we could protect each other. We loaded our rifles and put a single bullet in the chamber. Then we snapped off our rifle's safety. It was ready to fire. We agreed that if one

---

1 *Always First*

of the women pointed at anyone in our squad, we would all shoot her. Then the Army would have to deal with the problem. It was an amazing act of solidarity and brotherhood. I am not sure it was wise, but we were that close when we ended our time in combat together.

The women were led out by one of our officers. Neither was very attractive. It was carried out in full view of the enemy civilians who gathered to watch our formation. To me it was a moment of humiliation for all of us.

The women were asked to walk along the long ranks of the men in our battalion, a thousand in all. They paused a couple of times, but they never pointed out a man. I shuddered when they walked by me. If these women were Werewolves, they could execute an American soldier by pointing a finger. What an ignominious way for an innocent young man to die![2]

Either no one in our outfit had committed the crime, or these women lost their nerve. I will never know. I know that within our ranks there were men who were capable of rape, especially if it was an enemy woman. Only one man in our squad would be capable of such an act, the brutal Jimmy "Mac." He was capable of anything, but he had been with us throughout the night of the alleged rapes.

I do know that for a few weeks in combat and afterwards, I shared something very remarkable with the men in my squad. I hope they feel the same about me. We were truly comrades. While we were a diverse group and our skills and courage varied, we were a team. We trusted each other completely when the chips were down. They were good men. I will remember them always.

---

2   According to government statistics, from 1942-45 the United States Army carried out approximately 97 executions for murder and/or rape in the European/Mediterranean Theatre of Operations, 21 in the Pacific Area, 19 in the continental United States, two in (the US Territory of) Hawaii, one in Guadalcanal, and one in the China-Burma-India Theatre. All executions were performed under the authority of the *Articles of War* of June 4, 1920, an Act of Congress governing military justice between 1920-1948. Executions were either by hanging or firing squad. Only one soldier – Private Eddie Slovek, who was in the Battle of the Bulge in 1944 and claimed he was separated from his squad – was executed for desertion, shot by firing squad. Those who were executed in the ETO were buried in "Plot E" of the Oise-Aisne American Military Cemetery in France. This section is not generally open to the public and has no flag or headstones.

In recent years there has been some focus on the arrests and executions of U.S. military personnel in England during WWII since it appears that there was a disproportionate number of African Americans executed at Shepton Mallet Prison in Somerset, England, during this time. Eighteen American servicemen were hanged or shot – nine for murder, six for rape, and three for both crimes. Although the American army was 90% white, 10 of the 18 men hanged there were black and three were Hispanic.

THE SLAVE LABOR CAMP

On May 31, 2001, an article appeared in the *Des Moines Register* about German reparations to the slave laborers who were forced to work for the Germans during World War II. After reading it, I felt compelled to write a response based on my experiences at the end of the war. My article was written in the early summer of 2001 and published in the *Register*. It's an accurate account of an event that happened a few days after the war ended:

A FIERY NIGHT

When the war ended in Europe in the spring of 1945, I was an 18-year-old rifleman in a division attached to Gen. George Patton's Third Army. Late in May 1945, our platoon was assigned to guard a slave-labor camp in rural Germany. We wondered if we were going to protect the workers from a German resistance group called the Werewolves. It seemed like an easy assignment. It was not.

The camp was set in a small, shallow valley, a depression between two broad fields. There were two lines of wooden barracks, cheaply built, and there were barbed wire and guard towers around the area. Beyond was rolling farm country. Except for the camp, one could not tell a war had swept through the area.

In the camp was a mix of Russians, Poles, Italians, Slavs, Czechs, French and Greeks who had been forced to work on the area's farms. There they had worked as field laborers, some for months, some for years. They were euphemistically called "Displaced Persons."

Their job was to feed the German war machine while being restricted to eating as little as possible. If they did not work hard enough, they were punished. Some, we learned, had been beaten with chains when they became exhausted or ill and fell to their knees in the nearby fields.

A few died while we were on duty. Most were women and children. They were emaciated and weak.

On our arrival, we were allowed to look into the barracks, but we were told never to enter them, mainly because disease was rampant amidst the prisoners. The floors were covered with DDT and the people living there had ragged pallets, and not much more.

Men were in one barracks, women and children in another. Most of their bodies were emaciated, some from disease, some from hunger. Only a few retained their strength. In all, there were 200 people.

I suspect our officers did not want us to get to know our charges too well. To be honest, none of us really wanted to go into those barracks. The glimpses of what I saw still haunt me. The camp was not as bad as the extermination camps, but it was bad enough.

As a combat rifleman in the Infantry, I had seen many horrors before I was 19, but this was worse. These were helpless people who were unable to defend themselves as they were exploited by the Germans. In combat, we had been armed and could fight back.

In the week we spent guarding the camp, many of the male workers wanted to leave to gather food for their families and friends. Others wanted revenge. As young men who had been taught that our cause was moral, we understood their feelings and sympathized with them.

However, our job was to confine them to the camp. Two reasons were given by our officers: If they went into the countryside, they would spread disease. The other reason, and the one that seemed most important to our officers, was that they might take revenge on their masters by killing and destroying German property.

We were ordered to shoot anyone who tried to leave the perimeter we had set up around the camp.

We were faced with a moral dilemma. We no longer were allowed to shoot Germans, but we were told we must shoot those who had been slaves to the Germans. It seemed to us that German property was valued over everything else. This was hard for young men to understand.

Let's get one thing out of the way. The German farmers in that area knew what was happening. They used this slave labor on a day-to-day basis. Some protested their innocence – as all Germans did after the war. But there was no way they could not see the decline in the physical health of their slaves. Nor was there any way for them not to know they were using slave labor. And what about the beatings? If those rosy-cheeked German farmers did not do the beatings, they certainly saw it happen.

In the few days we were there on guard duty, we got to know those we were guarding. One night we could no longer resist the men's plea to seek justice. We let our charges out. There were fires throughout the area, and we heard gunshots in the distance.

The next morning, we were transferred to other occupation duty. The story I am telling has no conclusive ending. Who was killed that night? Who escaped and eventually returned home? And who might have been punished by the United States Army for leaving the camp? I will never know.

Has justice been done with the paltry reparations recently approved by the current German government? Or was justice done that fiery night in Germany 56 years ago just about this time of the year?

Sixty-six hundred dollars. Those who died of malnutrition and disease those nights many years ago will not collect. Those who died from their treatment too early in their lives will not be paid, either. Only a few must still survive. The toll then and over the years certainly has cut the German overhead for these reparations.

Will those who did survive receive the full amount of $6,600? Or will they receive $2,200 for working "under less onerous conditions?" And will their arbiter be one of those who enslaved them?

I think the Germans got a bargain either way.

An Epilogue About a Fiery Night

My story about the slave labor camp does not end there. Editorial constraints regarding space forced me to limit the length of my article so that there was a partial end to my experiences at the camp, but the story was never resolved. There is one aspect of this darker episode that I did not include in my newspaper article. I wish that I had.

While I stood daily guard, I made friends with a young Italian whose name was Giovanni. He spoke a few words of English. I had Army language guides in Italian, German, and French. We managed to piece enough together to tell each other about our lives back home. He was from a poor family in Naples. After the war we corresponded, but that slowly faded away. Post-war life in Italy was brutal. I suspect he couldn't afford stamps to mail me letters. I have a picture of Giovanni somewhere in my files.

Visiting us each day was a young Belgian man named Frédérique. He was very tall and strongly built. He had an effervescent personality and functional English. He brought us liquor and wine. He invited some of the men to his house. There he had parties that included German women. I never went, but some who did thought Freddy, as he was called, was a great guy.

One afternoon when we were on guard around the camp, an angry Freddy appeared and spoke in an agitated way to some of the men who lived in the camp. We learned that Freddy believed that one had attended his party and had stolen something of value.

Amidst the quarrel a massive Russian, literally a giant, lumbered into the area and started shouting at Freddy. I had seen the Russian playing soccer with the able-bodied men. His power and ability to kick the ball all the way out of that small valley that held the camp was awe-inspiring. His strength was almost superhuman.

Suddenly the Russian, his face livid with rage, charged Freddy and picked him up and held him over his head. Then he body-slammed Freddy straight into the ground. Freddy was strong, but this Russian was much, much stronger. Freddy, who was more agile, jumped up and ran away. He did not look back.

My Italian friend told me that before the war Freddy had been a boxer. During the war he had become a slave laborer like the rest of the men. But Freddy had turned on his considerable charm to be spared from hard labor. The SS had recruited him to fight exhibitions for their entertainment. He no longer had to work in the fields. In time, he became a foreman. I was told that to make those who were slow or ill more productive, Freddy had beaten them with chains.

It was then some of the men in the camp asked us to let them out of the camp for one night. They wanted revenge against their German oppressors and especially Freddy. Freddy, they wanted to kill.

As I wrote in the article, we were shipped out the next morning. I saw the distant fires and heard scattered gunfire. I never knew the end of this story, nor did the young Italian, Giovanni, ever mention what happened in the handful of letters he sent me after the war. We were on our way to other duty.

Many years later when my play, *A Stranger to the Past*, was entered in the American College Theatre Festival, one of the judges, a woman, chided me for lines I had written about this event. She said that the average German, a majority of them according to her, did not approve of the war and behaved well. She was somewhat younger than me and had not experienced the war. To her it was theory, pages in a history book. Those of us who were there knew without a doubt that those German farmers around that camp knew they were using slave labor. They also knew that their labor was being mistreated and that many were dying from their mistreatment. It was blatantly obvious to everyone.

Those average Germans knew and profited from that labor. Should they have been punished, too? How can you punish a majority of a nation? How can you explain a nation's evil behavior? I have thought about that many times. I believe that what happened in Germany was an orgy of violence that was driven by irrational hatred. The logical German mind, and it can be impressively logical, did not empathize, did not see another living breathing human being. Those that were persecuted and died were reduced to a subhuman status. Before we get too smug about this, remember a majority of Americans believed that Blacks and Native Americans were less than human. We see similar attitudes today regarding immigrants, Muslims, the LGBTQ community, the mentally ill, the poor, and the homeless.

It is this dark side of all of us that must be eliminated before we have a peaceful world. Is it the animal side of us, the predatory side of a carnivorous species? Or is it conditioned and taught? Those are questions I still wrestle with. The only solution I have come to is to work in the arts. Artists create empathy, understanding of others, and bring alive the evils the human race perpetrates.

Perhaps I learned that when I looked into the tearful eyes of my first German prisoner of war. He looked like my father, and he was terrified of me. I felt a surge of understanding and sympathy for the poor man. I could not have killed him, but Jimmy McElhanney was ready to castrate and then kill him. Mac was not afraid of the reality of brutality. Our leaders, however, abstract brutality and force us to be brutal with their causes.

The human race covers a wide spectrum. Perhaps we are all on different stages of the evolutionary scale. I hope I am on the high end. I must admit that my life would have been much easier if I had been on the lower end. With that in mind, I am glad that I am what I am. It may have caused me to suffer, to be less hedonistic and more self-centered in my pursuit of my life goals. But what would those goals have become? I think they would have been empty and materialistic.

I recently ran across this quote by the Hungarian-born author, Arthur Koestler:[3]

---

3   Arthur Koestler (1905-1983) was an essayist, journalist, and novelist. Born in Budapest, Hungary, he was educated in Austria. He joined the Communist Party in the 1930s, travelled to Spain to cover the Civil War as a correspondent, but was taken prisoner. He became disillusioned with Stalinism and resigned from the Party. He went to Paris during WWII, and eventually ended up in London where he worked for the Ministry of Information. His book, *Darkness at Noon,* was published in 1941. He wrote many books, articles, and essays on a number of subjects throughout his life – too many to mention in this footnote – and was interested in a broad range of subjects. He was diagnosed with Parkinson's Disease in 1976, and leukemia in 1978. He stated that he

War is a ritual, a deadly ritual, not the result of aggressive self-assertion, but of self-transcending identification. Without loyalty to tribe, church, flag or ideal, there would be no wars.

Koestler also included this quotation in his book, *Darkness at Noon*:

Show us not the aim without the way,
For ends and means on earth are so entangled
That changing one, you change the other too;
Each different path brings other ends in view.
    Ferdinand Lassalle: Franz von Sickingen

He also included this line:

Nobody can rule guiltlessly.
                    St. Just

I disagree. Until we find a way to rule guiltlessly, we will always have wars and injustice. If that is pessimistic, I believe it is a realistic assessment of the human condition.

---

was not afraid of death, but he was afraid of the process of dying. As his cancer began to metastasize, he and his third wife, Cynthia, committed suicide on March 1, 1983.

Dear Grandma & Grandpa

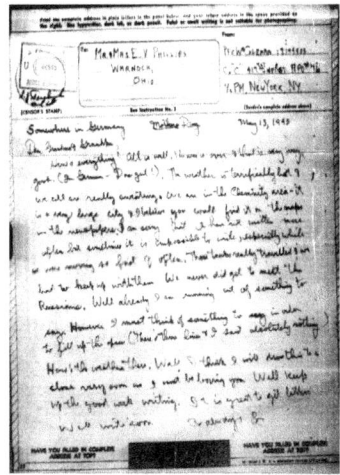

To: Mr. & Mrs. E.V. Phillips
Warnock, Ohio
From: PFC Wm Coleman 13194483 Co "C" 417th Inf. Rgt. APO #76
c/o P.M. New York, NY
Somewhere in Germany   Mother's Day   May 13, 1945

Dear Grandma & Grandpa,

How's everything? All is well. The war is over & that is very, very good. (In German – Das gut!). The weather is terrifically hot & we all are really sweating. We are in the Chemnitz area – it is a very large city & I believe you could find it on the maps in the newspapers. I am sorry that I have not written more often but sometimes it is impossible to write, especially while we were moving so fast & often. Those tanks really travelled & we had to keep up with them. We never did get to meet the Russians.

Well already I am running out of something to say. However, I must think of something to say in order to fill up the space (There's three lines & I said absolutely nothing!).

How's the weather there? Well, I think I will draw this to a close very soon as I must be boring you. Well keep up the good work writing. It is great to get letters. Will write soon.

As always
BC

Diversions Amidst Tragedy

As the war ended, hot food began to catch up to us most evenings, so our dysentery abated. Our mail also began to catch up with us. Mail call was a moment everyone waited for. A jeep would arrive, and its driver would stand on it and shout out the names of those who had letters. There was

Male Call

anticipation, but there was also dread. What if you had no mail?

My parents wrote almost daily, so I would get several letters at a call. My dad clipped articles from the local newspapers, especially about how our high school teams were doing. He often went to games and wrote me a letter about what he had seen. This was a side of him I had never seen before. In these letters I was truly close to him. Those touches of home were very important to me. Now I had time to be homesick. I yearned to leave the Army and return home. We all did.

Package from home

Letters from girls back home were prized. I had no serious girlfriend then, but I did have several friends from high school who wrote to me from time to time.

Our status with girls was indicated by a number of codes. If a stamp was upside down, that meant she cared for you. Some wrote SWAK[4] and planted a lipstick kiss across the seal. For me, these were few and far between.

With the food and letters came *The Stars and Stripes* and *Yank*. Packages were slower making their way forward. After the war ended, my mother sent me a box of orange

---

4　SWAK = Sealed With A Kiss.

cookies and other goodies. Orange cookies were among my favorites. There was also something called "economy bread," which was a Depression delicacy. It was a heavy bread filled with raisins.

Our free time allowed us to play a little. After seeing all that death and disease, we needed diversion and a chance to escape from the tragic realities surrounding us. Some of us found a railroad handcar. When we were off duty, we would take a ride down the tracks. It was not a safe pastime. We had no idea if remnants of the Werewolves were abroad, and we did not know when the trains would start running again. We were young and foolish, and it was a great feeling pumping away at the handles as we zipped along those rails.

Then one day we were going ahead at full speed when we heard a train whistle approaching us. We struggled to stop the car and reverse it. It seemed like forever. In the distance we saw a train approaching. We pumped away until we came to a "Y" in the tracks. I jumped off and switched the tracks, so we went off to a side track. Then I put the tracks in place, just in time to let the train pass us. It was a close call.

We were billeted in a German farmhouse. A rosy-cheeked buxom German woman of about thirty cleaned our house, or rather, her house. We learned her husband had been in Russia, and she had heard nothing about his fate.

Rooter saw an opportunity. The German wife had been without her man for years, and she seemed willing. She was. Soon Rooter had her in bed as often as possible. We sat in the kitchen as the headboard of their shared bed banged against the shared wall. We heard loud moaning and heavy breathing, sometimes for long periods of time. Rooter must have had amazing staying power. Their exertions reverberated throughout the house. We were annoyed and perhaps a little jealous even though none of us would have had anything to do with her once she had been with Rooter. Who knows? He may have contracted clap again somewhere else in the small village.

The woman beamed after these bouts. Her complexion became even rosier. One wonders if there were any offspring from her encounters with Rooter. More than a few German women became pregnant after the war, and with no husband was in sight. One of my college friends fathered such a child; but to his credit, he saw to the child's care after the war and even visited from time to time.

Rooter scrounged daily for any drink with alcoholic content. He was a prodigious drinker. He refused to share anything he found with anyone. One day we decided to get even. One by one we urinated in an old wine bottle until it was full. We placed a cork in it, sealed it shut with wax, and rolled it around in the dirt. It really looked like an antique bottle of Rhine wine. We hid it in the cellar behind some shelving. We hoped that Rooter would find it. Then we could have at least partial revenge for his failure to fire during combat.

Sure enough, Rooter emerged from the cellar, holding up the bottle, shouting in triumph. One of the guys asked, "Aren't you going to share it with us?"

"Hell, no," he replied, "I found it. It's mine."

Rooter held the bottle up to the light, exclaiming, "Look at that color!" Then he passed the top of the bottle past his nose. "And the aroma! This is *prima*! And it's all mine."

In response, we pled for a sip, knowing full well he would refuse. Other men would share their cellar finds with the rest of us. Rooter would not.

It was all we could do to suppress our laughter, but we did. We wanted to see Rooter drink our collective urine. While that would not pay for all his transgressions during the fighting, it would be a sizable remuneration.

After some byplay and taunting of the rest of us, Rooter took a big slug. He swallowed the unwholesome group pee of his comrades-in-arms in one massive gulp. He sat for a moment, rolling the wine on his pallet. Then his eyes bugged as a strange look of revulsion came across his face. He staggered about, his eyes rolling as he gagged and retched. Then he spewed out the revolting yellow liquid. And more. That included breakfast and lunch.

We were helpless with laughter. One or two of us rolled around on the floor.

Then Rooter realized what we had done. He was ready to kill any or all of us. He tried to find his rifle, but Larry had hidden it under a bed. He came after us as we fled in all directions. Some men fled to other rooms and locked the doors as Rooter rampaged about the house. A few of us jumped out open windows and fled into a nearby woods. We were fortunate that it was a warm spring. All our windows were open. His cursing was unusually eloquent.

When we returned Rooter was busy in bed with the German wife. Even now, I wonder how the poor woman stood Rooter's acrid breath that afternoon. In fact, I wonder how she stood him at all. Blind lust has always puzzled me. Perhaps that's because so few women blindly lusted after me.

OUR OWN PERSONAL CIRCUS

Just after the war ended some men in our outfit captured a circus. It was wending its way from the Russians to the east of us and, like so many refugees, they sought out American-occupied territory.

The circus was intact. It even had a smallish big top. It had a remarkable collection of clowns, jugglers, contortionists, trapeze, and tumbling acts. I have never seen their equal since. I remember one Asian juggler who managed to keep more than twenty objects in the air at the same time, and a young woman who placed her body in impossible positions.

The circus had few animals – a camel, a bear or two, and some horses that pulled their wagons and performed in riding acts. I hate to think what happened to the rest of their animals during the last hungry days of the Third Reich.

One of our officers had the excellent idea of making a deal with our captured circus. If we fed its performers at our mess and allowed them to charge the Germans admission, we would furnish our battalion jazz band to accompany their acts. They could keep all the money they took. GIs would be admitted free of charge.

The circus set up its small tent in the nearby town square. We went as often as we could when we were off duty. The almost-daily circus was a great improvement over the few films we got. During that time, I once again saw *Bowery to Broadway*.

One day a British officer rode up to our company headquarters. He was dapper and bemedaled. And highly indignant. It seemed that the circus was of British origin. It had been stranded in Germany throughout the war and survived by performing for Germans on the home front. The manager of the circus did not tell us their national origin, nor did we have any way of knowing it since its performances had a definite international flavor.

Our battalion was accused of enslaving allies for our entertainment. The truth of the matter was that the circus's performers wanted to be held by us. American Army food was much superior to that served to the British soldier, as I had discovered during my ocean crossing on the *Aquitania*.

Much to our – and their – dismay, our own private circus was released and moved into British occupied territory. There it had to endure British Army food until its performers were repatriated to their various countries.

Our jazz band, now without a permanent gig, performed just for us. They were quite good. Their music reminded us of life back home. There was one difference. Because of the non-fraternization rule we could not dance with German women. However, we were free to invite women who had been slave laborers to our dances in beer gardens.

One day when our band performed in the yard of a tavern, men danced with each other and a few DP women. The band really swung. The Germans, who had been forbidden to listen to "decadent" American jazz during Nazi rule, stood around the garden, craning their necks to see our wild jitterbugging and to hear this new music.

That day we truly celebrated our victory by playing our defiant, free-spirited music for those defeated Germans. The music that had been forbidden to them was a celebration of youthful American high spirits. That afternoon was one of my favorite moments while I was overseas. Somehow, that music made me very proud to be an American. Jazz is also at the heart of the American soul, and this was not nicely drilled big band commercial jazz. It was wild and free. At that moment, the Germans knew how futile their war had been. Americans will survive, even when they are damned fools. Is it because of our melting pot? Partly, yes. But it is especially true because of the great, vast land we have claimed as our own, combined with our inventive, adaptive, can-do mindset.

BOYS WILL BE BOYS
OR
CHOCOLATE, CIGARETTES, AND SOAP

Shortly after the war we moved into the sizable and beautiful city of Reichenbach. It had suffered some war damage, but it was almost intact. Our job was to stand guard and create an Allied presence until the boundaries of Germany were reestablished. In a few months it was handed over to the Russian Army and became part of East Germany. One of our tasks was keeping the Displaced Persons (DPs) from seeking vengeance against the Germans who had used them as slave labor. Despite the admonishments of our officers, we paid little attention to this duty.

Germans were moved out of their homes, and we moved in. The Army had the right to force billeting of troops in private homes. The Germans were allowed to come back daily and clean up after us. In general, we did little damage to the home our platoon took over. I am not sure how many of us were housed in this very typical German middle-class house. I do know that we had to share a bed with other soldiers. We rotated in and out of beds as we served our four-hour shifts of guard duty.

Most of occupation duty involved standing guard and walking guard posts. It was boring and dull and seemed pointless. We had our amusements. One day some of us went fishing. Our method was unusual. We threw armed hand grenades into a small river and harvested the dead fish that floated to the top. That evening we had a fish fry, cooking it in the kitchen of the German home that was our billet.

Another day, one of our squad, an expert hunter, brought in a deer he shot. He butchered it, and we each cooked our steak from the deer. I had tasted venison when I was a child, and bear meat, too; but this seemed very immediate. It was made all the more unique because I put what I thought was grease into the skillet. It proved to be honey. My venison had a sweet taste I will always remember.

Many of the men went foraging for wine and schnapps. One day we entered a cellar filled with casks that were almost as tall as we were. One of the men tried to tap one, hammering away at its plug with the butt of his rifle. It broke away and sent a wave of wine rushing into the cellar. We were half soaked in wine. It had been "served before its time." Fortunately, it was a white. If it had been a red our uniforms would have been hopelessly stained. For several days we smelled of wine. It was infinitely more pleasant than our ever-present body odor.

Our food improved as soon as the war ended. The company kitchen caught up with us and fed us very, very well. I remember the Germans standing nearby as we went through the chow line, filling our plates to the heaping. I could not help but feel sorry for them.

Finally, Special Services sent up softballs, a few gloves, and bats. We were able to play pickup games. Diamonds were laid out in flat and open fields. The competition was fierce. For an afternoon, at least, we seemed to be home. The Germans stood by and watched this sport that was strange to them.

One war ends, another begins...

Money was of little use during and right after the war. German money, of course, was worthless. The occupation money that was issued to us as pay was distrusted by the Germans. Goods were the main reason of barter. Americans had three things to barter – chocolate, cigarettes, and bath soap.

Cigarettes were the most common bartering object. I was told that European cigarettes were strong and bitter. As a non-smoker, I passed along the five cigarettes that came in our K rations to fellow squad members. At that time, I asked for nothing in return even though American cigarettes were very valuable. I learned that in France, where occupation marks were accepted, a carton of American cigarettes sold for the equivalent of two dollars a pack. Once purchased, they were sold on the black market for much more.

The Germans were desperate for food. Old men were even more desperate for a smoke. It was pathetic to see dignified older men following our smokers about, waiting for them to discard a smoking butt. They would drop to their knees to get it. Some of our smokers brutally stamped out the butt and ground what remained of it into the dirt.

There were also the continuing games of craps. Rooter continued to slide the dice to increase his odds of winning until someone called him on it. Some of us played hearts, and there were more than enough poker games. Blackjack was enormously popular, too. I tried my hand at it, but I never played for high stakes. Instead, I bet the cigarettes I did not smoke. They were welcome in the game.

After the war, when we had our own PX at company headquarters, I bought our weekly allowance of one carton of cigarettes. The cost was nominal, ten cents a pack. These I bartered with other soldiers for additional food or other goods.

Some men managed to secure nylon stockings and fancy women's underwear. Where they got these exotic items remains a mystery to me. Intimate apparel was even more valuable than chocolate and fine soaps. We did not dare to barter our GI issue clothing even though Germans tried to trade for parts of our uniforms. We refused. It was too easy to get caught.

Occupation duty - Chocolate!

Many years later I visited Russia. There, similar to what I encountered in postwar Germany, I saw barters being made, but by then it was for blue jeans, not the chocolate, cigarettes, or military gear. In the early 1990s the Russian ruble had little value, the dollar a great deal. The valuable lesson that I learned at the end of the war was that we put so much trust in money, we do not realize what a world without it would be like. It is a dangerous and unpleasant place.

*   *   *

The Germans had few things of value. Their most valuable possession was their women. We were forbidden to fraternize with the Germans. Any dealings we had were illegal, and it was illegal to have anything to do with young German women. That did not stop many of the men. Sex could be purchased easily from attractive young women who would, in ordinary times, have been virtuous. Women selling their bodies for food was not uncommon. It was also not uncommon for husbands to sell the only commodity they had, their wives.

Many of the German women were willing to have sex for a pack of cigarettes, a bar of soap, or a bar of chocolate. One of the mating calls was "Zig-zig for chokalat?" The Germans, who were fanatic about personal hygiene, valued our common bars of soap. It was gentler on their skin than what they had been used to.

I abstained. I'm not sure why. It was not for a lack of desire. Many of the young German women were very attractive and willing. Perhaps it was fear of venereal disease. As we had been told, the amateurs were more likely to be infected since they approached sex with enthusiasm and little caution. Perhaps I declined because I was a virgin and sex seemed both intimidating and something special to me.

Although I had gone through combat and killed many men by this time, I was still only 18 and sexually naïve (and more than a little insecure). Or perhaps I felt sorry for the German women who sold themselves so cheaply. At that stage in my life, I did not realize that many had been without men longer than we had been without women. Many of them wanted us as much as we wanted them. My friends told me their *Fräuleins* were passionate and inventive bed partners. They had no problem charging men who would pay for something they enjoyed too.

The younger German women got about town on bicycles. There were no shorts or slacks on view. Instead, they wore generous flowing skirts and peasant blouses; and one of the visual pleasures that spring was seeing those skirts flying in the breeze. Most never did anything to adjust them for modesty. They were quite enticing and knew it. Most of the women wore white panties. That combined with their pale German legs was a constant delight. Occasionally, a more brazen young woman wore no panties. Years later, I learned that most Europeans scorn excessive modesty.

Many of these German women, I suspect, hoped to land an American husband. Of course, that was impossible. If a soldier wanted to get married, he had to secure permission from his company captain. No Army officer was about to permit a marriage with a German. That sort of union was specifically banned by the Army's non-fraternization regulations. Even if a soldier was caught talking with a German woman, he could be sent to the brig.

Sometime after the war, the ban on German war brides was lifted. By now, I realized that European sexual attitudes, especially in wartime, were very different from the furtive necking and groping we experienced in high school, or even after the war. Most American couples I knew abstained from sex until their marriage was consummated. In Europe, if there was groping, there was sexual intercourse.

In time to come I became aware that romantic love did not play as large a part in European mating then as it did in the United States. Marriages were often based on economic or familial reasons. Some, I am sure, hoped that passion went along with the bargain. If passion lagged in marriage, affairs were accepted by European men and women as a reasonable alternative even as a marriage continued. Witness the behavior of more than a few royal personages over the centuries. European men, of course, were freer to dally; but European women had no compunctions about an extra-marital fling if they felt that it would be enjoyable.

Even with the non-fraternization strictures, we carried on conversations with German civilians as we wandered about the towns we occupied. Many spoke excellent English. I heard a great many stories – most long forgotten – about being a German in wartime. I soon found that most Germans wanted to justify themselves in our eyes. I never met one who admitted to having been a Nazi. Because of that, we took their declarations of innocence with a grain of salt.

While I later found that the French were less hygienic and often unpleasant in manner, I never admired the cleaner, more jovial Germans. Most of the French were fiercely independent. Only a few groveled. Most Germans did. Too many would sell anything – even their souls – if it meant a secure living standard. After the war the great German novelist, Thomas Mann, wrote the novel *Dr. Faustus*. It helped me understand why the Faust legend permeated the German soul.

What about the American soul? I am still trying to understand it. I see it as sitting on a single pillar that is the mind of Thomas Jefferson. On that pillar is a tripod. Its three sturdy legs are Nathaniel Hawthorne, Mark Twain, and Herman Melville. The metaphorical basis of the American soul is the seat that rests on this tripod. It is a very confusing metaphorical foundation that I find quite puzzling.

~~Somewhere~~ Reichenbach, Germany   27 May 45. Sun.

Dear Mom & Pop,   Rec'd June 8 th

How's everything? All is well here except that my
stomach is a trifle upset today.

I went to church this morning. It was a nice service.
Our Chaplain is quite young. He comes from Oklahoma.

Our company had a party & a chicken dinner.
— with of all things ice cream — the first I've
had since New York. The Division dance band
was there. It is pretty smooth.

The big treat was a young Bulgarian violinist,
Vasco Abajiew (or something in that effect) who had
reached the top as one of the greatest violinists in Europe
& was set for America when the war started. He
won the Fritz Kreisler Award a while back. He is
very young & as good as he was he must surely
have a wonderful future in store for himself. The
music teacher & violinist (Darnall of Paducah, Ky.) found
him by chance in this town & managed to get him.

He played Schubert's Serenade, Rhondo Capriccioso
by Mendelssohn, & a Rhondo by Puccini (one of the
most difficult pieces I have ~~to~~ ever heard let
alone seen played) & two American songs —
Stardust & I Cried for You. to keep audience
interest — you know how some are?

→

DEAR MOM & POP

~~Somewhere~~ Reichenbach, Germany   27 May, 45 Sun.

Rec'd June 8th

Dear Mom & Pop,

How's everything? All is well here except that my stomach is a trifle upset today.

I went to church this morning. It was a nice service. Our Chaplain is quite young. He comes from Oklahoma.

Our company had a party & a chicken dinner. – with of all things ice cream – the first I've had since New York. The Division dance band was there. It's pretty smooth.

The big treat was a young Bulgarian violinist, Vasco Abajiev[5] (or something to that effect) who had reached the top as one of the greatest violinists in Europe & was set for America when the war started. He won the Fritz Kreisler Award a while back. He is very young and as good as he was he must surely have a wonderful future in store for himself. The music teacher & violinist (Darnall of Paducah, KY) found him by chance in this town & managed to get him.

He played Schubert's Serenade, Rhondo Caprisoso[6] by Mendelssohn, a Rhondo by Paganini (one of the most difficult pieces I have ever heard let alone seen played) & two American songs – Stardust & I Cried For You to keep audience interest – you know how some are?

Anyhow it was a real treat. I received your box last night of Apr. 29 & Eurika another just as excellent one of April 10!! As glad as I was to get them, I cannot help but regret they came farther

---

5 Vasco Abadjiev (1926 – 1978) was born in Sofia, Bulgaria, the son of a violinist and pianist. He was a child prodigy, making his international debut at the age of six. He won many competitions and performed throughout Europe before World War II. At the beginning of the war his parents settled in Berlin, where he performed with conductors like Furtwangler, Bongarta, Abendroth, and Mengelberg. His father died in 1947, and his mother died in 1965. His personal life was a difficult one, filled with sadness, illness, and financial problems. Abadjiev died on December 14, 1978, in Hamburg, Germany.

6 SIC. Rhondo = Rondo, and Caprisoso = Capriccioso

apart. That's three I've gotten so keep them coming & they're always very welcome. Also include reading material!!

I got your letter of Sun. May 20 (only a week on the way) & 2 birthday cards Grandma Phillps & Bob & Anna.

Well I must close –

As always,

BC

P.S. Here is the order for our long march – beginning of our long trek across Germany.

Left Weibelsheim, motor convoy 2400, 29 March. Cross Rhine Buppart. Down E. side of River to St. Gorehaussen then NE thru Lerschied, Boyel, Olsberg to Nastulten where the troops were detrucks & commenced an approach march & then Due E. to a pt. N. of Frankfurt until heavy resistance is met. Order of March B, C, A, D, Hp. Co's Towns we passed thru & captured Hohernstein, Wustiomas, Treisberg, Brownback, Idstein, Rodaerg, Hunsre Arnsbach.

B Co. sustained most of the casualties as it was the point. We stayed in Arnsbruch for a few days & got on trucks & arrived near Kassel passing thru Eischwige. Stood division guard & took off once again. This time we met air resistance 4 or 5 times. There was heavy resistance in Zietz but we arrived in the closing phrases of the battle and the only trouble we had was a few mortar shells the night before we were dug in. Each squad was out in position 2 hours & off 4. We had been back about two hours when our 1st squad was counterattacked by around 50 Germans. The B.A.R. man stopped them with a rain of fire. We rushed out in position, but the trouble was over. We caught a couple Jerries. They wander around at night & it seems they can't see you in a foxhole & walk right up on top of you. A gun is stuck in their face & they usually surrender. One dumb bunny in our squad gets scared & shoots as soon as he sees them & scares them away as it is hard to shoot accurate at night. From Zietz we drove across the level plains of Germany coming very near Leipzig & then coming within sight of Chemnitz. Our furthest penetration into Germany. We left the 3rd Army, became part of the 1st and later the 9th Army. We are around 30 miles I would say from Chemnitz.

23

On Duty in Reichenbach

I WAS FIRST aware of young women in our house when I came back from guard duty in the middle of the night, exhausted and ready to sleep. In the bed I shared with three other GIs, I found two women. I realized that they had been brought in by some of the men. I ordered them out of the bed and let them sleep on the floor. They were half-clad, so I threw them some blankets and crawled into bed. We slept in our uniforms. There still was a potential of danger.

BATTLE OF THE BED

The women remained in our house for the food some of the men brought from the company kitchen. Good food was pure gold to the Germans. In return they had sex with any man who wanted it. I suspect these women were amateurs. I found the arrangement offensive, but there was nothing I could do about it. My chivalry was not due to a lack of desire. Deep inside me I knew that it was very wrong to have sex as a favor that grew out of a very human need for food and housing. Most other men did not feel that way. If sex was offered, they took it. If it was not, many bargained for it.

Sometime during the Occupation duty, a slightly older man joined our squad. I forget his name. He befriended a young German girl. She was no more than fifteen, or at least she seemed to be that young. Soon he was sleeping with her. We never knew if they had sex, but once I walked into his room and they were cuddled together in a baby crib. They were sound asleep. The Southerners had no problem with this. Women were said to be of marital age in many Southern states by the time they were fourteen. We Northerners were upset by this strange relationship. It ended when we shipped out to a new area. I forget the man's name. I believe he was married.

Some young German boys on the verge of puberty brought us a washtub of beer. Some were even younger. A few wore their *Hitler Jugend* uniforms.[7] Membership in this group was limited to boys between the ages of 8 and 14. They had been indoctrinated to worship force, and we were the force in town. These small boys hung around us, treating us like heroes.[8] We were replacements for the men of their defeated army. They offered to get us more beer, and a few offered their young sisters to us if the price was right. I am glad to say none of us accepted their offer.

One night a number of Displaced Persons got hold of weapons and went hunting for the Germans. They were intent on attacking those who had used them as slave labor. There was shooting all over the city. Our

---

7   The *Hitler-Jugend* (Hitler Youth) was an organization established by the Nazi Party for boys between the ages of fourteen and eighteen. It began in 1922 and continued until 1945. The Hitler Youth wore uniforms, and their emblem contained a swastika. The *Hitler-Jugend* was a way to indoctrinate the youth of Germany into being good Nazis and motivate them to fight for the Third Reich. By 1936 the membership had grown to more than five million, and by 1939 membership was mandatory for all "Aryan" youth. If a parent objected or refused to allow their child to join, they were investigated and punished. During WWII the *Hitler-Jugend* also evolved into a partially paramilitary organization. The Hitler Youth ceased to exist with the surrender of Germany in May 1945 and was outlawed by the Allied Control Council along with other Nazi Party organizations.

8   A chilling quote by Adolf Hitler says, "He alone, who owns the youth, gains the future." I have also heard this philosophy summarized as, "Give me your children until they are nine, and I'll have them until they are ninety."

officers sent us out to stop the violence. When we were a few blocks
away from company headquarters,
we entered an abandoned house and
holed up in its cellar for the night.
None of us were willing to risk our
lives to save a few Germans who had
committed war crimes. We never
knew how many were killed that
night. Everything seemed to return
to normal the next day. No one was
captured or punished. I suspect the
weapons that had been seized were hidden away for future use.

*Russian DPs at
Reichenbach pool.*

It was a warm spring, and there was a large public swimming pool that
was open to everyone. We often went there when we were off duty. Among
the swimmers were DPs, some of them young women. As Americans used
to modesty in our own culture, we were amazed to see Polish and Russian women come to the pool, strip off, and then put on their swimsuits
or what served as swimsuits. Often it was their rough underwear. Their
nudity lasted for a split second as they prepared to put on their swimming
suits. I have a blurry picture of some of those women. They were husky
women and far from the American ideal of beauty.

We had a table radio in our house. This allowed us to listen to stations
from some distance. The Armed Forces network played good jazz and
a lot of popular music. We got some news on the radio, but most of our
news came from the newspaper, *The Stars and Stripes.*

One day we returned to find our radio gone. Someone on another floor
said that a Sergeant Friday, who was attached to battalion headquarters,
had been in our house, probably to visit the women. He entered our billet
and took our radio away while we were on duty. We all knew that Friday
was a useless functionary who was impressed with his position at battalion.
Four or five of us found out where his billet was. With rifles in hand, we
entered his quarters. There he was, listening to our radio. We took our
radio back at gun point. Nothing was said about our vigilante action, even
though Friday was a favorite of the officers. He curried their favor with
many small tasks and favors, including the pimping of German women.

Now that we were out of combat, our squad sergeant, Mike Lipesky,
relaxed his air of command and became one of us. He had been a fine

squad sergeant and an excellent leader while we were in action. I liked Mike. He was devastatingly honest and a totally nice guy. He was from New Jersey and had a quiet sense of humor. It was enhanced by his dialect which was not unlike that of Corporal Schuler in basic.

Once Mike and I got into an amiable argument over a card game and ended up wrestling. As we tumbled about, we rolled to the head of a winding flight of stairs that led down from our garret billet. We rolled over and over down those stairs to the next landing, laughing, and slightly bruised. In a way, we were all becoming boys again. We never quite did. We had seen and experienced too much in our time in combat. When I could find a book, I would read it. Others in the squad read, too. Their interest ranged from westerns to mysteries. There were weekly arrivals of Armed Services Editions of a range of books. These paperbacks were two columns wide and compact in size. I managed to bring home a few of these paperbacks as souvenirs.

One of the most popular writers with the men was James M. Cain, a member of the hard-boiled school of fiction, a man that Edmund Wilson included in a group he called "the boys in the back room." We passed around his novel *The Postman Always Rings Twice* and reread it. Some of his sexual descriptions were candid for the time. Now they seem quite tame, but his writing remains crisp and fast moving.

One week I was late to the handing out of books. All that was left was a book of plays by Eugene O'Neill. At first, I was disappointed, but then I started to read the collection. I was swept away by the sea plays. I was too young to realize that some of them were melodramatic. *Anna Christie* was reality to me, a reality I had not seen before. A few years later I would understand its full power when I played a small role in it during a summer season at Penn State.

Another of O'Neill's plays, *The Hairy Ape*, amazed me with its expressionistic techniques. I had sampled professional theatre before I went overseas, but this exceeded what I had seen. Only Howard Richardson and William Berney approached O'Neill in theatricality with *Dark of the Moon*, and it wasn't even close in its reality or psychology. Little did I know that this small paperback of plays would lead me toward my life's work.

As soon as I got home, I bought a larger anthology of O'Neill's plays and read them all. I then began to track down his lesser-known plays. It is strange that in my long career in theatre I have only directed one of his plays, *Beyond the Horizon*.

I carried the paperback book of poetry I had brought overseas with me through all my time in combat. It is very battered, and its cover was lost a long time ago. I read many of the poems over and over again. It is a credit to the members of my squad that they never treated me as an oddball because I read so much and loved poetry.

My Life as a Cartoonist and Writer

During our extended stay at Reichenbach, battalion headquarters asked the company commanders if they had any artists. I had been drawing cartoons to send home to my parents and friends in my V-Mail letters. Remember that every letter we wrote home was read by an officer at the company level. If we wrote something that they considered inappropriate – mainly about military matters – it was blacked out. One of my friends, Eugene Cox, who came from West Virginia and was a farmer in civilian life, had copied my cartoons and sent them home to his wife.

Bill cartooning in Reichenbach.

Colonel Mette, commander of the 417th Infantry Battalion decided that he wanted to create a history of our rather young outfit, publish it, and distribute it to the members of our outfit after we got home. He needed men to illustrate and write the history.

Our company commander proudly told battalion headquarters he had not one but two cartoonists in one of his infantry platoons. Gene and I were sent to battalion headquarters which was housed in a huge mansion. There were two other artists on hand. One was Pvt. Donald M. Geil and the other was named Pfc. Arthur Buck. Geil was amazingly talented and was certainly the best of us. I am not bragging to say I was next best since Gene had been copying my cartoons and the other artist drew crudely.

We were certainly inspired by the work of Bill Mauldin.

I told Gene that I would feed him drawings since this looked like it was going to be soft duty. A tech sergeant, Clyde H. Horning, a tall kindly man, was put in charge of the project. We were given one of the mansion's kitchens as a studio. Its wide counters and big windows provided us with a true studio atmosphere. The drawing equipment we needed was "requisitioned" – some might say it was "liberated" – from a German art store.

By now, I had discovered that our platoon's billet had been the home of an artist who had served as a combat artist. I still have a copy of his books, most drawn while he was on the Russian front. He had not returned from the war, but there was some artists equipment in his study.

There we also found a ten-volume collection of pornography. It was filled with pornographic paintings, drawings, and photos of sculptures by major European artists over the centuries. With usual German efficiency, each volume was devoted to one aspect of sex or scatology. This encyclopedic work was often referenced in evenings by all of us. We had never seen pornography before. Some of the volumes were truly disgusting. Slowly, but surely, we were discovering European sophistication. Much of what Americans consider shocking, even now, they considered just another aspect of life.

Gene and I were taken off guard duty. Our job was to report to battalion headquarters right after breakfast. There we went to work. We were supplied all the logs of our daily actions. There was no typewriter, so we began to draft the story of our battalion.

Our battalion commander, Col. Mette, rarely visited us, but we had a daily visit from his adjutant, Maj. Verne E. Pate. One day he brought a German publisher and his wife to visit us while we worked. They were appalled that a military history was going to be illustrated with cartoons. The aging publisher's attractive young wife and Pate seemed to be unusually friendly.

The Major's assistant was 1st Lieutenant John Milliken, a curly haired, handsome young man who seemed to be quite impressed with himself. I never figured out what he did. Pate saw us daily, but Sergeant Horning was involved with our work page by page. Horning gave us a free hand in creating our drawings.

There was one hitch. The print factory had been bombed out. The publisher could still execute photographic plates, but his type setting facilities had been destroyed. The text had to be handwritten. Each of us gave a sample of our handwriting. Sergeant Horning had the best penmanship. He had the task of handwriting the history into its final form.

I was allowed to write several sections, including some major battles – and especially the one dealing with the young boys at the bridge. In glancing at the history as I write this, no mention is made that the defenders of the town and the bridge were boys in their mid-teens.

Into Horning's handwritten text we inserted thumbnail cartoons, along with full page cartoons. Geil and I did the lion's share of the drawing.

It was pleasant duty. We did not rush it because we were reluctant for our work to end. I slipped Gene a cartoon every day, so he seemed to be as productive as the rest of us. My sketchbook and the book itself survive. Major Pate seemed to enjoy the company of enlisted men and dropped by often. I think he liked our rowdy sense of humor. He was careful to examine all we were doing. Some of our artwork never made the book. Pate did not do the censorship himself. He sent our work on to regimental headquarters. There someone passed judgment on our work. On one sketch I did was written "No!" To the enlisted men and especially the combat infantrymen it was my funniest.[9]

In it a slovenly infantryman, holding a bottle in one hand and a German *Fraulein* in the other sees an officer approaching. In his mind he saw his Combat Infantryman Badge taking wing and flying away. Public drunkenness and fraternization with German women were forbidden. The penalty for this sort of misconduct was to take away the culprit's Combat Infantryman Badge. We considered this to be the same as a medal for bravery, and it

Occupation duty
Non-Fraternization

was. I value it more than my Bronze Stars. To take it away seemed like an injustice to all of us.

Major Pate understood our point of view, but he knew the Army would be most upset if it was criticized in one of its semi-official publications.

---

9 Another cartoon, "Spirit of the 76th," appears before the section titled "The Long Advance." (p. 225) In the upper right hand corner of that cartoon, the reader can see another "NO" written. Since it is not in Bill's handwriting, it is obviously another cartoon that didn't amuse the powers-that-be.

Another one that was rejected had three john doors. They were labeled "Men," "Women," and "Officers." This one almost got me court-martialed. Making officers a sex unto themselves was deeply resented! My best work was in the tiny thumbnail sketches and the frontispiece map showing the 76th's journey across Europe. While my cartooning now seems old fashioned, I found this part of my work expressive and humorous. My cartoons in India ink are stiffer. Pencil seemed to be my best medium.

Those few weeks at battalion headquarters were my most pleasant while I was in the Army. I was free of red tape, dull duties, and much of the code of conduct for soldiers. Becoming a writer and a cartoonist seemed like an attractive lifestyle to me.

Quite soon after the war, Major Pate sent each and every man in the battalion a copy of the book. I believe we all gave him a dollar or two in cash to cover expenses. It is an uneven effort. Some of the cartoons are quite good, some not so good, and much of the writing – while unemotional and withdrawn – has great clarity. My reading of Hemingway had paid off. I used his laconic style in the sections I wrote. I am not sure which are mine now. I think we all evolved in writing the book. Gene even managed an original cartoon or two of his own. It was a very good time. It was almost like being a civilian for a few weeks.

While I worked at Battalion headquarters, I got to see some of the inner workings of the military. I saw officers writing each other up for medals. Some were earned, most were not. A Bronze Star and especially a Silver Star advanced an officer's career. The officers involved were all attached to Battalion. There they had little opportunity to be in close combat. Officers at the company level did. In listing the medals, we also found that a disproportionate number had gone to officers and many of these to those who were technically in rear echelon jobs. We all found this back-scratching practice scandalous. Men who had been on the front lines were being passed over so officers who had rarely been near direct fire from the enemy could advance their careers.

ROOTER AGAIN

While we were creating our wartime history, Rooter had turned his attention to peacetime occupations. He still scrounged for anything containing alcohol. He had not learned his lesson. He fraternized with the German women. He was not, shall I say, very selective. He contacted gonorrhea. He went through the six-day cure and was released. Since he was promiscuous, we found out that even when he had sex more than once with a woman, he took the injection into his urethra every time.

One of our older men said he was going to burn his penis away with the constant medication. Rooter then decided that he could average his prophylactics and not use them for a few days. He contacted gonorrhea again. In all, to our knowledge, he caught it three times and was infected almost as soon as he was released from being cured three times.

None of us liked Rooter, so we took some joy in his constant cures. We all resented his attempts to rig crap games and the fact that he had never fired a shot in combat because he was too lazy to clean his rifle. In addition to that, he was a general annoyance.

Rooter was amazingly stupid. One day when we were sitting around bored, I decided to determine just how stupid Rooter really was. I found an old 78 rpm record in a German house that was our billet. I found a needle and a pencil. I put the pencil in the hole in the record, held the needle between my teeth, and spun the record with my finger as I pretended to listen to it. I even hummed a melody and nodded my head to a pretended rhythm.

Rooter, like an alley cat, was immediately curious and asked what I was doing. I told him I was listening to the record. I said that if I spun it at the right speed and held the needle in the groove the sound would go directly to my brain. Others in my squad watched this with great amusement.

"Gawdamn, you're really listening to music in yer haid?"

"I sure am."

Rooter then declared, "Gimme that goddamned thing, I'm going to listen to some music."

He spent the rest of the afternoon trying to get the needle and the record speed right. He asked me to show him how I did it. Then he tried again. He heard nothing. I told him he needed to get the needle at the right angle and the record moving at the right speed. He was determined to hear music in his head, and he kept trying. By supper time he was still unable to listen to music. Finally, he gave up. His long and unsuccessful efforts gave us an entertaining afternoon.

OTHER ART WORK

Since Gene and I were established as artists, we were assigned the task of creating a backdrop in a movie theatre for visiting USO troupes. Sgt. Friday, who by now had forgiven us for reclaiming our radio, took us about town in a jeep as we collected paint and brushes. We gave merchants slips of paper as receipts that said, "TS-POE." They accepted these as official. Of course, they were not. The abbreviation was based on a joke everyone shared before we left to go overseas – "Tough Shit, Port of Embarkation." "TS" was a common Army expression for not having good luck. The other was "chickenshit" which was a way of describing a non-com or officer who stuck too close to the rules.

We painted an enormous 76th Division patch on the beaded movie screen. The owner arrived in time to see that his screen was ruined. He was hysterical and for good reason. The screen was expensive, and he had no resources to replace it and go back into business.

The theatre owner had a beautiful teenage daughter that we lusted after. Sgt. Friday tried to get her alone at every opportunity. One day I managed to neck with her in the projection booth of the theatre. It went no further than advanced necking, but I proudly told Friday what had happened. He was not pleased.

The first and only attraction was Hal McIntyre's Band.[10] It was a solid second-rank big band of the time. The musicians were given a guided tour of life in occupied Germany. We were rewarded with a marvelous concert. To be perfectly honest, USO troops rarely ventured too far toward the front lines when the war was going on and they still tended to visit rear areas. There was still danger in Reichenbach.

---

10   Harold William McIntyre, or Hal McIntyre (1914 - 1959), was an American saxophonist, clarinetist, and bandleader. He came to fame in the mid-1930s when he joined the Glenn Miller Orchestra as a founding member. At Miller's encouragement, he founded his own group in 1941, and toured extensively throughout the United States. During WWII he played overseas for the troops. His group backed The Mills Brothers on their hit, "Glow Worm," in 1952. He died in 1959 as a result of injuries sustained in an apartment fire. His son, Hal Jr., later had a big band of his own, and performed many of his father's arrangements.

A Farewell

Now that the war was over, a few men with the most service were returned home to be discharged. Some were reassigned to serve in other outfits that had been decimated by combat. Among those who departed was Captain Walker, our C Company commander. He was immensely popular among the enlisted men and officers. He had treated us well and kept good discipline even while he was easy and understanding. He had lost a great deal of his hair during the war, perhaps from wearing the wool knit cap we all wore under our helmets in cooler weather or, as some of us theorized, perhaps it was from the stress of being in command during combat.

The company threw him a big farewell party. Someone found a hall, massive kegs of beer and bottles of wine, and food. The cooks managed to make it a special event. There was a great deal of joking during the dinner. The regimental band played for us. It was a great party.

One lieutenant told a ribald joke about a profane parrot that swore when parishioners came calling. Worse still, the parrot kept having sex with the neighbors' chickens. The parson threatened the parrot that he would pluck out all the feathers on its head if it happened again. It swore again during a Sunday school picnic, and the parrot's head feathers were plucked.

The parson had a church party one evening. He told the parrot to behave and do a small task for him. He wanted it to sit on a roost by the door and say, "The ladies cloakroom is to the left and the gentlemen is to the right."

For a while the parrot behaved, but a bald-headed church elder entered the door, escorting his wife. The parrot said, "The lady goes to the left; and you, you bald-headed chicken-fucker, get up here with me."

Everyone looked at Captain Walker's bald head and the room burst into laughter. It was quite a party and lasted into the wee hours of the morning.

The next morning, a jeep came to pick up our captain. The entire company gathered to bid him farewell. Then, as the jeep drove off, an enlisted man with one of those nasal country voices shouted, "So long, you bald-headed chicken-fucker."

The last we saw of Captain Walker he was rolling about on the jeep seat, helpless with laughter.

We felt much as the men in the film, *The Story of GI Joe*, felt about their captain.[11] I am glad our captain moved on to stateside duty. Of all the officers I met in the Army, he was the best by far.

Frightened Germans

Our occupation duty in Reichenbach was coming to an end. We were scheduled to pull back and turn the area over to the Russians. The Germans were upset by this decision. It changed their attitude toward us greatly. They did not want to live under Russian rule. Russians were reputed to be wild and dangerous. Decisions made at Potsdam[12] had determined their fate. We were now in what would later be called East Germany.

When the order for us to pull back came, the German publisher and his wife who had been working on our book asked Major Pate to take them with us or to kill them. Pate did neither. I heard of other instances where Germans, terrified of Russian rule, asked to be killed. To the best of my knowledge, none were. I suspect the affluent publisher and his wife had been Nazis. I might note that during my time in occupied Germany I never met a German who said he or she was, or had been, a Nazi. However, they were not shy about informing on their neighbors. For this, we despised them.

Near our billet, we saw a badly wounded German soldier who had returned home. One arm was missing, and he had a terrible limp. His face was terribly scarred. Helping him was his young wife. The German's

---

11   The film was based on Ernie Pyle's newspaper stories and days he spent with the troops as he covered the front line Infantry in Italy. In the movie, Robert Mitchum played a beloved captain who died on the line in Italy.

12   The Potsdam Conference, July 17 - August 2, 1945, was the last of the WWII meetings held by American President Harry S. Truman, British Prime Ministers Winston Churchill and Clement Attlee, and Soviet Premier Joseph Stalin. These talks established a Council of Foreign Ministers, and a central Allied Control Council for the administration of postwar Germany. Agreements on postwar order, peace treaty issues, land boundaries, punishment for war criminals, reparations, and the German economy were established. The three leaders also issued a declaration demanding the unconditional surrender from Japan. One of the results of the Potsdam Conference was that Germany and Austria were each to be divided into four occupation zones (earlier agreed to in principle at Yalta), and each capital would be divided into four zones.

first name was Willy. A few soldiers struck up a conversation with him – some, I fear, to explore whether his wife might be interested in straying.

One night after curfew, he invited some of us to their apartment. It was on the third or fourth floor. The ascent was by a winding staircase. He served us wine, and his wife had cheese and dark German bread. She was in her early thirties and was quite attractive. Even though there was the chill of spring in the air, she wore a light summer dress. It seemed that she wore nothing under it.

Willy's English was quite good. He told us how he had been badly wounded at Stalingrad and returned home.

After a few drinks, Willy said that if we could get him and his wife into American-occupied territory, we could have sex with his wife. She sat beside him, smiling in agreement. I was shocked to see people driven to this extremity. All about me I saw wives selling themselves to soldiers, but this was a reality where we saw how complicit German husbands were in bartering their wives for food and other physical needs.

There was no way we could smuggle a German couple into our fully loaded truck. We tried to explain this to Willy, but he asked us to try. No one took advantage of Willy's offer. At least, I think no one did. Fortunately, Rooter wasn't with us that sad evening.

I found this very upsetting. For a human being to be driven to such a point said something about the ravages left by all wars. Willy served his country bravely in Russia, and he had suffered greatly. He and his wife deserved a better fate. I hope that they had a good life in what was to become East Germany.

The evening went on and there was much drinking. I did not drink, so I decided to go back to our billet. The wife escorted me down the dark, winding stairs. With each step, she moved closer to me. When we arrived at the front door, she grabbed me in an embrace and kissed me. I withdrew, partly out of my shyness, and partly because I was shocked by this open offer of sex for a favor none of us could grant. I fled out the door and returned to my billet. Once there, I threw the prostitutes out of my bedroom.

I was not yet nineteen, and I was deeply upset in seeing the human race having to stoop so low just to survive. Even though the Germans were our enemies, people should not live like this. In years to come, I would learn that human existence could get much worse in the Third World.

We moved out and drew back. The duty at Reichenbach had been pleasant. However, my days as a cartoonist and writer were over. We got in trucks and drove out. The Germans waved to us, some with tears in their eyes. They had no idea how life would be under the Russians. I often wonder what happened to these people. Many had been Nazis or Nazi supporters. They got little sympathy from us. At the time we thought they were getting what they deserved.

* * *

DEAR GRANDMA & GRANDPA

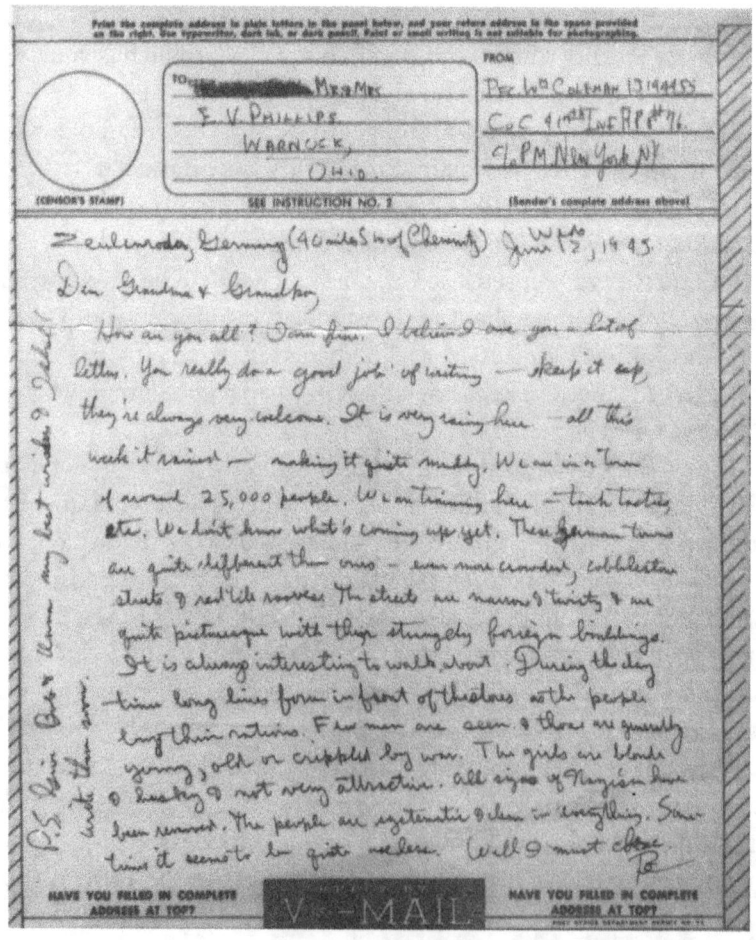

To:
Mr. & Mrs. E.V. Phillips
Warnock, Ohio

From:
Pfc. Wm Coleman 13194455
Co C 417th Inf APO #76
c/o P.A. New York, NY

Zeulenroda, Germany (40 miles SW of Chemnitz)
Weds June 12, 1945

Dear Grandma & Grandpa,

How are you all? I am fine. I believe I owe you a lot of letters. You really do a good job of writing – keep it up, they're always very welcome. It is very rainy here – all this week it rained – making it quite muddy. We are in a town of around 25,000 people. We are training here – tank tactics, etc., We don't know what's coming up yet. These German towns are quite different than ours – even more crowded, cobblestone streets & red tile rooves. The streets are narrow & twisty & are quite picturesque with their strangely foreign buildings. It is always interesting to walk about. During the day time long lines form in front of the stores as the people buy their rations. Few men are seen & those are generally young, old or crippled by war. The girls are blonde & husky & not very attractive. All signs of Nazism have been removed. The people are systematic & clean in everything. Sometimes it seems to be quite useless.

Well I must close. BC

P.S. Give Bob & Anna my best wishes & I shall write them soon.

24

THE 30TH DIVISION

THE 76TH DIVISION was broken up, and we were shipped out to older divisions. The war in the Pacific was still raging. Only those at the very highest levels knew there was an atom bomb that could end it all at Hiroshima and Nagasaki. The main body of the Army prepared itself to invade the Japanese mainland.

Some of the older veterans were sent home to be discharged. The rest of us lived with the fear that our new division would be sent to invade Japan. No one wanted to fight the Japanese on their home ground. Their tenacity in island warfare made them a dangerous foe. Certainly, they were more dedicated to their cause than the average soldier in the *Wehrmacht*.

By now, a point system had been devised to determine who went home first. Each month in service counted for one point. Each month overseas one point more per month. Each battle star counted for five points. I believe the Combat Infantryman Badge counted for five more. Medals for bravery counted five each, as did Purple Hearts (for being wounded). At that time my Bronze Stars were not registered or counted in my total. My time at VMI did not count as points since I was being educated by the Army. I may have the point system a little out of its correct time scheme, but I am sure it started before the war ended in Japan.

No one in our division had more than three battle stars or six months overseas, so the point total among even the most veteran among us was low. A few who had been wounded and received medals had enough points to be sent home.

The rest of us were assigned to the much older 30th Division. It had landed at Normandy less than a week after the invasion and had seen a lot of hard action. Its most veteran soldiers had five battle stars and a year overseas.

The division had a different feel from ours. Those combat veterans had seen much more violence than we had. When I

Hysterics in the Barracks

joined the outfit, they were living in a long room that was somewhat like a barracks. In one wall was a wide hole. When I asked what had caused it, it seemed that one soldier dared another to shoot a bazooka close to his head. The soldier complied and blew out the gaping hole.

Others had gotten drunk and drove jeeps through a Russian-occupied town, shooting it up Western style. They almost created an international incident. They had no intention of injuring Russians, and I suspect they didn't know they were riding through a Russian-controlled town.

Others told of visiting a site where Germans and Americans were experimenting with rockets. This must have been where Wernher von Braun volunteered to join in our space effort. Later when von Braun wrote his book, *I Aimed at the Stars*, some wag added, *But I Hit London*.

One day, we sat in our barracks watching a group of older German men loading one of the huge water heating systems the Germans had onto a horse-drawn wagon. It was an immense vat that weighed several hundred pounds. There were about a dozen men working on the project. Together they could have easily picked it up and put it on the wagon bed. Instead, they took an entire morning working out a ramp and pulley system. We sat together laughing at this very German display of efficiency.

In early June, I celebrated my nineteenth birthday. The war in the Pacific lingered on. As summer came, we were brought together for an address by General Edwin Walker. He told us that he knew we were fighting men who wanted to fight even more, and that he was going to make sure we were first on the beaches of Japan. He was roundly booed. He was removed from NATO command by Eisenhower when he advocated the far-right John Birch Society to his troops. Some years later, Edwin

Walker was arrested for public lewdness in a men's room in Dallas, having
fondled and propositioned a male undercover police officer.

*   *   *

DEAR BILLY

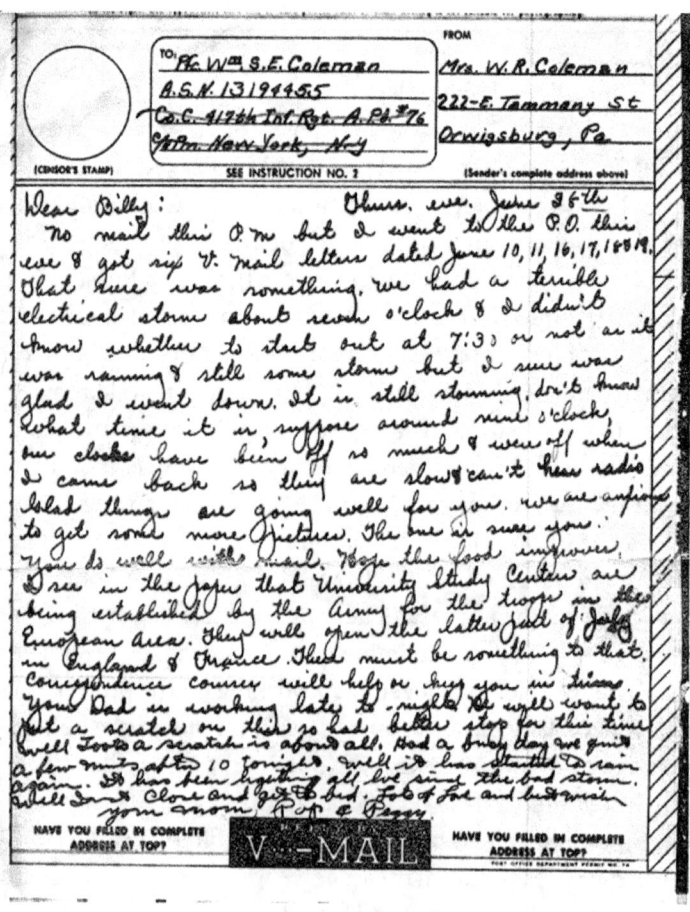

To:
Pfc Wm. S.E. Coleman
~~A.S.N. 13194455~~
~~CoC, 419th Inf. Rgt A.P.O. #30~~
~~c/o P.M. New York, N.Y.~~

From:
Mrs. W.R. Coleman
222 - E. Tammany St.
Orwigsburg, Penna.

Thurs. eve. June 28th

Dear Billy:

No mail this P.M. but I went to the P.O. this eve & got six V. mail letters dated June 10, 11, 16, 17, 18 & 19. That sure was something. We had a terrible electrical storm about seven o'clock & I didn't know whether to start out at 7:30 or not as it was raining & still some storms but I sure was glad I went down. It is still storming, but don't know what time it is, suppose around nine o'clock, our clocks have been off so much & were off when I came back so they are slow & can't hear radio.

Glad things are going well for you. We are anxious to get some more pictures. The one is sure you. You do well with mail. Hope the food improves. I see in the paper that University Study Centers are being established by the Army for the troops in their European Area. They will open the latter part of July in England & France. There must be something to that. Correspondence courses will help or keep you in time. Your Dad is working late to-night. He will want to put a scratch on this so had better stop for this time.

Well Toots a scratch is about all. Had a busy day. We quit a few minutes after 10 tonight. Well it has started to rain again. It has been lightning all eve since the bad storm. Will just close and get to bed.

Lots of love and best wishes.

Your Mom, Pop & Peggy[13]

---

13 Peggy was their dog.

EN ROUTE

Once again, we moved out. Only now we were heading south, back through the areas we had fought so hard to obtain. We were beginning the long journey home. On our way we got better looks at some of the bombed-out German cities. Frankfurt was a city without roofs. It had to be completely rebuilt. Mannheim was even worse. Many buildings were flattened. The city seemed lifeless. German civilians watched our trucks enter their city with empty eyes. They seemed thoroughly beaten even though the war had ended weeks before. No one expressed any pity for them. All of us had reasons to be angry with Germans in general, even though that was not rational. Certainly, some must have hated the war. Perhaps as it got worse most hated it, but there was little they could do to oppose it.

We stopped in Mannheim. I am not sure how long we were there, but we had time to see a movie, the ubiquitous *Bowery to Broadway*, in a theatre that had no roof. The stars loomed above us. During the last weeks of the war, while the 76th moved through the countryside and small towns – and one rather large city – in our movement forward, other units had fought through the streets of these cities. We all knew how brutal the street fighting had been. Now, as I looked at the stars and enjoyed the movie, I felt a mixture of gratitude and relief.

From Mannheim we rode a series of trains, this time toward France. Again, they were forty-and-eights. Some of the narrow-gauge tracks had been recently rebuilt. The bridges wobbled as we crossed over them. The devastation France had suffered was evident. As an eighteen-year-old boy, I brooded over the awful forces that make wars. Those that caused them lived much more safely and comfortably than those who lived in those ruins or those who fought through them. Many of the Germans who precipitated this destruction were caught. Some were imprisoned, some executed. They deserved a Hell, but I could not bring myself to believe in a God that would permit such a Hell to exist.

Eventually Europe rebuilt under the Marshall Plan[14] and the persistence of the European human spirit. The renaissance of Europe took years. Now all its countries prosper, some even more than the United States.

---

14 The Marshall Plan, officially named the European Recovery Program (ERP), provided aid to Western Europe following WWII. The United States gave over $12 billion dollars (in 2016 the equivalent would be nearly $100 billion US dollars) over a four-year period in economic assistance to help promote world peace and general welfare, rescue

I had no doubt then that there would be more wars. This, I believed, was a war that would generate more wars. It was the second World War in the first half of a century. I was right. Since then, there has not been a day of peace in our world. This tragic condition continues into the 21st century. The unending spiral of war after war that reaches back before recorded history continues. It seems to be part of our human nature. Too many people make money from war, and today's philosophy seems to be more about protecting profits than promoting peace. Just imagine what our world could be like if we focused our money and energies on improving the quality of life for the world and promoting peace rather than continuing hell-bent to find new ways to destroy the planet and each other.

As I rode through that devastation, I mourned my own comrades who had fallen, and I mourned for all those who were deprived of that most precious thing, life. I mourned for those who did not even dare dream amidst the privation. The dead were gone, but the living struggled to survive among the ruins about me.

That journey south was soul-searing. As we looked at the devastation, we also thought about what was ahead of us. We all believed that we would soon be on a boat that would take us to the beaches of Japan. At this point, the only thing we had to look forward to were day passes to French cities, and especially Paris. We tried to live in the moment, as our future was uncertain.

Some of the men sold or traded goods to the throngs that lined the rail lines just as they had when we rode toward Germany. It was like they had remained by the tracks waiting for our return.

One soldier had acquired a typewriter, probably stolen from an Army clerk. The trouble was that it was broken. Many of its keys were twisted and

---

and rebuild war-torn regions, modernize industry, remove trade barriers, and prevent the spread of Communism. The ERP was signed into law on April 3, 1948. It is still considered to be one of the most successful foreign aid programs instituted by the United States, and it had a considerable impact on Europe's recovery following the war. This plan was named for George C. Marshall, Jr., who rose through the US Army to become FDR's Chief of Staff, and then served as Secretary of State and Secretary of Defense under President Harry S. Truman. In 1949 Marshall was named president of the American National Red Cross. In 1953 he received the Nobel Peace Prize for his post-war work, the only career officer in the US Army to ever receive this honor. He died in 1959 at the age of 78 and is buried at Arlington National Cemetery.

even more were broken. He kept the lid half-closed to hide the damage. He sold it before our journey was over.

Our officers had their own car, a real railroad car. There they lounged in relative luxury. We rarely saw them during our journey. They again became the privileged class they had been before they went into combat with us. We could only imagine the perks they enjoyed.

Our train approached the outskirts of Paris. We inquired about passes to tide us over while the train wended its way through the shattered French railroad system around Paris. None were offered. I awoke our first morning to realize that one third of the forty men in our box car were gone. The same was true throughout the train. A very large percentage of the 30th Division went AWOL during those few days. There was no way our officers could cope with this mass exodus. Too many had fled to the pleasures and sights of Paris. The war was over, so their absence meant fewer men had to be fed in our mess tents. Most rejoined the train three days later as it exited the Paris yards. I regret I did not join them, but I was afraid of being sent to the brig, so I dutifully stayed on board. No one took roll, so none of those who jumped train and returned were punished.

We moved south from Paris to a large rural area near Reims. There the 30th occupied a vast tent city that sprawled across rolling hills. It was a hot summer. As July progressed, we waited for shipment back to the United States. Would it be a brief furlough at home and a trip to the Pacific? Would we be among the first to storm the beaches of Japan? We were apprehensive and angry. Hadn't we done enough?

SIGHTSEEING

Daily trucks took us into Reims.[15] There was a fine indoor city swimming pool that we enjoyed. We delighted in the young French women whose bathing suits were far more daring than anything we had seen on American beaches. We flirted with them, but our trucks waited to take us back before twilight.

---

15   Also known, in English, as Rheims, but Reims is the more common spelling today. The city of Reims is 80 miles east-northeast of Paris.

I seized time to visit the famous cathedral every day I went into town. This was the first Gothic cathedral I had ever seen. I was hypnotized by its beauty, the lift of those columns and arches, and that vast echoing space.

I brought home a print of Reims Cathedral. My mother appropriated it and framed it. It hung in her living room until she had to leave her home and move to Des Moines. Now we have it hanging in our dining room. While it is not a great print, it marked the beginning of my fascination with Gothic architecture. Eventually, I saw dozens of Gothic cathedrals in England, France, Italy, and Germany.

On another day we were taken to Deauville and Trouville to enjoy a day on its famed beach. This rich resort area was too expensive for us. We decided to go to a vast sand beach near town. There we first saw the swimming suits that were later called bikinis. They revealed more of the female form than I had ever seen before on a beach. Again, I observed European women who were not shy about changing into their swimsuits on a beach in full view of everybody. They would strip entirely, then put on their swimming suits. Here and there a few women sunbathed topless.

On one of these excursions, our truck convoy stopped for a break. Many of the men had to urinate, but we were in the middle of a French town. Someone found a door to a courtyard that enclosed a large French house and its outside buildings. It was completely enclosed. Within a few minutes, dozens of men were urinating on the green grass of the courtyard. Others from the convoy joined them. In all, two or three hundred soldiers were relieving themselves on the green patch.

The angry French owner charged out of his house with a pitchfork. He was disarmed by a couple of men who promptly broke his pitchfork over a rock as the dozens of men continued urinating. I have often wondered how many weeks it took to get rid of the stench of that mass urination in his enclosed courtyard. We did no good for international understanding that day.

While I am on the subject of the French, their enthusiasm for Americans had declined in the months since France was liberated. Once the euphoria of the Liberation waned, the French immediately resumed their traditional rude ways. We did nothing to soothe that attitude. No one much liked the French men, but most of us were enchanted by the women. Young French women had a special beauty that is unique. It is Latin in look, but less robust than that of Italian, Spanish, and Greek women. The younger women had slender figures and modest breasts.

The men, on the other hand, were often uncivil and churlish, and the French merchants were ruthless in their dealings. Waiters in restaurants were chronically rude and, I am told, still are. I'm sure that the French men felt the same as the British did about American GIs – "They're over-dressed, overfed, oversexed, and over here."

Occupation Duty. Bill at Parade Rest.

25

PASSES TO PAREE

I MADE TWO trips to Paris, each on a one-day pass. My first
trip was alone. I managed to explore Paris with a guidebook
I purchased. My squad leader, a man named Gus, generously
lent me occupation francs and some actual French francs. It was
more than enough for a day in Paris. I also carried two cartons
of cigarettes I'd purchased at the PX. They represented twenty
dollars each. I sold the cigarettes to a very shady looking French
man. That twenty dollars gave me a nice day and evening in Paris.
When I returned the money Gus lent me, he chided me for not
spending it all.

The reason I was short of money was that paymasters were slow to
catch up with us as we moved about in combat. Then, after the war, this
was further complicated because outfits were being terminated and collapsed into other outfits.

When we finally were paid, the money we received was in occupation
money. It was backed by the United States, but locals did not trust it. They
wanted goods. The money of the day was cigarettes, soap, silk stockings
(if you could get them), and chocolate.

We were up long before dawn. A convoy of trucks hauled us into
Paris along narrow roads. I dozed off. I knew I was going to need all
my energy for the day ahead. By now, I was an expert in sleeping under
difficult conditions.

We pulled up with dozens of other trucks from other units in the
spacious *Place de la Concorde.* Dawn was breaking, and Paris was just

awakening. We were told we must be back here at two in the morning.
The trucks would not wait for stragglers; if you didn't catch your truck,
you would be considered AWOL.

I was thrilled to be in Paris even for a few hours. The first thing I did
was to purchase a map. I had heard much about the city from others who
had passes there while they were in combat. I moved about on the Metro,
their subway system. I had mastered the New York system. I quickly found
out the Paris system was less complicated.

On this trip, I visited the Louvre the first day it was open after the
war. Not everything had found its way back to the museum, but many of
its major works were on view. I wandered through the galleries, seeing
paintings and sculptures I had heard about all my life. I experienced the
hypnotic effect of Leonardo da Vinci's *Mona Lisa* and the soaring feeling
of the *Winged Victory* statue.

On both my trips to Paris, I spent hours in those galleries while my
comrades were out chasing French women and drinking wine. I wandered
through the rooms, but I found myself drawn back to the *Mona Lisa* again
and again. She was not beautiful by modern or Hollywood standards,
but she cast a spell on me. She represents the mystery of all women. We
men never quite know them. Perhaps they feel the same way about us?

There were other paintings that enchanted me. I fumbled my way
through the galleries. There were no art appreciation classes in high school.
However, those trips to the Carnegie Museum in Pittsburgh gave me a
toehold on artistic greatness. My parents had done well by taking me to
those Art in America exhibits.

After coming out of the Louvre, I asked directions from a petite French
woman my age. She seemed friendly and her English was passable. She
wore a skirt and light summer blouse. Her small breasts were visible
through the fabric of her blouse. She had large brown eyes and dark hair.
She had a special Gallic beauty.

I knew a few French phrases. We tried to converse for a few minutes.
We communicated at a basic level. Suddenly that hideous shyness I had
in high school returned. I wanted to, but I failed to ask her to spend at
least part of the day with me. It's odd that I still have a strong image of
her. I remember most vividly standing on the steps in front of the Louvre
as we tried to understand each other.

Over the years, I remember so many "what might have been" possibilities when it comes to young women. What if I had mustered the courage

to ask her to spend that day with me? There have been others along the way. It is odd that once in a while you feel that sudden connection to another person. That French girl was one of those.

J.B. Priestly wrote a rarely produced play called *Dangerous Corner*. In it, people make a turning in time that leads toward disaster. Then they are returned to where they made that turn and continue on their real-life courses. Those dangerous corners haunt me even now. Somehow, I felt that if I had turned that corner with that young French woman, it wouldn't have been dangerous. I have turned many corners in my life. Some were lucky escapes, some remain unanswered, and all give me no regrets. My life has been interesting, even when things have not gone well. Why? They led to a more pleasant, rewarding corner.

Paris was full of wheeler-dealers. Some bought American goods for resale on the black market. On each of my arrivals in Paris, I found a black marketer and sold my carton of cigarettes and received the equivalent of twenty dollars in return. Further down the street a scrawny Frenchman sidled up to me and flashed a packet of photos. It was just enough to give me a glimpse. They were pornographic. Then he said, with a mouth full of saliva, "Feelsy peektures?"

I moved on. I had better use for my newly acquired cash.

With me on my second trip to Paris were two other GIs. One was a man named Boggart. He was openly a Communist, the first I had ever met. He and the other soldier, whose name I forget – I'll call him Dave - amused themselves off duty calculating how we could travel to the moon and planets. It was the first time I became aware of some of the laws involved with physics in relation to space travel. They even talked about the slingshot effect needed for propelling us to further distant planets.

Boggart never hid his politics. In fact, he freely admitted them, even though the Army looked dimly on Communists. For that matter, most officers – and especially West Pointers – looked down at those with leftist leanings of any sort.

When Boggart was shipped overseas, he was assigned as a stevedore who unloaded ships coming into French harbors. It was grueling, heavy work. He tried again and again to volunteer for combat. Eventually he was assigned to the 30th Division and saw a considerable amount of combat in a rifle company.

Once again, we arrived in Paris just before dawn. Boggart showed us where the main sights were and went off on his own to see some European friends. Dave and I set out to see as much of Paris as we could. We went up the Eiffel Tower as far as they allowed. Access to its very top was limited.

There are many monuments in Paris, but not much survives from the realities of the country's past. France's military history is undistinguished. Even their most successful general and emperor Napoleon was eventually defeated after causing much pain and suffering throughout Europe. I almost felt as though I should have spit on his tomb. Fortunately, I did not!

We were joined by another GI for part of the day. He was a Southerner. As we stopped to look at some statues, he remarked, "My, my, men weren't very well hung in those days."

One of the oddities of Paris were its street *pissoirs*. These were large cages on sidewalks. Inside were dozens of urinals. For modesty, there was a steel band at waist level. If you had the urge, you entered and relieved yourself while pedestrians walked by. After the war, I read that these were huge sources of bribes. A *pissoir* would be placed in front of a restaurant – especially a café with street tables. Customers would avoid the place, but if the restaurant owner offered the police a bribe, the *pissoir* would be moved on down the street – and probably in front of another restaurant.

Indoor toilets were unisex. Most were nothing more than two feet marks and a hole. There one squatted and did his or her business. I was shocked when a young woman walked in, lifted her skirt, lowered her panties, and let it fly beside me.

The Metro – the Paris subway – was always crowded. It whisked us about the city efficiently and quickly once you got the hang of it. At that time fares were subsidized and amazingly cheap.

When I was in college, I wrote an essay describing a memorable ride:

A RIDE ON THE METRO

Night and a city, a city of light. After a glorious day, night fell, and a far different city emerged. Gay Paree had not been gay since it fell to the Nazis; but after it was liberated, this great city rebounded. The Paris I visited twice was shabby, but it bore a semblance to that legendary City of Light. However, there were shadows where dangers lurked.

The main streets became more crowded, crowded to the point shoulders were rubbed. They were filled with a polyglot of humanity. The triumphant armies that had freed Europe were on leave.

The Metro was packed. Tempers flared. Gallic curses were launched. Some were directed at the scattering of Americans, others at Brits, even more cursed at each other. Any gratitude for their liberation was gone. Body sweat half-covered by cheap perfume permeated the crowded car. The French lived up to their reputation of a lack of physical hygiene. I was too young, too American, to realize that soap was a luxury and that tap water had to be conserved.

As the Metro sped along, bodies rubbed against each other. I faced a woman who was a little older than me. She was quite pretty. Her hair was brown, her eyes even browner. The packed car forced our bodies together. Her eyes probed mine as her soft body pressed against mine. She moved against me as the train jounced ahead. Her movements were overtly sexual. She straddled one of my legs. Her crotch ground against it, her breasts were pressed against my chest. Not a word was said.

It was midsummer and she, like many young Parisian women, wore little or nothing under her summer dress. One of the pleasures during my two leaves to Paris was watching young women walk by. Their bodies were unfettered, their walks insolent and inviting.

As our bodies meshed in that crowd, I felt the normal stirring of a nineteen-year-old. She seemed to be enjoying this intimacy, and I know I did. That seemed to provoke her movements against my leg even more. I remember those liquid brown eyes burning into mine as she ground against me. No hands were involved. One of my hands clung to the strap; the other, pressed by my side, was on my wallet. Could she be a lure for a pickpocket behind me?

Was she a prostitute seeking business? I was wary. I certainly wasn't interested in paid sex, and I knew that amateurs were often diseased. I remembered that young woman I talked with outside the Louvre. I regretted not asking her to share the day with me.

While we were in combat, a member of our squad went AWOL during a leave in Paris when he found an accommodating young woman. He returned a few days late. He was stripped of his sergeant's rank and returned to combat as a private. He soon was promoted back to his old rank.

Now that the war was over, the penalty for briefly going AWOL would be even less. What was there to do at our camp? We were only waiting, waiting, waiting at our dusty camp for a ship to take us home. While I was tempted to follow her out that sliding door, I didn't want to miss my ship home. It could come any day. Other men took that risk during our Parisian leaves. As for me, I was a cautious young man, so I continued our rubbing together.

Then the train drew to a stop. She smiled, but she said nothing. Then she turned and pushed her way toward the open doors. Had that departing smile meant that she wanted me to follow her? There was no time for that because the doors closed behind her. I was on my way to another station. There the Folies Bergère waited for me.

Had our exchange been only for momentary pleasure? Other men related similar experiences. A fleeting moment like that was safer than a street encounter. Could she be going home to a husband? Had she lost her man in the war and wanted a brief moment of male contact? I'll never know. Perhaps one of the reasons I became a storyteller was my way of filling out all those enigmatic moments in my life. Life is so incomplete, but there is completion in imagining what could have happened.

I caught on that few of these subway intimacies ended with a sexual encounter. If the women had been prostitutes, they would have grabbed our crotch instead of rubbing against it. By now I had begun to realize that European attitudes toward sex were quite different from ours. They recognized it as an ongoing need and acted accordingly. It was one of those hedonistic European moments that were then alien to our American sensibilities. Of course, all that changed in the 1960s.

As for my essay, I never turned it in to my composition teacher. While it seems mild today, it was a little too candid then.

THE FOLIES BERGÈRE

Gay Paree

In the evening, I attended a performance of the Folies Bergère. It was lavishly produced and featured bevies of bare-breasted young women. Its performers managed to entertain us with a mix of several languages. There were frequent musical and dance numbers. I had grown to love the sound of French popular music. I still love it. Interspersed were short comedy and vaudeville routines. All were geared to its international audience. Like burlesque in America, the men, at least, were there to see the half-naked women.

Among the Folies' wonders were the sets that transformed into another setting right before our eyes. A lush boudoir would slowly start moving, its walls folding and its levels shifting as it transformed into a formal garden. Out of a running fountain rose two lovers, posing as statues. The man wore a jockstrap, the woman was topless and wore a G-string. Their skimpy costumes were flesh-colored to make them appear to be nude. Slowly they came to life and performed an erotic dance that was quite beautiful. That was only one of several elaborate sets used during the performance.

Later I found that the Folies' stage was extremely shallow and that those sumptuous designs had to be ingeniously devised so all those sets could fit on stage.

Just before intermission, the entire company came on stage. Many came down steep stairs, others came in from the wings. Some stood around a ramp that circled the front of the first balcony. To make them even more visible, the ramp was made of glass. It was truly a grand finale. I had never seen that many bare breasted women at one time. In fact, I had seen few before that evening; and they were at the swimming pool in Reichenbach while Slavic women changed into their swimming suits and at Deauville-Trouville. Those were sturdier and less attractive to me than these lovely French chorines.

The lobby at intermission was filled with a polyglot of foreigners. Champagne cocktails were sold as well as souvenirs. They were expensive. I did not partake.

I had never seen such spectacle, even in the Broadway shows I saw before I shipped out. My friends told me that the nearby Casino de Paris was even more spectacular. Years later, in the late-1960s, I returned to Paris and saw another performance at the Folies Bergère. The scenic effects were different, but the miraculous set changes were based on the same mechanical principles. Of course, by then the lithesome, high bosomed young women I saw in 1945 had become matrons and were replaced with equally attractive young women.

The Folies Bergère managed to survive and even prosper during the German occupation. During the war, audiences were made up of Germans and their allies. It managed to shift gears at VE Day and continued to perform for several more years. Now I understand that the Folies is closed. It's a pity. A pale shadow of it was performed in Las Vegas. I saw it once on television in an HBO production. The only similarity with the original is that the women were bare-breasted.

I managed to save the program for that evening's entertainment. It now sits on a shelf in my study along with a program when I saw the Folies again in 1966. Among my books is a paperback history of the Folies. The French music hall tradition is gone. Now it would be too expensive to build such elaborate scenery and to hire such a large company. Even the most elaborate Broadway musical cannot match the lavish Folies at its peak.

In London there was a counterpart at the Windmill Theatre. Now it is a strip bar. Then it was a musical hall entertainment that featured stationery nudes. In London at that time, women could be naked on stage as long as they did not move. If women wore G-strings, they could move and dance. Of course, all that has changed. Nudity even turns up at the

Royal National Theatre and the Royal Shakespeare Company. I never saw the Windmill, but my friends told me its production numbers and scenery were less opulent.

By now, my ideal of feminine beauty was firmly implanted. These young French women fitted that ideal better than their German counterparts. Most men of that time lusted after big breasted women. I preferred those whose body type resembled that found in classic sculptures. I also preferred brunettes over blondes. Perhaps this all fits in with the idea of a chemical attraction between men and women. One of the ironies of my adulthood is that blondes and redheads seemed to be attracted to me, while most brunettes couldn't have been less interested. Fortunately, there was an exception to this. In fact, my only long-term relationship with a brunette has been my forty years with Linda.

At this moment in time, it is considered in bad taste, and even sexist, to discuss ideals in beauty, and especially feminine beauty. The fact is that we all have our physical ideal of beauty, and that includes women. That has been imprinted on all of us as we grew up.

More often than not, we depart from these lofty ideals when it comes to permanent mating. Perfect beauty is intimidating. Over the years I became friends with a few startling beauties. All had problems with their looks and would have been happier if they looked more ordinary. All told me that they feared that men saw them only as an ornament. They were more insecure than less spectacular women whose beauty wore well – and longer – on the eye.

There has to be much more than a violent chemical reaction when it comes to a stable married life. It is a mystery that still confounds me. Why do we see and pursue a particular mate? I still don't know. Linda says it was destiny that brought us together. Whatever it was, I remain grateful.

The trucks to transport us back to our camp did not arrive at the *Place de la Concorde* until the early morning hours. After the show, we had two or three more hours of leave remaining before we returned to our camp. We made our way to the *Place de la Pigalle* – commonly called Pig Alley. It was the center of prostitution in Paris. Along a long main street were carnival attractions. Soldiers from many nations crowded the street and side street. Women of all ages solicited us. They did so crudely, grabbing us by the crotch when we weren't looking. When I say the women were of all ages, I mean they ranged from girls in their early teens to quite aged women. Most were unappealing, or worse still, pathetic. A few were very apparently diseased.

Dave was married and, like me, uninterested. We started up a side street to get away from the teeming crowd. Two pimps stood in a dark doorway across the street from us. A young woman approached us. She headed straight for me with one hand lowered. I pointed at Dave, indicating she should approach him. She grabbed him firmly by the crotch. He howled in pain and surprise and as a reflex action back-handed her, sending her sprawling into the street. The two pimps drew knives and headed for us as we fled back into the crowded main street. They did not dare follow us. There were too many soldiers crowded together. We quickly left the area and headed back to *Place de la Concorde.*

I enjoyed my visits to Paris, but I did not like the Parisians very much. Paris is a beautiful city to look at, and it was virtually untouched by the war.[16] I was interested in more walks through the Louvre, but otherwise I had little interest in returning. Later trips confirmed that feeling. I feel it is a city of monuments, many to failed policies and wars.

At the end of each leave, *Place de la Concorde* was crowded with weary and drunken soldiers waiting for their truck to arrive. Once in a while men would not get there in time. A few willfully stayed in Paris. Those who did were court-martialed. Some were sent to the brig. If they did not stay too long, most officers were lenient and reduced the punishment to extended KP duty. The war was over, and an absence meant very little.

I only remember the first name of a gentler, mature man in our unit. Darryl was about thirty and was a high school music teacher in a small town in Appalachia. When he found a violin, he played jazz for us. I fondly remember his version of "I Cried for You." His personal tragedy was that he was slowly going deaf after being under intense shell fire. He was quiet and never spoke of his oncoming deafness.

---

16 Paris was an "open city" during WWII. This happens when a city, knowing that capture and occupation are imminent, declares that it has abandoned defensive measures in order to try and preserve the city and its citizens from destruction. In June 1940, the French government declared Paris an open city during the Battle of France. Other open cities during WWII included Krakow, Poland; Brussels, Belgium; Belgrade, Yugoslavia; Rome, Italy; Athens, Greece; and Manilla, the Philippines. Some cities still suffered damage and casualties both prior to and after being declared open, but the protocol of the Geneva Conventions forbade the attacking party to "attack, by any means whatsoever, non-defended localities."

At the end of my last trip to Paris, Darryl did not meet up with our truck at the end of the day. This was not like him. Darryl, of all of us, was reliable, and he was a solid family man. Even so, he stayed in Paris a few days before he voluntarily returned by meeting one of those late trucks. Our compassionate captain never brought charges against him. We learned that Darryl had become enamored with a French woman and lingered on for a short affair before he decided to rejoin his outfit. He never said anything about his transgression. Instead, he sat in one corner of our tent and played "I Cried for You," this time without the jazz emphasis, but with a more plaintive air.

DEAR BILLY

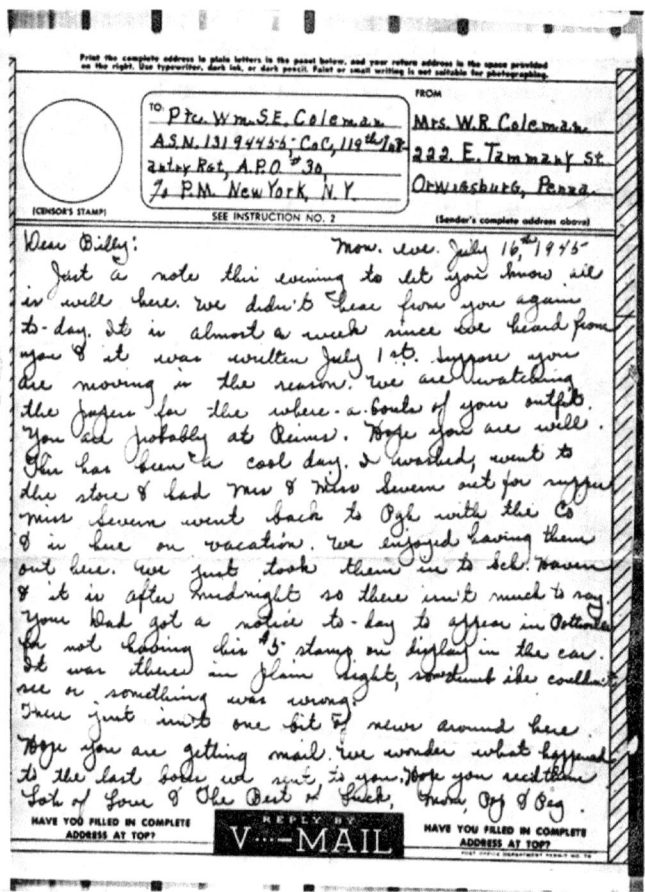

TO: Pfc. Wm. S.E. Coleman
A.S.N. 13194456. Co C, 119th Inf.
Intex Rct, A.P.O. #30
P.M. New York, N.Y.

FROM
Mrs. W.R. Coleman
222. E. Tammany St
Orwigsburg, Penna.

Dear Billy: Mon. eve. July 16th, 1945

Just a note this evening to let you know all is well here. We didn't hear from you again to-day. It is almost a week since we heard from you & it was written July 1st. Suppose you are moving in the reason. We are watching the papers for the where-a-bouts of your outfit. You are probably at Reims. Hope you are well. This has been a cool day. I washed, went to the store & had Mrs. & Mrs. Severn out for supper. Miss Severn went back to Ogk with the Co & is here on vacation. We enjoyed having them out here. We just took them in to Sch. Haven & it is after midnight so there isn't much to say. Your Dad got a notice to-day to appear in Pottsville for not having his #5 stamp on display in the car. It was there in plain sight, somehow the couldn't see or something was wrong. There just isn't one bit of news around here. Hope you are getting mail. We wonder what happened to the last book we sent to you. Hope you recd them. Lots of Love & The Best of Luck, Mom, Pop & Peg.

HAVE YOU FILLED IN COMPLETE ADDRESS AT TOP?

V····MAIL

HAVE YOU FILLED IN COMPLETE ADDRESS AT TOP?

To:
Pfc Wm. S.E. Coleman
A.S.N. 13194455 – Co C,
119th Infantry Rgt A.P.O. #30
c/o P.M. New York, N.Y.

From:
Mrs. W.R. Coleman
222 E. Tammany St.
Orwigsburg, Penna.

Mon. eve. July 16th, 1945

Dear Billy:
Just a note this evening to let you know all is well here. We didn't hear from you again to-day. It is almost a week since we heard from you & it was written July 1st. Suppose you are moving is the reason. We are watching the papers for the where-a-bouts of your outfit. You are probably at Reims. Hope you are well.

This has been a cool day. I washed, went to the store & had Mrs. & Miss Severn out for supper. Miss Severn went back to Pgh with the Co & is here on vacation. We enjoyed having them out here. We just took them in to Sch. Haven & it is after midnight so there isn't much to say. Your Dad got a notice to-day to appear in Pottsville for not having his $5 stamp on display in the car. It was there in plain sight, some dumb ike couldn't see or something was wrong.

There just isn't one bit of news around here. Hope you are getting mail. We wonder what happened to the last boxes we sent to you. Hope you rec'd them.

Lots of love & The Best of Luck. Mom, Pop & Peg

A WAITING GAME

The Thirtieth's Last Stand

We had little else to do as we waited for shipment home. A trip to Paris or some other nearby city broke the monotony. I had the good fortune of liking to read. Many of the men gambled incessantly. Money flowed back and forth, and a few of the more skilled gamblers amassed small fortunes by gambling with men from different units. One bragged to me that he had won enough to buy a house for his family when he got home.

Again, I stayed out of the games. I did enjoy watching them. The ebb and flow of men's fortunes fascinated me, but I had no desire to lose my own money. I tried blackjack a few times when we were on occupation duty. I lost more often than I won.

Occasionally there was a fight, but there were only a few. This, I think, is remarkable since all our nerves were frayed by what had happened to us in the war and the apprehension of what was to come. In general, men who had seen combat became less violent and prone to macho fighting.

We had no idea that the war would end very soon.[17] Instead, we accepted the fact we were headed to the Pacific and the beaches of Japan.

---

17 What we did not know was that the first atom bomb was tested at Alamogordo, New Mexico, on my 19th birthday. A little more than a month later, the first detonation of an atom bomb took place in the New Mexico desert 120 miles south of Santa Fe. The tower holding the bomb was vaporized. Less than a month after that, two cities in Japan would be unimaginably devastated by atomic bombs. The war would soon be over.

Buddy Blackjack

No one wanted to be in such an invasion. We knew that the Japanese code did not allow for surrender. We also knew they were quite willing to fight with bayonets and knives. Of course, it had been indoctrinated into us that the Japanese soldier was treacherous and brutal.

I occupied myself for several days by creating a huge cartoon mural in a PX on base. There was a vast white expanse on one wall, so I filled it with a large cartoon mural of GIs behaving badly while they were on leave in French cities. I spent a little time each day adding to it until it covered the entire wall on one side the tent. No one objected. In fact, many GIs came in to watch me draw with my charcoal sticks. Some told me tales of their adventures on leave. I added some of these to my emerging mural.

The PX sold light beer and soft drinks, candy, and cigarettes. They also sold other goods that were worthy of bartering when we went on leave. We were reminded from time to time that it was illegal to sell PX goods to civilians. No one obeyed that order.

In time, all the tents were torn down and thrown away. They were not valuable enough to merit shipment home.

Popular music began to catch up with us. One song was almost an anthem for us. It was Les Brown's version of *Sentimental Journey* with Doris Day singing the vocal in that unique smoky voice of hers.

The waiting seemed interminable. Our almost-daily trips to Reims broke up the monotony but that was only for a morning or an afternoon. Trips to Paris were strictly limited. The Army did not dare to send in whole units. The city was crowded even as leaves were rationed.

JANE FROMAN

During those few weeks we waited for transfer to ships, no more than half a dozen USO shows visited us. On other nights movies were shown. Many were films that had not been released in the United States. We did not know that until we came home and saw the same films in theatre that we had seen in that field in France.

Most of the USO troupes consisted of female singers and dancers, an accordion player, and one or two comedians. Many were entertainers who had failed or whose careers were on the wane. None had names we recognized. Some were quite entertaining, others less so. There has been a lot written about all the famous performers who toured with the USO. I am sure many did, but our outfit never saw any great names – except one, and that one was worth all those long waits and the mediocre performances we endured during those summer evenings.

The USO performances took place in a natural amphitheater on a sloping hillside. At its base was a rough stage. Like everything else military, it was the same configuration as many others that were scattered about France that summer. In July it was a hot, dry place. When the hundreds of men arrived near twilight, dust rose and finally settled before the performance began.

When the USO acts were bad, the rowdier members of the audience became very rude. One incident stands out in my memory when some men in the audience blew up condoms and played volleyball with them during a young woman's song. She broke down and fled from the stage, weeping. I was furious, and many others were, too. Only the best performers got complete and undivided attention. They were few and far between.

Then came Jane Froman, the noted Broadway singing star. She had made many recordings and was often heard on the radio, but I don't remember her being in motion pictures. She was unknown to many in her GI audiences, yet she had become legendary. In February 1943, while traveling to a USO performance in Portugal, she was in an airplane crash and had suffered severe leg injuries. Of the 38 people on the plane, only 15 survived. Less than a year after the crash, after having endured 13 operations for her injuries, she returned to Broadway. Before she was fully healed or rehabilitated, she insisted on touring again.

She came out on stage with the aid of crutches. She was dressed in a beautiful formal dress, but you could see both of her legs were in casts.

Troops listening.

She was a pretty brunette woman. She radiated grace and warmth as she came on stage. We also sensed she was still in great pain. Many of the men seated about me had been wounded and had returned to combat after a brief rehab. They understood courage under pain.

A silence spread across the vast field packed with GIs, all combat veterans. Articles in *The Stars and Stripes* reported that she had demanded that she be allowed to tour again. That alone gained our respect and admiration. Soon she would command our rapt attention.

She stepped to the microphone and sang a medley of recent hits. They were pop favorites, all romantic. Each was greeted with tumultuous applause. She told no jokes and had no routines. She just sang the songs we all loved. They spoke to older men away from their wives, and they spoke to those of us who were little more than boys. She sang about their realities, and she sang about our dreams. She was the epitome of womanhood to all of us.

The rowdies were stilled. She had her audience in the palm of her hand. She sang of love, lost love, and loneliness. As a mature woman, then in her late 30s, she understood loss and sadness. Even the most hardened among us listened, our eyes locked on that solitary figure on stage. Finally, she sang "Embraceable You." She sang it simply and directly. There were no embellishments. She sang it so each and every one of us felt it was just for us. That moment remains in my memory. It cannot be erased. I will always treasure that moment in time.

Hardened infantrymen wept unashamedly. I did, too. They saw courage, femininity, and grace combined in the slight, elegant woman, that enchanting being singing out every man's wishes upon his return home.

Encore followed encore. Finally, Froman reluctantly left the stage. Masses of men rushed to the rear of that crude stage and waited for her to go to her waiting jeep. Hands reached out in the hope of touching her, but her hands were on her crutches. As she drove away hundreds of men stood and cheered her. We were reluctant to give up that wonderful moment. That night we were ready to go home.

In the years to come, little I have seen in show business matched that evening in a French field.

THE LONG VOYAGE HOME

Before we shipped out home, we had one last duty. A young man in the 30th, Technical Sergeant Francis Sherman "Frank" Currey, had been awarded a Congressional Medal of Honor.[18] We heard that he had gone crazy during an intense moment in combat, ran berserk, and used every weapon available in a front line Infantry company at least once. In the process, he had killed more than one hundred Germans.

The parade in his honor was a disaster. It was the height of summer, and the heat was intense. Men fainted as they stood in ranks waiting

---

18   During World War II, 464 United States military personnel received the Medal of Honor. Of those, 266 were awarded posthumously. Technical Sergeant Francis Sherman "Frank" Currey (June 29, 1925 – October 8, 2019), was presented his medal on July 27, 1945, by the 30th Infantry Division commander, Major General Leland Hobbs, near Reims, France; and it was officially awarded to him on August 17, 1945. Currey's actions at Malmédy, Belgium, during the Battle of the Bulge on December 21,1944, earned him the United States military's highest decoration for valor. For his heroic actions during and after the war he also was awarded a Silver Star, a Bronze Star, 3 Purple Hearts, and the Belgian Order of Leopold. Following WWII, Currey worked as a counselor at the VA Medical Center in Albany, New York, from 1950 until his retirement as a supervisor in 1980. He then owned a landscaping business and worked at a hotel booking conventions until his retirement from that in 2002. A wonderful YouTube interview with Currey, including footage of the presentation of his Medal of Honor, can be viewed at https://www.youtube.com/watch?v=iRXNpeHyTDY

Currey lived in Selkirk, NY. He and other WWII Medal of Honor recipients were featured on a US Postage Stamp in 2013.

I might note that I was able to catch a glimpse of PFC William Coleman in the YouTube footage of the Medal of Honor presentation. Bill was in the back row of the assembled soldiers.

to pass by the reviewing area. The field was rough and uneven, so the marching ranks were ragged and uneven.

When I passed by the reviewing area there stood the hero. He was a short, thin young soldier. He was not an epic figure. In today's terms he would be called a nerd. But there he stood, the bravest of the brave. He watched us march by with wondering, almost uncomprehending eyes. I saw a smile pass across his face. I suspect he was amused by the chaos his parade presented. I also believe he felt a surge of pride. There were bigger and stronger men honoring him and envying him. I hope he had a good life.

THE BOMB AND V-J DAY

We heard the atom bomb had been dropped, first on Hiroshima, Japan, on August 6, then on Nagasaki on August 9. At Hiroshima 70,000 died immediately or shortly after the bomb was dropped. Many more have died over the years. At Nagasaki 60,000 to 80,000 died; about 40,000 died instantly.

According to the Encyclopedia Britannica:

> The explosion, which had the force of more than 15,000 tons of TNT, instantly and completely devastated 10 square km (4 square miles) of the heart of this city of 343,000 inhabitants. Of this number, 66,000 were killed immediately and 69,000 were injured; more than 67 percent of the city's structures were destroyed or damaged. Some place these estimates much higher.
>
> The next atomic bomb to be exploded was of the plutonium type; it was dropped on Nagasaki on August 9, 1945, producing a blast equal to 21,000 tons of TNT. The terrain and smaller size of Nagasaki reduced destruction of life and property, but 39,000 persons were killed and 25,000 injured; about 40 percent of the city's structures were destroyed or seriously damaged. The Japanese initiated surrender negotiations the next day.

While the death toll from the atomic bombs was shocking, Japan had endured nightly fire bombings that took an enormous death toll on the civilian populations of many Japanese cities.[19] There was no escape from these in bomb shelters. There was even less escape from an atomic bomb.

We did not know then that thousands more would die in the days and years following these horrendous bombings. We did not know about the lingering aftereffects of radiation burns and poisoning. The horrors of this were not brought home to the American public until John Hershey wrote his vivid *Hiroshima*. That small book created a discussion about the morality of dropping the bomb that continues to this day. I believe that the terrible fire bombings would have persuaded the Japanese to surrender without an invasion of Japan.

If we add the nightly fire bombings to the death toll of two atomic bombs, our Air Force killed more than a quarter-million Japanese civilians.

In retrospect I question the fire bombings of large civilian populations. Our major firebombing in Germany was at Dresden. The horrors of that bombing – which some say was strategically unnecessary – are still being debated by historians. One thing is certain: The bombing of civilians at Guernica on April 26, 1937, started this carnage.

These days our military and politicians talk euphemistically about "surgical strike" bombings by "smart" bombs that exempt civilian populations. I doubt that is possible. Then and now, the mass bombing of large cities with any sort of bomb is an abstraction to Americans. Perhaps that is why it has been so easy for us to support the seemingly perpetual wars that followed World War II.[20]

When I was in France waiting for shipment back to the States, I read about that terrible death toll at Hiroshima and Nagasaki in *The Stars and Stripes*; but I saw this as a step toward ending a Pacific war I would be joining all too quickly. I was little more than a boy, and I saw

---

19 According to the U.S. Strategic Bombing Survey, from January 1944 until August 1945, the U.S. dropped 157,000 tons of bombs on Japanese cities. It estimated that 333,000 people were killed, including the 80,000 killed in the Aug. 6 Hiroshima atomic bomb attack and 40,000 in Nagasaki three days later. Other estimates are significantly higher. Fifteen million of the 72 million Japanese were left homeless.

20 That, plus the fact that since the conflict in Vietnam, and especially since we invaded Iraq in 2003, we no longer see the images or the horrors of war on our news media or in newspapers and general news magazines. I find it ironic that, in an age where there is more communication and connectiveness than at any time in history, the American public is isolated from the realities of our government policies and undertakings and shielded from the consequences of U.S. activities throughout most of the world.

the world only from my point of view. Perhaps all of us were little more than boys. I do know we were frightened when we were told we would "be the first on the beaches of Japan." None of us wanted to fight the Japanese. They did not surrender, and they fought with cold steel when they were cornered. Besides, we all felt we had done our share and taken enough risks in the combat we saw in Germany.

We began packing to return home. Our company kitchen had kept a sump pit that was about fifteen by fifteen feet and just as deep. The cooks had stolen a jeep from another outfit and used it for their own personal transportation. To avoid being caught with it as they packed up the kitchen, they drove it into the deep pit, letting it sink amidst the reeking garbage. Somewhere in France, a rusting jeep lies beneath French soil.

Some men left before us. One was a pitiful case. His first name was Jess. He was a tall, lanky man who looked like he had walked out of a Western movie. He walked about camp muttering to himself. He had been wounded at least five times. Each time he was sent back, even though he had been broken. He acquired more than enough points for immediate discharge since Purple Hearts earned five discharge points.

As the news of the terrifying new bombs broke, we shipped out to Le Havre and embarked on a Coast Guard ship, the *USS General W.M. Black*.[21] We were given back all the equipment that had been stored and not used during combat. Why we had carried it to Europe is beyond my comprehension. All that stuff was a major waste of the taxpayer's money. I am happy that I did not have to carry it all in my walk across Europe. Among that stored stuff was a package from my parents. It arrived after I left for the front. In it were orange cookies my mother had baked, a favorite delicacy in my boyhood. They were crumbled, dried, and hard, but there was a semblance of the taste I loved.

Once we were at sea, we encountered stormy weather. The *General Black* was a large troop ship. We were told it was more than five hundred feet long. It was smaller than the *Aquitania* by almost four hundred feet, but it was still very, very big. It had been built for the war effort and was launched in 1943. Even so, the waves were so high our screw (propellers) emerged from the water as we plowed homeward.

---

21 Named after Major General William Murray Black (1855 – 1933), the U.S. Army General who had served in the Spanish-American War as Chief Engineer of the 3rd and 5th Army Corps. He received a Distinguished Service Medal for his work as the Chief of Engineers during World War I, mobilizing and training some 300,000 engineer troops.

Many of us became violently seasick. During the occupation and the waiting to go home, we had been well fed. Our company kitchen worked hard to prepare solid American food for us, and my dysentery faded away. The food on board the ship was not as good.

There was some discussion of feeding the worst seasick cases intravenously. In mid-voyage, some of us were assigned to work in the Chief Petty Officers' mess. The food was drastically better there than it was in the enlisted men's mess. Their kitchen was deep in the bowels of the ship. The motion was less perceptible, and the good food stabilized our seasickness.

They showed movies in the messes. Only a hundred could see the film at one sitting. Sure enough, there was a copy of *Bowery to Broadway*. A young, bumptious Donald O'Connor later earned my forgiveness when he performed "Make 'em Laugh" in the 1952 movie musical *Singin' in the Rain*. Another evening there was another repeat, *Rhapsody in Blue*. That was one I enjoyed seeing over and over again. I even believed it told me something about Gershwin's real life.

One night, while we slept, the intercom came on. An officer announced that Japan had surrendered.[22] A few of us let loose some feeble cheers. The rest of us sighed with relief. There was no further celebration. We went back to sleep.

In the United States crowds celebrated in the streets. We were just relieved that our war had ended.

---

22 The surrender of Imperial Japan was announced on August 15, 1945. The Instrument of Surrender was formally signed by Japanese foreign affairs minister Mamoru Shigemitsu on board the *USS Missouri* on September 2, 1945.

PART VII

ODYSSEY'S END

Not even when the rolling seasons brought in the year
the gods chose for Odysseus' homecoming was he
safe among friends and free of his troubles.

Homer, *The Odyssey*

East and west on fields forgotten
Bleach the bones of comrades slain,
Lovely lads and dead and rotten;
None that go return again.

A. E. Housman, *A Shropshire Lad*

— POST WAR PLANS —

26

STATESIDE

W E LANDED IN Boston on August 15, 1945. I remember seeing water spouting from tugs in the harbor and hearing ship whistles to celebrate our homecoming. There was no time to tarry. We disembarked and were whisked onto a troop train. By afternoon we were headed south. I don't remember where the train stopped or where we waited for our passes home. I do remember taking a train home. There, my parents waited on the train platform. In my life I have had few greater moments of joy. I was home. I babbled on about my experiences. I spared them many details. It was odd that now I was sheltering them from the realities I had faced.

Home on leave.

As we walked to the car, I looked at my parents. Mother seemed to have grown a little older in the months I had been overseas, but Dad had aged a lot. His hair was gray, and he seemed like a much older man. Only then did I realize how much I meant to him.

They now lived outside of Pottsville in a smaller town, Orwigsburg. It was thoroughly Pennsylvania Dutch. It was close enough to Pottsville that I managed to see some old friends and girlfriends.

One night we went to a country auction. One auctioneer was Jewish and proud of it. He had a quick wit and a ready comeback. He and the Dutch flung epithets back and forth. The Dutch were openly anti-Semitic, he was openly disdainful of the results of more than a century of inbreeding among the locals. Somehow, it came off as amiably contentious. While they attacked him, I noticed that he always got the better of the deal. I pondered if there was something within the German character that was inherently anti-Semitic.

My leave lasted two weeks, if memory serves. I was ordered to report to Fort Knox, Kentucky. There, I received a crash course in occupational counseling. After the course finished, I was transferred to the Adjutant General's Department – the pencil-pushing branch of the Army – and assigned to the discharge center.

Those of us who had higher test scores were given intensified training. It could not have been more than two weeks. The Army had a cookie-cutter way of teaching. When we finished our course, we qualified as occupational counselors. I still shudder to think that at nineteen I was entrusted with advising men – many older than me – what to do with the rest of their lives. Actually, I was relieved that I did not have that responsibility since my own input was very limited. The Army had reference books that translated their past education and Army experience into civilian occupations. It was all neatly laid out. I was assigned this job because I had tested high and had one semester of college. To put it more bluntly, I could read and write!

As the Army was slowly releasing soldiers back into civilian life, the economy was slowly readjusting from wartime production to peacetime pursuits. We did not understand it at the time, but if the ten million men and women serving in the Armed Services at the end of the war had been released all at once, it would have been an economic disaster. Unemployment would have been rampant, perhaps rising to the levels of the Great Depression. We were released slowly, not because of fear of another war, but out of a sensible economic policy.

Fort Knox was an old Army post famed for training armored units. It also housed most of the gold of the United States in a veritable fortress on the post. To those of us who served in the Third Army this was an appropriate posting since we had been involved with armored units. Many of its buildings were built of brick. Ours were not since we were not housed where the regular Army men stayed.

I was shocked at the level of education in the country prior to the war. Indeed, I had led a sheltered life. Only a small percentage of the enlisted men being discharged had finished high school. Many had not finished grade school. A rare college graduate passed through our center. Anyone who had graduated from college usually became an officer, usually with a desk job.

There were many cases of injustice. Homosexuals, if caught, were given what was called a Blue Discharge. It was not as bad as a Dishonorable Discharge; but they were lumped together with men who had committed crimes in the Army.

One sergeant in his mid-twenties was given a Dishonorable Discharge. I examined his record. He had two Silver Stars, a Bronze Star, and two Purple Hearts. He had been in infantry combat for more than six months. He made one bad mistake. Shortly after the Invasion during the brutal Hedgerow Campaign he went AWOL long enough to be considered a deserter. I knew from talking with the older veterans in the 30th Division that this was one of the most terrifying infantry battles. Each row hid an unknown enemy, each row taken was taken at great expense. Many considered this worse than the Battle of the Bulge.

During the Bulge he left his Parisian mistress and returned to his outfit. He won his final Silver Star after his desertion, and he also was awarded his second Purple Heart. Then, when the war ended, charges were brought against him. He was shipped home. He had served longer than most infantrymen in spite of being AWOL for month. He was the most decorated soldier I interviewed. With a dishonorable discharge he lost his voting rights, had limited citizenship, and no benefits. He was virtually unemployable. His life was ruined long before he was thirty even though he had valiantly served his country. There was nothing I could do to help him. I could only fill out his forms and send them along for processing. I will never forget his haunted eyes. He knew his life had ended just as it was supposed to be beginning. He was dead before he could live again.

I interviewed men who were illiterate, and many who were mentally challenged. One man looked forward to returning to his job as a garbage man. Others had been psychologically damaged by their experiences and had received no treatment. The Army considered these men psychos. They received Section 8 Discharges. Their rights as citizens were abridged. Military justice was harsh and often irrational.

One man freely admitted he had stolen cars for a living and planned to do so again. Each man had his own story. During my months as an occupational counselor, I got an even broader glimpse of the broad diversity of our country. The diversity was all White, though. No Blacks came through our center.

Most men just wanted to go home and get on with their lives. A few had ambitions beyond those they had before they went to war. Assisting them was one of the most noble programs ever devised by our government – the GI Bill of Rights. Soldiers who could be admitted to colleges and universities received a basic twelve months of free education. More was available for longer service and for service overseas. I had enough credits for the full four years of college.

The free college education guaranteed under the GI Bill of Rights changed our society. Before the war private schools were reserved for the rich and privileged. State schools offered lower tuition and lower standards. A few like my dad managed to attend a private university. Now hundreds of thousands of men and women who would not have been able to go to college, and especially name colleges, did so. Their skills transformed our country and changed our view of how society was structured. Republican politicians never forgave the Democrats for putting this program in action. It made life much more competitive to the children of the rich. How the Republicans fear the competition they demand in so many aspects of our lives!

Even so, the elite remained elite, but their power was diminished. At their posh schools they were confronted with highly motivated veterans whose mission was to get ahead in American society. Some intermarried into the upper levels of society. The end result of World War II was that it leveled what had been a strictly tiered society. That leveling was not enough to completely democratize our society, but it was a step forward. A few of the men passing through our center had received a high school equivalency certificate. Most could enter a state college, and many did.

Our section was made up of above-average men and women, people who were well read and cultured. All had registered high on the Army aptitude test. Some of us had seen front line combat, some had not. The WACs who worked with us tended to be older than we were. Many viewed us an innocent boys needing the protection of an older woman. They could not bring themselves to think of what we had seen in combat.

The counselors worked in a long line of cubicles. I would finish my paperwork and advising and pass my documents along to a WAC who would type it onto discharge forms. By the end of the day, a soldier was on his way home. I interviewed a soldier every half hour.

There were few breaks in our work, but when there were, we had marvelous conversations and exchanges of jokes. I remember one older soldier who had lost his eye and had it replaced with a glass eye. Three or four men and two WACS were on break. One of the more beautiful WACs walked by. One of the younger soldiers remarked, "I'd give my right arm to get into her pants."

The WACs looked shocked. The older soldier reached to his eye socket and took out his glass eye and said, "I'd give my right eye."

I thought the two WACs were close to fainting. It seems they did not know the guy had a glass eye!

Louisville

We took passes to nearby Louisville whenever possible. Like most towns and cities near Army bases it had its dives and prostitution. The vice districts tended to be isolated along a specific street, probably to keep them away from those who lived in the city. Usually, these areas were close to where buses coming from the base unloaded. I avoided the sleazy temptations and moved on to other attractions. Mainly it was to see the most recent movies.

I remember seeing *Cluny Brown*, a light comedy based on a popular novel. Jennifer Jones played a poor young woman who had taken up plumbing. When a rich man asked her if it was difficult to be a plumber, Jones replied, "No, it's very easy. I roll up my sleeves, roll down my stockings, loosen up the joint, and bang! bang! bang!" The mostly GI audience exploded into laughter.

While its cultural assets were less than those on the Eastern Seaboard, Louisville had a budding symphony orchestra. The hall was a large circular auditorium with side boxes that caught the isolated sound of specific instruments and reflected them out to the main audience. One weekend I saw the touring Chicago Symphony Orchestra conducted by Désiré Defauw. Later I would learn he was considered an average conductor and one who held back the Chicago Symphony during his short tenure there. The CSO was on the verge of its great future, which was unleashed by Fritz Reiner who left the Pittsburgh Symphony after a long term there.

This was my first experience with live symphonic music. I was swept away. I don't remember the program, but I remember the effect of hearing the massive sound of a live symphony orchestra. This was different from what I heard on those scratchy 78 rpm records. Even now with digital sound, live concert sound far exceeds anything the best sound system can produce.

Of all the events I saw in Louisville, the most moving was a personal appearance of Bill "Bojangles" Robinson. Born in 1878, he was 67 and aged for a tap dancer, but he still was vital. I had seen him in Shirley Temple movies when I was a child. In person he was magical. I have never felt such warmth coming from the stage toward an audience. When he did his stair dance, he looked over his shoulder, smiled that broad smile he had, and exclaimed, "Yah!"

The temperature in the theatre rose several degrees. Even in this marginal southern city, he played to packed houses. I stayed through the movie – long forgotten – to see him dance again. That evening has to be counted as one of the great theatrical moments in my life.

I enjoyed Louisville's cultural life. I even ventured out of the city for short bus trips. One weekend a friend, whose name I forget, and I took a bus trip into Bluegrass country. We rode by the white-fenced farms where racehorses were bred. I wasn't able to get away long enough to go home to Orwigsburg. Short weekend passes were available, but extended leaves were handed out after several weeks of service.

A Spring and Summer of Discontent

Seeing so many men being discharged gradually got on our nerves. There they went while we stayed in the Army. Our duty was not very difficult, or even very military, but we were still in the Army. I realized that it could be as long as a year before I was discharged. The desk duty got to me, and I longed for something more active. For a brief moment I even considered asking for a transfer to join the military police. I know that sounds stupid, but I wanted out to somewhere else, and I grew bored with my relatively cushy job. Remember, I was ambidextrous and could write with both hands, so I worked faster than most counselors. I willfully let my handwriting disintegrate. I hoped that I would be declared inept and transferred. Unfortunately, the WACs adapted to the change in my handwriting. They offered no complaints.

One WAC who was well into her 40s took a motherly view of us. Before the war she headed

"Oh, that's for combatting infantrymen."

housekeeping at the prestigious Palmer House in Chicago. Circulating among us was a "dirty book" called *Erotic Edna*. She saw to it that none of us 19-year-olds got a look at this story of Mussolini's mistress. One day on break some of us were exchanging dirty jokes. One was particularly lurid. Suddenly a copy of *Erotic Edna* flew over the partition. Our protector realized that the war had taken away our innocence.

I dated two WACs. One was Mildred, a vivacious, tall, lanky Texan. She was approaching thirty. We often went into Louisville. When we stayed over, we booked separate rooms. To her, I was an interesting boy; to me, she was an older woman, a friend. We wrote for a while after the war.

Another was Eileen. She was Irish, darkly pretty, and enjoyed classical music. We passed books back and forth and went to the Louisville Symphony together. We, too, wrote for a while after the war.

We were attracted to each other, but she was a devout Catholic and much older than me. Marriages between Catholics and Protestants were rare. At that time Catholics who married Protestants were expected to bring their children up as Catholics. I did not want to impose any religion on my children. I wanted them to find their religious beliefs – or lack of them – on their own.

Once Eileen said she had no intention of ever marrying. In retrospect, I wonder if she became a nun. It is difficult to think these three women, if they are still alive, are well into their nineties or beyond. I owe a lot to these older women.

At that time, I was terribly shy with women. In high school my experiences went to close dancing, a good night kiss, and a little light petting. For me to venture anything with these older sophisticated women was unthinkable. I often wonder if they took my shyness for gayness?

ART FOR ART'S SAKE

My closest friend at Fort Knox, Art Chicoine, was a French Canadian from Vermont. He was tall, loose-limbed, and had a bit of a wild streak. He had been a basketball player in high school. His approach to life was exuberant. I was quiet, a contrast to his raucous nature. Nobody in our section was as wild as Art. Despite his wildness, he was intelligent and quick witted. We quickly became friends. I think he needed a quiet counterpart, a balance to his joyful exuberance.

We had another French Canadian in our section. He was nicknamed "Short Fuse," which was a referral to his smallish genitals. All of us took group showers, so we were all familiar with our physical attributes or inadequacies. I forget Short Fuse's real name, but he was a small, amiable guy who often joined our forays into Louisville. These were less than cultural.

Once when Art and I were on pass into Louisville, we walked by a cellar bar. Art, who had been drinking, picked up a chair that sat by the door at the top of the stairs and flung it down into the bar, shouting, "Faggots!"

It was a working man's bar, a rough place we had visited earlier that evening. Art took off running. I managed to keep up with him as a group of irate workers came storming up the stairs and out of the bar. By that time we were around a corner and up a dark alley. After waiting for a while, we ventured out and made our way to the bus stop.

On our way to the bus stop, Art stopped to urinate against a gasoline pump at a late-night service station. The irate attendant came running out of his office, screaming obscenities at Art. Again, he took off running. I can still visualize his long-legged galloping gait. It was all I could do to keep up with him. Fortunately, I had drunk very little that night.

Later, upon our return to the base, Art picked up two garbage can lids and marched along a row of barracks playing them like cymbals. When a non-com came storming out a barracks, Art was off and running again. Once again, I barely kept up with his loping gait. Again, we escaped.

I know this makes Art seem to be anti-social or a troublemaker, but somehow there was an amiable good will about his practical joking and high spirits. In quieter times he was thoughtful, well read, and a good friend. Let's say he was filled with youthful high spirits. We wrote for a while after the war. He went off to college, as I did; and our friendship drifted away.

Exuberant Art with garbage can lids.

Bored young men who spent their days discharging other soldiers were full of pranks and practical jokes. One Saturday night when Art, Short Fuse, and I returned a little earlier than usual, we unfastened the springs of an upper bunk that belonged to one of our largest soldiers. He staggered in, stripped to his skivvies, and vaulted into his bunk. He and his mattress fell down on the man sleeping below.

There was much cursing, but our two victims decided to join the prank. We fixed another bunk; another man fell on a sleeping man below. Again, there was much cursing. Then we reassembled the mattress strings, again using string. As we did, we shuffled the bunks about. Short Fuse did not notice we had disassembled his bunk's springs. When he leaped into bed, he too fell on the man below. No one got much sleep that night.

There was a camaraderie among us. Most of us had been in Infantry combat. None of us had served in the same outfit. Still, we had that respect infantrymen have for each other. In a way, our outfit of occupational counselors became another Infantry outfit. We only bothered to follow orders that suited us. How could they discipline us? We had seen the worst, and our stateside barracks non-coms had never been overseas. I think some feared that we would revert to the violence of combat if we were pushed.

Our original barracks non-com, who took a tolerant attitude toward our pranks, was discharged. He was replaced with an older Southerner, a barely literate regular Army corporal. He decided he was going to discipline these "young college-educated sumsabitches." He put some offenders on KP and turned in others.

Then, in the middle of the night after a visit to Louisville's bars, one of our men pried open the door to the corporal's private room. He held a bottle of lighter fluid and a Zippo lighter as he shook the corporal awake. Then he gestured as though he was going to pour the lighter fluid on the corporal and snapped on the flame of his lighter. The terrified corporal screamed and ran out into the night. He did not return.

No one would testify against the man. No charges were pressed. The terrorized corporal demanded another assignment for some vague reason and was reassigned. A new corporal was assigned. He was as amiable as we were. The barracks settled down into its old merry ways. Our captain was a genial, forgiving man. He knew that many of us were still coming down emotionally from combat.

We had access to two kitchens. One was run by a famous chef who worked in a Washington D.C. hotel before the war. Using Army issued food supplies, he cooked wonderful gourmet meals. Each meal was different. Nothing was repeated. He even added a touch of his own to breakfast omelets. All his meals were incredibly good and unlike any other Army food I had during my service. After every meal the chef stood by the door to be congratulated on his cooking. We were glad to stroke his ego.

Soon no one went to the other mess kitchen. Our officers devised a system so that we alternated between the two mess halls. Nobody wanted to endure ordinary Army cooking after our culinary experiences with that magnificent chef. Sadly, we had to settle for this excellent cuisine only every other day.

POWs

German prisoners of war served as janitors for our barracks. These POWs were limited to their work and their own area. They were not allowed to attend our movies and other entertainments. They might have had radios in their barracks, but they had lonely lives.

Most became expert ping pong players. We were not so bad either. There were rec halls around the base. If one wanted a real challenge, the German POWs were an ideal match. They did not want to lose to us, and we did not want to lose to them. Our games were extended and spirited exchanges.

One young German named Hans was particularly good at ping pong. He was a demanding opponent and gave no edge to us, even though we were his captors and he was our forced labor. He was blonde and boyish, and he spoke passable English. He was also the horniest young man I ever met. He begged us to tell him about our adventures in town. I had little to tell since I was not interested in the young women who lived near the base. Most were typical Southerners, many were poorly educated, and a few were prostitutes.

To entertain Hans, we made up elaborate tales of sexual adventures that had never happened. He would sit, his

Von Fritz and Ping Pong

eyes bulging, exclaiming his amazement at our fictional sexual exploits. Yes, it was cruel. In some ways it was our last little revenge against the Germans.

Near the end of my service, the Germans were allowed to go into town on passes. I wonder how Hans did!

ANOTHER MOMENT OF SOLIDARITY

One of the non-coms who ran our barracks was a sergeant. He was a tall, slender, balding man who left us alone once the corporal had fled. He was a quiet man in his mid-thirties. We heard he had worked for our captain's father before the war. While he had been in the Army for four years, he had always been in a training situation and never shipped overseas.

The sergeant befriended a quiet young corporal from Philadelphia. Soon they were going into town together on weekend passes. Then one night someone walked into the sergeant's quarters and saw him in bed with his new friend. I am not sure who reported the incident. It was probably one of the sergeant's Regular Army corporals.

We all feared the two men would receive Blue Discharges. A Blue Discharge was one without honor. It was one step above a Dishonorable Discharge. If a soldier received one, his civil rights were impaired, and he was virtually unemployable in civilian life. We liked the sergeant and his friend and felt the punishment that awaited them far exceeded any moral transgression. We were upset. I can say that almost every man in our barracks felt the same way. Most of us valued a single life over our acquired prejudices.

Our captain, a humane man, ordered us to rush the sergeant's papers through the discharge process before a report was filed with the military police. We worked together to rush their processing through. While homosexuality mystified most of us, we realized that this sergeant was a kind, gentle man who deserved a full civilian life. Late the next afternoon both men received Honorable Discharges and were on their way home. For once, the unforgiving Army policy against gays was sidestepped.

This event strongly influenced my growth as a human being. I think that whatever prejudices I had in my life, my sense of injustice overrode them when it came down to a critical moment of choice.

If this event seems atypical, there was a good reason for this solidarity. Most of the men involved had been in the combat Infantry. To them, external forces were the enemy. Infantrymen stood with their own. Many of the men who sided with the sergeant were probably homophobic; but they stood with a member of their unit, just as a different group of men resolved to stand together during that rape line-up months before.

As I said before, infantrymen create their own laws. Sometimes I think we formed our own nation, a nation forged out of fire and death. That solidarity lingered after the war. Gradually, it faded away as we were assimilated back into civilian life.

Most infantrymen became gentler after seeing war. Only a few became more brutal. I suspect they were brutal to begin with. After a war, time mutes our experiences, and many revert to how we were. A few grow and become wiser. I hope I am one of them. I believe we all have inner prejudices we hate to admit. Our virtue may be determined by our ability to fight back those small hatreds and mistrusts that well up from our subconscious. What has been implanted in us when we are very young is hard to erase, but we do have the capacity to shunt the dark side of our nature aside and do what is right.

After the war there was a period in my life when I was overtly homophobic. I am deeply ashamed of that time. It faded away as I began to realize that some of the friends I valued most were gay. At least two heard me express homophobic views. They valued my friendship over that aspect of me. Both know where I am now, and they contributed in a major way to my growth, understanding, and compassion. I thank them for that. Years later, my wife Linda's kind and loving attitude towards people also helped me grow.

I look back to the basis of my prejudices at that time and realize that my prejudices were based on societal stereotypes and the actions of two or three unpleasant gays I had worked with in theatre. I later realized that they would have been mean little people whatever their sexual orientation was. I made the mistake of basing a belief on a particular rather than a generality. I was suckered into an anecdotal evidence approach to certain things in life. In time, I pushed all that aside. If one applies broader statistics to one's inner prejudices, most are untenable. As a cross-section we are all pretty much the same when it comes down to our basic needs and feelings. What we do with our private parts has little to do with our inner reality as human beings.

A tanker's furlough.

Passes and Furloughs

Unless we were inundated with a shipment of troops, we worked more or less normal hours. There was time for passes into town, and on occasion we got overnight and weekend passes. We could save up time and exchange our times to extend a pass long enough for a long weekend. These exchanges were illegal, but our supervisors overlooked these extended passes. As long as someone manned every cubicle, they had no reason to complain. At times I worked two eight-hour shifts in a row, one for myself, one for a friend who would owe me a day's work.

As winter worsened and Christmas approached, I applied for a Christmas leave. I wanted to go home for at least a day. My application was turned down. Finally, I arranged to work for friends if they would work for me. I did double shifts so three days of my work assignments were covered. I had a standing pass that allowed me to go into Indianapolis any evening I was free. However, I was not supposed to go any farther. To do so could mean a charge of being AWOL.

On Christmas Eve, when my work was covered, I took the post bus into town and headed to the railroad station. There I found that all trains East were full. Dozens of soldiers and civilians waited ahead of me. A friend and I took a bus to the edge of town and stuck out our thumbs. A moving van pulled up and stopped. We climbed into the back of a truck and got under the heavy cloth mats used to protect the furniture. We got another hundred miles and were left off. It was late and there was no traffic heading east. Half frozen, I gave up on my efforts to spend Christmas at home. So did my comrade. We thumbed our way back to Indianapolis. I sent a telegram to my parents telling of my change in plans. Then I saw a movie and returned to the post.

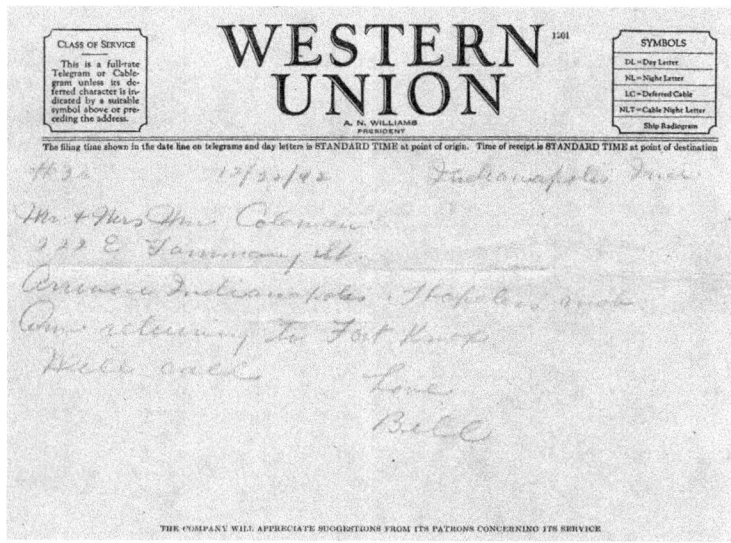

WESTERN UNION

#36   12/25/45   Indianapolis Ind.

Mr. & Mrs. Wm Coleman
225 E Tammany St.
Arrived Indianapolis. Hopeless mob.
Am returning to Fort Knox.
Will call

Love,
Bill

This was my second AWOL Christmas. No one caught me either time. I came back, went to my job, and kept the substitute hours ready for future use.

Christmas Party, 1945.

27

Another Transfer

As the separation of soldiers accelerated, another discharge center was needed. Our unit was moved 130 miles north to Camp Atterbury, Indiana. It was about twenty miles outside of Indianapolis. Atterbury was an installation built during the war and was vast, flat, and quite drab. It was GI in its nature. By that, I mean it was built like every other post in the country. It was a vast collection of standardized wooden barracks set on an empty plain. During winter that plain was swept by bitter winds. It was my first experience with winter in the Midwest. In Pennsylvania we were cold, but the hills broke up those incessant winds. Years later I learned to live with these windswept winters in Iowa.

Atterbury was pleasant duty once we were out of the winter months. Even though we were all non-coms by now, we lived in an open barracks. I was now a T/4, a Technician Fourth Grade. It was the same as a buck sergeant when it came to pay. To that was added my continuing ten dollar a month combat Infantry pay. By now I was making more than fifty dollars a month. It was good money for that time. In fact, I was almost affluent. Tax and social security came out of that, but I had more than enough spending money. All that I made was spending money since everything else was taken care of by the Army. Even so, I was not a big spender. I found little that was worth spending money on.

I had none of the vices of most soldiers. I drank a little beer, I didn't smoke, and I went to as many movies as I could. I purchased a few books when I was in town, but I found most of these in bargain bins. Mainly I relied on the well-stocked post library for my reading material. I limited

First pay as a T-4.

my possessions. My slot in the barracks gave me little room for things other than those the Army issued to us. As a result, I managed to save a little money during my final months in the Army.

It was during this time my education began to gain sophistication and depth. Some of that was due to those older WACS, some to friends and their breadth of interest, and some to my own inquisitive mind. Even without guidance, I seemed to have a knack for finding the right things to read and appreciate.

Our work did not change. However, I did acquire a new set of friends. I believe Art was transferred elsewhere, as were some other members of our section and my WAC friends. It was like starting over again.

One of the first people I met was Bob Meade. He shared my sense of humor and excelled it. His sense of the absurd was always amusing. Sometimes it was gut-bustingly funny.

Meade was a civilian musician without a musical group. His interest in music ranged widely. He introduced me to more classical music at the post library. We'd sit in a listening booth enjoying staples from the classical repertory. Though Meade was my age, he had not served overseas because he married straight out of high school. For this reason, his induction was delayed until near the end of the war in Europe.

One of Meade's friends was another musician who happened to be the brother of a new movie star. The star was Jane Russell. Her first film, *The Outlaw*, managed to open without the imprimatur of the Hays Office. It was scandalous then – overwrought, melodramatic, and sexy in a heavy-handed way that would not earn it a PG-13 rating now. Adding to its risibility was the use of Tchaikovsky's Sixth Symphony, the *Pathetique*, for underscoring. Of course, we all went to see it.

It was greeted with wild laughter, even in its serious moments. The main attraction of the film was Jane Russell's ample bust. Howard Hughes, who had directed the film, advertised the film on posters with the logline, "Two reasons to see *The Outlaw*." Above it was a picture of Jane Russell in a low-cut – for then – peasant blouse.

Bill with Bob Meade

Her brother grumbled, "I wish Jane would give it up. She can't act, and she's making a damn fool out of herself." She went on to star in more than 20 films during her career and was one of the leading sex symbols in Hollywood during the 1940s and 1950s.

Our unit included other soldiers from the Chicago area. One was Hannity,[1] a burly guy who loved to get into fights. He was smart, but he also had a mean streak. I never crossed him, so we got along well.

Once, as a group, we all went into town and went roller-skating. I was shaky on skates and struggled along. A civilian buzzed me and sent me sprawling. As a reflex I swore at him. By now, profanity came easily to me. He turned back, ready for a fight. Suddenly there was a mass of civilians and ex-30th Division men confronting each other. Striding into the middle Hannity loomed hugely. He took a massive swing at the civilian who was ready to swing at me. Hannity hit him hard, and the civilian skidded into the seats surrounding the rink.

Then everybody was swinging punches at everybody, and everybody was on roller-skates. It was an absurd versions of a John Ford bare-knuckled fist fight. Within minutes military police arrived and everybody took off in all directions. No one was arrested.

Years later Meade wrote me that Hannity was still picking fights in mill town bars outside of Chicago. Most combat infantrymen I knew were gentle men who avoided fights. I often wondered if Hannity was over-compensating for the fact that he had been too young to see combat.

---

1 Not his real name.

Survivors of the Battle of the NCO Club.

He lived in Calumet City, then one of the roughest cities in the United States. He was bred to brawl, and he was formidable. I was glad he was there in that rink to bail me out.

On post we took advantage of the NCO club. I was not interested in the 3.2 beer, but the food was good. As the evening progressed many got drunk, and then even drunker. At a table next to us, I heard a very drunk and singularly ugly WAC ask in a slurred, complaining voice, "Who's got their finger up my snatch?"

A burly master sergeant shouted, "Who's fucking around with my woman?"

Why anyone would admit she was their woman or have a sexual interest in her still puzzles me. The master sergeant took a wild swing at the digital explorer and decked him. A corporal jumped on the master sergeant's back and tried to strangle him while others, for no good reason, threw punches indiscriminately.

Our table, which was made up entirely of combat infantrymen, backed away, ducking punches as we retreated to a safe distance. There we watched the brawl develop. Finally, the MPs arrived; and everyone abruptly stopped. No one wanted a trip to the brig.

I must inject here that most of us who had seen combat avoided the Saturday evening brawls among the regular Army non-coms. We had seen enough fighting.

Meade and I amused ourselves with writing satirical articles. We also found a recording booth in town and soon we were writing mock radio shows and sending them to our families. One of our recorded skits was called "Teakettles Over Dog Bone," another was titled, "A Drunkard in the Apparition Mountains." These three-minute recordings are mercifully lost.

Clowning around.

There were frequent passes into Indianapolis. Big bands played at one of the larger movie houses. There was a feature film, a break, and then a name band played a set. Meade and I went often. We saw Spike Jones and his band in a raucous concert. Jones' orchestra was filled with skilled musicians, but the music they played was a parody of recent hits.

Tex Beneke had assembled the old Glenn Miller Orchestra and played its old charts. Beneke had a large chin and looked a little like a typical country boy. When the curtain opened to reveal him fronting the band, Meade, who had no inhibitions, exclaimed loudly, "What a hick!"

The audience roared, and Beneke looked bewildered.

On another occasion, Shep Fields and his Rippling Rhythm Orchestra appeared. After an opening number he introduced his lead singer, a young woman with an awesome figure. Meade enthusiastically proclaimed, "Look at them knockers!"

The audience was stunned for a second. Then the entire theatre broke out into raucous laughter. The woman looked shocked and embarrassed.

Meade's ribald outbursts only happened once a performance. He dared not repeat them. If he had, ushers – yes, they had ushers in those days – would have discovered who the troublemaker was and eject him.

One weekend both Meade and I managed to get a short leave and I went home with him to Chicago. There I got my first taste of the Windy City. I remember little of that since it was a brief visit. Much of it was spent at Meade's home. His family, like him, were jokers. Their sense of humor was wild and free ranging.

* * *

There were several on-post movie theatres at Camp Atterbury. Each unit had one. Films were rotated about the post with changes every two days. Admission was a quarter. One could follow a good movie around the several posts and see it many times. We went to the movies indiscriminately. There was nothing else to do on evenings during the week.

There were nights with bad double features. I remember United World Pictures as a production company that was even lower than Monogram and Republic Pictures. One of their efforts starred Rondo Hatton as the misshapen "the Creeper" in the film *House of Horrors*.[2] Mr. Hatton suffered from acromegaly, a curious gland condition that gave him a Neanderthal look. The low budget films he starred in caught the look of dark, damp streets but little else. I still retain the image of his misshapen figure scuttling along one of those dark, rain drenched, cobblestone studio streets that were more real to me than real streets in my own hometown.

There were good films, too. MGM was in the midst of its golden age of musicals. We also enjoyed the many action films. *O.S.S.*,[3] starring Alan Ladd and Geraldine Fitzgerald, was one of our favorites. It dealt with American intelligence activity with the French Underground. It was written by Richard Maibaum, a WWII veteran who would later write twelve of the first fifteen James Bond films. Another film, *The Stranger*, directed by Orson Welles and starring Edward G. Robinson, Loretta Young, and Welles, had a unique power and visual beauty. It was the first Hollywood film to deal with war criminals. Welles' genius is stamped all over it. I am puzzled that it is so rarely mentioned by critics and film historians.

---

2 A short-lived effort between J. Arthur Rank, Universal, International Pictures, and Kenneth Young, this company began in 1945 and dissolved in July 1946. *House of Horrors*, directed by Jean Yarbrough, produced by Ben Pivar and Universal Pictures, and distributed by Producers Releasing Corporation, was one of two films that Rondo Hatton appeared in as "the Creeper." It was filmed in September 1945 but wasn't released until March 29, 1946. A series of "Creeper" films had been planned, but after filming the second in the series, *The Brute Man* (released on October 1, 1946), Hatton died, and the series was discontinued.

3 O.S.S. stands for Office of Strategic Services. Formed as an agency of the Joint Chiefs of Staff during World War II to coordinate espionage activities behind enemy lines for all branches of the Armed Forces, it was the predecessor of the modern Central Intelligence Agency (CIA).

Welles also starred in *Jane Eyre*, a wonderful Gothic film released in 1943 that some say he helped direct. Perhaps this is true. Welles managed to give his Edward Rochester striking entrances throughout the film. I liked *Devotion*, a moody Warner Brothers film about the Brontë family. It was set in a studio copy of Haworth, England. Many years later when Linda and I visited this village, I realized that the motion picture sets were amazingly accurate. The film itself was wildly romantic. I loved the storm-swept moors, fog, and cobblestone streets. Franz Waxman's score still reverberates in my mind as does Arthur Kennedy's brilliant performance of the half-mad Branwell Brontë.

By now there were fewer war movies. We were critical of most. They did not reflect the reality of war. One was the poetic *A Walk in the Sun*. While it featured some of Millard Lampell and Earl Robinson's phony "folk" ballads, it had unusual dialog and vivid characters. Some of the dialog was written in blank verse. The combat scenes were suggested and never graphic. Like so many other films, there were many errors in how we dressed and moved as an Infantry squad. Many of its stars were blacklisted in the 1950s.

Most of the other postwar films blur in my memory. The true Hollywood golden era was before the war. There was no need to raise morale or to revile a vanquished enemy. Hollywood quickly turned to escapism. We did not know that neo-realism was emerging in Italy.

*   *   *

Final leave in the Army.

I made it home to Pennsylvania once. Now my parents were living in nearby Schuylkill Haven, a small town about five miles from Pottsville. I have no idea why my parents moved there. One evening we went into Pottsville and saw the movie version of Oscar Wilde's *The Picture of Dorian Gray*. It was directed by Albert Lewin, who also adapted the screenplay, and starred Hurd Hatfield in the title role and George Sanders as Lord Henry Wotton. Others in the cast included Angela Lansbury, Donna Reed, and Peter Lawford. It is an elegant film that uses Wilde's dialog intact. I think my parents were puzzled by it, and maybe a little shocked. Its elegance in look, acting, and dialog and its sophistication gave me a glimpse into a world I had not seen. Of course, I began to read Oscar Wilde.

I am not sure when I acquired a collection of his writing. I read Dorian Gray and was not disappointed. I read *The Importance of Being Earnest* and much of Wilde's poetry. *The Ballad Reading Gaol* moved me once I knew it was a reflection on Wilde's imprisonment. His short poem "The Harlot's House" had been a favorite of mine in that book of poetry I carried during the war. I reread it again and again and committed it to memory.

I remembered the Albright brothers painting at the *Art in the United States* exhibit I had seen before the war. A favorite of mine was a painting of a decayed funeral wreathe on an aged door by Ivan Albright. Its title was long – *That Which I Should Have Done I Did Not Do (The Door)*. Its portrayal of decay was most lovingly detailed. The brothers, who were said to be as strange as their paintings, were ideal candidates to paint the portrait of Dorian Gray as it deteriorated while Gray remained young and vital. For one moment in the film there was a burst of horrific color that moved down to the dead Dorian's horribly dissipated face. This magnificent film is all but forgotten.

DIVERSIONS

I continued to fill my sketchbooks with cartoons, but now it was for the amusement of my friends. Most were passed about or posted. Most were irreverent enough that the officers did not approve of them. When I was promoted and needed new stripes sewn on my uniform, I would draw a WAC a personalized cartoon in exchange for her help as a seamstress. Most of my friends wanted one of my cartoons, and I gave many away. Some of these cartoons still exist in two sketchbooks that I have saved. Some of my drawings reach back to my work on the battalion history while we were on occupation duty. Some of my cartoons still stand up, some are interesting curiosities that reflect another time.

Kids and G.I.

One of our hangouts was the PX. Post Exchanges were places that were the equivalent of duty-free shops, but they were exclusively for the military. They also had light refreshments. Working at one of our PX counters was an attractive young woman named Ila Jean. We struck up a conversation, dated a little, and wrote for a while after the war. She traveled all the way from Michigan to my senior prom at Slippery Rock State Teachers College.

I made one trip to visit her in Michigan. Our interest in each other drifted away with time. It is just as well. By the time I finished college we shared few interests. I hope she found happiness.

A college friend of my father and his family lived in Indianapolis. My parents drove out and I came into town for a weekend pass. Mamie, the mother, was one of those stout, well corseted talkative women who never stopped moving about. She was tense as she constantly talked about nothing in particular. I am sure she was goodhearted, but she certainly was the most aggravating woman I ever met, and there have been more than a few of those in my life. By the second day of my visit, my stomach was so tense that I had to go into the bathroom and throw up.

The father, Charles, was a tall, quiet man. He had survived the Depression cuts in the Pittsburgh offices. My dad harbored a resentment of that, but on the surface, they remained friends. Their two sons were younger than me. All I remember about them is that they were nice kids who spoke with a harshly nasal Southern Indiana accent. A few weekends after that, as a courtesy to my parents, I stayed with them again. Again, my stomach was a mess by the time the weekend was over.

Atterbury: Spring day.

Indianapolis was a pleasant city. Fort Knox had been a better posting, but we were now solidly in the North. To many of us that was comforting. The overt racism and Jim Crow laws offended me. I resolved to never again live in the South.

I managed to enjoy Indianapolis' cultural life. It had touring plays, a good amateur theatre, and a budding symphony orchestra. I saw a touring company of Maurice Evans' GI version of *Hamlet*. Born in 1901 in Dorset, England, Evans had enlisted in the US Army at the start of World War II and had risen to the rank of Major by the end of the war. He was in charge of an Army Entertainment Section in the Central Pacific where he toured his two-hour adaptation of the play. By this time, the 45-year-old actor was a little too chubby and middle-aged for the youthful Prince of Denmark. He also intoned his lines with a quavery voice in a Nineteenth Century style of Shakespearean acting. He attempted to generate deep emotions with that vibrator tremor. The King was played by Thomas Gomez, who usually played villains in Hollywood films. I don't remember the rest of the cast. This was my first full evening of live Shakespeare.

Later, Evans was the first actor-producer to put Shakespeare on network television. He remounted his *Hamlet* and then *Macbeth*. Judith Anderson[4] wiped him off the screen in their scenes together. Both productions were clear readings of those great plays, but they never reached the summit of the greatness they deserved. It's a shame that Evans wasn't a better actor.

I managed to injure myself again while off-duty. Some of us cut across the barracks lawns one evening in a race to get back to the barracks. We were full of boyish enthusiasm and leapt fences and dashed around buildings. I missed one low fence and hit my shin, cutting it badly. It was not enough to put me in the infirmary, but I still get creaks and twinges in that injured shinbone. I am always reminded of the war by the creak in my ankle and my battered shin and knee.

---

4 Judith Anderson (1897 – 1992) was an Australian-born British actress who had a successful career in stage, film, and television. She won two Emmy Awards, a Tony Award; and was nominated for a Grammy Award and an Academy Award. She is considered one of the great classical stage actors of the 20th century. Some of the more notable films she appeared in were *Rebecca* (1940), *Kings Row* (1942), *Stage Door Canteen* (1943), *Laura* (1944), *The Ten Commandments* (1956), *Cat on a Hot Tin Roof* (1958), *A Man Called Horse* (1970), and *Star Trek III: The Search for Spock* (1984). She was created a Dame Commander of the Order of the British Empire (DBE) in 1960 – and thereafter billed as Dame Judith Anderson. In 1991 she was appointed a Companion of the Order of Australia (AC). She died in 1992 at the age of 94.

The Battle of the Mops.

By early summer my point total came up and I was discharged. I went through the process I had been a part of. Before my paperwork was complete, I joined the enlisted Reserves. In doing so, I kept my status as a non-com in the Adjutant General's Department. My thinking at the time was that there would be more wars. I hoped that my new personnel skills would keep me from being in the Infantry again.

I said good-bye to Bob Meade. Along with Art Chicoine, Larry Freeman, and Mike Lipesky, he was among my closest friends in the Army. Actually, Meade was probably the closest. He brought out my own humor, something I had kept within myself, or only let out in my cartooning.

For a while Meade and I remained in contact, but eventually our friendship faded away. He had a keen mind and a quick sense of wit, but he never went to college. Instead, he worked in one of the steel mills. He divorced and remarried. I fear that his life didn't turn out very well. If so, that is sad. If he had found a niche for his energy, wit, and imagination, he had all the talents for success.

I called him once when I passed through O'Hare Airport in Chicago. He sounded much the same. But that was more than forty years ago. As of this writing, I don't know if he's still alive.

Atterbury: Goofing off.

GOIN' HOME

I walked to the post gates on July 1, 1946 and waited for the bus into Indianapolis. There I would catch a train to take me home. While I waited, a young medical officer drove up and offered me a ride into town. He remains one of those memorable characters I met during my time in the Army. He was a medical doctor, a proctologist, whose assignment was to examine dozens – more probably, hundreds – of male rectums a day. When he mentioned his duty, I remembered that physical examination when I was inducted.

All the way into Indianapolis the young doctor complained, in graphic detail, about how horrible it was to do his job during the summer months. I was amused, but I was also thoroughly revolted. I held back my laughter throughout the ride. It was no easy task. I got out of his car, thanked him for the ride, and entered the railroad station. My Army career ended on a most bizarre note with that ride and barrage of graphic anatomical complaints. In his peacetime life I hope he was able to concentrate on other parts of the human anatomy.

Somehow that last ride away from my final post provided a ribald end punctuation to my life in the Army. I think it's only fitting since it also furnishes a coarse metaphor for my feelings toward all things military and just where they can put them.

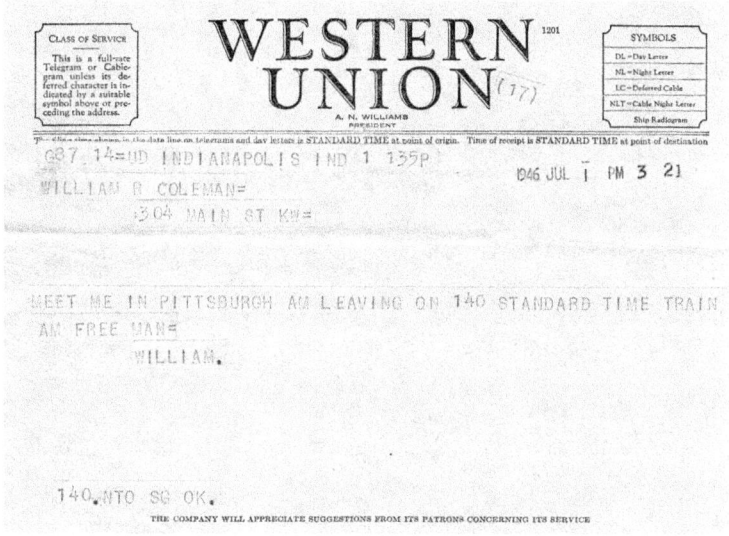

PART VIII

REFLECTIONS

They were human beings, they had their weaknesses
and their flaws and their good sides and bad sides.
The only thing they had in common was they were
a little too young to die.

Bill Mauldin

William S.E. Coleman

Reflections

O N THAT BRIGHT summer day as I boarded the train to go home after my discharge, what lay ahead of me was a mystery. I did not fear entering that mystery. My courage had been tested. Never again would I know the fear I had known in combat. Never again would another human being truly intimidate me. Why should I be afraid? I had faced maiming and death. I felt I had no superiors. I was an equal in a world that conspires to make us unequal. That fearlessness persisted throughout my life. It allowed me to act on principle when I felt the need.

The boy who had listened to the radio broadcast about the bombing of Pearl Harbor less than five years before was no more. I had seen the darkest side of humanity close up. That would affect me. I knew now that humanity – if I can apply that word to the human race – bent easily under some pressures. On the other hand, I saw nobility and bravery. Violent pressures seemed to strengthen us. Subtle economic pressures seemed more persuasive. If people were touched right, I saw firsthand that they would do anything to eat and continue their lives. This capacity for evil doing certainly defined my values and what I considered important.

I looked forward to my civilian life. I mourned for those who were not coming home. It was terrible to think that they would not enjoy the mysteries of life that lay ahead of me. My hope was that I would add something to the world I had helped destroy.

After what seemed like an eternity, the train finally left the station and I began my 600-mile journey back home. Soon the cityscape of Indianapolis was replaced by farmland. As I watched the scenery sweep by, I alternated between reading and musing. I remembered another train ride – could it have been only two years prior? – when I wondered where I would be sent. Would I even have a future? Would I live long enough to find myself? Those questions had been answered. I was here. The future was now. I was beginning the journey to find my life's course and discover my next self.

Thoughts bombarded me. New questions sprang to my mind. My imagination raced far ahead of the train towards whatever was waiting for me. However, I did arrive at one conclusion. Our lives continue on because of a split second's difference or a decision we unwittingly make. A bullet missed me because I had just moved a fraction of an inch in more than one instance. Had Larry and I decided to dig our foxhole a few feet from where it was the night of the brutal shelling, we would have received a direct hit and become unrecognizable corpses. Such a slight variance in time and space determines whether we frail mortals live or die. This determination of our existence is with us every moment of our daily lives – in traffic, in accidents, and in civic violence.

In combat there were also many "ifs" along the way, plus the luck of the draw. If I had learned to type and drive, I would have never been in combat to begin with. If I had not sprained my ankle and shipped out in early November, I would have been in the midst of the bloody Battle of the Bulge. I had other delays after that month of recovery. Not having two pairs of glasses when I arrived at the POE gained me another week – a time when there was heavy fighting around Trier. Then, when I approached the front, I gained two more days with dental work. If my teeth hadn't had those eight cavities, I might have been assigned to B Company – possibly ending up next to Flynn on the side of the road.

Our C Company was rarely the point company in the heavy actions we were in. They had borne the brunt of casualties before I arrived at the front lines. We took few casualties after I joined the company. I was spared because brave men had died before me.

*   *   *

Decades after the war, my mother told Linda that a growth she carried in her womb should have prevented her from carrying me to full term.[1] I was born against all physiological odds. She called me her "miracle baby."

---

1 This tumor was apparently a rare benign uterine teratoma that shared the womb with Bill. It did not attach itself to him as is often the case with parasitic twins. The tumor was surgically removed later, along with the uterus. As a result, Bill was an only child.

Linda has said many times that she finds it incredible that I don't believe in miracles. Her argument is that my whole life has been nothing short of miraculous. As I approach the end of my life, I think I might have to agree.

As I look back now, one thing I do know: If I had been killed, neither of my sons would have existed, nor would my grandchildren. Each of the women who would become my wife would also have had a significantly different life. Much that happened because I was alive would not have happened.

*   *   *

Other thoughts crowded my mind. Why did we fight? We fought because we were trapped within a great war machine and we had no other choice. Once we were within that cruel mechanism, our main intent was to protect each other as we were commanded to advance. Here and there the ability of young men to stand and meet the bloody challenges of battle changed the course of civilization. What would the Western World be like had not those Spartans stood at Thermopylae? Or thousands of other armies who stood at other places throughout the millennia? Or Bataan? Normandy? Stalingrad? Leningrad? The Bulge?

Yes, I was proud that I stepped up and did my duty. But underneath that pride smoldered a deep resentment. A select group of people had not joined in that fight. Many profited from the war. As I marched through Germany and witnessed the destruction of towns and cities, I had seen the names of numerous corporations that would come out on top regardless of who won the war. Greed, not good, was their motivation. Many continue to dominate the economy to this day. Industrialists prospered and bought politicians that did their bidding. Many of those profiteers also managed to get their sons deferred from the draft or attached to stateside or rear echelon units. The human race can be so gullible. It never learns.

Before I went to war, I believed that there should be no profits in wartime and that the entire nation should be conscripted to the service of the war. I was convinced then, and I remain convinced to this day, that wars are fought for economic reasons. There can be moral issues, and there were many of those in World War II, but at the center of that war and every war is a fight for material things. Religion is often used as an excuse for war, but it is used as a cruel rationalization for the need for un-Christian behavior. If you took profit out of wars, I believe there would be fewer wars. Some will label this idea simplistic. It is certainly unrealistic.

Some say World War II was a necessary war, and while I cling to my pacifism, I tend to agree. I was proud to play a small part in stopping the murder of millions more than the millions that were savagely killed in camps, bombings, and battles. Winning the war meant that we freed many who were about to be executed in concentration camps. We freed slave laborers, and entire countries that had been occupied by the Germans. Even so, I remain convinced that it is wrong to kill another human being.

I am glad that the vast majority of Americans do not experience the realities of war. We as a nation have not done so since the Civil War. Being on a continent far away from the wars of the 20th century and the perpetual state of war that we now accept in the 21st century gives war an abstraction.

Many say that the brutal television views of the Vietnam War contributed to the resistance against that unjust and meaningless war. As brutal as those pictures were, they were less than a tenth of the reality the men who fought in Southeast Asia faced.

In the 21st century, especially following the 2003 invasion of Iraq, most of the images of our wars have been removed from newspapers and the media. Many are culpable for this removal – politicians, media, corporations, etc. – and for a variety of reasons. It is not a stretch to say that most people in the U.S. have little or no awareness of what is happening in countries where armed forces are actively deployed and engaged. As a result of this, we do not have to face the consequences and realities of war. War is also removed from our social and moral consciousness, even as our military is touted as the definition of patriotism at sporting and other public events. This growing disconnect is evidenced by the fact that, while medical and mental health support for returning veterans is shamefully inadequate and generally tolerated by the voting public at the polls, an athlete "taking a knee" during the National Anthem is loudly decried. To the average American, war has become abstract – images limited to video games and entertainment programs on television and in the movies.

Perhaps selected citizens – the civilians who stay home and watch our wars on television or promote them on social media – should be transported to a battle zone for a few days. There they could witness the reality and then come home and tell others what they had seen. That, too, is a suggestion many will label impractical or even naive. I argue that one can never be too naive about solutions to stopping the plague of war that has scarred every century of human existence.

* * *

A great many men functioned well and bravely in World War II. Some went far beyond any reasonable expectation in impossible situations. When things get rough and the situation is hopeless, the best of the best become existentialists. It is better to act than do nothing.

Throughout my life, I have thought a lot about what courage is. I am glad that I was never pushed to the extremities of my own courage. And what is bravery? Bravery against great odds moves me to tears when I have seen it in life and on film. I have never thought of myself as a particularly brave person. I'm not sure about how courageous I have been during my life's crises. In combat, an act of courage often arises from an inescapable situation, a situation where one must act.

Some years ago, I scribbled down a sentence. It goes, "There comes a time when life is less important than the moment. At that moment heroes are born." I have seen that happen. I am glad it never happened to me. I never considered myself a hero. I believe that I only did what I had to do in a desperate situation. I had no other choice.

In looking back, I believe that we are all allotted a certain amount of courage. When it runs out, we become cowards. Life wears us all down. I have known men who had deep wells of courage. Some fought from the hedgerows of Normandy to the end of the war on the banks of the Elbe River.

Other men break easily and quickly. Why? I cannot venture to say why this happens. At the time, we all looked in disdain on the less than a handful of men who broke under the tension. Now, as I look back, I have great compassion for them. Most men endured and fought just as men had stood against other men from the dawn of civilization, or what we call civilization.

When you are in a group of men who have become your friends, you stick with them. You cannot give up, even when you want to. We were not heroes. We did not fight for our country. We fought for our friends. We were a group of ordinary men who did what we had to do. We became a "band of brothers."

I do know that once I moved into civilian life, my courage was tested many times. I admit that I bent a few times, but I can also say that I bent because the well-being of my family was at stake. That, I believe, is at least a partial explanation of why Germans allowed the horrendous deeds that went on around them. If this ever came to pass in the United States – and it could – I hope that I would act with courage.

I am proud that I was accepted into the comradeship of my Infantry squad. It took me a long time to come to the conclusion that I behaved bravely – or was at peace with my two Bronze Stars and what they symbolized. I am still uneasy about that. I find it ironic that a bookish and not very athletic young man did something brave and doesn't have a clear recollection of what he did. At this late date, it doesn't really matter. After all, the medal that I am proudest of is my Combat Infantryman Badge. However, these awards also symbolize the death of enemy soldiers who had families, men who were loved and mourned, and men who fell from the bullets I fired.

*   *   *

The men in the front line Infantry were remarkable human beings. They paid a great price. Not the least was that horrible memory of killing another human being. What the soldier brings home is not so much honor and glory, but a haunting guilt of things he had to do in order to stay alive and come home. I feel that sense of guilt.

Once I flippantly said that war was open season on humanity. But the reality was that there are men who lost the privilege of coming home to their loved ones, and I am the reason they did not. I had killed other human beings. I have spent my life dealing with that. That memory goes with one to the grave – and perhaps far beyond. I pass it off lightly when I talk about it. I have to. "That way madness lies."[2]

There's a great line in the 1992 Clint Eastwood film, *Unforgiven*: "It's a hell of a thing, killin' a man. You take away all he's got, and all he's ever gonna have."[3] When I heard that line a few years ago, I again had that

---

2   From *King Lear*, Act III, Scene IV, Line 21, by William Shakespeare.

3   Clint Eastwood's line as the character William "Will" Munny in the movie, *Unforgiven*, written by David Webb Peoples, and produced and directed by Clint Eastwood. The film won four Academy Awards, including Best Picture and Best Director.

sense of mourning those who died in my war and the wars that came before and after.

I am sometimes filled with sadness; but I do know that at the moment of killing I had no other choice. I was an eighteen-year-old boy caught in the midst of events I never fully understood. I was not about to give up my own life so that an enemy soldier could live.

How did I assuage that guilt? I do know that my choice to be a teacher is part of my penance. Giving something to the sum of things seemed important to me then. It still does now. I spent my working life trying to make a positive contribution to the world, to add to the sum of good things as a teacher and an artist. I have tried to live the lives of the men I killed as well as my own. I hope I have done well for them. I mourn them as well as my fallen comrades. That, to me, is the tragedy of being in a world filled with wars and violence.

The guilt has also made me a workaholic much of my professional career as a teacher, theatre director, historian, and playwright. That in itself made me difficult to live with at times. I apologize to those who got short shrift from me as a son, husband, father, and friend. I hope all those who were affected will understand that I had no other choice.

*   *   *

World War II had shaped and defined me. I was not aware that many of my ideas were formed by the time I entered the Army. My politics were liberal to left. I would spend the rest of my life moving from a moderate center position to further left. At that time, my thoughts about sexual morality were highly theoretical given that I remained inexperienced in such matters.

I have always been a very conventional person at heart. My noncon-formity is limited to my thoughts and my art. There were many rough edges in my character and behavior that needed to be smoothed off. There still are some. Some are essential to my identity. Adding to that complexity was a mix of clumsiness and sophistication, a sophistication that was growing with each book and play I read. They are the quirks an artist needs to look at the world afresh and from a slightly skewed angle.

By the end of the war, the conventional religious beliefs that were given to me were gone. I have never felt the hand of an omniscient God on my shoulder. To think that seems a great impertinence to me. However, I have felt a sense of destiny – and even fate – guiding me along as I drifted through my life. Perhaps our existential necessity arises out of the observable fact that we are all linked together even when we do nothing that is remarkable. I do know I have always been fascinated by how I fit into the overall scheme of things just by living as one of billions of others on this insignificant planet in a vast universe where a myriad of suns light an infinite number of planets.

I have led a productive life, I helped a few people, and I hope I helped more than I hindered. However, that sense of fate drove me in my early manhood.

*   *   *

The young man who ran down that train platform to greet his parents was an odd mix. I had been forced to become a man while I was in combat, but the vestiges of a boy remained inside me.

I knew then that I was fortunate to survive combat and come home. I felt an obligation to do more with my life, to live at least one extra life for those who died during the war. I wanted to add something to a world I had helped destroy.

As I considered the future, I hoped that I would find love and happiness. I wished to be a father, too. I wanted to move the Coleman name into a new, and hopefully more peaceful, generation.

In looking back, few of the young women that I grew up with would have fit in to the life that lay ahead of me. Indeed, if I had settled on one of them, they would have settled me. I did not know then how fortunate I was that no woman had decided to love me at that time in my life. I wanted marriage and its permanency, but I also was fumbling toward a life that was not yet defined to me.

I was not alone in this. Most of those single veterans I knew that were college-bound stayed unencumbered. A few got engaged. Only a very few married and tried to manage college and marriage at the same time.

On my return, I decided that I would go to college. The GI Bill furnished free higher education to all who qualified for college admission. For the first time in American history, the masses were able to pursue a dream that before had been limited to only a few – a few who had money, and those who had the determination to work their way through college in a tough pre-war economy. With the Depression lingering until the war was underway, working one's way through college was very difficult. Now millions went to college. The face of America was forever changed.

I enrolled at Slippery Rock State Teachers College. I would major in history and English, and train to be teacher. I was excited by the world of ideas, past and present. I wanted to become a writer, but the idea of a life in the theatre was still beyond my wildest dreams. Why did I choose teaching? First, after being a child of the Great Depression, I wanted security; but more than that, I felt a desire to make the world about me more humane.

*   *   *

Over the years, I have written about the war in a discarded attempt at a novel, a few essays and articles, two or three short stories, a very short play, two longer plays, and a screenplay. All combine fact with fiction. As a writer, one takes pieces of truth and reassembles them into what one hopes is a fictional truth. A good fictional truth can be more truthful than reality. Why? Because it is organized and structured in a way so that a human situation is intensified.

Yes, there is much of my inner self in my writing. There are also many incidents from my life, but it is all reshaped, placed in differing contexts, and in rearranged sequences so I can construct a stronger narrative. Life rarely has a coherent structure. Those who argue that one can replicate reality are dead wrong. What passes for reality in art is something greater than reality. Perhaps in being greater, it is a more intense reality than any of us has experienced.

*   *   *

Today I know no one who was a combat infantryman with me. I hope all my friends had good lives, and I hope they are all still with us.[4]

---

4 Linda's note: I have researched most of the people Bill served with and mentions in this book. Sadly, by 2018, among those I were able to find, only three remained among the living (including Mel Brooks). In 2015, at the time of his death, Bill also appeared to have been the last surviving member of his combat outfit, C Company.

As I write this, nearly 1700 veterans of World War II die each day.[5] That is one reason why I am filling so many pages with memories of my modest experiences in the war. Our memories of World War II, and of that whole era, need to be preserved. It was a unique and dramatic time in world history. Our individual microscopic views of the war could eventually be assembled into a broad panorama, a very human one reflecting what happened to all of us.

Journalist Tom Brokaw described us as the "Greatest Generation." I find that flattering, but I truly believe that we only did what had to be done. There was no escaping our obligation to our country and to humanity. That, to me, makes us less remarkable, but much more human. I salute my brave friends.

As I write this in my eighties, I can say I dodged a lot of bullets in my life, figuratively and literally. I am past the average age of life expectancy for Americans. Is there a reason I survived? No, I don't think I'm that important in the overall scheme of things. However, I am grateful to have lived as long as I have.

Every day is a bonus now. Every moment is precious. In fact, every day of our lives from birth onward is a bonus we should appreciate. It is our obligation to use our life well and not to waste it. If we do waste some time now and then, we should do it for enjoyment and pleasure. Too many people put off living. That is tragic. As many have said, "The greatest risk is to take no risk at all." How right they were – and are.

Life is very good, even at its worst. Feelings of all kinds are valuable, even the bad ones because they are part of our divine mortality. Even when I am being a damned fool, I am living. Besides, I believe there is nothing wrong with being a damned fool once in a while. It puts the rest of life into its proper perspective.

---

5   The 1700 figure was quite a few years ago. As of 2017, of the 16 million Americans who served in World War II, only about 558,000 were still living, and veterans were dying at the rate of about 362 per day. As of September 30, 2018, it was down to 496,777 surviving veterans – less than 5% of the 16 million – and they were dying at the rate of 348 each day. By May 2020, on the 75th anniversary of VE Day, only 300,000 WWII veterans were still alive. By September 30, 2021, only 240,329 veterans survived, with 234 dying each day. By 2025, estimates are that only about 61,000 veterans will still be living. Within a decade, only a few hundred veterans will still be alive, and all will be centenarians. The last living American veteran from WWII is projected to die in 2044. That is why the National World War II Museum in New Orleans, LA, is trying to preserve as many oral and written histories of those who served as possible.

Peace!

It seemed wonderful. Little did I know that there would not be a single day of peace in the world throughout what was left of the 20th century. The 21st century looks to be even more violent.

What brutes we are! How complacent we are in the face of our mass brutishness.

As I leave my experiences in the war behind, I must quote one of the pieces of writing that got me through the war:

> No man is an island, entire of itself; every man is a piece of the continent, a part of the main; if a clod be washed away by the sea, Europe is the less, as well if a promontory were, as well as if a manor of thy friends or of thine own were; any man's life diminishes me, because I am involved in mankind; and therefore never send to know for whom the bell tolls; it tolls for thee.
>
> John Donne,
> *Devotion upon Emergent Occasions* (1624)

Good men and women leave such messages behind them, but few pay heed to them. Those who do rarely find a place within the power structure of their countries. Most are called subversive and immoral. Their counsel would be to avoid war at all costs. That would be counter to that most pernicious of all phrases – the national interest.

*   *   *

Not long after I returned home, the Cold War began. While I was still in college, the Korean War began. It was brutal and long. It was followed by another war, then another, and many others throughout the world. As I write this, we are trying to extricate our armed forces from Iraq while we dive deeper into Afghanistan. No one has ever won a war there. As this continues, myriads of large and small wars flare in Africa, Asia, and the Middle East. The endless cycle of war goes on. We are in a perpetual state of war.

Has there been even one moment of peace in this world during my long life? I don't think so.

494

Will we ever find peace?

* * *

Don't rejoice in his defeat, you men.
For though the world stood up and stopped the bastard,
The bitch that bore him is in heat again.
Bertolt Brecht
The Resistible Rise of Arturo Ui

A hero is no braver than an ordinary man,
but he is brave five minutes longer.
Ralph Waldo Emerson

The best soldiers were men who didn't want to be there.
William S.E. Coleman

ACKNOWLEDGMENTS

P EOPLE WHO DON'T know us very well have asked why, if this is Bill's "memories and a memoir," my name appears as co-author. Bill said, "It might be *my* story, but it's *our* book." *Boyhood's End* was our final project. I wish that he'd lived long enough to see it through publication, but since that wasn't possible, it is up to me to see it through. To me this has not been work, but a labor of love. I am honored to be entrusted with his story.

Bill and I worked together throughout our entire relationship. At times it was difficult to know where the professional ended and the personal began. Many people said that we were "joined at the hip." Some of his students referred to us as "Doc&Linda" as if we were one name, one person. Especially during our early years, he taught me most of what I know about research, writing, editing, and composing. He shaped me and molded what I would become. We brought out the best in each other. And regardless of how pissed at the other we might be at any given moment, we *always* knew that we had each other's back no matter what. Thanks to Bill, I have exceeded any and all of my childhood dreams and imaginings. Thanks to me, he was able to achieve more than he thought possible, especially in his later years. We were soulmates and true partners in every sense of the word.

I have also been asked how much of me is in this book. I want to be very clear. This is Bill's life, as told in his own words. Even though my fingerprints are on every page, it is Bill's voice and his story. The illustrations are his. My job was to take more than 600 pages of *his* chapters, stories, memories, reminiscences, and illustrations and to turn them into *our* book. My own words will be found mostly in the footnotes, clarifications, and some of the historical explanations and summaries. I do not differentiate between his and mine because this was truly a team effort every step of the way.

With Bill's blessing, I changed many names. In some cases, it was to protect privacy. Other names were changed for those who might not have behaved in ways that would make their wives or grandchildren proud. Some names are real, especially relatives and people whom Bill admired but are now deceased. Our hope was that if a member of those families ever came across this book, it might bring a smile to their lips and comfort to their heart.

I would like to express my appreciation to A. Zee, author of numerous books including *Fearful Symmetry, On Gravity,* and *Fly by Night Physics.* Our meeting was serendipitous. Tony was looking for a reader who was not a scientist for his new book and I wanted to learn about quantum physics. I am honored to be mentioned in his acknowledgments in *Quantum Field Theory, as Simply as Possible,* published by Princeton University Press (January 2023). Added benefits were that I made a new friend, plus I learned a lot about the process of book publication. Thank you, Tony, for expanding my horizons, especially into the world of quantum physics!

When looking for people to read *Boyhood's End,* I wanted to include someone who loved history, belonged to a younger generation, and could provide a more objective opinion than our close friends or immediate family. Carl H. Hanson was a perfect match. He had met Bill a few times, but they weren't close. Carl is a military veteran, loves history, and is very well read. He is also the son of one of my favorite cousins. Thank you, Carl, for your experience, insight, perspective, and thoughts.

To Eileen and Ronald Bowerman, who have been part of my life in one way or the other since I was fourteen years old, my profound thanks and deepest gratitude seem inadequate. Ron was Bill's best friend and baseball buddy and has been like a brother to me. Eileen is my adoptive sister. She also was and is my teacher, colleague, mentor, and friend. Ron came to Bill's bedside every day during those last few weeks just to sit with him and provide the calm friendship we both needed. The steak and ice cream were most welcome, too.

Eileen and Ron were also the ones I called before I alerted Hospice of Bill's death. They dropped everything and came to my side, providing love and support as I endured the love of my life being taken away in a body bag. I don't know what I would do without them.

Eileen's sister, Jane Harbers Baumgardner, has been in my life for fifty years. She was my best friend throughout college and the bridesmaid at my wedding. Bill and I always loved her sense of humor and her compassionate heart. While I don't see her as often as I would like, I know that her love and friendship are always there.

Wanda Bryant has been a constant in my life for nearly half of a century. She, Jane, and I were classmates at Drake, and she and Jane were roommates. A couple of years after graduation, our friendship really took hold, and she became part of our extended family. Words are inadequate to describe the role she has played in my life. She challenges me in ways that are necessary to my development, she supports me in ways that nurture my confidence and calm my fears, and she keeps me grounded and growing. I'm not sure that I would have survived this long without her.

One of Bill's talents, as a teacher and a friend, was that he saw potential in people and found ways to draw it out. Wanda's brains and talents were being wasted in Des Moines. Bill encouraged her to pursue a graduate degree, and much to our delight, she did. Our sadness at her departure was offset by our pride and admiration at her doctorate in ethnomusicology from UCLA, resulting in a successful and rewarding career. Thanks to plane tickets, telephones, and the internet our close-knit bonds were never broken. She remains one of the most vital and important people in my life to this day.

To someone not in theatre or higher education, and even to those who are, it's difficult to adequately describe Bill's impact on the people he taught and worked with. I have never seen anything quite like it. In fact, I'm still amazed at how many kept ties with Bill – known to his students as "DOC" – once they graduated or moved away. People were always stopping by or calling, often to get suggestions for audition materials, recommendations on plays, or advice about production issues. Sometimes they called to discuss personal decisions or challenges they might be facing, other times they would happily report a new job, marriage, or the birth of a child.

Perhaps the happiest call came from a student who had graduated in the 1980s. Now living in Australia, Robert Shook wanted to let Doc know that he and his wife Sue-Ellen just had their first baby. "And DOC! We're naming him Coleman!" A decade later we were able to meet this fine young man. It was a joyful meeting and a heartfelt reunion.

It should be no surprise that Bill's ability to have a positive impact on people began long before he arrived at Drake. From his first college teaching job in West Virginia in the 1950s until he retired from the classroom in 2002 to fully explore his talents as a playwright and screenwriter, he was always growing, exploring new things, and reaching out. In fact, as he lay dying, one of his plays won a cash award and was in the middle of a professional production in Toronto, Canada; another play had just closed after enjoying performances in Australia; a third play was chosen for a production in Arizona; and a fourth was given a staged reading in England at the same time it was being scheduled for a full production by a regional theatre closer to home.

At the same time, as former students, colleagues, and friends learned of Bill's terminal diagnosis, we began receiving cards and letters, emails, phone calls, and even a few spontaneous visits from people who wanted to let him know the impact he'd had on their lives. Witnessing these good-byes was difficult, yet profoundly moving and reaffirming. In those final days, through tears and smiles, Bill said, "I am amazed and overwhelmed. I guess that I've made a difference after all." I assured him that he had. I know that it gave him peace as he slipped from this life into the next.

Even so, I found it quite remarkable that shortly after his death, hundreds of people, representing five decades of Drake alumni and faculty, independently raised money to establish a memorial fund in Bill's name.

Then, in 2016, more than 150 returned to campus to celebrate the results of their efforts – the renaming and dedication of the William S.E. Coleman Studio Theatre at Drake University and the establishment of a guest artists series in his name. A lovely portrait titled "DOC, *In loving memory*" was painted by Drake art alumnus (and occasional Drake theatre actor) David Marcet. It proudly hangs in the lobby of the Performing Arts Hall at the Harmon Fine Arts Center. I just wish that Bill had been able to enjoy that magical weekend and see the ongoing impact of his legacy. I will carry those memories in my heart forever.

Two of Doc's former students have been especially helpful over the years, and especially so as I completed *Boyhood's End*. Sean Gannon is a wonderful playwright, screenwriter, filmmaker, actor, and so much more. His movie *Something Blue*, shot and produced in Iowa, has been shown at numerous film festivals and theatres throughout the USA. Bill was so honored to be a consultant on the film. Even when Sean lived in L.A., he kept close ties to Iowa. We were overjoyed when he moved back home and brought lovely Kate with him. Sean is family.

Bridget Flanery is the brilliant author of the screenplay for *Gossamer Folds*. This independent movie has been shown at film festivals and was nominated for a 2022 GLAAD award. She is even better known for her numerous film, television, and theatre acting credits. Years ago, she paused a successful acting career to complete a graduate degree at Yale. She then returned to L.A. to widen her horizons and enjoy even more success. Bridget is Doc's adoptive daughter. She has truly followed in his footsteps, first as a visiting faculty member in the Drake Theatre Department, and more recently as a full-time faculty member and Chair at the American Academy of Musical and Dramatic Arts in Los Angeles. I am deeply grateful to both Sean and Bridget for valuable feedback on the book, and for their continuing love and friendship.

What can I say about Deanna Lehl? Brilliant, beautiful, intelligent, compassionate, kind, and fun only begin to describe this incredible human being. We've been friends for more than forty years. She is my opera and concert buddy. She inspires me on so many levels. Her late husband Allan came to Drake the same year Bill did, so I initially knew her as a fellow "Drake Dame" faculty wife. Their oldest son Philip was one of Bill's students and remains a close friend. Deanna sat with Bill the day before he died when I had to run an errand. Since then, she has picked up shattered pieces of my psyche and glued Humpty Dumpty back together again more times than I can count. I trust her. Everyone should have a friend like Deanna.

My profound gratitude goes to Robert and Rosalie Shultz. Bob was Bill's oldest friend and colleague. Bob was also my mentor. In truth, he was so much more than that. For almost fifty years he filled many roles in my life: adoptive father, professor, *mensch*, advisor, teacher, colleague, counselor, and friend. It was Bob and his late wife Janet who sat us down one day early in 1977 and said, "When are you kids going to get married?" Three months later that question was answered when Bill took a night off from rehearsals for *Romeo and Juliet* to tie the knot.

What BobDad has given me would take volumes to describe. Even so, it would be incomplete and inadequate. Bob celebrated his 102nd birthday in 2021. He was also a World War II Army veteran. His knowledge of that era was vital to me. Since Bill and my mother are gone, *Boyhood's End* had to pass "the BobDad test" before I showed it to anyone else.

Rosalie was one of my first piano teachers. She is a lifelong friend who became part of my extended family. I am grateful for my part in bringing Bob and Rosalie together more than twenty years ago. Their love and marriage have been an inspiration throughout the years. Rosalie became my grammar angel. She caught my capricious or elusive commas, corrected my punctuation and grammar mistakes, and provided crucial comments on content. What she did "for fun" (her words) was invaluable and desperately needed by me.

I knew that I could count on Bob and Rosalie to be totally honest and objective about the book. If they liked it, I knew that I would survive any other type of reaction I might receive. Their help and encouragement were critical to this project and to my life. They saved me many times over and helped pull me out of the darkness of grief and self-doubt and into the light. My eternal love and thanks go to these two. Sadly, in 2021 Bob joined Janet and my Bill. He will remain in my heart forever.

As he mentioned throughout *Boyhood's End*, family was important to Bill, as is the Coleman name. This book would not be complete without mentioning Bill's son Eric and his wife Lizzie, and our grandchildren Ian, Jared, and Reilly. My only regret is that Bill didn't live to see the next generation of the Coleman family arrive with Ian and Katie's daughter, Isabelle. I know that her GreatGrandPaDoc would have doted on her. Her smile lights up a room, and her laughter brings joy to the world.

My deepest thanks go to Bill's eldest son Wim and his wife Pat Perrin for all of their help throughout this journey. Their encouragement and guidance were critical to this project. Wim's emotional support and assistance with editing the first hundred pages during those final weeks of Bill's life were critical to his father's comfort and joy.

Wim and Pat have had impressive careers as writers, artists, poets, and publishers. Their work has won numerous awards. I am eternally grateful for their friendship throughout our lives, and especially for their love and support since Bill's death. Special appreciation goes to Pat for her guidance and help during the final steps of preparing *Boyhood's End* for publication. Their wonderful daughter, our beloved granddaughter, Monserrat Perrin Coleman, is a joy in our lives.

Finally, I want to thank all our family and friends, along with all the colleagues and alumni who helped Bill and me throughout the years and especially during this process. It takes a village to raise a child, and many doulas and midwives to give birth to a book. My appreciation is ongoing, and my gratitude is eternal.

It has been an honor and a privilege to work on this book, on my beloved husband's story.

His story is history.

I hope that I have done it justice.

I hope that I have done him proud.

Photographs and Illustrations

PART VI OCCUPATION DUTY BEGINS

ACKNOWLEDGMENTS

PHOTOGRAPHS AND ILLUSTRATIONS

ABOUT THE AUTHORS

ABOUT THE AUTHORS

WILLIAM S.E. COLEMAN dropped out of high school and enlisted in the US Army in 1944 at the age of 17. One of the last age groups to see front-line combat in World War II, he was awarded the Combat Infantryman Badge and two Bronze Stars for his service. After the war he attended college through the G.I. Bill of Rights and enjoyed an illustrious career as an award-winning playwright, screenwriter, historian, author, director, and professor emeritus of theatre arts at Drake University.

As a writer, Coleman received numerous awards and international recognition along with more than 100 productions of his plays in New York (including Off-Broadway and Off-Off-Broadway), Toronto, Sydney, Melbourne, Chicago, Los Angeles, Pennsylvania, Massachusetts, Florida, Washington, Iowa, Stratford-Upon-Avon, and various regional and university theatres.

In 2015 his play *Border Lines* won top prize in Canada's largest one-act competition. It was awarded a cash prize and produced by Theatre Inspirato in Toronto. *A Future Imperfect*, his dystopian suite of satirical plays, enjoyed a critically praised run Off-Broadway as an official selection of the 2013 New York International Fringe Festival.

Odyssey's End, Coleman's World War II drama, was one of four finalists out of more than 2,000 submissions in the Eugene O'Neill Theatre Center's New Plays for the Media competition. It received Equity Showcase readings at the Minskoff Theatre Studios in New York, and by the 4th Wall Theatre Company in Houston, Texas.

His two-act romantic comedy, *One Golden Moment*, won the annual Mountain Playhouse International Comedy Competition, and was produced with a New York Equity cast and ran to full houses in 2010. A screenplay version has been optioned twice.

Recognized here and abroad as one of the leading experts on the life and career of William F. "Buffalo Bill" Cody, Coleman's historical comedy, *Buffalo Bill to the Rescue!* was workshopped by the StageWest Theatre Company in 2012, and by Nichols-Langdon Productions in Stratford-Upon-Avon in 2016. His acclaimed two-hour mixed media show *Buffalo Bill's WILD WEST* was presented throughout the United States and Europe. He appeared on NPR and BBC radio and television; and served as a consultant for the *National Geographic* magazine, other books and publications, and several Cody museums and collections.

For 36 years "Doc" Coleman served first as Chair and later as the senior professor of theatre at Drake University where he taught playwriting, screenwriting, acting, history, and directed more than 200 stage plays. His lifelong interest in developing new playwrights and screenwriters resulted in his creation of the Drake Playwrights Acting Company. This became a model for playwriting companies in universities throughout the nation. He was playwright-in-residence for Drake Theatre and the Central Iowa Repertory Theatre, and co-founder of the Friends of Drake Arts and the Iowa Scriptwriters Alliance.

In 2016 Drake University renamed their black box theatre the William S.E. Coleman Studio Theatre and established a guest artist series in his name. More than 250 alumni spanning 50 years at Drake participated in honoring him.

After spending more than twenty years researching and collecting information and documents, Coleman and his wife Linda created their critically praised non-fiction book, *Voices of Wounded Knee*. It details the events and attitudes leading to the 1890 Massacre and the end of the Plains Indian Wars. Published by the University of Nebraska Press in 2000, it was the first book to give equal weight to the testimony of the Native Americans and is considered the definitive book on this topic. The book remains available in bookstores and online.

Boyhood's End is the culmination of William and Linda's forty-year-long personal and professional partnership. Over the years they collaborated on more than thirty theatre productions, dozens of scholarly articles, books, plays, and music. Their advocacy and contributions to non-profit arts organizations and individual artists has been celebrated here and abroad.

L INDA ROBBINS COLEMAN is a composer, pianist, writer, research associate, and arts ambassador whose music is regularly performed and broadcast throughout North America and Europe. She became the first Iowa woman to have music performed by a major symphony orchestra and to serve as Composer-in-Residence with any orchestra. Her residencies included Drake Theatre, the Wartburg Community Symphony, and Orchestra Iowa. Career highlights include more than 75 commissions, and honors from Drake University, Sigma Alpha Iota, the ACTF at the Kennedy Center, and the Houston International Film Festival. Her music is listed in *Daniels' Orchestral Music*, published by Rowman & Littlefield.

In 2021 her symphonic poem *For a Beautiful Land* was included on the *American Discoveries* cd by Reuben Blundell and the Lansdowne Symphony Orchestra. This recording was awarded the American Prize for Orchestra Performance. That year also saw the premiere of *Diversions*, a concerto for one soloist, three flutes and orchestra, commissioned by Robert McConnell and the Southeast Iowa Symphony. In September 2022, it was featured on flutist Rose Bishop's cd, *Diversions*.

Coleman co-founded the Friends of Drake Arts and the Iowa Composers Forum and has served on committees and boards for numerous organizations including the International Conductors Guild. Her educational credits include working as an adjunct in the theatre department at Drake University, serving on the Iowa Arts Council performing artist and education rosters, and participating in the visiting artist program at a magnet elementary school in Des Moines' inner city.

Since 1976 she has owned Coleman Creative Services, specializing in composing, performance, promotion, publicity, research, and consultation. She is a published poet and writer, and has worked as an editor, historian, publicist and coordinator for numerous organizations and groups throughout the USA and abroad. Additionally, she served as a caregiver to elderly relatives for more than thirty years.

For four decades she served as collaborator, research associate, and editor with Professor William S. E. Coleman, working on materials related to William F. (Buffalo Bill) Cody and the 19th century Lakotas, the escape of the Danish Jews from Nazi persecution in 1943, and modern productions of ancient Greek plays by the Greek National Theatre. From 1977-2000 she worked with her husband researching and editing their book, *Voices of Wounded Knee*. It details the events and attitudes leading to the 1890 Massacre and the end of the Plains Indian Wars. Published by the University of Nebraska Press in 2000, it is considered the definitive book on this topic, and remains available in bookstores and online. In 2016 she was interviewed for an article about Cody for the March-April issue of the *Iowa History Journal* magazine.

Boyhood's End is the culmination of William and Linda's forty-year-long personal and professional partnership. Over the years they collaborated on more than thirty theatre productions, dozens of scholarly articles, books, plays, and music. Their advocacy and contributions to non-profit arts organizations and individual artists has been celebrated here and abroad.

www.ingramcontent.com/pod-product-compliance
Lightning Source LLC
Chambersburg PA
CBHW071130130626
46553CB00004B/1325